Manufacturing Systems

This reader is one part of an Open University integrated teaching system and the selection is therefore related to other material available to students. It is designed to evoke the critical understanding of students. Opinions expressed in it are not necessarily those of the course team or of the University.

Manufacturing Systems:

Context, Applications and Techniques

*Edited by Victor Bignell, Mike Dooner,
John Hughes, Chris Pym and Sheila Stone
at the Open University*

Basil Blackwell
in association with
The Open University

Selection and editorial material © Open University 1985

First published 1985

Basil Blackwell Ltd
108 Cowley Road, Oxford OX4 1JF, UK

Basil Blackwell Inc
432 Park Avenue South, Suite 1505,
New York, NY 10016, USA

All rights reserved. Except for the quotation of short passages for the purposes of criticism and review, no part of this publication may be reproduced, stored in a retrieval system, or transmitted, in any form or by any means, electronic, mechanical, photocopying, recording or otherwise, without the prior permission of the publisher.

Except in the United States of America, this book is sold subject to the condition that it shall not, by way of trade or otherwise, be lent, re-sold, hired out, or otherwise circulated without the publisher's prior consent in any form of binding or cover other than that in which it is published and without a similar condition including this condition being imposed on the subsequent purchaser.

British Library Cataloguing in Publication Data

Manufacturing systems : context, applications
   and techniques.
   1. Production management.
   I. Bignell, Victor   II. Open University
   658.5   TS155

ISBN 0-631-14377-7
ISBN 0-631-14378-5 Pbk

Library of Congress Cataloging in Publication Data

Manufacturing systems.

   Includes index.
   1. Production Management.   2. Production engineering.
I. Bignell, Victor.   II. Open University.
TS155.M3337   1985   670′.68′5   85-9144
ISBN 0-631-14377-7
ISBN 0-631-14378-5 (pbk.)

Typeset by Downdell (Typesetting) Ltd.
Printed in Great Britain by
TJ Press, Padstow, Cornwall

Contents

Introduction

Part 1 Manufacturing in Context 7
Introduction
1.1 The Finniston Report: Engineering, Manufacturing and National Economic Needs 9
  Sir Monty Finniston
1.2 The Demise of the British Motorcycle Industry 27
  B. M. D. Smith and N. M. Rogers
1.3 How Wadkin Worked Clear 43
  G. Foster
1.4 Manufacturing in the 1980s 51
  C. New
1.5 The Focused Factory 62
  W. Skinner
1.6 How Should You Organize Manufacturing? 76
  R. H. Hayes and R. W. Schmenner

Part 2 Opportunities for Change in Manufacturing 99
Introduction
2.1 Advanced Manufacturing Systems in Japan 103
  R. Shah
2.2 Classification of Flexible Manufacturing Systems 111
  J. Browne, D. Dubois, K. Rathmill, S. Sethi and K. Stecke
2.3 Design of a Flexible Assembly System for a Small Company 120
  S. J. Mallin and P. J. Sackett
2.4 The Use of Commercial Local Area Network in Distributed Machine and Process Control Systems 127
  R. H. Weston, P. D. Hanlon and A. Salihi
2.5 Cellular Manufacturing Control 137
  T. J. Greene and R. P. Sadowski
2.6 Kanban versus MRP II – Which is Best for You? 151
  W. Goddard
2.7 Computer-aided Manufacture 164
  J. Hatvany

Part 3 Change: How Techniques Can Be Used 177
Introduction 181
3.1 Plant Layout in Practice
  L. M. Nicol and R. H. Hollier
3.2 Capacity Planning System 196
  J. Black

3.3	Decision-making in Operations Management *R. Wild*	204
3.4	Technical Investment Planning of Flexible Manufacturing Systems – the Applications of Practice-oriented Methods *H. J. Warnecke and G. Vettin*	215
3.5	The Design of an Automated Material Handling System for a Job Shop *G. K. Hutchinson*	232
3.6	The Use of Modelling and Simulation Techniques in the Design of Manufacturing Systems *J. M. Kay*	242
3.7	Inventory Control: Models and Problems *G. Urgeletti Tinarelli*	254
3.8	IGES: a Key to CADCAM Systems Integration *B. Smith and J. Wellington*	272
	IGES Update *B. Krauskopf*	276
3.9	Capturing Production Engineering within a CADCAM System *R. G. Hannam and J. C. S. Plummer*	278
3.10	An In-company Study of NC Machine Utilization and its Improvement by a Systems Approach *B. R. Kilmartin and R. G. Hannam*	294
Index		309

Acknowledgements

The editors wish to thank Madeline Tasker and Glen Back for researching articles; and Ruth Iley for preparing the manuscript.

The editors also wish to thank Sara Burt and Margaret Wingrove for their secretarial work, John Taylor for publishing advice, and the staff at Basil Blackwell for seeing the book through the press.

As members of the *Structure and Design of Manufacturing Systems* (PT611) course team at the Open University, the editors finally wish to acknowledge the financial support given by the Science and Engineering Research Council which has enabled the Course and its Reader to be prepared as part of the Open University's Manufacturing Programme.

Introduction

A new awareness of a need for change in manufacturing is the setting for this book. Industry can no longer bask in complacency, relying on routine production in a seller's market. Competition, rising costs and wary customers are driving out the inefficient manufacturer and the inappropriate product, so that if today's manufacturing companies are to exist at all tomorrow, they need to recognize where they stand, decide where they would like to be going, evaluate alternative policies and practices for going there, then act. The selection of articles in this book has been designed to assist in this process, by assembling in one volume the pick of recently published papers on relevant themes.

In the past, manufacturers have not felt a great need to study a wide range of literature beyond trade journals; production engineers have been able to confine their reading to the technical press and specialist journals; business has, by and large, operated independently of advice from the academic world. This state of affairs must now be put firmly in the past because, in taking on change in and around manufacturing, the need for timely and relevant information and guidance is as great for the people steering change as it is for the machines they will select for the factory of the future. Only the best of opinions and the most practised of ideas will do to aid the effective seizing of opportunities from among what is on offer. This applies to all methods of organization, from the establishment of business objectives and parameters down to the smallest subassembly routine, or the changing of a worn-out tool.

To do this requires that a systems approach is adopted explicitly or implicitly in order to take stock of manufacturing as a socio-technical activity set in the context of a business enterprise. Each part of the manufacturing system includes concerned individuals whose role shapes their viewpoint and differentiates it from that of others. But assistance must be drawn from many sources and harnessed to improve manufacturing performance, so mutual understanding is essential. This begins by extending the range of sources to include those which a routine reading of published work in only one field would not encounter. The recognition of foreseeable change is neither the sole province of the engineer at operations level, nor that of the business entrepreneur far above. Manufacturing is too important to be left to the generals, or indeed to any one level above or below this either.

To address these needs the articles here have been selected, edited and arranged in sections to set out ideas on systems, factory organization, automation, flexible manufacturing systems, networks, simulation, inventory control and many more relevant subjects. Some are state-of-the-art papers, others are on where we might or ought to go in manufacturing. Others in the techniques section show what to do and how to go about it, with better chance of success than if experience is ignored.

More than ever before, manufacturing has an international forum, and rather than being beaten by a foreign competitor we can actually learn from the best of practices worldwide. Thus the book contains articles on developments abroad, including that long-standing fount of lessons in the implementation of innovation, the USA, and the strong young newcomer to industrial competition, Japan.

We have already explained that manufacturing requires sensitivity to different viewpoints, and these have been kept in mind in selecting articles for a correspondingly wide readership. The same audience of key personnel has been aimed at in the Open University course which this book accompanies, and for which it has been compiled. The course is entitled 'Structure and Design of Manufacturing Systems', and is part of a programme of courses in manufacturing, satisfactory completion of which can lead to a diploma or Masters degree of the Open University.

The course draws on the papers in this book in order to proceed through the several stages of consideration of change in manufacturing. The course examines the options available in traditional and modern manufacture. It explains how to arrive at a rational basis for choice, particularly with regard to seeing manufacture as a business enterprise. The course concludes with the design of new systems in detail, and case studies of implementation.

The book follows a different scheme, as may be seen from the contents list and the explanations and commentaries which precede each part. The first article sets the scene. It comes from the Finniston Report of 1980, part of the largest investigation into the professional activity of engineering ever undertaken in this country. Surrounded and impelled by portents of doom the government of the day (1977) had set up a Committee of Inquiry into the Engineering Profession (Chairman Sir Montague Finniston). As the application of engineering is mainly in manufacturing the Committee's work took it strongly into this area. Evidence was accumulated from home and abroad; witnesses were invited and questioned; surveys were conducted. The Committee spent £400,000 on its work, representing a monumental effort that can hardly be repeated for some time. The Committee's recommendations were directed at the organization of the engineering profession and the education of engineers; its highlighting of the need for continual up-dating of engineers led to a Science and Engineering Research Council initiative of financing and setting up a programme of

Introduction

Open University courses for industry; the course that this book serves is part of that programme.

Using the book to accompany a postgraduate course does not preclude its use in other ways. In a subject which is changing as fast as the application of new ideas in manufacturing the articles will be of use in courses at other levels, while the book gives the general reader involved in manufacturing access to articles he or she might otherwise not be aware of.

The editors are indebted to the authors who allowed their work to be republished, and to all those people inside and outside the Open University who helped in the selection and preparation of material.

Part 1

Manufacturing in Context

Introduction

The group of articles in Part 1 of this book sets the scene for later parts dealing with the possibilities of change in manufacturing. Efficient and effective means of commercial production of goods are vital to the life and wealth of the nation, and if manufacturing industry is to survive in this country it will be a slimmer and more agile creation, due in part to the spirit of changes established on the basis of views similar to those set out here.

This part begins with a brief extract from the early pages of the Finniston Report, referred to in the Introduction to this book. What the Finniston Report did was to point out the condition of British manufacturing, and urge that narrow engineering excellence is but one part of the much larger setting of their work that engineers and manufacturers must now recognize. The term 'engineering dimension' was coined, and although the nomenclature has not captured the imagination and survived into the 1980s, the new breadth of interests, involvement and concern that the expression represents gives a key to current progress, summed up by the need to be wide-awake and ready and able to change so as to pursue those policies and practices that ensure survival and lead in the direction of restored prosperity.

The second article concerns what can be regarded as an open and shut case – the virtual disappearance of the British motorcycle industry. The story can be told as if it were that of a now-vanished civilization. In earlier times the failure of the sedan-chair and the horseshoe industries could be laid at the door of technological progress. There was an element of this in the demise of our motorcycle makers but really they were beaten by a rival in a contest which they thought they had the means and opportunity to win. The full story of all the influences at work is a complicated one; it is hard to summarize so the account is set out in some detail. Based on work done at Birmingham University, itself at the regional heart of the industry, the investigation ranges from the study of technical features of the motorcycle to manufacturing, business and political factors. Maybe the industry, its owners and backers lacked the internal will and outside support needed for survival, but the agile firm, in an alert and aware industry does not get caught out like this; it dodges one blow and strikes back another way.

One such firm was chosen as the subject of the third article, though many others could have been used. The account tells the recent history of Wadkin, which triumphed to survive, when in theory it should have died. The firm's success is characterized by 'adaptation', active corporate reflex, design for efficient manufacture, production to a short lead time, market selection, cash monitoring, and careful information-fed decisions. The management shows a willingness to take counter-intuitive decisions such as slimming the catalogue when orders are falling. But detail apart, the major impression is one of acceptance that 'upheaval has become a way of life' at Wadkin.

The fourth article 'Manufacturing in the 1980s' is significant in several ways. First it generalizes the special lessons derived from experience. Here we can see echoes of historical study of failures, as in the motorcycle case, and indicators from success stories such as Wadkin. The article also takes up the Finniston 'engineering dimension', develops it for application in manufacturing and shows the route towards ways of handling it usefully in a firm. Lastly, the appearance of detailed articles like this in the glossy magazine *Management Today* indicates action on the turn-round recommended in other articles in this book. The article comes from an academic pen, but is a long way from specialist offerings on details of tool speeds, economic batch-size formulae or queuing theory.

The article by Wickham Skinner in typical American assertive style is one from a series of oft-quoted papers commenting on the broader issues of where manufacturing should be going. In deciding on what, how and when to manufacture, there will be the need to establish a profile that satisfies a number of aspects of policy without violent transgression of others. It all comes down to trade-offs, in the context of knowing what the firm can do well. Skinner sees task focusing as a way to avoid excessive and damaging compromises.

Hayes and Schmenner follow Skinner in advocating a focused manufacturing plant, matching a properly determined corporate strategy embodying a 'manufacturing mission'. Fine tuning of the system is done to remove bottlenecks rather than increase efficiency locally where it cannot affect the overall outcome. The authors further pursue the notion of factory focus to the extent that each manufacturer should recognize a 'product focus' and a 'process focus' in the firm. Their respective opportunities and organization are quite different, so to try to mix the two is a pitfall to avoid. Separating them as much as possible will reduce confusion and in the end produce a better overall unity.

1.1

The Finniston Report: Engineering, Manufacturing and National Economic Needs

Sir Monty Finniston

Manufacturing and National Prosperity

The relative industrial decline of this country is now widely seen as a matter of grave concern. If allowed to continue it would seem only too likely to lead to growing impoverishment and unemployment in years to come.[1]

For many years Britain's performance as a manufacturing and trading nation has been in relative decline with her major competitors. Many reasons can be identified as to why this is so, but a central cause of our decline must be our failure to unlock the full contribution of those working in manufacturing industry – or to attract into manufacturing those with a contribution to make.[2]

1.1 These statements, the former from the Bank of England and the latter from the TUC, illustrate the deep concern of widely diverse organizations at the condition into which the British economy has declined, and the widespread but less universal recognition that reversing this decline is possible only through the regeneration of Britain as an advanced manufacturing nation.

Manufacturing in the UK Economy

1.2 The importance of manufacturing to Britain's prosperity, and hence to the welfare and living standards of her people, cannot be overstressed.

Sir Monty Finniston is Chairman of the Committee of Inquiry into the Engineering Profession.
Source: Report of the Committee of Inquiry into the Engineering Profession (HMSO, 1980).

1. Bank of England, *Quarterly Bulletin*, September 1979.
2. Trades Union Congress, evidence to the Committee of Inquiry into the Engineering Profession.

Manufacturing industries, including process industries like steel and chemicals as well as industries making capital and consumer products, generate 30 per cent of the nation's wealth and employ 32 per cent of the British working population (see table 1).

Furthermore, almost every sector of the economy has close links with manufacturing either through the provision of raw materials, the distribution and sale of goods, or by supplying finance or other services which add value to manufactured products. One study has suggested that half of those employed in non-manufacturing sectors depend for their jobs on these links with manufacturing industry.[3] Since these other sectors are also important customers for manufacturing industry, the dependence is mutual.

1.3 The manufacturing sector also occupies a key role in the international trading performance of the economy. Britain exports over one-third of her gross domestic product, a higher proportion than any other large industrial nation;[4] 66 per cent of these exports come from manufacturing industry (table 1) and the remainder from natural wealth (including North Sea oil) and traded services.[5]

TABLE 1   MANUFACTURING IN THE BRITISH ECONOMY

Year	Contributions to Gross Domestic Product by manufacturing industry[a] (%)	Proportion of total numbers in employment in manufacturing industry[b] (%)	Proportion of exports of goods and services contributed by manufacturing[c] (%)
1963	33	37	69
1968	32	36	68
1973	29	35	67
1978	30	32	66

Sources: [a] National Income and Expenditure (before providing for depreciation and stock appreciation).
[b] *Department of Employment Gazette.*
[c] Department of Industry.

1.4 As in almost every other industrial nation, the proportion of the labour force working in manufacturing industry has fallen over recent years (table 1). Some economists have postulated from this trend that Britain is moving into a 'post industrial' stage of development in which traded and public services will become the main source of future growth in employment.[6] This shift into services has important implications for the pattern of

3. J. Gershuny, *After Industrial Society?* (London: Macmillan, 1978).
4. Department of Trade, *Memorandum to NEDC*, NEDC (78) 57.
5. Department of Trade, 'Export Performance – No Room for Complacency', *Trade and Industry*, 1 September 1978.
6. Moore et al., 'A Return to Full Employment?', *Cambridge Economic Policy Review*, March 1978; 'Traded services' excludes such areas as government administration, education and public welfare provisions which, while important as employers and also vital to national wealth-creating abilities, do not themselves add significantly to wealth creation or overseas earnings.

employment and income distribution within the UK economy but it in no way diminishes the importance of maintaining a strong manufacturing capability. This is because:

(1) manufacturing exports in 1978 amounted to £30 bn, but exports of traded services to only £12 bn; a 1 per cent fall in export earnings from manufacturing thus requires 2.5 per cent offsetting rise in earnings from traded services to maintain the balance of payments. Although tourism, the financial and insurance institutions of the City of London and the traded services sector generally have long provided a surplus on their balance of payments, they have only limited capability to fund a large deficit from trade in manufactured products.

(2) The value of an industrial sector to national wealth creation need not correlate with its importance as an employer, since it is in the nature of manufacturing that increased output and/or improved efficiency often rest upon the introduction of more capital-intensive, and hence less labour-using, processes; for example, in 1978 the chemicals sector provided 10 per cent of total manufacturing output and 15 per cent of manufacturing exports, but employed only 6 per cent of the manufacturing work force.

(3) Personal incomes will inevitably be spent in part on manufactured goods, whichever sector provides those incomes. Indeed, as incomes rise, the discretionary element of consumer spending (after taxes, rents and rates, heating and lighting, essential foodstuffs and clothing) tends to rise first on purchases of manufactures, some of them substituting for spending on services (e.g., motor cars for public transport, washing machines for laundries, television or hi-fi equipment for 'live' entertainment).[7]

(4) To the extent that extra spending also goes on services, then the demand for manufactured goods is indirectly stimulated through the service sector, growth in which depends to a greater or lesser extent upon the availability of manufactured products required in the provision of such services; these products range from major capital investments, often in technologically sophisticated ones such as computers or aircraft, to more prosaic but no less essential items like furniture.

1.5 Notwithstanding the growing importance of the services sector as an employer and generator of prosperity, the long-term growth of the economy depends upon the value of domestic output of manufactured goods continuing to rise to meet a substantial share of domestic demand, both to meet those demands and to earn sufficient currency from sales abroad to pay for the imports of raw materials, food, fuel, manufactured products and services. Since Britain is firmly established as virtually an open market within the European Economic Community and within the General Agreement on Tariffs and Trade so the distinction between home and export sales has blurred. British producers must therefore be competitive in international

---

7. J. Gershuny, *After Industrial Society*.

terms since their products are in direct competition with the best on offer in the world in both overseas and home markets.

Indicators of Manufacturing Performance

1.6 Viewed in the perspective of its own past record, the performance of British manufacturing industry in meeting this requirement has not been without merit.

As table 2 shows, the value of manufacturing output rose 43 per cent in real terms between 1963 and 1973 (since when it has declined), with exports as a proportion of that output rising from 16 per cent to 25 per cent between 1963 and 1978 and thereby contributing greatly to the growth in national income. These gains were achieved notwithstanding a fall in the total work force employed in manufacturing and with an improvement of over 50 per cent in productivity in the period.

TABLE 2 UK MANUFACTURING PERFORMANCE

Year	Index of production[a] (1975 = 100)	Index of numbers employed[b] (1975 = 100)	Index of output per head[c] (1975 = 100)	Ratio of exports to total sales[d] (%)
1963	76	111	69	16
1968	94	110	86	17
1973	108	104	104	20
1978	104	97	106	25

Sources: [a-c] *Monthly Digest of Statistics*.
[d] Department of Industry, *Economic Trends*.

1.7 But although British manufacturers have achieved commendable gains, they have not done as well overall as their major overseas competitors. Manufacturing industry in Britain has been markedly less productive and less profitable than in other industrial countries.[8] Moreover the pattern of UK exports has been moving on trends increasingly divergent from those obtaining overseas. In the decade to 1977 exports of manufactures from all the major industrial countries together rose by 9 per cent each year, while British exports of manufactures rose by only 5 per cent per annum.[9]

As table 3 shows, the UK share of 'world trade' in manufactures fell from 15 per cent in 1963 to under 9 per cent in 1973 (since when it has remained around this level), while – excepting the indigenously wealthy USA – all the other individual nations cited have held or even expanded their world market shares.[10]

8. F. Blackaby (ed.), *De-Industrialisation*, Economic Policy Papers 2 (Heinemann/NIESR, 1979); C. Saunders, *Engineering in Britain, West Germany and France – Some Statistical Comparisons*, Sussex Papers no. 3 (1978); M. Panic (ed.), *UK and West German Manufacturing Industry, 1954–72*, NEDO Monograph 5 (1978); Department of Industry, 'Britain's Pattern of Specialisation' (mimeo, 1978); Barclays Bank/BOTB, *Report on Export Development in France, Germany and the UK* (1979).
9. Department of Industry, *Trade and Industry*, August 1978, p. 500.
10. British Overseas Trade Board, *Annual Report, 1978* (published 1979).

1.8 Market shares have declined for almost every UK industrial sector: between 1964 and 1976 the world market shares of British cars fell from 11 per cent to 5 per cent, of ships from 8 per cent to 4 per cent, of steelmaking from 6½ per cent to 3 per cent, of chemicals from 13½ per cent to 9½ per cent, of non-electrical machinery from 16 per cent to 10 per cent, and of electrical machinery from 13 per cent to 7½ per cent. Some previously thriving UK industries, such as motorcycles and cutlery, have all but disappeared.[11]

TABLE 3   SHARES OF WORLD TRADE[a] IN MANUFACTURES[b] (%)

Year	UK	West Germany	France	Italy	USA	Japan
1963	15	20	9	6	21	8
1968	11	20	8	7	20	11
1973	9	22	10	7	16	13
1977	9	21	10	8	16	15

Source: Monthly Review of External Trade Statistics.
Notes: [a] 'World Trade' is defined as the exports of 12 major manufacturing countries.
[b] 'Manufactures' is a narrower group of goods than the products of manufacturing industry referred to elsewhere, mainly because it excludes manufactured food and fuel.

1.9 While the proportion of UK manufacturing output going to exports has been increasing (see table 2, col. 4), this increase has gone hand-in-hand with growing import penetration of home markets, often in the same product categories. Both trends are common to other industrial countries (except Japan), but they have been more pronounced in Britain. Imported manufactures now take over 24 per cent of the total UK market, and in certain sectors foreign producers supply two-thirds or more of the home market.[12] In recent years, whenever UK domestic spending has risen, imports of manufactures have risen disproportionately more, reflecting a combination of UK producers' inability to raise output sufficiently to meet increased demand and UK customers' increased preference for foreign products. Efforts by successive governments to encourage domestic industry by stimulating consumer demand have often proved more beneficial for overseas than for British manufacturers, and once lost to foreign manufacturers, markets have proved very difficult to regain.

1.10 The implications of the growing disparity between British and European growth rates in manufacturing output and national prosperity have been graphically stated by the Bank of England:

> The consequences of failing to arrest this country's industrial decline are likely to become more pressing and obvious as time goes on. Now condemned to very slow growth, we might later even have to accept, if present trends continue, decline in real living standards.[13]

11. Ibid.
12. Department of Trade, *Memorandum to NEDC*, NEDC (78) 57; Department of Trade, 'UK Imports' (mimeo, 1978).
13. Bank of England, *Quarterly Bulletin*, March 1979.

If this inadequate national trading performance in manufactures seems remote from individual welfare and prosperity, table 4 illustrates how British income levels have failed to grow at the rates achieved in other EEC countries.

Since 1966, when Britain was among the richest European nations, it has slipped to become one of the poorest.

TABLE 4   PER CAPITA GDP: EEC COUNTRIES (UK = 100)

Country	1966	1977
UK	100	100
West Germany	109	129
France	99	124
Italy	69	77
Netherlands	97	117
Belgium	93	119
Denmark	115	129

Source: Statistical Office of the European Communities (1978); indices of GDP/head at market prices shown at purchasing power parities.

1.11 Until the 1960s Britain continued to be one of the most prosperous countries in the world, thriving on her strengths as a trading nation and her position at the centre of the Sterling Area. From our meetings and discussions around the country during this Inquiry, it is clear to us that notwithstanding repeated warnings over many years *very many people in this country do not fully appreciate that those days are past; that Britain is now poorer than many of the countries she formerly outperformed; and that both the roots of that relative decline and the seeds of future recovery lie with the performance of her manufacturing industries.*

The Need for Growth

1.12 The decline of British manufacturing competitiveness relative to her major competitors has progressed insidiously over many years and *radical and fundamental improvements in UK manufacturing performance are required if the rising levels of private and public consumption to which the British people have become accustomed (and expect to continue) are not to fall further behind those in other industrial countries. There is no prospect that the contributions from natural resources (including North Sea oil and gas or coal) or growth in other sectors of the economy can generate wealth on the scale which can be earned by manufacturing industry;* for example the contribution of North Sea oil to GDP in 1978 was £2.3 bn, equivalent to 8 per cent of the contribution made by manufacturing to total national value-added.

1.13 Growth in the economy as a whole and in manufacturing industries in particular, must be restored if Britain is to become a high-earning economy on a par with its main competitors, and one in which sufficient jobs are available for the young people entering the work force for the first time and

Engineering, Manufacturing, Economic Needs

for the workers displaced by improved productivity in existing activities. That growth must come not only from existing activities but also from new enterprises emerging to replace traditional industries which have rationalized, declined or disappeared. In 1975 Britain produced only 5.6 per cent of total OECD output although her population was 7.5 per cent of the total within OECD (which includes a number of much less industrially developed economies than Britain). For Britain to raise her per capita industrial output to a level commensurate with her share of OECD population, which would still be much lower than that achieved in Germany, France or Japan, would require a rate of growth in industrial output 3 per cent higher than the rate of all OECD countries together, sustained for 10 years. By comparison, industrial output in Britain has risen by little more than 6 per cent overall, or well under 1 per cent p.a., in the nine years since 1970, and current forecasts predict no improvement.

Britain as an Advanced Industrial Nation

The Structure of UK Industry

1.14 A number of studies[14] have compared the characteristics of British manufacturing industry with those of competing industrial countries, to see whether differences emerge which might explain Britain's relative weaknesses. Characteristics considered include the relative sizes of British and overseas enterprises, the extent to which output is concentrated in a few leading companies, the categories of products in which different countries specialize, the sizes and types of export markets sought, the relative capital-intensiveness of British companies compared with their overseas competitors, and so on. A consensus emerges from these studies that, in respect of these measures, although the UK displays some differences, they are not so large individually or collectively to provide an explanation of why Britain has been less efficient and hence less successful than its competitors and other reasons must be sought.

Productivity and Profitability

1.15 Change and growth in industry depends on the level of effective investment in new plant for manufacturing new products or for making current products better; this in turn depends in large measure on the availability of finance through profits earned from existing plant and products. As table 5 illustrates, although the profitability of manufacturing industries has been steadily declining in each of the major industrial nations over the past 25 years the fall has been very much more pronounced in Britain than in other countries.

The declining profitability of manufacturing industry reduces the availability of internal funds for the development of better products and for

---

14. Op. cit. (see note 8).

TABLE 5   INTERNATIONAL COMPARISONS OF PROFITABILITY, 1955-77 (NET RATE OF RETURN[a]: MANUFACTURING)

	Canada (%)	United States (%)	Japan (%)	West Germany (%)	United Kingdom (%)
Averages for years[b]					
1963-7	18.5	31.7	26.7	18.7	13.6
1968-71	15.5	21.6	28.4	19.0	10.7
1971-5	17.0	17.4	15.7	12.5	5.6
Years:					
1975	14.5	14.5	13.9	11.0	2.1
1976	13.3	18.1	n.a.	13.5	2.5
1977	12.5	19.0	n.a.	13.3	3.9

Source: Department of Industry (1979).
Notes: [a] Defined as net operating surplus as percentage net capital stock of fixed assets (excluding land).
[b] Each of these groups of years covers a cycle in UK rates of return. Figures for other countries for the same years may cover more or less than a complete cycle, and in this sense provide only a broad comparison with UK.
n.a.: not available.

more efficient manufacturing systems and deters external investment in manufacturing. Real levels of investment in industry (in terms of the amount spent per employee) have fallen behind comparable levels in other countries, further weakening UK competitiveness.[15]

1.16 Furthermore the benefits accruing from such investment as has been made have all too frequently been attenuated by slow construction, with consequential high costs and delay in commissioning, and by the manifestation of poor industrial relations, manning levels markedly higher than those employed on comparable plant in other countries, and low output rates interrupted by industrial disputes.

1.17 Table 6 illustrates how far UK levels of manufacturing productivity have fallen behind those in competing nations over the last decade.

In 1970 the UK level of productivity was 65 per cent of that in West Germany and only 47 per cent of that in Japan but by 1977 the comparison showed a further deterioration to 61 per cent of the German level and 38 per cent of the Japanese.[16]

1.18 The wide spread between the levels of productivity achieved in the best UK firms and the worst in particular industries emphasizes the considerable scope which exists for securing significant improvements in output from existing human and physical resources in UK manufacturing.[17] Indeed

15. D. Jones, 'Output, Employment and Labour Productivity in Europe Since 1955', National Institute Review (1978); J. Barnett/HM Treasury, 'The Nuts and Bolts of the Economy', *The Sunday Times*, 25 June 1978.

16. See also memorandum from the Secretary of State for Industry to NEDC, NEDC(79)59: *Productivity and Manufacturing Industry*.

17. Wragg and Robertson, *Post-War Trends, by Industry in the UK, 1950-73* (HMSO, June 1978)

Engineering, Manufacturing, Economic Needs

TABLE 6 RELATIVE INDICES OF MANUFACTURING[a] PRODUCTIVITY, 1970-7 (level of productivity[b] UK = 100)

	1970	1973	1975	1977
UK	100	100	100	100
Belgium	156	146	160	n.a.
France	177	185	197	205
West Germany	153	146	151	165
Italy	138	117	111	120[c]
Netherlands	178	173	182	n.a.
Japan	215	238	233	263
US	340	336	338	360

Source: After NIESR Review, February 1979.
Notes: [a] The definition of manufacturing used here varies slightly – but not significantly – from that used in other tables.
[b] Value added per employee, measured at $ purchasing power parity rates of exchange in 1970.
[c] 1976.
n.a.: not available.

several studies of production methods in British companies supported by much technical literature and many 'awareness' programmes[18] have indicated specific measures which could raise productivity, reduce manufacturing costs and increase profits, thereby increasing the flow of funds for investment in innovation and new industries catering to world markets as well as improving the total climate for investment in manufacturing industry.

Product Qualities

1.19 Labour productivity (in terms of value added per employee) is, however, not just a function of the efficiency of manufacturing production, but reflects the market appeal and value of the products being made, since companies selling high-value products on rising markets may well prove more profitable than those with more efficient and harder-working work forces producing less attractive or lower value products. An important difference between UK and overseas manufacturing industries in this respect is indicated by evidence that British manufacturers have not shared fully in the international trend for advanced nations to trade up-market, that is, to increase the 'value added' represented by their output.[19] Studies by the National Economic Development Office and others of the relative selling prices of closely comparable products, have suggested that the UK shows a tendency

18. C. New, 'Managing Manufacturing Operations', *British Institute of Management* (1976); D. Smith, 'Managing for Productivity', *Management Today*, October 1977; Centre for Interfirm Comparisons, 'Management Policies and Practices, and Business Performances' (IFC, 1978).

19. Op. cit. (see note 18); Department of Industry, 'International Competitiveness and R&D Policies' (mimeo, 1978).

to 'export cheap and import dear' in manufactured products.[20] For almost every product group in the Standard International Trade Classification (SITC) the 'unit values' of UK exports are lower than those of exports from other industrially advanced nations, and also lower than the 'unit values' of UK imports of manufactures. In a study of 86 product groups accounting for one-third of British exports, the values per tonne of the British products in 1978 were 20–40 per cent lower than those of comparable German and French products.

This disparity, already wide, appears to be growing, as table 7 illustrates for mechanical engineering products. As table 7 shows, the ratio of the unit values of UK exports to those for imports of comparable products has fallen from 60 per cent in 1970 to 47 per cent in 1977 while the ratio for France, although also less than unity (i.e., France too has been exporting relatively cheap and importing relatively dear), has been improving and that for Germany has strengthened from 106 per cent to 113 per cent.

TABLE 7   EXPORTS AND IMPORTS – MECHANICAL ENGINEERING INDEX OF UNIT VALUES[a] (UK exports 1970 = 100)

	Exports 1970	Exports 1977	Imports 1970	Imports 1977	Exports/Imports a/c	Exports/Imports b/d
UK	100	138	165	290	0.61	0.48
France	99	220	125	246	0.79	0.89
West Germany	121	297	114	262	1.06	1.13

Source: NEDO (1979).
Note: [a] $000s/metric tons.

1.20 The high 'unit values' of competing exports and of imports into Britain relative to those of British exports suggests that the source of the relative weakness of British producers in world markets has not generally lain in unduly high UK selling prices. There is no evidence of a decline in the price competitiveness of British goods during the period in which UK market shares fell most steeply;[21] if anything, until very recently the reverse has been true, with producers in other countries often winning sales from British companies despite their higher selling prices. The key differences between Britain and her competitors appear to lie in the differing emphasis given to the specification and qualities of the products made and in the way they are manufactured. While other advanced industrial nations have concentrated on producing high-value, high-quality products (in respect of performance, reliability, finish and ease of maintenance) to sell at competitive prices in rising markets, Britain has struggled with a product range for which world demand, including that from home customers, has grown

20. D. Connell, 'UK Export Performance – Some Evidence from International Trade Data' (NEDO mimeo, 1978); D. Stout, 'International Price Competitiveness, Non-price Factors and Export Performance' (NEDO, 1977); see also op. cit. note 18.
21. Department of Industry, 'Manufacturing Industries – UK Performance since 1963', *Trade and Industry*, 8 September 1978.

relatively slowly; for example, in 1975 the UK and West Germany both sold about 22 per cent of their total exports of metal-forming machinery to developing countries, but whereas the unit value of the British machines was $1628, that of the German products was $4951, and the total value of the German sales was over four times greater than that for the UK.[22]

Market Trends for Manufacturing Economies

Implications of Spreading Industrialization

1.21   The advanced industrial nations compete for markets mostly with each other but also to an increasing extent with producers from newly industrializing countries. The patterns of trade and competition between the advanced nations and these newly industrializing countries are changing and will continue to change rapidly as the world becomes increasingly industrialized. As current products and processes mature and more effective designs and production techniques are established, so manufacturing methods become standardized and amenable to automation and routine procedures. The less advanced newly industrializing countries – which are not in general able to compete in the non-routine, highly knowledge-intensive skills required at the outset of innovative cycles – are at this stage well placed to enter the market with modern plant and with significant advantages in labour and total operating costs over the established producers. The increasing sophistication of industries in some newly industrialized countries, employing modern plant and new technology, has meant that the area of comparative advantage for the advanced countries is being progressively eroded by this 'product cycle'.

1.22   The strengths of advanced countries lie in inventing and exploiting *new* products and processes, incorporating high levels of human skill and knowledge, most often at the leading edge of technology, and in *continual incremental improvements* to current products and processes through reducing production costs. Their advantages lie particularly in devoting attention to *non-price factors*, for example, in up-rating the performance, reliability and general 'fitness for purpose' of their products, improving quality control, providing greater assurance and promptness of delivery, and otherwise attending flexibly and readily to customer requirements before and after sale.[23] The advanced countries must move up-market, in this way, continually seeking new ways to maintain their advantages by identifying, developing and accelerating the introduction of new technologies and potential growth products. They must also be prepared to move out of product areas in which their earlier comparative technical and commercial advantages have been irrevocably lost.

---

22. F. Blackaby (ed.), 'De-Industrialisation'.
23. K. Corfield, 'Design for Manufacture' (NEDO, 1979): J. Pilditch, Evidence to CIEP from Allied International Designers; R. Feilden (Chairman), 'Report of Committee of Inquiry on Engineering Design', (HMSO, 1963).

The Importance of Non-price Factors

1.23 Customers' evaluations of value-for-money from manufactured products, particularly for consumer durable and capital goods, have increasingly stressed the relative importance of 'non-price' factors based upon the expected total cost of the purchase over its useable life. Factors in this market trend have been the rising labour costs of servicing, maintenance and repairs, a shortage of skilled technicians to do such work and the rising cost of down-time on highly productive modern plant. Partly as a result, both corporate and private customers have come to insist on long warranties and guarantees from suppliers, and have often proved willing to pay a higher initial price if they are persuaded that later costs and inconvenience will be minimized. Furthermore, progressively more rigorous worldwide standards concerning safety, pollution control, energy consumption and other aspects of product performance have forced products which do not meet these specifications out of many markets. This reflects the international growth in 'consumer power', and in associated legislative controls (particularly those concerning product liability) which penalize inferior designs and unreliable products.

1.24 Studies of the performance of particular groups of UK manufacturers[24] have identified areas where British companies have not adjusted sufficiently in adapting the quality and specification of their products to meet these and other changes in market requirements. Sectoral studies, from shipbuilding to electronic components, have cited opportunities missed and markets lost due to non-price factors. These range from failure of British producers to innovate or to match changed requirements through specific shortcomings in the design or performance of products to a general reputation of British goods for inferior quality, late delivery and unreliability in service (e.g. over the provision of spares). 'Made in Britain' was once synonymous with high quality, internationally sought-after products. This is still so for products from many UK companies but not for all. Such excellence must be reinstated as the norm for UK manufacturing industry, capitalizing upon the successful experience of its best companies. Notwithstanding the shortcomings we have described there is much in current UK manufacturing industry to justify confidence that overall performance could be greatly improved by more companies building upon the 'best practices' exemplified by the leading UK companies and emulating these companies' successes in relating their products to market needs.

Engineering and Market Trends

1.25 We cannot stress too strongly the need to meet change with change nor can we over-emphasize how much engineering pervades activities in in-

24. K. Pavitt (ed.), *Technical Innovation and British Economic Performance* (Macmillan/Science Policy Research Unit, 1980); Central Policy Review Staff, *The Future of the British Car Industry* (HMSO, 1975); CPRS *The Future of the UK Power Plant Manufacturing Industry* (HMSO, 1976); Department of Industry/Boston Consulting Group, *Strategy Alternatives for the UK Motor Cycle Industry* (HMSO, 1975); National Economic Development Office, 'Survey of Investment in Machine Tools' (NEDO, 1975).

Engineering, Manufacturing, Economic Needs

dustry, the home, and even in leisure through manufactured products and systems based on them. The opportunities afforded by recent technological achievements present rich markets to companies with the market perception and engineering capabilities to exploit them[25] but to outline a particular scenario for manufacturing industry in the 1980s and 1990s would be a fruitless exercise. None the less, the central, critical and growing place of engineering and engineers within *any* scenario is illustrated by considering emerging developments in:

- the availability and real cost of *basic resources*;
- the evolution and impact of *new technologies*;
- the intensification of *competition* between industrial nations;
- the economic impact of *social and political trends*.

1.26 Fundamental changes calling for engineering-led responses are already being experienced in the demand for and supply of basic resources:

(1) *Food* Continuing (if less rapid) growth in world population, coupled with rising expectations of people in the developing countries, demand engineering-based responses for machinery, chemicals and civil engineering systems for raising agricultural productivity, for manufacturing synthetic foodstuffs for human and animal use and for improving efficiency of food processing, storage and distribution.

(2) *Energy* Rising real costs of conventional energy sources have created an urgent need for engineering solutions to the problems of minimizing the energy consumed by products, processes and systems, exploiting hitherto inaccessible or uneconomic fuel sources and developing economically viable alternative sources of energy.

(3) *Materials* The increasing scarcity and rising real costs of industrial raw materials raise new engineering problems in the design and manufacture of products and plant particularly in the optimum use of these materials, in their recycling and in substitution.

1.27 Major advances in technology are radically changing industry's potential to meet these and other market challenges, as well as creating new opportunities in themselves. Particular applications of new technologies, together with new applications for established knowhow, are increasingly altering the character and scale of world markets. Among the most pervasive and ubiquitous of these are advances being made in applications of microelectronics; others, to name but a few, include communications, transportation and alternative energy:

(1) In *communications*, technical advances in both hardware and software, associated with computing systems and modes of data transmission, are revolutionizing the transfer, control, storage, access and display of information. As costs decline and allow economic

---

25. D. Stout, *Industrial Policy in the Longer Term – An Approach Through Investment*, NEDO/NEDC (74)31; Nabseth and Ray, *The Diffusion of New Industrial Processes – An International Study* (CUP/NIESR, 1974).

applications in an ever-extending range of functions these developments will transform business, industry, distribution, entertainment, education, health-care and the home.

(2) In *transportation*, the movement of people and freight by land, sea and air is undergoing a revolution built upon developments in vehicle designs, rapid mass-transit systems, traffic control, navigation and safety systems, and other changes deriving from and implemented by engineers.

(3) In *products and processes* the choices before customers are continually increasing in number and sophistication, and even the most recent innovations are liable to be rendered obsolete in a short time by competitors' applications of new knowledge and techniques.

1.28 The market opportunities opened by these developments will be enormous. For example, the world market for telecommunications equipment, worth $30 bn in 1977, has been estimated at $45 bn in 1982 and $65 bn in 1987.[26] Competition for world markets will be concomitantly fierce. As more countries industrialize, so the number of competitors for each market will increase but with the advantage in the initial stage resting with the advanced countries. Developments in communications and transportation and international political pressures for free trade will continue to erode distinctions between home and export markets, so that domestic producers must keep abreast of best world practice in the engineering of their products and processes and in the management of both. Competition for markets will be further intensified between established industrial nations, as each seeks to maintain growth in new product areas to provide solutions for the structural unemployment which will inevitably arise as more and more traditional employing industries become obsolete or capital intensive.

1.29 Engineering responses to these market developments must take into account the growing impact of social and political considerations and constraints upon technical decisions. Examples are:

(1) *Consumerism* Not only are the customers for manufactured products becoming more sophisticated in their separate appraisals of the quality and value-for-money of those products, but they are collectively demanding greater controls over their production and performance, as is manifest in the spread of statutory regulations regarding energy consumption, emission and noise levels, safety, and in the introduction into the legal framework in some countries of 'strict liability' upon manufacturers for every aspect and application of their products in use.

(2) *Politics* The rise of consumerism and the impact of resource and technological developments on people's jobs, their physical environment and their 'quality of life' generally have brought engineering issues into the centre of the political stage and demand a forceful, informed and coherent engineering input to national debates and policy counsels, to ensure that ill-informed and emotional reactions do not predominate in shaping policies and action in these areas.

26. Arthur D. Little Inc., quoted in *Financial Times*, October 1979, p. 20.

(3) *International collaboration* The scale of intellectual and material resources demanded to meet the emerging challenges posed by technological and market changes is now often beyond the capabilities of individual companies, or even individual countries. The engineering expertise of several countries has been mobilized already upon some major projects by initiatives either at Governmental level or by private companies (often multinationals). Only those companies whose engineering capabilities are of world class will become involved in these potentially highly rewarding ventures and collaborations.

The Challenges for UK Industry

1.30 *The changes outlined above in the competition for world markets in manufactures are inevitable, inexorable and international. Since producers in other countries will undoubtedly respond to the challenge and opportunities presented, the British response must be more energetic and purposeful than it has been hitherto. Britain's survival as an advanced industrial nation depends critically upon her manufacturing companies moving up-market into the production of high quality, high value-added goods, utilizing the best of current knowledge and technology, and directed towards areas where world demand is growing or can be generated most rapidly and where competition from newly industrializing countries is initially least severe.*

1.31 *The response to these developments, which afford unprecedented opportunities for growth and regeneration, demands market-oriented engineering excellence, managed and translated using the best of current technology and knowhow into the types of high quality, high value-added goods and services sought by world customers.*

The Engineering Dimension

1.32 There are few – if any – areas of manufacturing where the competitiveness of a company's products and processes does not depend upon its corporate engineering capabilities. We would not suggest that changes regarding engineering and engineers are all that is needed to achieve the dramatic improvements demanded of manufacturing performance. Account must also be taken of a whole range of complex and interrelated factors, including:

- the size, buoyancy and accessibility of world *markets*;
- the impact of policies and priorities determined in the *political* sphere;
- the availability of *finance* for industry and in particular for innovations;
- the competence of company *managements*;
- the *support and commitment* of employees at all levels for the changes needed.

Each of these factors has been the subject of intensive analyses and reviews. Underlying and largely shaping them all are the intangible influences of

British attitudes towards change, industry and engineering, and the legacies of economic and social history. The interplay of these factors has bred an economic and cultural environment in this country frequently inimical to engendering the radical changes needed in national behaviour and priorities. However, the successes of the many British companies which have overcome these supposed handicaps to progress show that changes are feasible, and that they can pay, bringing prosperity to the companies and those who work in them and to the nation as a whole.

1.33 Among those manufacturers in this country and overseas who have prospered in world markets, we found a common characteristic in the way they had built upon excellent engineering, integrated into enterprising and forward-looking market and product strategies. Management in these companies clearly regarded engineering as the common factor linking the inputs of the various specialist functions within the organization to its overall objectives. Engineers were involved in each stage of the manufacturing process, from the technical appraisal of world-market opportunities and the translation of those appraisals to the design of products and systems to exploit the opportunities through to the development, manufacture, sale, delivery and service of the products. There was thus achieved a continuous interplay between marketing, design, research, manufacturing and selling, with all concerned seeking to ensure that the company's products met the demands of world markets.

1.34 The engineering performance of manufacturing enterprises depends not only upon the numbers and qualities of engineers employed but equally, if not more, on the effective priority accorded to engineering in the enterprise, and on *the capability of the organization as a system for translating engineering expertise into the production and marketing of competitive products through efficient production processes.* This capability involves many of the non-engineering factors mentioned above. *To convey the interaction of engineering with non-engineering factors in determining manufacturing performance, and to emphasize the importance of considering the whole manufacturing system and not just aspects of it, we have adopted the concept of the 'engineering dimension'.* The engineering dimension involves all the factors and activities concerned in relating the technological capabilities and expertise of an organization to its overall objectives, which in manufacturing are to prosper through the sale of products and systems in the world market. They should also be borne in mind in government – both national and local – where the importance of engineering and engineers has hitherto been badly neglected.

1.35 *The engineering dimension in manufacturing industry determines the impact of engineers on companies' responses to world markets, particularly in:*

- *assessing and/or anticipating market needs and opportunities;*
- *assessing the company's potential to meet or create these opportunities;*
- *conceiving, designing and continually developing products and systems to meet market requirements;*
- *developing, operating and improving processes for manufacturing such*

Engineering, Manufacturing, Economic Needs 25

products profitably, making optimum use of materials, energy, capital and human resources;
- ensuring that engineering support for products is efficiently sustained throughout product life; and
- adapting flexibly to particular market requirements, and responding quickly to changes in those requirements or in the technical potential needed to meet them.

1.36 *The engineering dimension is understood and well developed in successful manufacturing companies, but there are too few such companies in the UK to produce sufficient wealth to match the social and economic expectations of the nation.*

Summary

1.37 (1) The future of the UK economy and the employment and living standards of its population depend critically upon the extent to which British companies can prosper in international competition for markets for its manufactures.

There is no prospect that growth from natural resources or from other sectors of the economy can generate wealth on the scale which can be provided by manufacturing industries. Past relative declines in UK manufacturing competitiveness and output must therefore be stemmed and reversed if expectations of continually rising living standards are to be maintained and the socially untenable consequences of very high levels of long-term unemployment averted.

(2) Prosperity for the advanced industrial nations depends on the production of high-quality, high value-added goods, utilizing the best of current knowledge and technology. There is evidence that British manufacturers have not shared fully in the international trend among advanced nations to trade 'up-market', and that room exists for greatly improving the efficiency of much of British production. Close attention must be paid to the market appeal of the products of British industry and to the efficiency with which they are made, building upon market-oriented engineering, so that 'Made in Britain' can once again become synonymous with high-quality internationally sought-after products.

(3) Changes in the world market for manufactured products are increasingly emphasizing the need for companies to develop and maintain an advanced engineering capability to meet the challenges posed and to exploit the opportunities being presented; we have no doubt that producers in other countries will respond to this need and it is imperative that UK manufacturers do likewise.

(4) While engineering excellence is not the only determinant of manufacturing prosperity, the example of the most successful companies shows that it is *essential* to continuing competitiveness. That excellence derives from the effective priority accorded to engineering in manufacturing

enterprises, and the capability of the organization as a system for translating engineering expertise into the efficient production and marketing of competitive products, which capability depends upon companies' understanding and development of the 'engineering dimension'.

The Finniston Report printed herein is Crown copyright 1980 reproduced by permission of the Controller of Her Majesty's Stationery Office.

1.2

The Demise of the British Motorcycle Industry

B. M. D. Smith and N. M. Rogers

[. . .] The purpose of the research has been to provide some understanding of why the British motorcycle industry, and the great names of BSA, Triumph, Norton, Royal Enfield, Matchless, AJS, Sunbeam, etc. declined from the apparent prosperity of the early 1960s to almost total oblivion by 1975. This historical study has identified the late 1950s and early 1960s as the key period when events occurred and decisions were taken that caused, or failed to provide the means to combat, the later decline. Yet, at the time, these were years of limited success, lost opportunities and complacency; minor, step-by-step improvements in motorcycle designs were introduced but not the needed revolution in design, production and marketing and, above all, not in management and drive; this failing affected all the companies equally – as well as much of the rest of British manufacturing.

The attack on the British motorcycle industry came from two opposed directions. First, there was the fall in usage and demand for motorcycles in Britain that lasted for the decade 1960–9. Second, there was the advent of competition in home and export markets, most specifically from the Japanese. The word 'opposed' was used because the Japanese certainly did not thrust themselves so forcibly into a market inevitably in decline but set to work to generate new demand. This they succeeded in doing even in the car-hungry United States and Great Britain. While, in the developing world, as need turned into demand with rising incomes, new demand and new producers have appeared. [. . .]

The decline of the British and rise of the Japanese motorcycle industry (aside from the rise of the car industry) represents a prime example of the power and speed of capitalism to generate uneven development and structural change. But, then, the issue moves on to why the relative advantages

B. M. D. Smith and N. M. Rogers wrote from the Centre for Urban and Regional Studies, University of Birmingham.

Source: From B. D. Smith, 'The History of the Motorcycle Industry, 1945–75', Occasional Paper no. 3, 1981, and N. M. Rogers, 'The British Motorcycle Industry, 1945–75', Working Paper 67, 1979, Centre for Urban and Regional Studies, University of Birmingham.

switched so easily and, disaggregating from these macro trends, one is back with seeking explanations relating to events at individual concerns in Britain, Japan and elsewhere and back asking why, if motorcycle competition became too severe for British concerns at a time of falling demand, none of them diversified successfully into other products or localities?

Amongst the other events and trends adverse to the industry to be borne in mind can be listed these: postwar American policy towards German and Japanese industry and the urgent need in Japan for a low-cost, low-petrol-consumption form of personal transport; the expansion of the motorcar industry (that took markets, workers and suppliers away from the smaller motorcycle industry); the conglomerate and merger fashion (that led BSA into many diverting and ultimately unrewarding alternatives to motorcycles and obscured its vision of its main function); variations in vehicle licensing and taxation systems (that, in Britain, used hire purchase and purchase tax as controls on consumption without much consideration of the harm done to the particular products and producers affected (Dunnett, 1980) and treated a scooter or motorcycle as a kind of car rather than as a kind of bicycle as in many other countries); regional policy that hindered alternative manufacturing industries and firms from developing in the West Midlands to replace motorcycles; the blind and often suicidal devotion of British governments and their officials to free trade (exemplified in the 1962 Anglo-Japanese trade agreement which failed to extend to motorcycles, even temporarily, the quotas and voluntary controls put on imports of textiles, radios, etc., despite the lobbying of the British Motor Cycle Industries Association); and the persistent British business failure to pay enough attention to marketing, investment and productivity improvements to retain, let alone extend, markets. [. . .]

Two main approaches have been employed in reaching our conclusions. The first has been concerned with the capabilities of the Japanese motorcycle producers and the second with the deficiencies of the British motorcycle companies. These deficiencies were such that, with or without Japanese competition, they would have generated problems for British motorcycle sales in a period of change in transport, leisure and spending choice. The first approach has suggested that the British industry was murdered by the Japanese onslaught; the second that it committed suicide by neglect or accident rather than conscious choice before that onslaught was actually completed. Either approach involves an emotive metaphor but, together, they state the dilemma for detectives seeking to explain the events of the decline and fall of the British industry. [. . .]

Home Market

The use and demand for motorcycles in Britain, the British industry's home market, rose to about 1960 and then fell steadily for a decade before recovering in the 1970s. This contrasted with the situation in the private car industry where current licences and new registrations have risen steadily. [. . .] On every indicator, the British industry shows sharp decline in the 1960s com-

The Demise of the British Motorcycle Industry

pared to the 1950s, with the 1954 Census return representing the peak in size. By 1958, four factories and nearly 4000 employees had left the industry which was producing 50,000 fewer complete motorcycles. However, this reduction in employment had been accompanied by a small increase in output per employee (in numbers of machines and value) and this was not improved upon in future years as far as we can tell.

In 1954, the British industry produced just enough motorcycles to meet home demand as reflected in new registrations in 1955. Thereafter, imports were necessary to meet this demand. [. . .] In the late 1940s, virtually no motorcycles had been imported into Britain and 66 per cent of home production was imported. By 1955, while one-third of home production was exported, imports had risen to equal exports in numbers of machines though not in value. By 1960, imports had grown to exceed exports; the surge of imports in that year was exceptional, presumably generated by the sharp rise in new registrations in 1959.

While home production and, to a lesser extent, exports fell, this was not initially because of lack of home demand but because buyers increasingly chose imported machines. In particular, they bought smaller capacity machines from abroad in the 1950s and 1960s, mainly from Europe not Japan, and smaller and larger capacity machines in the 1970s. These came increasingly from Japan. By 1973, when the last Census of Production figures showed three British establishments surviving, all small capacity sales in the home market were being met by imports, two-thirds of them from Japan, and half of all large capacity sales were also being met by imports, again largely from Japan. In twenty years, the Japanese had entered and virtually taken over the British home market in motorcycles.

World Supply and Trade

World production of motorcycles (mainly but not exclusively over 50 cc) was five times larger in 1975 than in 1953. Moreover, the centre of production had ceased to be Western Europe. In 1953, three-quarters of all machines were made in Western Europe; in 1975, only one-third. By then, half of world production came from Asia, and Eastern Europe was producing a fifth of all machines. One in three of all motorcycles were, in fact, produced in Japan, with the USSR and France (mainly mopeds including many presumably below 50 cc) producing about one million each in 1975.

Within this production and its implied demand context, world trade in motorcycles changed. Firstly, the Japanese came to dominate world trade in motorcycles. Secondly, markets peripheral to Europe and the US were developing and it is to these markets particularly that the Japanese exports were directed. But third-world markets remained small into the 1970s despite their need for low-cost transport. This may have been a matter of purchasing power, foreign currency or home production. Nevertheless, the USA remains outstanding as a market, followed by the UK, the latter having switched to being a net importer of motorcycles. Furthermore, aside from the USA and Canada and Australia–New Zealand, most of the trade occurred within Europe. While Japanese imports were important in the UK and USA, most European countries – Italy, France, Austria and even West Germany – retained their exports even if in 1975 importing more than hitherto. Japan's markets were mainly elsewhere though the situation was changing in 1975. Thus, while the UK had lost its home market to Japan and others, the process was proceeding more slowly elsewhere in Europe, notably in France and Italy due to restrictions placed on Japanese imports. [. . .]

The American Market

Much of the action in the world and British motorcycle industry occurred in the US (and Canadian) market because of its size, its preference for large, expensive motorcycles, and its openness to imports in the virtual absence of home production and exports. After a fall in the 1950s, usage of motorcycles (as represented by registrations) surged upwards in the early 1960s, doubling between 1964 and 1967 and again between 1967 and 1973. In 1967, about 18 per cent of all registrations were in the one state of California. Imports doubled every five years and rose from 10 per cent of registrations in 1965 to 17 per cent in 1975 and probably represented virtually all the new machines brought into use. In 1965, the US market took three-quarters of all British exports and, in 1975, 57 per cent. For the Japanese, the proportions were similar at 67 per cent and 47 per cent but the scale was rather different. In 1975, the Japanese provided 87 per cent of American imports. After the UK, West German and Italian imports ranked next in importance.

Japanese exports to the USA absorbed 40 per cent of all world trade in motorcycles in 1975.

The Japanese Onslaught

The British motorcycle industry was virtually eliminated at a time of mounting Japanese competition and declining demand. This competition (and decline) suddenly hit the British and American markets in the early 1960s (within months of the trade agreement). British motorcycle firms were in varied positions economically and reacted variously but nearly all succumbed over the next fifteen years. [. . .] Moreover, the American, German, French and Italian motorcycle industries were also seriously affected by Japanese competition – though great names like BMW (in Germany) and Harley Davidson (in the USA) at least survive and the French moped industry continues. The Italian industry is in better fettle; it was astute and influential enough to obtain tariff protection for the smaller motorcycle and scooter market from imports. [. . .] This generality of decline, however, indicates that explanations for the British collapse should not be confined to deficiencies in British management, unions, labour, consumers, government or industrial locations, although these, separately or in combination, may have worsened the British response to Japanese competition and declining demand.

The Demise of the British Motorcycle Industry

It is relevant to examine the Japanese onslaught carefully. It was sudden and sharp in its force in the market-place (in 1963, the Japanese exported almost 50,000 motorcycles to Britain, providing 89 per cent of all such imports and close to two motorcycles imported for each one exported from Britain; also at that time Britain imported 70,000 mopeds, 66 per cent coming from France, and 21,000 scooters, 84 per cent coming from Italy with negligible exports going out from Britain) (British Cycle and Motor Cycle Industries Association circulars, 1963-4). But several points need to be made in relation to this. First, the Japanese invasion had in a sense been building up for a decade in the development of the Japanese *home* market and it seems surprising that motorcycle producers outside Japan seem to have overlooked both the opportunity offered by the Japanese (and Third World) market in the 1950s and the build-up of the Japanese industry (and its consequent economies of scale) to meet that opportunity.

However, British manufacturers in the 1950s were working to capacity. Several chose consciously not to expand capacity and sales (because they believed that shortage added a premium to their prices and a certain cachet) through either advertising (Kelly, 1978, p. 174) or pushing into new overseas markets or, for some time, entering the scooter market in competition with continental producers. They thus missed the chance to establish themselves, their names and economies of scale in design and production at the critical time (1954-62) - for this was a relatively more favourable time for successful expansion than was to occur again as, in practice, the Japanese seized these advantages instead. Such a decision, of course, would have involved a considerable imaginative and financial leap for any British producer.

Secondly, it has been suggested that the Japanese export onslaught occurred in motorcycles (rather than in some other goods) specifically because opposition abroad was weak in resistance and so encouraged rather than effectively stifled incipient Japanese competition (Magaziner and Hout, 1980, pp. 13, 19, 21 and 26). The importance of the Japanese home market to the Japanese producers until the mid 1960s as a base from which to work cannot be exaggerated. Even today, with eight million motorcycles in use in Japan and the home market saturated, a third of production goes to the home market even if the kind of motorcycles exported differs from the bulk of those sold on the home market (much larger capacities are sold abroad than are wanted at home where noise and pollution standards are higher in view of the narrow Japanese streets). Moreover, apart from their own large home market, the Japanese were aware that the North American market had no indigenous producers for any motorcycles under the 1000 cc ones produced by Harley Davidson. Therefore, there was plenty of opportunity to develop further sales there before real competition from home producers in another country's home market had to be encountered in obtaining further expansion. In 1975, one-fifth of Japanese production was exported to the USA; only one-twentieth to the United Kingdom.

Thirdly, the Japanese export onslaught started off quite mildly in the early 1960s, with a few poor and unsuccessful models in smaller engine sizes. But, rapidly, within a year or two, the Japanese had learnt the essential lessons and had earned the essential returns to venture, first, successfully into the small-engine markets and, then, gradually, to move up the engine range to massive motorcycles and total command of the market in the 1980s. Opposition in Britain was not quick off the mark when the Japanese arrived, and later it was not concerted across all motorcycle sizes, companies or the national industry and such opposition as there was proved ineffective.

Fourthly, the collective term 'the Japanese motorcycle industry' must not obscure the fact that there were, and are, many Japanese producers competing amongst themselves for the home market and export markets and, thus, these were challengeable individually by British producers. The competition *within* Japan was severe enough to cut the number of producers from the 1950s to the present position in the 1980s when Honda, Yamaha, Suzuki and Kawasaki are the largest and most successful. Fuji and Mitsubishi withdrew from the trade in 1968 and 1965 respectively (though they survived in other trades). There have been, therefore, unsuccessful Japanese motorcycle concerns to line up with the British and other failures.

Fifthly, Japanese motorcycle producers as good capitalists seized their opportunities through new thinking, new demands and new technology. Individually and collectively, they saw new marketing opportunities in their own country and in South-East Asia; in motorcycling for pleasure and excitement as well as merely to get to work or to market; in clean, reliable, attractive machines that did not assume a 'manly' attitude to oil drips, vibration, kickstarts and the need for regular mechanical adjustments; in harnessing *existing* (prewar British in some cases revamped for the 1960s) designs and features and in establishing themselves and their excellent after-sales service in the smaller machines long used in Japan before invading the larger capacities to push the world demand to want capacities unthought of before at prices above those of many motorcars; in new orientations for advertising campaigns, so finding new markets throughout South-East Asia and the developing world as well as in leisure use in existing markets. They also harnessed research and technology to revolutionize combined design and production so that motorcycles ceased to be hand assembled and fitted (the fitting being essential when components did not fit together automatically but needed careful adjustment and filing down) and, thus, became mass produced mechanically at low cost, consistent high quality and with relatively unskilled labour. In this way, prices were cut, extending markets and enabling economies of scale to be obtained with massive improvements in productivity year after year as the effects accumulated and combined. Such economies absorbed the transport and marketing costs involved in selling Japanese-made motorcycles in Britain, Europe and the USA. It also opened up the possibility of production in the developing world where there are now many motorcycle factories. [. . .]

British Firms' Policies

Even if British motorcycle producers had noticed the Japanese threat and begun to plan to meet it around 1960, were they capable of finding the

The Demise of the British Motorcycle Industry

resources to meet it in terms of finance, ideas and management capability and implementation? British motorcycle models in design terms seem to have been capable of meeting competition (though there was a distinct tendency to abandon models quickly that failed to attract management or the market rather than to promote, or make minor alterations to emphasize, their virtues, thus wasting design resources, and we have noted in the motorcycle industry as elsewhere in British industry an undue concentration on *short-term* returns – or rather their absence – when persistence and planning might have produced *long-term* results such as the Japanese engineered). The problem lay in production investment. This had several facets in the motorcycle industry. It entailed finding, or obtaining the board of directors' permission to use, the necessary money and management resources to lay down adequate production facilities to produce motorcycles at a low enough price, at the right season of the year, and in the required quality and quantity. This proved demanding even to meet existing plans. In practice even eager customers were often unable to obtain motorcycles that met these conditions, let alone other customers who had to be won over to justify the much larger production needed to compete with the Japanese. We cannot say with confidence that the resources were there or that, if they were, they would have been invested in the necessary revolution in motorcycle productivity and marketing. The former is more likely than the latter.

In any case, the differences in productivity and, therefore, in costs between Britain and Japan were enormous by 1973 as table 1 indicates. While British output per worker per year had almost halved in 1973 compared to 1961, that in Japan had doubled. Starting from a more favourable position in 1956, British output had fallen to one-fifteenth of the Japanese average or one-twentieth of Honda's record figure by 1973. It is difficult to believe that government investment, the merger, the new models or rationalization down to one or two works was going to counter or meet the competition that this productivity differential implied, even allowing for the undoubted difference in the capacity of the motorcycles being produced.

TABLE 1 ESTIMATES OF RELATIVE PRODUCTIVITY
(output per worker per year)

	UK	Japan
1956	19	16
1961	23	86
1966	16	116
1971	19	162
1973	13	195

	Meriden	Honda	Yamaha	Suzuki	Kawasaki
1973	14	262	200	114	159

Source: Based on our estimates and those of Boston Consulting Group (1975). It assumes UK employees of 6500 in 1956–66 and 4500 in 1967–73, and assumes Japan employees of 21,000 in 1956–73; it ignores any differences in the size of the motorcycle being produced.

The British Retreat

Thus, we have come up against a second series of key questions which relate to the deficiencies of the British motorcycle producers in the 1960s and 1970s that, irrespective of one's answer to the first key question above, prevented them from surviving the Japanese onslaught in practice. Thus, ignoring the Japanese, it is possible to identify factors that help to explain the decline of the British motorcycle industry in the history and behaviour of individual companies and in government policy towards the industry, trade and the economy generally.

However, here too, it is necessary to recall that the British motorcycle industry comprised a number of private enterprise concerns presumably motivated by the profit motive, and to ask whether failure to invest in more advanced and expanded motorcycle production (as distinct from new models) was explained simply by the existence of poor relative returns and prospects in that industry even in the days before Japanese competition. Our findings, however, suggest that returns and funds were available in the 1950s in the motorcycle companies but that investments were not made on anything like the scale necessary to advance and expand motorcycle production and that this was not due to lack of a market at least until the 1960s. [. . .]

But, as so often in Britain, investment proved to be of an unproductive kind. [. . .] Thus, production facilities were only maintained rather than improved, let alone revolutionized, in the early 1960s and the limited attempts to do this in the late 1960s at BSA failed. Evidence from both BSA and Enfield indicate that new motorcycle designs had to be suitable for production on existing machine tools and, thus, were changed marginally and not fundamentally in their method of production. When decisive production changes were introduced – the Woolwich engine plant in 1955 or at Andover in 1969 for Associated Motor Cycles (AMC) or in 1968/9 at BSA – they failed to work the miracle; at Woolwich and BSA this was because the particular product proved defective. This failure was largely through weak management and decision-making and a grave failure of communication and cooperation between departments and companies. For instance, within BSA, the proposals of the motorcycle division seem to have met a poor response in interest and understanding at group board level, where non-executive and non-motorcycle directors were in the majority at all times, quite apart from failures between departments and the deep and sustained division between Triumph/Meriden and BSA/Small Heath. Again, throughout the industry, customers for Villiers' engines experienced indifference to their wishes and needs from Villiers; it was this that led AMC to the fateful attempt to make its own small-capacity engine.

It was errors of these kinds that brought the individual companies down. Japanese competition was only relevant in the sense that it produced the situation that, with falling home demand, gave rise to some of these errors. Thus, decline was not *caused* directly by Japanese competition. The British concerns that made up the industry had already taken decisions with fatal

The Demise of the British Motorcycle Industry

consequences for each of them. These decisions were various in content, time scale and justification. While it is attractive to find one explanation in a panic reaction to the Japanese threat, this seems to have had no justification in practice; British top motorcycle management were too complacent and unaware to appreciate fully the Japanese threat. At least one top manager, Edward Turner, visited Japan and motorcycle factories there in 1960 and reported back on the Japanese 'menace' (Davies, 1980, p. 199). His report was outspoken and clear even if he did not expect the Japanese to 'eclipse the traditional type of machine that the British motorcyclist wants and buys' (ibid., p. 204). However, his warnings fell on deaf ears and he himself failed to act. Quite how this happened or how the 1962 trade agreement came to omit reference to motorcylces is difficult to understand, for the Japanese were already established producers and exporters. It was even suggested in *The Times* and on television that the Japanese small motorcycle revolution in the USA was having a beneficial effect on British heavy motorcycle sales. Vast sums were being spent on advertising by the Japanese, particularly by Honda. The initial impact was viewed as improving the general image of motorcycles as well as to filter some new riders through to BSA/Triumph's more powerful machines. However, by 1964, it was accepted that Britain could not produce machines below 350 cc to compete with the hordes of Japanese lightweights reaching the USA; and Britain was next on the invasion list.

It does seem that most British companies almost committed suicide by errors of judgement or by apparent indifference to the Japanese threat and the state of the industry or, indeed, went out of business for independent reasons (such as asset-stripping). It is a sad story of enthusiasm, loyalty and teamwork at the middle level being undermined, it seems to us, by a succession of significant failures and wrong (with hindsight) decisions at the top of each company.

Some of these are literally incredible and large scale. We refer here particularly to the fateful decision of AMC to make its own engines at Woolwich rather than continue to buy from Villiers, for these AMC engines were never in practice satisfactory and the process, before engines were again purchased from Villiers, merely served to discredit and weaken the James and Francis Barnett marques. [. . .]

New men failed to learn from the experience of the old and they failed to see that designs were adequately tested before going into production. There was also much designing by committee with subsequent modification and delay; the 1971 750 cc triple Triumph Trident was based on a 1964 prototype and could, according to Hopwood, have gone into production in 1965 (Hopwood, 1981, pp. 216 and 230). There were other disasters. There was the BSA 650 cc twin-cylinder model whose saddle was three inches higher than normal and suitable only for giants (Hopwood, 1981, pp. 236-7 and 249). There was the Ariel Three shoppers' tricycle, launched with an enormous flourish in July 1970 and backed with a new production line at Small Heath to produce 25,000 a year but which sold only 2500 as it was too expensive for its market and failed to meet most countries' legislative requirements. This was another sizeable investment of an unproductive kind that, also, served to delay improvements in other machines. A third disaster involved machines of 'abominable' and 'unacceptable' design that reached the US market too late for the American buying season and, on more than one occasion, both badly corroded and without forks. [. . .]

At a less dramatic level, mergers in the British motorcycle industry were not followed by integration and economies of scale. Instead, the individual plants and marques were maintained separately and encouraged to compete with each other as well as with outsiders. This was a short-sighted practice common to concerns in other British industries. It neglected the benefits of economies of scale, especially in rationalizing overheads and sales forces. Thus, BSA and Triumph had for many years separate and competing sales organizations in the USA and little was shared between Meriden and Small Heath, which were distinct and jealous empires. Practices and wages differed; personnel were difficult to transfer. The same was true at AMC between Norton and AJS in larger machines and James and Francis Barnett in smaller ones. Similar independence was maintained between product divisions within BSA. It was a leader in sintered components, non-corrosive steel and monochrome finishes, quite apart from machine tools, but failed to apply these in motorcycle development – where corrosion and chrome finishing were particular problems. [. . .]

Product Market Area

A motorcycle is a consumer durable – a word introduced at BSA in 1964 as part of the McKinseyization so hated by Hopwood (Hopwood, 1981, p. 206) – in both the transport and the leisure market. Demand fluctuates sharply both seasonally and from year to year. More consideration of the leisure field could well have directed the British motorcycle producers to new opportunities and customers and reshaped publicity and model range.

As a form of transport, motorcycles have competed with scooters, bicycles, mopeds and the small car. New successful small cars were produced in Britain undoubtedly replacing a motorcycle for some. The sidecar has disappeared. The transport market, however, offered an opportunity to provide a motorcycle on two or three wheels for women and older men to use on shopping trips though this would have required more attention to safety, cleanliness and reliability – qualities not present in many postwar British motorcycles geared (perhaps mistakenly) to a different image. British producers failed to enter seriously the step-through scooter market; models were produced soon after the war (BSA developed one in the 1940s – Hopwood, 1981, p. 97) but always seemed to be abandoned with a wasteful lack of persistence.

The leisure market, on the other hand, offered almost unlimited potential as a consumer good with a new social image (such as was exploited by the Japanese), a status symbol (e.g. the very big motorcycles), or in new sporting activities like motocross, etc., and at a time of increasing spending, especially on the part of youth, being owned in addition to a car. [. . .]

Economic Policy

Like the motorcar industry, the motorcycle industry in Britain has suffered from the instruments of economic policy and the regulation of the economy persistently upsetting its markets. Controls on hire purchase, purchase tax, taxes on petrol, etc., quite apart from taxation of profits and investment subsidies, affected sales and prevented forward planning. The harmful effects are commented on constantly in chairmen's statements to shareholders and in the trade press. It is particularly significant for the motorcycle industry that the Budget in April coincides with the start of the selling season, too late for adjustments in production to take place. Thus removal of taxes could leave markets unmet whereas their introduction on other occasions could leave a company loaded down with unwanted stocks. By way of illustration, BSA considered tighter hire purchase regulations had cut their sales by one third in 1959/60 and noted that these changes were the tenth such change in eight years. [. . .]

Seasonality in Demand and Supply

Immediately after 1945, motorcycles could be sold readily throughout the year. A decade later, a return to the seasonality in sales common in the 1930s was noted. This seasonality derived from the weather and usage of motorcycles. The season was even more severe in the US market. This transmitted itself to production (at BSA, Small Heath, output in August on average between 1965/6 and November 1971 was only 46 per cent of that in May) but not fully into numbers of employees and overtime (the number of employees in August was 88 per cent of that in May and overtime hours were 44 per cent when one would have expected them to be nil given the lower output). As a result, it took twice as many hours to make one motorcycle in August as it did in May even allowing for holidays and, for the slack six months of each year, 50 per cent more hours were spent on each machine than in the busy half of the year. Such operations were uneconomic, and it is our view that more marketing effort should have been directed to extending the season, possibly by selling at lower margins and/or in India, Pakistan, Australia, etc., where the seasons were more favourable or complemented those of the north. This seasonality was common to other producers and to trade in motorcycles; its cost implications for producers was considerable.

Two other issues need mentioning even if this is not an entirely appropriate place.

Productivity

In conjunction with the work on seasonality at Small Heath just mentioned went a study of employment, hours and output for the years 1965/6 – 1970/1. This has shown that Small Heath output peaked in 1966/7 when 43,500 motorcycles were produced but that subsequently overmanning and falling productivity per man hour must have imposed an enormous cost burden on the firm, superimposed on the seasonality costs already mentioned. The ins and outs of it are not entirely clear; one is suspicious simply because the statistics are so frightening. For instance, these indicate that, in 1965/6, Small Heath took about 130 hours to make a motorcycle (or each worker produced one a month); in 1970/1, when all the difficulties were experienced with the models, it took 330 hours to make a machine, though these were probably larger, more complex machines and each man made only 80 per cent of a machine in a month. There was, therefore, falling productivity at a time when it is hard not to think the Japanese were improving their productivity by 10 per cent p.a. or more (see table 1).

Trade Unions, Wage Demands and the Problems of the Industry

We wish to make the point that industrial relations in the British motorcycle industry at factory level do not provide an explanation for its demise. We have examined this popular explanation and consider that industrial relations had little or no impact on the well-being of the industry until the last few years. Although there were a series of harmful strikes at suppliers, a search of the records shows virtually no strike action (of the degree recorded by the Department of the Employment) at all pre-1969 at Small Heath[1] or Meriden,[2] wage demands in the mid 1960s at the latter being granted without dispute in order to maintain production (Hopwood, 1981, p. 207). We have, however, been told of worsening industrial relations at Small Heath in the late 1960s and this is confirmed by the Department of Employment records. In the uncertainties of the time, apparently there were work stoppages over many minor matters such as when the wages were late on a Friday morning. Between 1968 and 1973, there were 6 strikes at Triumph and 11 at BSA. We find that the issues were basically management issues or involved problems within companies which came under management control. No revolution in production methods was attempted, and redundancy (e.g. at BSA in August 1967 and 1969 and November/December 1971 or at Woolwich) was not much of a problem when unemployment rates were very low.

Conclusion

Finally, we would say that the simplistic explanations that are often suggested all have an element of truth in them but it has become clear to us that a full explanation needs to integrate all these elements rather than to rely on merely one. There is no one feature (apart from relative unit costs and that is an effect of other decisions not a cause) that explains the decline of the British motorcycle industry. It is therefore difficult to be sure that we have the measure of the problems and fully understand why decisions were taken as they were. In so far as other industries fall into these patterns, the factors involved are likely to be of the same kind and as diverse.

The motorcycle industry faced a mixture of international, national and company structural problems and it is the conjunction of events at each of

1. There was only one strike between 1945 and 1968 and that was in 1962; there were many strikes in 1969 and thereafter.
2. There were 10 strikes between 1945 and 1968, involving a total of 18,455 working days. Based on Dept. of Employment original record books at Public Record Office (1945–60) and Dept. of Employment Statistics Division, Watford (1961–75).

The Demise of the British Motorcycle Industry

these three levels that caused the problems for individual companies. Nevertheless, too much emphasis should not be placed on the problems of individual companies because, clearly, a number of these companies were affected adversely at about the same time. Thus, importance must be attached to the wider events and, undoubtedly, amongst these, the key event is the arrival of Japanese motorcycles on the British and American markets in the mid 1960s and the scale of production and export of individual Japanese concerns. The second key event is the fall in demand for motorcycles in the 1960s in Britain and America. While, at the time, this seemed to be a structural change brought on by the advent of lower cost car transport, the revival of demand from a somewhat different customer and activity throws that decline into a rather different perspective as the revival of demand was a response to more determined marketing. This was undertaken by the Japanese but, perhaps, might as easily have been introduced earlier by more dynamic British manufacturers when they led the world in the 1950s. Could that opportunity have provided a different end for the study? We shall never know.

APPENDIX

Production Methods

The case for studying the production process has been discussed elsewhere (Smith, 1980), but here we present some initial reasons. The ability to sell in a competitive market and realize a profit is founded on the cost competitiveness of the product. The cost of a product is a result of levels of productivity per man hour. Productivity in labour-intensive industries depends on the intensity of labour. However, once brought into a capitalistically organized process productivity largely depends on the method of organization and the productivity of the plant provided. Finally, the quality of the work experience and industrial relations can be directly related, at least in part, to the nature of the work process. Thus, on all counts, the success of a company originates in the production process, although there are obviously additional factors to consider, e.g. advertising, distribution, etc.

The empirical conclusion of the Boston Consulting Group's (1975) Report was that there was a very marked difference in the production processes in the British and Japanese industries.

> The British motorcycle industry has three rather antiquated factories in the Midlands. Investment has been low for many years and the equipment in the factories is old and mostly general purpose in nature. As a result, it is difficult to maintain product reliability and impossible to use modern, high volume, highly automated, low cost methods. (Boston Consulting Group, 1975, Appendix, p. 211)

The general nature of the equipment is borne out by the Chairman's appeals for work to be found for BSA's spare motorcycle capacity. This would only be possible on the most general of machinery. The reliance on skilled labour, i.e. the lack of automation, is also revealed by BSA's constant reference to its shortage and the effect it was having on production (see Chairman's 'Report to Shareholders', various years, and reports of the apprentices' annual dinners from 1960 onwards). BCG also estimated 80 per cent of the plant in Britain to be over fifteen years old (Boston Consulting Group, 1975, Appendix, p. 211).

In contrast they summarize the Japanese system as follows:

> The Japanese production system is modern and growing. High and increasing productivities are achieved through the use of capital intensive methods, the introduction of which is facilitated by the high model volumes and overall growth. The general level of production technology is very high, and much of it in the machining area may be proprietary since each of the major manufacturers have their own specialised machine tool designing and building operations.

> They also mention the high productivity of, and close relationships with the parts industries, e.g. cross holdings, loan finance, etc. Furthermore, the labour-intensive activities, e.g. assembly, are increasingly located 'offshore', i.e. in low-wage countries, relative to Japan.

> Overall, it seems that the highly competitive costs of the Japanese motorcycle industry are based on high productivity in both the parts supply industry and the motorcycle manufacturing operations themselves. (Boston Consulting Group, 1975, Appendix, pp. 222-3)

Two examples can be given to illustrate these points. In 1959 total motorized two-wheeler production in the UK (motorcycles, scooters and mopeds) was 235,452 machines. Honda's total production for that year was 317,000 machines (*Business Monitor*, Carrick, 1976, p. 20), and this was primarily in the lightweight classes, i.e. up to 250 cc.

The second example is the techniques used for producing frames for small motorcycles. Boston Consulting Group report (1975, p. 229) that the Japanese industry use pressed steel frames or subassemblies, using automated, conveyor-based techniques wherever possible. Assembly times are about one minute per frame. An article in BSA's *Group News* in the early 1960s, under the heading 'How It Is Done', shows the equivalent stage at Small Heath. The brazing up of the frames was done as follows. Align all the tubes; 'paint' on a mixture of black lead and molasses to those areas not to be brazed; put the relevant joint into a vat of molten brass; remove, cool, and chip off the 'black lead toffee'. This was all done manually by about seven men, most of whom had over twenty-five years service with the company. The comparison needs qualification, in that the situations compared are about ten years apart, but it demonstrates the attitude to production technology in either case. BSA, for instance, were not investing in more modern technology, as such investments would certainly have appeared in their *Group News*.

The Demise of the British Motorcycle Industry

British and Japanese Producers

Postwar, there were two major amalgamations in Britain. AMC was a specialist motorcycle producer whereas BSA was involved in many other lines of business. However, both these amalgamations were simply collections of companies. In neither case was there any real attempt to rationalize either the model range or the methods of production. Production technology was based on skilled labour and general machinery. Consequently, low levels of output were achieved. The management and often the ownership of the companies was drawn in the main from pioneers and enthusiasts.

The postwar Japanese developments were different in origin. Only Honda, himself an engineer, was a specialist motorcycle producer. Suzuki, Yamaha and Kawasaki were all long-established companies in other industries before they diversified into motorcycle production. The difference in approach is dramatically shown in the amount and form of investment in production technology, as well as the careful development of distribution networks and advertising. The basis for this difference would seem to be the Japanese willingness to invest, and their ability to do so on a large scale.

A further point of interest is the British attitude to rival producers. AMC had an isolationist attitude to seeking designs outside the company (Grant, 1969, p. 38). BSA rejected Honda's application for tools. Both cases imply an insularity that may well account for subsequent under-estimations of the situation. For example, the loss of sales in the early 1960s was seen as due to a temporary recession (see the various Chairmen's Statements for the period), not an all-out attack on the UK market by bigger firms. This can be contrasted with Lucas's tactics of constantly visiting rivals to minimize the technological lead gained with a new process, and the extra profits that it gave rise to.[3]

In many ways the case of BSA is the most interesting. Of all the British companies BSA was the most similar to the Japanese. It was large, long established, the world leader at one point and involved in many complementary industries. Furthermore, in the Docker era it definitely had boardroom experience of finance and banking as well as in its component industries. Yet its attitude and strategy (if one can be discerned) to motorcycle production was illogical or at least short-sighted. Instead of restructuring production using their expertise in machine tools, combined with new steels, sintered components, etc., the strategy was to boost production by promoting intercompany rivalry. One corollary of promoting worker loyalty to the companies in the group was the later problems experienced in trying to rationalize production.

The MBH interventions, first in buying AMC and then in Norton Villiers Triumph, appear to be the first attempts to match the Japanese production technology. However, the gap was by this time so great that the scale of redundancies was enormous. Furthermore, the implications in terms of deskilling were commensurately large, with a great loss of worker control of the labour-process. When seen in the context of the stress on company

---

3. I am indebted to P. Embley of Birmingham Polytechnic for this point.

loyalty and the many supportive references to the high quality of British workmanship, the MBH proposals, in particular the two-factory plan, were clearly going to generate political tensions. The fundamental difference between Japanese and British rationalizations has been that while the Japanese were expanding, British firms were contracting. This, however, was inevitable if the basic supremacy of Japanese firms had been established by 1962.

The provisional conclusion would seem to be that the problem lies in a lack of investment and restructuring in the 1950s that might have maintained the British industry's position.

References and Works Consulted

Boston Consulting Group (1975) *Strategy Alternatives for the British Motorcycle Industry* (HMSO, H. of C. 532).
British Cycle and Motor Cycle Industries Association Circulars (1963–4).
Business Monitor Production Series, Board of Trade.
Carrick, Peter (1976) *The Story of Honda Motor Cycles* (Cambridge: Patrick Stephens).
Carrick, Peter (1978) *The Story of Kawasaki Motor Cycles* (Cambridge: Patrick Stephens).
Davies, Ivor (1980) *It's a Triumph* (Yeovil: Haynes).
Dunnett, P. J. S. (1980) *The Decline of the British Motor Industry: The Effects of Government Policy, 1945–1979* (London: Croom Helm).
Glueck, W. F. (ed.) (1980) *Business Policy and Strategic Management* (Tokyo: McGraw-Hill) 3rd edn; see esp. W. R. Sandberg, 'Norton Villiers Triumph and the Meriden Cooperative', p. 427 and seq.
Grant, Gregor (1969) *The History of a Great Motor Cycle* (Cambridge: Patrick Stephens).
Holliday, Bob (1972) *Norton Story* (Cambridge: Patrick Stephens).
Holliday, Bob (1978) *The Story of BSA Motor Cycles* (Cambridge: Patrick Stephens) with foreword by Jeff Smith.
Hopwood, Bert (1981) *Whatever Happened to the British Motorcycle Industry* (Yeovil: Haynes).
Kelly, J. W. E. (1978) 'A History of Veloce Ltd', unpublished PhD thesis, University of Bradford.
Louis, Harry and Currie, Bob (1975) *The Story of Triumph Motor Cycles* (Cambridge: Patrick Stephens) with foreword by Dennis Poore.
Magaziner, I. C. and Hout, T. M. (1980) *Japanese Industrial Policy*, Policy Studies Institute, no. 585.
Ryerson, Barry (1980) *The Giants of Small Heath: The History of BSA* (Yeovil: Haynes).
Rogers, N. M. (1979) *The British Motorcycle Industry 1945–75: Programme Notes for an Epic Still to be Written*, Centre for Urban and Regional Studies Working Paper 67.
Smith, Barbara M.D. (1980) 'Decline in a Core Region: the British Motorcycle Industry, 1945–75' End-of-grant report to SSRC.

1.3

How Wadkin Worked Clear

G. Foster

How's this for a quick thumbnail sketch of the middle reaches of British engineering? Products – technologically a bit dated; manufacturing methods – ditto; controls – fairly rudimentary; management – middle-aged, not over-burdened with imagination; labour – disinterested or disaffected; productivity – poor by international standards; customer service – ditto; environment – cramped, old-fashioned buildings in dreary back streets; prevailing ethos – anything for a quiet life.

Unfair, perhaps – in one or other particular – if applied to a given company; but as a generalization it can just about stand. It's a lot less true than it was, however, partly because a good number of firms that fitted the description are no longer there. Among the survivors, hopes of tranquillity have been severely shaken by the experiences of the past five years; and productivity, if nothing else, will have improved. Those which survived as anything more than shadows of their former selves obviously demonstrate some capacity for adaptation, even though many came through by the skin of their teeth. Wadkin of Leicester is one of these.

As a capital goods producer with an annual turnover of £26.6 million (in 1983), Wadkin is hardly a household name. Yet to the joinery and sawmilling trades, it is an industry giant, accounting for around 50 per cent by value of the UK market for woodworking machinery. (In the absence of statistics, market share is at best a rough estimate, but it is clear that Wadkin dominates the sector.) The company also reckons to be the biggest force in the most buoyant segment of the home market for metalworking machine tools. However, that claim is of recent date, and machine tools remain a secondary activity. For the present, as in the past, Wadkin lives or dies by woodworking equipment.

Until the end of the 1970s, this tucked-away corner of engineering brought Wadkin a fairly comfortable existence. During the middle years of the

G. Foster is deputy editor of *Management Today*.
Source: G. Foster, 'How Wadkin Worked Clear', from *Management Today*, May 1984.

decade, revenues of £13–16 million generated a steady annual £1.6–1.7 million of profit before tax. Yet the company was all too clearly stagnating. Foreign competitors – mainly from the EEC – were chipping away at the points where Wadkin's market coverage was weakest, especially in machinery for furniture manufacture; and profit margins and return on capital were both declining from their historically high levels. Even a record in calendar year 1978, when turnover broke the £20 million barrier and pre-tax profit exceeded £2 million for the first (and, so far, only) time, hardly arrested the downward trend.

What followed stopped just a little way short of disaster. A wave of strikes (national and local), closely followed by runaway inflation, the appreciation of sterling against other currencies, and the steep downturn in UK industrial production, cut the ground from under Wadkin – as from innumerable other manufacturers. (Given the importance to Wadkin of joinery equipment, the company was particularly sensitive to the condition of the housebuilding sector.) Profits went into a dive in 1979, turned into a loss the following year, and went on plunging to a deficit exceeding £1.3 million pre-tax in 1981.

As the haemorrhaging continued undiminished into 1982, the banks became understandably nervous, and were threatening to require security for the mounting overdraft when the turning-point came a little over 18 months ago. (Amazingly, although Wadkin's borrowings climbed well past the £3 million mark, they remained unsecured throughout.) 'We got into fairly deep water', comments Chairman Michael Goddard with masterly understatement. Perhaps more accurately, he acknowledges that 'In theory, we shouldn't now exist.'

In the light of the modest surplus (just announced) of £465,000 for 1983, and in expectation of progress towards the levels of the mid 1970s this year, Wadkin is currently being rated a recovery stock. What's ironic is that this rise from the deathbed is largely the result of an expensive course of treatment which the company prescribed for itself *before* it was hit by the full force of the recession. In the 1970s, management had tried to protect itself against foreign infiltration by importing equipment in areas where its own range was deficient: large panel-making machines for the furniture industry were brought in from Italy, for example, and small power tools from Japan. The company simultaneously attempted to hit back at competitors through its own sales subsidiaries – augmenting the usual distributor network – on the Continent.

Unfortunately, Continental techniques of joinery, like butchery, frequently differ from those of the UK. The present marketing director, John Nutt, points out that only a small part of Wadkin's range was of the right specification for Germany – Western Europe's biggest market. In 1981 the company there was closed down, leaving a substantial bad debt. A loss-making subsidiary in France, where Italian manufacturers had made considerable inroads, had ceased trading two years earlier.

During most of the postwar period Wadkin demonstrated a corporate reflex commonly seen in businesses accustomed to being dominant forces in their own worlds; it progressively extended, and elaborated, its catalogue.

How Wadkin Worked Clear

Back in the 1950s, not long after it went public, the company acquired a competitor in the north of England, with factories near Durham and near Colne in Lancashire. Although the group sales organization became centred on Leicester, the northern works (which mainly produced simpler 'classical' woodworking machines, such as saw benches and surface planers, under the name Bursgreen) always enjoyed a good deal of independence. The proliferation of products in semi-autonomous centres had a predictably adverse effect on costs. Stocks and work-in-progress, for example, reached 40 per cent of turnover by 1975, and went on rising.

Wadkin's rather turgid performance through much of the 1970s hardly escaped the shareholders or senior management. Chairman Bill Sims eventually retired at the start of 1980, when well into his seventies. (Now honorary president, he had joined the company as a young engineer 52 years before, reportedly to convert machines from belt to motorized drive.) The new chairman, Michael Goddard, was by far the youngest member of the board, and a real rarity at Wadkin's level of engineering – an Oxford graduate. But his association with Wadkin goes further back than that of some of the man-and-boy corporate servants. His father was chairman for many years, and his grandfather was one of the company's early backers around the turn of the century. The family still holds a significant, but now very minor, stake in the equity.

Certain measures introduced after Goddard took the chair were obviously dictated by the company's rapidly deteriorating financial position. Thus, a mounting succession of redundancies cut the payroll from a 1979 high point of over 1900 to 1100 at the end of 1982. But many other changes, although they also often produced short-term savings, were the result of strategic decisions agreed as soon as Goddard became chairman – and in some cases before.

Actions may have been speeded up under pressure of events, but the policies they reflected were 'intended to carry the company forward, rather than pull it through'. In other words, they were conceived as means of combating problems that had been building up in the 1970s, rather than as desperate remedies for the crisis of the early 1980s. This was not so much sang-froid as a repeated failure (shared with countless other manufacturers) to foresee how deep and how far the recession would go. Had Wadkin known in advance, Goddard admits, 'we probably wouldn't have had the courage to see the programme through'.

Goddard details the corporate strategy adopted since 1980 under five headings: (1) products – modernize and redesign for lower-cost production; (2) manufacturing – rationalize facilities, and invest in new equipment; (3) higher quality – of product and of service to customers; (4) marketing – review distribution channels and internal procedures to create a more responsive organization; (5) people – devolve responsibility and encourage individual development.

Set out like that, the objectives look a little too pat, and in some ways now standard. No doubt they were slightly modified as time went by – shaped by evolution as well as by inspiration. But it is clear that the five-point plan indicates fairly accurately the priorities adopted by management at the beginning of the decade. Goddard's office contains a bundle of visual aids that he has used for getting the message across within the company. In any case, progress of the plan can be seen in the record.

Action on the product front was pioneered by the machine tool division, because, from the mid 1970s on, 'metalworking was under greatest siege'. Wadkin's involvement in metalworking tools – indeed, its specialization in woodworking machines, for that matter – derived from wartime manufacture of aircraft parts. In World War I, Wadkin engineers had developed an 'automated' propeller shaper; before World War II, the company was asked to design new types of woodworking machines for aircraft production, but also equipment for cutting aluminium. Postwar, it moved from aircraft into general engineering with a range of drilling machines. Then, in the 1970s, like every competing manufacturer, Wadkin added a tool-changer to a numerically controlled drill and, hey presto, it had vertical machining centre.

This was no commerical breakthrough, however. While the Japanese were coming out with good, standard, competitively priced machine tools, Wadkin (not alone among UK producers) concentrated on specials: the customer could have any spindle speed, any control system; 'It was not really profitable business', recalls Rod Charles, who was then a production manager and is now general manager of the machine tool division. 'Margins were terrible. Delivery and quality were poor. . . . We spent most of the time getting the things to work.'

At the end of 1978, management realized that, out of 38 machines produced that year, 36 were substantially different from one another. 'It brought us to our senses', says Charles. 'We decided that if we were going to compete with the Japanese, we had to sell at their sort of prices, and specification and delivery must be as good.' Obviously, matching Japanese prices called for a fierce attack on manufacturing costs. Goddard, who took a special interest in NC machines while deputy chairman to Sims, points out that 'design does predicate production methods – 80 per cent of the cost of a product is fixed when you've finished drawing it'.

So Wadkin set out to design a machine for speed and simplicity of construction. (Value engineering became a management obsession: the current expression is DEM – design for ease of manufacture.) A critical path exercise indicated that it should be possible to assemble the new product within 12 weeks of the receipt of parts, compared with the customary 20 weeks, but that took no account of floor space or man hours – or cash flow. Today, the typical cycle time for assembly and testing (most of which takes place simultaneously) of a machine tool is 20 days.

The first of the new family, a medium-size CNC vertical machining centre, appeared in 1980. A second model, half as big again, followed in late 1982; and three smaller machines were launched last year. Together, it is reckoned, they cover about 80 per cent of the market for vertical CNC machines; and sell at a fraction of the price of earlier designs. One of the new generation, listed at £39,750, replaces a product which used to be offered at £84,000 in 1979. Moreover, according to Charles, warranty costs are below 20 per cent of previous levels.

How Wadkin Worked Clear

Wadkin's range of woodworking equipment is far more varied than its machine tools. Nevertheless, the woodworking side has had much the same treatment to simplify production and compress the manufacturing cycle. Redesign of one product, a simple saw bench, allowed its price to come down 28 per cent from £2500 to £1800. (Inflation and an oil-supported currency lent added urgency to such price-cutting: Goddard is fond of preaching that a 33 per cent cost reduction is needed to offset a 50 per cent decline in price competitiveness.) Several of the bigger machines have simultaneously been upgraded and equipped with sophisticated microprocessor controls. 'The technologies we've been developing in the machine tool division are applicable to woodworking products', says Goddard, 'It's a happy case of incest.'

Many other machines (and permutations of machines) have been discontinued. 'We were making everything in too small numbers. We dropped about a third of the product range. . . . It's a hard thing to rationalize when the order book is falling in a recession – most people do the opposite.' But Wadkin still has most of the market covered, from the needs of the small woodworking shop to those of the high volume producer. At the very bottom of the scale, the power tool division has been sold. Elsewhere, the company continues to augment its own range by factoring a few Italian imports.

The rationalization programme extended to the factories themselves, to increase specialization and output, and reduce overlap and stockholding. Moulding machines and cross-cuts are built in Leicester; routers at Colne; bandsaws at a Cleveland factory opened in 1978; classical machines at Durham. Some 20 CNC machine tools (including some of Wadkin's own manufacture) were commissioned between mid 1980 and the end of 1981, and there were further investments in computing for administration and production control – totalling £2 million in all. 'Quite a dose for a company this size', comments Goddard.

This high-risk policy of product innovation and capital investment in an increasingly unfavourable economic climate was at least launched on the basis of a fairly strong balance sheet. Wadkin's profitable, if unimpressive, performance in the 1970s had left the company with little in the way of borrowings. Goddard expected to be able to recover the £2 million almost immediately from a reduction in stocks; and he was very nearly right. Work-in-progress in December 1982 was £1.3 million lower than a year before; while raw materials and finished and factored goods released a further £600,000 of much-needed capital.

The substantial reduction in the pay roll contributed to a 25 per cent-plus improvement in productivity over three years. But the fall in volume, of a similar 25 per cent order, made mounting losses, plus the mounting debt, unavoidable. Goddard points out (hardly necessarily) that the company kept the banks informed, 'and they gave us support in what we were doing'. Yet their patience was evidently wearing thin by the time a finance director was appointed in October 1982.

It is an astonishing fact that Wadkin had no top-level finance officer during the critical period between the arrival of the new man, Max Hall, and the 1979 retirement of his predecessor, a characteristically venerable company servant of 33 years' standing. (Accountant Frank Dixon was appointed to the board in a non-executive capacity, however.) Hall remarks, wryly, that the shortage of orders in 1982 at least simplified the task of installing management controls, which had been very largely lacking. 'Michael Goddard was flying blind, without instruments, when I joined.' But, happily, the order book had just begun to pick up. The inflation and sterling exchange rates were both coming down, and Wadkin ended the year on an improving trend: redundancy costs aside, the loss at the pre-tax level was half that of 1981, and the company was again trading profitably.

The recovery in the cash flow, which came back sharply in the final quarter of 1982, enabled a hefty level of spending to be maintained last year. The cash position is now monitored weekly ('Cash reporting was particularly lax', says Hall); other reports come in from the divisions at the usual monthly intervals. There are some 15 operating divisions, implying a surprisingly complex structure – that is, again, for a company of Wadkin's size. But this is partly a consequence of Goddard's deliberate policy of thrusting responsibility down the line to encourage initiative and 'put decision-making where information is most plentiful'.

Before Goddard took over, the company consisted of a handful of manufacturing and trading divisions based on Leicester, while the northern factories remained separately incorporated. At the beginning of 1980, the subsidiaries were converted to divisions, bringing a marginal saving in administrative expense. The divisions vary enormously in size, and are organized into three groupings under different chairmen. The northern group, headed by Wadkin's deputy chairman, Leslie Robinson, has three woodworking divisions, at Durham (with around 150 employees), Colne (with 60) and Cleveland (maybe a dozen); also a couple of metal fabricators, and a foundry in Scotland. The latter supply components to other divisions, and generate what business they can outside the group.

In the Midlands, the dominant woodworking machinery division (some 400 employees) shares the same roof as high-tech NC woodworking (with 15 or 20). A tooling bits and pieces division is also located in Leicester, and the machine tool division occupies a more modern factory on an industrial estate at the further edge of the town. In addition, the Midlands manufacturing group includes a small division specializing in electronic drive systems. Finally, there are the commerical divisions: factoring, project engineering (currently working on a contract to equip a complete, highly automated woodworking factory in Egypt), and a machine rebuild operation, trading as Wilkinsons.

The devolution policy can show some positive results. The tiny Cleveland division, for example, developed a novel, and highly successful, type of bandsaw – and is currently 'the most profitable division in the group'. The principal complication stems from the fact that sales and marketing (at least of woodworking machines) are handled from the centre, by a separate pyramid under John Nutt.

Management recognizes the problems posed by a matrix formula; at the same time, it would clearly be impractical (and defeat the aim of 'a stripped-down organization') for each division to function as a self-contained business. The solution has been to appoint divisional marketing staff, linking in to Nutt's group marketing board. 'Central marketing takes the lead in market planning,' Goddard explains, 'but we are expecting the divisional boards to take a more active part in marketing.'

Nutt's top priority is 'to defend the UK against foreign competition – but we *have* to produce for world markets'. Wherever possible, the company is anxious to deal directly with its customers. Encouraging designers of machines to get out and talk to users is one way of involving the divisions in marketing; but it also reflects the current distribution strategy. 'We've questioned the traditional method of distribution through agents', says Goddard. There are risks entailed here, too, for in the UK, as elsewhere, a large proportion of orders are generated through stockists.

Overseas, Wadkin's sales are now surprisingly evenly spread across five continents. Export volume has lately declined even more sharply than home sales: typically a little under 40 per cent of group turnover, exports dropped to under 30 per cent in the first half of 1983. As Nutt's statement implies, the main promotional effort is currently directed at the domestic market, but in future years the balance is expected to change. In foreign markets, of course, the company's size ensures that it must remain largely dependent on an agency network; the more so since the French and German outlets have closed their doors. Europe – notably Northern Europe – still contains important outlets for the group's woodworking machinery, but the geographical focus has already shifted. So has the approach to selected markets: Basil Thornley, the main board director responsible for exports, says that 'Instead of doing the world as a global thing, we are dividing and concentrating.'

A couple of years ago the company acquired its distributor in New South Wales; it also opened a branch in Greensboro, North Carolina, a centre of the US furniture industry. High hopes are entertained of the US, where houses, too, are usually built of wood; where the exchange rate has moved decisively in Wadkin's favour; and where the local woodworking machinery manufacturers are said to be many years behind the Europeans, who provide the stiffest competition. Although it will significantly increase the cost of sales, Wadkin now intends to set up a string of satellite operations across the US – seven or eight before the end of the 1980s, according to Thornley.

Such plans belong to an uncertain future, however. Wadkin's recovery still has a long way to go, even to get back to the position reached in 1978. Moreover, in the nature of things, the recovery has so far been uneven. With the introduction of new models, output of machine tools has more than doubled since the beginning of last year; even so, the division is at present unable to keep up with the order intake, and delivery dates are stretching out far beyond the eight-week target. (Machine tools are so far for domestic consumption only; this year Wadkin expects to capture 30–40 per cent of the UK market for vertical machining centres in its own size categories. Further ahead, there could well be export opportunities – several approaches have already been received from US distributors.) The Leicester woodworking equipment factory is back to three shifts in certain departments, and management is talking of putting a fourth, unmanned shift on its CNC investment.

On the other hand, the Durham division – which was hardest hit in the recession – is not fully loaded. And there is a fourth northern woodworking machine factory at Thornaby on Tees, which has never been in production since it was optimistically acquired by Wadkin at the turn of the decade. As Goddard remarks, 'There is plenty to go for.' The recent Budget will do the company no harm in the short term, however, by encouraging investment on the part of UK customers before capital allowances come to an end.

There is plenty to go for, too, on the design and engineering fronts. On the woodworking side, Wadkin is thinking less about standard products, and more about integrated systems. Machine tool automation is being carried one step forward this year, with the launch of multi-pallet models that will shorten the machining cycle yet again. The company is half-way through a study into the potential for flexible manufacturing methods in its own factories. Goddard anticipates that the project will cost at least as much as the £2 million spent on CNC and related equipment, but that it will bring about further significant reductions in stockholding and working capital.

Wadkin's way ahead is still far from distinct; and indicated as much by hopes and assumptions as by present and foreseeable reality. But that is true of most businesses. Having come through the worst slump in half a century, management believes that the policies it has applied in the past three years or so make the company a match for any competition. 'We have surpassed the Japanese [machine tool builders] on design for economic manufacture': yet, even with the protection of voluntary import restrictions, Wadkin remains vulnerable to Japanese decisions on pricing. 'We have designed [woodworking] products to offset our competitive disadvantage vis-à-vis the Italians' but the Italians, too, often enjoy advantages of scale (besides possessing 'a mysterious ability to defy gravity'). 'Our social costs are below the Germans', but the Germans are acknowledged to be highly efficient manufacturers. The claims may be fair – but so are the qualifications.

In three and a half years, Wadkin has not been able to eradicate all the traces of age and mental weariness, the complacency and drabness and making-do that were almost the hallmarks of British engineering. But it has unquestionably seen great changes for the better and that's fairly typical too. Goddard's truthful assertion that 'upheaval has become a way of life' offers the best hope that there is a healthy future ahead of Wadkin – and of a once dominant and still vitally important sector of British industry.

1.4

Manufacturing in the 1980s

C. New

There has been no shortage of 'explanations' for low growth in the UK, including the old favourites of management deficiencies, the UK educational system, social attitudes, restrictive practices of trade unions, national apathy, insufficient investment and government intervention. Professor Kaldor, in his inaugural lecture, *Causes of the Slow Rate of Economic Growth in the UK* (1966), put forward a different explanation, which later became known as the 'structural problem' of the UK economy:

> Fast rates of economic growth are associated with the fast rate of growth of the 'secondary' sector of the economy – mainly the manufacturing sector – and . . . this is an attribute of an intermediate stage of economic development. It is the characteristic of the transition from 'nonmaturity' to 'maturity', and . . . the trouble with the British economy is that it has reached a high stage of 'maturity' earlier than others, with the result that it has exhausted the potential for fast growth before it had attained particularly high levels of productivity or real income per head.

This explanation comes down to the fact that, for many years, the UK had no surplus labour supply available from the primary (that is, agriculture and mining) sector of the economy. By 1972, for example, the UK primary sector employed only 2 per cent of the population and produced 3 per cent of the gross domestic product, while in France 13 per cent of the population produced only 6 per cent of the GDP, and in West Germany 8 per cent of the population produced only 3 per cent of the GDP.

Of course, in the period 1954–64, when the average annual growth rate of the UK in real terms was 2.7 per cent, compared to 4.9 per cent in France

---

C. New is Professor of Management at the Cranfield Institute of Technology.
Source: From Professor New's inaugural lecture at the School of Management, Cranfield Institute of Technology; first published in *Management Today*, October 1979.

and 6 per cent in West Germany, concern over these differentials was high. It continued to be felt thereafter. However, in the period 1972-5, these annual growth rates all slowed dramatically, to 1.3 per cent in the UK, 2.5 per cent in France and 0.7 per cent in Germany; and slower rates of growth have now become the norm in the advanced industrial economies. Moreover, these slow rates of growth have been associated not with *increases* but with *reductions* in the level of employment in manufacturing in each case: 0.9 per cent per annum in the UK, 0.3 per cent in France and a hefty 3 per cent in Germany in 1972-5. Naturally, attention has turned to comparisons in balance-of-payment terms, and of levels of unemployment and of the *level* of productivity being achieved – rather than the rate of growth in output itself. How should British manufacturing industry respond in these circumstances?

In order to remain successful, a manufacturing company must have a coherent manufacturing strategy which matches its market and corporate strategy: in short, it must have a manufacturing structure which is appropriate to the manufacturing task which it has set itself. This principle can be applied to the UK economy as a whole in the context of the structural pressures which will be present in the 1980s.

Almost all the scenarios put forward for the 1980s and beyond point to even greater problems in the manufacturing area of the business than today's. The major pressures include: (1) the *social*: higher educational standards, rejection of the work ethic, growing levels of violence, higher expectations of employees, rising unemployment, expectation of greater social responsibility of companies to maintain employment; (2) the *environmental*: pollution restriction, control of dangerous processes, raw-material supply, cost increases and shortages (particularly from growing militancy in the Third World); and (3) the *technological*: higher levels of automation both in product design and in manufacturing facilities (e.g. the impact of microprocessors), leading to lower labour requirements with different skills.

The key to the possible effects of the so-called microprocessor revolution lies in the cost reduction of feasible control systems: the F-100L microprocessor (the first of European manufacture) will do for £50 what the 1960 computer would do for £200,000, at a fraction of the power consumption and at negligible size. The effects of the microprocessor on the telecommunications industry perhaps cannot be read across into other sectors – there will clearly always be a need for mechanical control systems in the traditional products of UK engineering industries. Nevertheless, these effects on telecommunications are a pointer for the future.

For instance, in the Switching Equipment Division of the US Western Electric, over the period 1970-80, these impacts are expected: (1) reduction in direct employees of 55 per cent from 39,200 to 17,400; (2) reduction in factory space from 4.7 million sq ft to 3.1 million sq ft; (3) at the same time, an increase in unit output of 13 per cent from 5.4 to 6.1 million lines per annum; therefore, (4) an increase in unit output per direct employee of 154 per cent from 138 to 351 lines.

Even these figures do not tell the whole story: the labour remaining is of a different skill mix; maintenance engineering is revolutionized, the bought-

Manufacturing in the 1980s

out content has risen from 20 per cent for the old Strowger exchanges to nearer 75 per cent for the latest electronic systems. Most important of all, perhaps, for the individual companies is the requirement for cash. First, redundancy payments: one UK company has estimated the loss so far at £27 million: overall it could run to perhaps £100 million. Secondly, for new investment in plant and equipment Western Electric has spent £18 million on updating a single plant, and the European plants are much older.

Some key questions are raised by these problems: (1) should corporations accept responsibility for employment – if automation and high technologies create unemployment, should this be offset by creating new labour-intensive, that is, craft operations within the company? (2) What level of 'participation' (in the true sense) is going to be appropriate in a radically changed environment? (3) What will be the consequences of a zero growth economy – not just in the UK, but in the world as a whole? (4) In what ways will greater sensitivity to material and energy costs affect product design, product life, servicing and manufacturing requirements?

The manufacturing manager will be a major factor in determining the effectiveness with which organizations cope with these problems. In particular, it will be essential for the manufacturing function to play a much greater role in developing overall corporate strategy than in the past. Only if this is done can change be managed within the constraints which the social and environmental pressures seem likely to place on corporate activity.

The key prerequisites for market success are:

(1) *Reliable delivery.* Although a plant may not offer as short a delivery time or as low a price as competitors, its reputation for meeting delivery quotations can be a major strength, particularly where capital goods are supplied to a construction schedule.

(2) *Delivery lead-time.* In some markets, such as the supply of urgent spares, it will not be enough to offer reliable delivery; it will have to be fast as well.

(3) *Product quality and reliability.* In certain markets, such as nuclear power equipment, product reliability is a *sine qua non*; in other cases, the product may not be the cheapest or the best designed or have the shortest delivery time, but is guaranteed to work when you get it, and, in the rare case of failure, redress is immediate. Actual product quality, in terms of both product design and manufacture, is essentially a balance with price, unless competitive products are indistinguishable. A plant must choose either a high absolute quality level or simply one which is consistent with market price.

(4) *Product design flexibility.* Product design may be either internally controlled or specified by the customer. In some markets, a plant can choose to offer a standard product range or to specialize in custom-built, non-standard products.

(5) *Output volume flexibility.* It may be an essential ingredient of market success to be able to vary total output very quickly in relation to market needs. Such flexibility is usually required of service systems, such as restaurants and hotels, on a relatively short time-scale. It is, however, also

a characteristic required in plants competing on price, in highly cyclical industries. A plant may choose to have inflexible capacity, but, if it does, it cannot also choose to be both a low unit-cost producer and to offer a short and reliable delivery.

(6) *Price*. Price is rarely as isolated a competitive variable as some economists believe. Price and quality are directly related, except in commodity-type markets, but delivery times and delivery reliability also have price implications. The UK economy relies extensively on the export of capital goods, in which direct price comparability is difficult to establish, and where non-price competition is dominant.

In addition to these six external elements, two internal ones can be added: (1) *Capital investment*. The company may wish to operate in a market without investing too much in capital plant; and (2) *Learning*. The prime reason for operating in a product market may simply be to learn about the market. The most important thing to realize about all eight elements is that they contain implied trade-offs both within themselves and against the others. A plant cannot pursue all the elements for success simultaneously. If it attempts to do so, it will inevitably fail to perform satisfactorily on any individual issue.

Each requirement has then to be considered against the background of the company's corporate strategy, the market in which it operates, competitors' strategies and the environmental pressures. Out of this should come clear statements of, first, *a corporate product strategy*. This should cover which products to sell in which markets, and the associated marketing mix; that is, the basis on which the products are to be sold into these markets. Second, *a corporate manufacturing strategy*: i.e., which products to manufacture in which plants and the associated manufacturing mix (or structure); that is, the physical manufacturing facilities required and the key decisions on control systems and personnel relating to each plant.

Generally speaking, the first of these statements is spelt out fairly concisely (even if not optimally) in most companies, if only because it must be in order to sell anything at all. The second statement is rarely made explicit enough to be of any operational significance. When it appears in statements of corporate policy, it often takes the form of: 'Deliver on time on the shortest possible lead-time a superior quality product, making anything the customer asks for in any volume required at the lowest possible price, while not investing any capital and learning all you can about the market while you do it.' In such cases, the corporate strategy, as it concerns manufacturing, can best be described as a set of pious, incompatible hopes.

If, after much heart-searching, the current corporate strategy does not seem to meet all the requirements, there is a choice of solution: (1) change the strategy; (2) sacrifice some of the requirements; (3) be at least as creative as your competitors; (4) manage each segment differently.

Perhaps the clearest statement of the three basic truths of manufacturing strategy is that of Wickham Skinner ('The Focused Factory' *Harvard Business Review*, May–June 1974): (1) there are many ways to compete besides producing at low cost; (2) a factory cannot perform well on every yardstick; and (3) simplicity and repetition breed competence. The traditional model seems to be that corporate strategy is often set with little reference to the existing manufacturing structure. While the overall strategy is carefully translated into product strategy and marketing mix, the manufacturing function is simply expected to cope with the outcome.

No marketing director would consider using the same marketing mix to sell a high-reliability, custom-built, critical-delivery product as he would for a low-margin, standard product ex-stock. Yet nobody seems worried when a single manufacturing facility is expected to produce such products, equally effectively, using the same facilities, systems and people. If you hand the manufacturing people an inherently impossible task, it is small wonder that they cannot achieve it.

My proposed model provides for a coherent statement of corporate, market and manufacturing strategy set around the criteria for success. From the market strategy comes a statement of the marketing mix, and from the manufacturing strategy comes a statement of the manufacturing structure. It does not matter which comes first, but you do need *both* for survival.

Any feasible set of market success requirements will translate into: 'what does the manufacturing activity have to be good at, if the company is to succeed in the market place?' This might be defined as a manufacturing task: 'The *unique* manufacturing competence demanded by the combination of the firm's *corporate strategy*, its *marketing policies* and any *constraints* imposed by the technology and *financial* resources.'

Perhaps this is more palatable if translated into specific cases. Task 1: to produce a standard product line at high volume for sale ex-stock selling on the basis of low price; and Task 2: to produce high-quality/high-reliability products, incorporating customer-specified modifications on reliable lead-times substantially shorter than the competition's, at a premium price. A manufacturing system set up to carry out Task 1 is unlikely to be very successful at carrying out Task 2. In order to remain successful, a company must match each task with an appropriate internal manufacturing mix (more often termed a 'manufacturing structure').

Definition of a manufacturing structure involves two types of interacting decisions: asset decisions, which define the physical structure; and systems decisions, which define the control, personnel and organizational structure. Two problems arise from this: first, it is necessary to analyse an *existing* manufacturing structure to assess its suitability to perform a particular manufacturing task; and secondly, an *appropriate* manufacturing structure must be defined to meet a particular task.

Again, within the manufacturing structure, choices must be made on each dimension. Each choice generally restricts the possible choices on other dimensions and has a major impact on matching task and structure. (1) *Plant and equipment technology*. Plant size and location, the balance chosen between general purpose and special machinery, the level of automation, and the nature of production tooling; (2) *production systems*. The load planning and control systems, choice of inventory break points, the sophistication of plant scheduling and quality management; (3) *personnel policies*. The payment systems, skill levels, training provisions, supervisory levels and degrees of unionization; (4) *product design/engineering*. The width of the product line, degree of custom work, attitude to technological risk in using unproven processes, the level of manufacturing engineering; and (5) *organization and management*. The form of organization, value systems, use of central staff functions, performance measures.

It should be obvious from this description of the elements of the manufacturing structure that changes can take a considerable time, and that the whole process of defining and maintaining a structure is not a 'one-off' exercise. In particular, movement along a product life-cycle involves changes in the 'manufacturing task', which inevitably produce a need to modify the manufacturing structure. Moveover, these trade-offs between performance requirements must be made somewhere. If they are not made at the level of manufacturing strategy, they will be made *ad hoc* at an operating level, with no consistency either with corporate strategy or with each other.

An example of the problems which arise when a mismatch exists between manufacturing task and structure is the entry of the US Babcock and Wilcox into the large-scale manufacture of pressure vessels for nuclear power. In the late 1960s, as a major producer in the steam pressure vessel field, B&W thought it had found a potentially very profitable niche in the nuclear power business: production of the large pressure vessels required for each reactor. To cater for the expected high demand, B&W set up a brand-new $25 million plant on a greenfield site at Mount Vernon on the banks of the Ohio River to take advantage of cheap barge transport. In terms of physical requirements, nuclear pressure vessels are simply larger versions of products which B&W has been making for many years for the power-generating industry, and the Mount Vernon plant was a rather more sophisticated version of its older plants.

In comparing market criteria for success, however, the products are not so similar. In the nuclear business, reliable delivery is essential, but delivery lead-time is not a major factor; the product must be individually designed with absolute product reliability; and, if you can make the product properly for a reliable delivery date, price is almost immaterial. On the other hand, the steam pressure vessel market is mainly a replacement market, demanding a standard product on a short and reliable lead-time, of a quality consistent with its price and sold in a highly price-competitive market. While it is easy to be critical in retrospect, a manufacturing structure suitable for the production of the steam vessels seemed unlikely to be particularly successful in producing nuclear ones.

In fact, Mount Vernon produced three pressure vessels in the first three years of its operation: it should have produced over 20. By May 1969, every one of the 28 pressure vessels under construction was late by up to 17 months, even on renegotiated due dates. At this stage, two of the main contractors, General Electric and Westinghouse, which had between them 21 vessels on order, took the almost incredible step of moving 14 of the part-processed 700-ton vessels out to B&W's competitors: three to US rivals, two to Japan, two to France, and two to Rotterdam. The total value of the work shipped out was probably around $40 million, and total company profits dropped from a peak of $33 million in 1967 to $5 million in 1969.

Manufacturing in the 1980s

It is true that labour disputes, and a minor earthquake which upset sensitive machinery, caused some delays, while others could be traced back to late delivery of sophisticated machinery. However, the overriding failure was almost certainly that the manufacturing structure at Mount Vernon was designed to meet a manufacturing task totally different from that which it really faced.

The key elements of the structure required were probably skilled welders, high supervision levels to ensure high quality, a job-shop approach to scheduling and production planning, a capacity/load balance which allowed for a high re-weld rate, and a high-pay/low-turnover labour policy. Instead, as in the traditional steam vessel business, production planning and control were based on flow type manufacture, and cost pressures were high in a lean organization; so capacity was over-committed, while supervision and quality assurance were insufficient. Tight control of labour costs (taking advantage of the greenfield site) back-fired into high turnover and growing militancy. Even a management victory in contract negotiations was somewhat shallow – all it did was raise the turnover rate even further and cause even more delays.

The three common problems which arise in matching manufacturing task and structure could be summarized as: (1) multiple tasks required of the same structure; (2) structure inappropriate to the current task; and (3) a structure which is inconsistent within itself. Thus, the company which attempts to produce customer specials on a quoted lead-time, and standard products for supply ex-stock on the same set of facilities, is asking its plant to be all things to all men. Thus, too, the product innovator with a 'tweak-it-and-see' plant may find himself shut out of a mature market, because he has become uncompetitive on price, and will be replaced by the mass-producer with a purpose-built plant. Thus, too, a plant in which the formal performance system concentrates on unit cost, while the production control system is dedicated to meeting delivery promises, is basically inconsistent.

Why do so many companies have such mismatch problems, and how can they be avoided? The first answer lies in the role which the manufacturing function plays in the business. In most companies, manufacturing is viewed as a cost sink, rather than a profit source – the corporate millstone effect. What is needed is a positive input from manufacturing, based on an objective appraisal of its existing capability. Many senior managers involved in setting corporate strategy will have little, if any, experience in manufacturing. On the other hand, the senior manufacturing manager has traditionally been given little say in setting corporate strategy. His contribution must be positive, rather than negative – what manufacturing can do well, rather than why its management cannot do what is asked.

In the short term, possible market strategies will inevitably be constrained by the existing manufacturing structure; but, in the long term, the manufacturing structure must change to meet market needs. It is tempting to interpret this as 'stick to what you are good at', but as market characteristics will inevitably change over time, such a policy is as naïve and dangerous as having no policy at all. Too often senior management regards manufacturing's input to corporate profitability as being no more than achieving high output and low cost. It is apparent that routine manufacturing decisions, made without proper recognition of corporate goals and market strategy, can tie a company into facilities, personnel policies and systems which are highly inappropriate and will take many years to change.

In much the same way, on the national scale, decisions made without reference to overall national goals or world market strategy have tied British manufacturing industries into facilities, personnel policies and systems which are inappropriate for a developed economy and will unfortunately take many years to change. Some UK companies are indeed among the best in the world in particular sectors. The problem is rather at the level of national policy; although this doesn't only mean government policy.

It is true that the UK share of world trade in manufactures has dropped from 18 per cent in 1958 to 9 per cent in 1977, but this in itself need be neither surprising nor worrying. What is of much more concern is the lower level of sophistication of British engineering exports compared to Continental rivals. Christopher Saunders' researches (*Engineering in Britain, West Germany and France: Some Statistical Comparisons*, Sussex European Papers) have been discussed before in *Management Today* (March 1979). In summary, they showed that across 46 product groups accounting together for a third of British exports, the value per tonne in 1975 was 20–40 per cent lower than for comparable French and German exports. There were just a few exceptions: in telecommunications; thermionic valves, transistors and tubes; watches and clocks; and printing and bookbinding machinery. For at least 22 of the groups, the gap had been steadily widening over the previous 20 years – and there is no evidence that the trend has altered since 1975, as shown in table 1.

TABLE 1

	Median value per tonne of exports ($)		
	1963	1971	1975
UK	2280	3080	4790
West Germany	2580	4080	7610
France	2530	3430	6730
West Germany/UK Ratio	1.13	1.32	1.59
France/UK Ratio	1.11	1.114	1.41

Not only has the gap between the UK and both West Germany and France widened, but it appears to be widening at an increasing rate. Take two typical groups for 1975 in a little more detail: metalworking machinery, and machinery for special industries (i.e., paper making, printing, food processing, etc.). For metalworking machinery, both the UK and West Germany sold about the same proportion of their total exports to the developing countries – 22 per cent – but the overall unit values were very different: $1628 for the UK and $4951 for Germany. Moreover, the total value of West German exports was over four times the UK figure.

Manufacturing in the 1980s

Similarly, in trade in machinery for special industries, the UK figure is $3172 per tonne compared to the German figure of $4861, while the UK export value is less than half that of West Germany. In addition, in this group, a much higher proportion of UK trade goes to developing economies. Again, taking the same two product groups and looking at the trade between the UK and Germany, there is a similar pattern: in both cases, a large UK deficit and a significantly higher value per tonne for the West German goods, thus contributing to the UK's total net deficit on this trade of $1263 million in 1975.

This pattern is not confined either to trade in these two product groups or to trade with West Germany. It is a general characteristic of all trade in UK engineering products. This is shown clearly by comparing the export value per tonne to the import value. For a highly developed economy, the expectation might be that exports would be of a higher 'technology' than imports, and the ratio should therefore be greater than one. Within a particularly narrow product group, this argument becomes complex: for example, a country capable of exporting highly sophisticated numerically controlled machines should surely be able to produce standard machine tools for home consumption without having to import these low technology products. But this argument returns to the original proposition: a plant capable of producing the high technology product will not be suitable for producing the standard product as well, and high labour costs and resource constraints will probably lead to concentration 'up-market'.

Across the whole engineering sector, the UK is a relatively poor performer on this criterion, although the situation has improved marginally over the period 1963–75. Across the 46 engineering product groups, export value per tonne for 1975 was only 85 per cent of import value per tonne, compared to 120 per cent for West Germany and 107 per cent for France. Indeed, in 1975, only nine product groups showed a ratio above 100 per cent, and these groups accounted for only 23 per cent of total engineering exports. The only significant groups are: internal combustion engines (non-aircraft); heating and cooling equipment; telecommunications equipment; thermionic valves, transistors, etc.; and automotive electrical equipment. (The first and the last of these probably reappear in the import statistics as parts of Granadas, Volvos and the like.) To be scrupulously fair to the UK, it should be added that the 46 product groups do not include road motor vehicles, aircraft or ships – all groups in which the UK had substantial trade surpluses in 1975. Aircraft in particular earned the UK $796 million in exports for 1975.

The practical consequences of exporting low technology are readily visible in UK manufacturing plants: where do you buy high-speed packaging machinery or sophisticated high-speed production machine tools? A recent report on UK textile companies' buying habits reveals all: the appropriate machinery is either not available from UK suppliers, or the foreign equipment is simply more advanced or provides better performance. The UK textile machinery manufacturing companies do a good job of selling abroad – Britain exports almost three times as much as it imports – but it is the same story: the UK exports cheap and buys dear.

Returning to the prerequisites for success, exporting engineering goods from a developed economy probably demands reliable delivery; short delivery times; high product quality and reliability; high design flexibility; volume flexibility; and a premium price – in short, high technology products competing on design and special features, with short reliable delivery, at a price premium. In contrast, the current market characteristics for many UK engineering exports are: uncertain delivery; long delivery quotations; low-level (but not necessarily poor) quality and reliability; low design flexibility; inflexible response; and low price. In short, low technology products competing mainly on price.

This is a simplification, and unfair to many UK manufacturers; but there are inevitable conclusions inherent in the overall picture. The UK is still exporting far too much in relatively low technology products to developing and advanced developing countries, which will soon be able to produce such products for themselves. That is one reason, apart from history, why UK exports have the lowest proportion among EEC countries of total exports going to EEC partners: 32 per cent compared to 44 per cent from West Germany and 49 per cent from France in 1975.

The blame for this must clearly be carried by manufacturing companies themselves, but a major portion can also be related back to long-term government policies. First, there is the problem of misguided regional policy. Despite enormous amounts of government spending, management time, and use of scarce resources, the regional balance is probably no better than in the 1930s. Aid has gone primarily to regions with the highest unemployment, without any real attempt to focus on the development of new industrial activities involving capital-intensive processes or high technology. Indeed, as late as 1972, priority industries for investment grants included textiles, clothing and footwear, shipbuilding and metal manufacture. The net effect seems to have been to rob the formerly 'strong' regions.

Then there is the central redirection of expenditure – robbing Peter to pay Paul. The telecommunications sector is one in which the UK still has significant strengths, a sector in which major investment is required to cope with the changing technology. But in just one company, the £27 million paid out in redundancy payments must have considerably reduced the capital available for reinvestment. *The Times* of 2 August 1978 reported that the Government was to invest £70 million *over the next five years* in development work on the manufacture of microelectronics products. However, in the same issue, it was announced that £85 million was to be made available to Britain's shipbuilders – this being only a further tranche *to last until the end of the year* in order to make UK shipbuilding prices competitive in world markets. The latter funds did come from EEC sources, but this hardly represents a viable strategy for the restructuring of UK manufacturing industry.

The personal and political problems which will be created by major switches in industrial employment must not be underestimated, but sooner or later they must be faced, and the sooner they are faced, the more planned the changes can be. The simple fact is that, if the UK wishes to become a high real wage economy, it cannot continue to lock scarce skilled resources

Manufacturing in the 1980s

into decaying industries which are easily duplicated in the advanced developing countries.

There is also the question of the direction and size of government-sponsored research and development funds. The UK shows a pattern of R&D expenditure which is totally out of balance with the size of the industrial sectors concerned; this is particularly true of aircraft and defence electronics, paid for by central government. In essence, money is siphoned off from other sectors, via taxation, to pay for the imbalance. True, the industries concerned are in high technology, and thus meet this important criterion: but they operate in markets dominated by the USA, which vastly outspends the UK in R&D. In Japan, the pattern of spending is much more closely in line with the relative size of the sector and its export importance. One consequence has been to direct the best of UK engineering talent into these glamorous sectors at the expense of the rest of manufacturing industry.

Finally, as a highly developed economy, the UK cannot put up with a university educational system that, to quote a now notorious statistic, produces more graduates in Welsh than in manufacturing engineering. Directed education may not seem very equitable or very palatable, but it is necessary. There are relatively painless mechanisms, such as two-tier grants linked to continued UK residence: or recourse to the traditional school of management approach of high advertising expenditure to attract students. There are 25,000 notified vacancies for electronics engineers against a total output of 2000 a year: against such a background, education for education's sake has become a luxury that the UK can simply no longer afford.

The needs are: (1) Replacement of the current regional strategies by an industry-based national plan, with a guaranteed life of at least 10 years, and redeployment costs built in. (2) Phasing out low-technology industries, unless they can support themselves in a free market. (3) Abandoning prestige aircraft and electronics defence projects which have little chance of being self-funding. (4) Introducing two-tier grants for university education and redirecting the educational effort towards education for real national needs.

To quote finally from Professor Kaldor:

> there is the question how far a mature economy could continue to reap the benefits of economies of scale, not through a fast growth in manufacturing industry as a whole, but through greater international specialisation . . . benefits could continue to be secured by concentrating our resources in fewer fields and abandoning others.

1.5

The Focused Factory

W. Skinner

The threat posed by foreign competition, the problem of industries suffering from 'blue-collar blues', and the increasing complexity and frustration of life in the factory have forced public attention back to the industrial sector of the economy. Many years of taking our industrial health and leadership for granted abruptly ended in the 1970s when our declining position in world markets weakened the dollar and became a national issue.

In the popular press and at the policy level in government, the issue has been seen as a 'productivity crisis'. The National Commission on Productivity was established in 1971. The concern with productivity has appealed to many managers who have firsthand experience with our problems of high costs and low efficiency.

So pessimism now pervades the outlook of many managers and analysts of the US manufacturing scene. The recurring theme of this gloomy view is that (a) US labour is the most expensive in the world, (b) its productivity has been growing at a slower rate than that of most of its competitors, and therefore (c) our industries sicken one by one as imports mushroom and unemployment becomes chronic in our industrial population centres.

In this article, I shall offer a more optimistic view of the productivity dilemma, suggesting that we need not feel powerless in competing against cheaper foreign labour. Rather, we have the opportunity to effect basic changes in the management of manufacturing, which could shift the com-

Author's note: This article is an analysis based on my cases written in the electronics, plastics, textile, steel and industrial equipment industries, supplemented by recent project research in the furniture industry. Financial support for this work provided by the Harvard Business School Division of Research and course development funds is gratefully acknowledged.

W. Skinner is James E. Robinson Professor of Business Administration at Harvard Business School.

Source: W.Skinner, 'The Focused Factory', from *Harvard Business Review*, May–June, 1974, reprinted by permission. Copyright © 1974 by the President and fellows of Harvard College; all rights reserved.

The Focused Factory

petitive balance in our favour in many industries. What are these basic changes? I can identify four:

(1) Seeing the problem not as 'How can we increase productivity?' but as 'How can we compete?'
(2) Seeing the problem as encompassing the efficiency of the *entire* manufacturing organization, not only the efficiency of the direct labour and the work force. (In most plants, direct labour and the work force represent only a small percentage of total costs.)
(3) Learning to focus each plant on a limited, concise, manageable set of products, technologies, volumes, and markets.
(4) Learning to structure basic manufacturing policies and supporting services so that they focus on one explicit manufacturing task instead of on many inconsistent, conflicting, implicit tasks.

A factory that focuses on a narrow product mix for a particular market niche will outperform the conventional plant, which attempts a broader mission. Because its equipment, supporting systems and procedures can concentrate on a limited task for one set of customers, its costs and especially its overhead are likely to be lower than those of the conventional plant. But, more importantly, such a plant can become a competitive weapon because its entire apparatus is focused to accomplish the particular manufacturing task demanded by the company's overall strategy and marketing objective.

In spite of their advantages, my research indicates that focused manufacturing plants are surprisingly rare. Instead, the conventional factory produces many products for numerous customers in a variety of markets, thereby demanding the performance of a multiplicity of manufacturing tasks all at once from one set of assets and people. Its rationale is 'economy of scale' and lower capital investment.

However, the result more often than not is a hodge-podge of compromises, a high overhead and a manufacturing organization that is constantly in hot water with top management, marketing management, the controller and customers.

A simple but telling example of a failure to focus is uncovered in this case study of a manufacturer, the American Printed Circuit Company (APC). APC was a small company which had been growing rapidly and successfully. Its printed circuits were custom-built in lots of 1 to 100 for about 20 principal customers and were used for engineering tests and development work. APC's process consisted of about 15 operations using simple equipment, such as hand-dipping tanks, drill presses and manual touch-ups. There was considerable variation in the sequence and processes for different products. Delivery was a major element for success, and price was not a key factor.

APC's president accepted an order from a large computer company to manufacture 20,000 printed circuit boards – a new product for the company – at a price equivalent to about one third of its average mix of products. APC made the decision to produce these circuits boards in order to build volume, broaden the company's range of markets, and diversify the line. The new product was produced in the existing plant.

The result was disastrous. The old products were no longer delivered on time. The costs of the new printed circuit boards were substantially in excess of the bid price. The quality on all items suffered as the organization frenetically attempted to meet deliveries. Old customers grew bitter over missed deliveries, and the new customer returned one third of the merchandise for below-spec quality. Such heavy losses ensued that the APC company had to recapitalize. Subsequently, the ownership of the company changed hands.

The purpose of this article is to set forth the advantages of focused manufacturing. I shall begin with the basic concepts of the focused factory, then follow with an analysis of the productivity phenomenon, which tends to prevent the adoption of the focused plant concept. Finally, I shall offer some specific steps for managing manufacturing to accomplish and take advantage of focus.

Basic Concepts

From my study of approximately 50 plants in six industries, I can pinpoint three basic concepts underlying focused manufacturing. Consider:

(1) *There are many ways to compete besides by producing at low cost.* This statement may be self-evident to the reader (particularly to one in an industry which has been badly hit by low-priced foreign imports and has been attempting to compete with better products, quality or customer service and delivery). Nevertheless, it still needs saying for two reasons.

One is simply the persistent attitude that ways of competing other than on the basis of price are second best. The other is that a company which starts out with higher manufacturing costs than its competitors is in trouble regardless of whatever else it does.

While these assumptions may be true of industries with mature products and technologies, they are not at all true of products in earlier stages of their life cycles. In fact, in many US industries, companies are being forced to shift to products in which technological innovation in the form of advanced features is a more critical element of competitive advantage than cost.

(2) *A factory cannot perform well on every yardstick.* There are a number of common standards for measuring manufacturing performance. Among these are short delivery cycles, superior product quality and reliability, dependable delivery promises, ability to produce new products quickly, flexibility in adjusting to volume changes, low investment and hence higher return on investment, and low costs.

These measures of manufacturing performance necessitate trade-offs – certain tasks must be compromised to meet others. They cannot all be accomplished equally well because of the inevitable limitations of equipment and process technology. Such trade-offs as cost versus quality or

The Focused Factory

short delivery cycles versus low inventory investment are fairly obvious. Other trade-offs, while less obvious, are equally real. They involve implicit choices in establishing manufacturing policies.

Within the factory, managers can make the manufacturing function a competitive weapon by outstanding accomplishment of one or more of the measures of manufacturing performance. But managers need to know: 'What must we be especially good at? Cost, quality, lead times, reliability, changing schedules, new-product introduction, or low investment?'

Focused manufacturing must be derived from an explicitly defined corporate strategy which has its roots in a corporate marketing plan. Therefore, the choice of focus cannot be made independently by production people. Instead, it has to be a result of a comprehensive analysis of the company's resources, strengths and weaknesses, position in the industry, assessment of competitors' moves, and forecast of future customer motives and behaviour.

Conversely, the choice of focus cannot be made without considering the existing factory, because a given set of facilities, systems and people skills can do only certain things well within a given time period.

(3) *Simplicity and repetition breed competence*. Focused manufacturing is based on the concept that simplicity, repetition, experience and homogeneity of tasks breed competence. Furthermore, each key functional area in manufacturing must have the same objective, derived from corporate strategy. Such congruence of tasks can produce a manufacturing system that does limited things very well, thus creating a formidable competitive weapon.

Major Characteristics

Five key characteristics of the focused factory are:

(1) *Process technologies*: Typically, unproven and uncertain technologies are limited to one per factory. Proven, mature technologies are limited to what their managers can easily handle, typically two or three (e.g., a foundry, metal working and metal finishing).
(2) *Market demands*: These consist of a set of demands including quality, price, lead times and reliability specifications. A given plant can usually only do a superb job on one or two demands at any given period of time.
(3) *Product volumes*: Generally, these are of comparable levels, such that tooling, order quantities, materials-handling techniques and job contents can be approached with a consistent philosophy. But what about the inevitable short runs, customer specials and one-of-a-kind orders that every factory must handle? The answer is usually to segregate them. This is discussed later.
(4) *Quality levels*: These employ a common attitude and set of approaches so as to neither overspecify nor overcontrol quality and specifications.

One frame of mind and set of mental assumptions suffice for equipment, tooling, inspection, training, supervision, job content and materials handling.

(5) *Manufacturing tools*: These are limited to only one (or two at the most) at any given time. The task at which the plant must excel in order to be competitive focuses on one set of internally consistent, doable, non-compromised criteria for success.

My research evidence makes it clear that the focused factory will outproduce, undersell and quickly gain competitive advantage over the complex factory. The focused factory does a better job because repetition and concentration in one area allow its work force and managers to become effective and experienced in the task required for success. The focused factory is manageable and controllable. Its problems are demanding, but limited in scope.

Productivity Phenomenon

The conventional wisdom of manufacturing management has been and continues to be that the measure of success is productivity. Now that US companies in many industries are getting beaten hands down by overseas competitors with lower unit costs, we mistakenly cling to the old notion that 'a good plant is a low-cost plant'. This is simply not so. A low-cost plant may be a disaster if the company has sacrificed too much in the way of quality, delivery, flexibility, and so forth, in order to get its costs down.

Too many companies attempt to do too many things with one plant and one organization. In the name of low investment in facilities and spreading their overheads, they add products, markets, technologies, processes, quality levels and supporting services which conflict and compete with each other and compound expense. They then hire more staff to regulate and control the unmanageable mixture of problems.

In desperation, many companies are now 'banging away' at anything to reduce the resulting high costs. But we can only regain competitive strength by stopping this process of increasing complexity and overstaffing.

This behaviour is so illogical that the phenomenon needs further explanation. Our plants are generally managed by extremely able people; yet the failure to focus manufacturing on a limited objective is a common managerial blind spot. What happens to produce this defect in competent managers? Engineers know what can and cannot be designed into planes, boats and building structures. Engineers accept design objectives that will accomplish a specific set of tasks which are possible, although difficult.

In contrast, most of the manufacturing plants in my study attempted a complex, heterogeneous mixture of general and special-purpose equipment, long- and short-run operations, high and low tolerances, new and old products, off-the-shelf items and customer specials, stable and changing designs, markets with reliable forecasts and unpredictable ones, seasonal and non-seasonal sales, short and long lead times, and high and low skills.

The Focused Factory

Lack of Consistent Policies

It is not understood, I think, that each of the contrasting features just noted generally demands conflicting manufacturing tasks and hence different manufacturing policies. The particular mix of these features should determine the elements of manufacturing policy. Some of these elements are the following:

- Size of plant and its capacity.
- Location of plant.
- Choice of equipment.
- Plant layout.
- Selection of production process.
- Production scheduling system.
- Use of inventories.
- Wage system.
- Training and supervisory approaches.
- Control systems.
- Organizational structure.

Instead of designing elements of manufacturing policy around one manufacturing task, what usually happens? Consider, for example, that the wage system may be set up to emphasize high productivity, production control to maximize short lead times, inventory to minimize stock levels, order quantities to minimize set-up times, plant layout to minimize materials handling costs, and process design to maximize quality.

While each of these decisions probably looks sensible to the professional specialist in his field, the conventional factory consists of six or more inconsistent elements of manufacturing structure, each of which is designed to achieve a different implicit objective.

Such inconsistency usually results in high costs. One or another element may be excessively staffed or operated inefficiently because its task is being exaggerated or misdirected; or several functions may require excess staff in order to control or manage a plant which is unduly complex.

But often the result is even more serious. My study shows that the chief negative effect is not on productivity but on ability to compete. The plant's manufacturing policies are not designed, tuned and focused as a whole on that one key strategic manufacturing task essential to the company's success in its industry.

Reasons for Inconsistency

Non-congruent manufacturing structures appear to be common in US industry. In fact, my research revealed that a fully consistent set of manufacturing policies resulting in a congruent system is highly rare. Why does this situation occur so often? In the cases I studied, it seemed to come about essentially for one or more of these reasons:

- Professionals in each field attempted to achieve goals which, although valid and traditional in their fields, were not congruent with goals of other areas.
- The manufacturing task for the plant subtly changed while most operating and service departments kept on the same course as before.
- The manufacturing task was never made explicit.
- The inconsistencies were never recognized.
- More and more products were piled into existing plants, resulting in an often futile attempt to meet the manufacturing tasks of a variety of markets, technologies and competitive strategies.

Let me elaborate on the first and last set of causes we have just noted.

'Professionalism' in the plant. Production system elements are now set up or managed by professionals in their respective fields, such as quality control, personnel, labour relations, engineering, inventory management, materials handling, systems design, and so forth. These professionals, quite naturally, seek to maximize their contributions and justify their positions. They have conventional views of success in each of their particular fields. Of course, these objectives are generally in conflict.

I say 'of course' not to be cynical. These fields of speciality have come into existence for many different reasons – some to reduce costs, others to save time, others to minimize capital investments, still others to promote human cooperation and happiness, and so on. So it is perfectly normal for them to pull in different directions, which is exactly what happens in many plants. This problem is not totally new. But it is changing because professionalism is increasing; we have more and more experts at work in different parts of the factory. So it is a growing problem.

Product proliferation. The combination of increasing foreign and domestic competition plus an accelerating rate of technological innovation has resulted in product proliferation in many factories. Shorter product life, more new products, shorter runs, lower unit volumes, and more customer specials are becoming increasingly common. The same factory which five years ago produced 25 products may today be producing anything from 50 to 100.

The inconsistent production system grows up not simply because there are more products to make – which is, of course, likely to increase direct and indirect costs and add complexity and confusion – but also because new products often call for different manufacturing tasks. To succeed in some tasks may require superb technological competence and focus, others may demand extremely short delivery, and still others, extremely low costs.

Yet, almost always, new products are added into the existing mix in the same plant, even though some new equipment may be necessary. The rationale for this decision is usually that the plant is operating at less than full capacity. Thus the logic is, 'If we put the new products into the present plant, we can save capital investment and avoid duplicating overheads.'

The result is complexity, confusion, and worst of all a production organization which, because it is spun out in all directions by a kind of cen-

The Focused Factory

trifugal force, lacks focus and a do-able manufacturing task. The factory is asked to perform a mission for Product A which conflicts with that of Product B. Thus the result is a hodge-podge of compromises.

When we may have, in fact, four tasks and four markets, we make the mistake of trying to force them into one plant, one set of equipment, one factory organization, one set of manufacturing policies, and so on. We try to cram into one operating system the ability to compete in an impossible mix of demands. Each element of the system attempts to adjust to these demands with variation, special sections, complex procedures, more people and added paperwork.

In my opinion this syndrome, starting with added market demands and ending with incongruent internal structures, to a large extent accounts for the human frustrations, high costs and low competitive abilities we see so much of in US industry today.

Who gets the blame? The manufacturing executive, of course, gets it from corporate headquarters for high costs, poor productivity, low quality and reliability, and missed deliveries. In turn he tends to blame the situation on anything which makes sense, such as poor market forecasts, subpar labour, unconcern over quality, inept engineering designs, faulty equipment, and so forth.

Probably all such factors contribute and, undoubtedly, they all add to the pressure on production people. But what is not perceived is that a given production organization, as we noted earlier, can only do certain things well; trade-offs are inevitable. Experience accomplishes wonders, but a diffused organization with conflicting structural elements and competing manufacturing tasks accumulates experience and specialized competence very slowly.

Towards Manufacturing Focus

A new management approach is needed in industries where diverse products and markets require companies to manufacture a broad mix of items, volumes, specifications and customer-demand patterns. Its emphasis must be on building competitive strength. One way to compete is to focus the entire manufacturing system on a limited task precisely defined by the company's competitive strategy and the realities of its technology and economics. A common objective produces synergistic effects rather than internal power struggles between professionalized departments. This approach can be assisted by these guiding rules:

- Centralize the factory's focus on relative competitive ability.
- Avoid the common tendency to add staff and overhead in order to save on direct labour and capital investment.
- Let each manufacturing unit work on a limited task instead of the usual complex mix of conflicting objectives, products and technologies.

This management approach can be thought of as focused manufacturing, for it is the opposite of the under-one-roof diffusion process of the conventional factory. Instead of permitting the whirling diversity of tasks and ingredients, top management applies a centripetal force, which constantly pulls inward toward one central focus – the one key manufacturing task. The result is greater simplicity, lower costs, and a manufacturing and support organization that is directed toward successful competition.

Achieving the Focused Plant

In my experience, manufacturing managers are generally astounded at the internal inconsistencies and compromises they discover once they put the concept of focused manufacturing to work in analysing their own plants.

Then, when they begin to discern what the company strategy and market situation are implicity demanding and to compare these implicit demands with what they have been trying to achieve, many submerged conflicts surface.

Finally, when they ask themselves what a certain element of the structure or of the manufacturing policy was designed to maximize, the built-in cross-purposes become apparent.

At the risk of seeming to take a cookbook approach to an inevitably complex set of issues, let me offer a recipe for the focused factory based on an actual but disguised example of an industrial manufacturing company which attempted to adapt its operations to this concept. Consider this four-step approach of, say, the WXY Company, a producer of mechanical equipment:

(1) *Develop an explicit, brief statement of corporate objectives and strategy*. The statement should cover the next three to five years, and it should have the substantial involvement of top management, including marketing, finance and control executives.

In its statement, the top management of the WXY Company agreed to the following:

> Our corporate objective is directed toward increasing market share during the next five years via a strategy of (1) tailoring our product to individual customer needs, (2) offering advanced and special product features at a modest price increment, and (3) gaining competitive advantage via rapid product development and service orientation to customers of all sizes.

(2) *Translate the objectives-and-strategy statement into 'what this means to manufacturing'*. What must the factory do especially well in order to carry out and support this corporate strategy? What is going to be the most difficult task it will face? If the manufacturing function is not sharp and capable, where is the company most likely to fail? It may fail in any one of the elements of the production structure, but it will probably do so in a combination of some of them.

To carry on with the WXY Company example, such a manufacturing task might be defined explicitly as follows:

The Focused Factory

Our manufacturing task for the next three years will be to introduce specialized, customer-tailored new products into production, with lead times which are substantially less than those of our competitors.

Since the technology in our industry is changing rapidly, and since product reliability can be extremely serious for customers, our most difficult problems will be to control the new-product introduction process, so as to solve technical problems promptly and to maintain reliability amid rapid changes in the product itself.

(3) *Make a careful examination of each element of the production system.* How is it now set up, organized, focused and manned? What is it now especially good at? How must it be changed to implement the key manufacturing task?

(4) *Reorganize the elements of structure to produce a congruent focus.* This reorganization focuses on the ability to do those limited things well which are of utmost importance to the accomplishment of the manufacturing task.

To complete the example of the WXY Company, table 1 lists each major element of the manufacturing system of the company, describes its present focus in terms of that task for which it was implicitly or inadvertently aimed, and lists a new approach designed to bring consistency, focus and power to its manufacturing arm.

What stands out most in this table is the number of substantial changes in manufacturing policies required to bring the production system into a total consistency. The table also features the implicit conflicts between many manufacturing tasks in the present approach, which are the result of the failure to define one task for the whole plant.

The reader may perceive a disturbing implication of the focused plant concept – namely, that it seems to call for major investments in new plants, new equipment and new tooling in order to break down the present complexity. For example, if the company is currently involved in five different products, technologies, markets or volumes, does it need five plants, five sets of equipment, five processes, five technologies and five organizational structures? The answer is probably *yes*. But the practical solution need not involve selling the big multipurpose facility and decentralizing into five small facilities.

In fact, the few companies that have adopted the focused plant concept have approached the solution quite differently. There is no need to build five plants, which would involve unnecessary investment and overhead expenses. The more practical approach is the 'plant within a plant' (PWP) notion in which the existing facility is divided both organizationally and physically into, in this case, five PWPs. Each PWP has its own facilities in which it can concentrate on its particular manufacturing task, using its own work-force management approaches, production control, organization structure, and so forth. Quality and volume levels are not mixed; worker training and incentives have a clear focus; and engineering of processes, equipment and materials handling are specialized as needed.

TABLE 1 CONFLICTING MANUFACTURING TASKS IMPLIED BY INCONGRUENT ELEMENTS OF THE PRESENT PRODUCTION SYSTEM

Production system elements	Present approach (conventional factory)	Implicit manufacturing tasks of present approach	Changed approach (focused factory)
Equipment and process policies	One large plant; special purpose equipment; high-volume tooling; balanced capacity with functional layout	Low manufacturing costs on steady runs of a few large products with minimal investment	Separate old, standardized products and new customized products into two plants within a plant (PWP). For new PWP, provide general purpose equipment, temporary tooling and modest excess capacity with product-oriented layout
Work-force management policies	Specialized jobs with narrow job content; incentive wages; few supervisors; focus on volume of production per hour	Low costs and efficiency	Create fewer jobs with more versatility. Pay for breadth of skills and ability to perform a variety of jobs. Provide more foremen for solving technical problems at workplace

Production scheduling and control	Detailed, frequent sales forecasts; produce for inventory economic lot sizes of finished goods; small, decentralized production scheduling group	Short delivery lead times	Produce to order special parts and stock of common parts based on semi-annual forecast. Staff production control to closely schedule and centralize parts movements
Quality control	Control engineers and large inspection groups in each department	Extremely reliable quality	No change
Organizational structure	Functional; production control under superintendents of each area; inspection reports to top	Top performance of the objectives of each functional department, i.e., many tasks	Organize each PWP by program and project in order to focus organizational effort on bringing new products into production smoothly and on time

Each PWP gains experience readily by focusing and concentrating every element of its work on those limited essential objectives which constitute its manufacturing task. Since a manufacturing task is an offspring of a corporate strategy and marketing program, it is susceptible to either gradual or sweeping change. The PWP approach makes it easier to perform realignment of essential operations and system elements over time as the task changes.

Conclusion

The prevalent use of 'cost' and 'efficiency' as the conventional yardsticks for planning, controlling and evaluating US plants played a large part in the increasing inability of many of the approximately 50 companies included in my research to compete successfully. However, such goals are no longer adequate because competition is getting rougher and, in particular, because a strictly low-cost, high-efficiency strategy is apparently becoming less viable in many industries.

While the economy has moved towards an era of more advanced technologies and shorter product lives, we have not readjusted our concepts of production to keep up with these changes. Instead, we have continued to use 'productivity' and 'economies of scale' as guiding objectives. Both feature only one element of competition (i.e., costs), and both are now obsolete as general, all-purpose guides in manufacturing management.

But I have concluded that the focused plant is a rarity. With the mistaken rationale that the keys to success are limited investment, economies of scale and full utilization of existing plant resources to achieve low costs, we keep adding new products to plants which were once focused, manageable and competitive.

Reversing the process, however, is not impossible. In most of the cases I have studied, capital investment in facilities is not difficult to justify when payoffs that will result from organizational simplicity are taken into account. Resources for simplifying the focus of a manufacturing complex are not hard to acquire when the expected payoff is the ability to compete successfully, using manufacturing as a competitive weapon.

Moreover, better customer service and competitive position typically support higher margins to cover capital investments. And when studied carefully, the economies of scale and the effects of less than full utilization of plant equipment are seldom found to be as critical to productivity and efficiency as classical economic approaches often predict.

The US problem of 'productivity' is real indeed. But seeing the problem as one of 'how to compete' can broaden management's horizon. The focused factory approach offers the opportunity to stop compromising each element of the production system in the typical general-purpose, do-all plant which satisfies no strategy, no market and no task.

Not only does focus provide punch and power, but it also provides clear goals which can be readily understood and assimilated by members of an organization. It provides, too, a mechanism for reappraising what is needed

The Focused Factory

for success, and for readjusting and shaking up old, tired manufacturing organizations with welcome change and a clear sense of direction.

In many sectors of US industry, such change and such a new sense of direction are needed to shift the competitive balance in our favour.

1.6

How Should You Organize Manufacturing?

R. H. Hayes and R. W. Schmenner

Introduction

Manufacturing organizations tend to attract the attention of general managers the way airlines do: one only notices them when they are late, when ticket prices rise, or when there is a crash. When they are operating smoothly, they are almost invisible. But manufacturing is getting increasing attention from business managers who, only a few years ago, were preoccupied with marketing or financial matters.

The fact is that in most companies the great bulk of the assets used – the capital invested, the people employed, and management time – are in the operations side of the business. This is true of both manufacturing and service organizations, in both the private and public sectors of our economy. These resources have to be deployed, coordinated and managed in such a way that they strengthen the institution's purpose; if not, they will almost certainly cripple it.

The problems and pressures facing manufacturing companies ultimately find their way to the factory floor, where managers have to deal with them through some sort of organizational structure. Unfortunately, this structure often is itself part of the problem. Moreover, problems in a corporation's manufacturing organization frequently surface at about the same time as problems in the rest of the company, and they surface in a variety of ways. For example:

(1) A fast-growing, high-technology company had quadrupled in size in a ten-year period. Its manufacturing organization was essentially the same at

R. H. Hayes is Professor of Business Administration at Harvard Business School; R. W. Schmenner is Assistant Professor of Business Administration at Harvard Business School.
Source: R. H. Hayes and R. W. Schmenner, 'How Should You Organize Manufacturing?', from *Harvard Business Review*, January–February 1978, reprinted by permission. Copyright © 1978 by the President and Fellows of Harvard College; all rights reserved.

the end of that period as before, dominated by a powerful vice-president for manufacturing and a strong central staff, despite the fact that its product line had broadened considerably, that the company was beginning to make many more of the components it formerly purchased, and that the number of plants had both increased and spread into four countries. A sluggishness and sense of lost direction began to afflict the manufacturing organization, as overhead and logistics costs soared.

(2) A conglomerate had put together a group of four major divisions that made sense in terms of their financial and marketing synergy. But these divisions' manufacturing organizations had little in common, little internal direction, and no overall coordination. The parent company was confronted with a series of major capital appropriation requests and had little understanding of either their absolute merits or the priorities that should be attached to them.

(3) A fast-growing company in a new industry had for a number of years operated in a seller's market, where competition was based on quality and service rather than price. Its manufacturing organization was highly decentralized and adept at new product introduction and fast product mix changes. In the 1970s severe industry overcapacity and price competition caused corporate sales to level off and profit to decline for the first time in its history. Manufacturing efficiency and dependability clearly had to be improved, but there was fear of 'upsetting the corporate culture' and 'crippling the golden goose'.

Why did these companies' manufacturing arms get into trouble? And to what extent were these problems the outgrowth of poorly designed organizational structures? In attempting an answer to these questions, we will begin with a review of the concepts of 'manufacturing mission' and 'manufacturing focus' that were first defined and explored in a series of articles by Wickham Skinner beginning in 1969.[1] These concepts, and the conclusions that flow logically from them, have since been polished, elaborated, and tested by him and a number of his colleagues in conjunction with various manufacturing companies over the past several years.

After this review we will evaluate the advantages and disadvantages of different approaches to organizing a company's manufacturing function and then apply our concepts to recommending the type of organizational design that is most appropriate for a given company. Finally, we will discuss the various kinds of growth that companies can experience and how these expectations should affect the organization of the manufacturing function.

Basic Elements of Strategy

The concept of manufacturing strategy is a natural extension of the concept of corporate strategy, although the latter need not be as rational and explicit as management theorists usually require.[2] As we use the term, a corporate strategy simply implies a consistency, over time, in the company's preferences for and biases against certain management choices as shown in table 1. We use the term company to refer to a business unit that has a relatively homogeneous product line, considerable autonomy, and enough of a history to establish the kind of track record we refer to here. Such a 'company' could, of course, be a relatively independent division within a larger enterprise. The following four 'attitudes' shape those aspects of a company's corporate strategy that are relevant to manufacturing.

TABLE 1 CORPORATE ATTITUDES THAT IMPLY STRATEGIC PREFERENCES

Dominant orientation
  Market
  Product or material
  Technology

Pattern of diversification
  Product
  Market (geographic or consumer group)
  Process (vertical integration)
  Unrelated horizontal (conglomerate)

Corporate attitude toward growth
  Growth sought explicitly
  Growth viewed as a by-product of successful management of the 'core' business

Competitive priorities
  Dependability
  Price
  Product flexibility
  Quality
  Volume flexibility

Dominant Orientation

Some companies are clearly market oriented. They consider their primary expertise to be the ability to understand and respond effectively to the needs of a particular market or consumer group. In exploiting this market knowledge, they use a variety of products, materials, and technologies. Gillette and Head Ski are examples of such companies. Other companies are clearly oriented to materials or products; they are so-called steel companies, rubber companies, or oil companies (or, more recently, energy companies). They develop multiple uses for their product or material and follow these uses into a variety of markets. Corning Glass, Firestone, DuPont and Conoco come to mind. Still other companies are technology oriented – most electronics companies fall into this class – and they follow the lead of their technology into various materials and markets.

  A common characteristic of a company with such a dominant orientation is that it seldom ventures outside that orientation, is uncomfortable when doing so, often does not appreciate the differences and complexities associated with operating the new business, and then often fails because it

How Should You Organize Manufacturing?

hesitates to commit the resources necessary to succeed. A recent example of a company that ventured, with considerable trauma, outside its dominant orientation was Texas Instruments' entry into consumer marketing of electronic calculators and digital watches.

Pattern of Diversification

Diversification can be accomplished in several ways: (1) product diversification within a given market, (2) market diversification (geographic or consumer group) using a given product line, (3) process or vertical diversification (increasing the span of the process so as to gain more control over vendors and/or customers) with a given mix of products and markets, and (4) unrelated (horizontal) diversification, as exemplified by conglomerates. Decisions about diversification are closely interrelated with a company's dominant orientation, of course, but they also reflect its preference for concentrating on a relatively narrow set of activities or, alternatively, its willingness to enter into a wide variety of activities, products, and/or markets –and which ones it will enter.

Corporate Attitude Toward Growth

Does growth represent an input to or an output of the company's planning process? Every company continually confronts a variety of growth opportunities. Its decisions about which to accept and which to reject signal, in a profound way, the kind of company it prefers to be. Some companies, in their concentration on a particular market, geographic area or material, essentially accept the growth permitted by that market or area or material consumption. A company's acceptance of a low rate of growth reflects a decision, conscious or unconscious, to retain a set of priorities in which a given orientation and pattern of diversification are more highly valued than growth.

Other companies, however, are so structured and managed that a certain rate of growth is required in order for the organization to function properly. If its current set of products and markets will not permit this desired rate of growth, it will seek new ones to 'fill the gap'. Again, this decision will closely reflect its attitudes regarding dominant orientation and diversification. One obvious indication of a company's relative emphasis on growth is how growth is treated in its planning, budgeting and performance evaluation cycle, and particularly the importance that is placed on annual growth rate, compared with such other measures as return on sales or return on assets. It is necessary to differentiate between a company's stated goals – words on paper – and what actually moves it to action.

Choice of Competitive Priorities

In its simplest form this choice is between seeking high profit margins or high output volumes. Some companies consistently prefer high margin products, even when this limits them to relatively low market shares. Others feel more comfortable with a high-volume business, despite the fact that this commits them to severe cost-reduction pressure and often implies low margins. An interesting article describes David Packard's attempts to redirect Hewlett-Packard away from the latter approach, where it was nose-to-nose with Texas Instruments, and back toward the former approach.[3]

This concept can be expanded and enriched, however, since companies can compete in ways other than simply through the prices of their products. Some compete on the basis of superior quality – either by providing higher quality in a standard product (for example, Mercedes-Benz) or by providing a product that has features or performance characteristics unavailable in competing products. We intend here to differentiate between an actual quality differential and a perceived difference, which is much more a function of selling and advertising strategy.

Other companies compete by promising utter dependability; their product may be priced higher and may not have some of the competitive products' features or workmanship. It will, however, work as specified, is delivered on time, and any failures are immediately corrected. IBM has been cited as an example of a company that competes on this basis; in a sense, so do AT&T and Sears, Roebuck.

Still others compete on the basis of product flexibility, their ability to handle difficult, non-standard orders and to lead in new-product introduction. This is a competitive strategy that smaller companies in many industries often adopt. And, finally, others compete through volume flexibility, being able to accelerate or decelerate production quickly. Successful companies in cyclical industries like housing or furniture often exhibit this trait.

In summary, within most industries different companies emphasize one of these five competitive dimensions—price, quality, dependability, product flexibility and volume flexibility. It is both difficult and potentially dangerous for a company to try to compete by offering superior performance along several competitive dimensions. Instead, a company must attach definite priorities to each that describe how it chooses to position itself relative to its competitors.

Practically every decision a senior manager makes will have a different impact on each of these dimensions, and the organization will thus have to make trade-offs between them. Unless these trade-offs are made consistently over time, the company will slowly lose its competitive distinctiveness.

Without such consistency, it does not matter how much effort a company puts into formulating and expounding on its 'strategy' – it essentially does not have one. One test of whether a company has a strategy is that it is clear not only about what it wants to do but also about what it does *not* want to do – what proposals it will consistently say no to.

Toward a Manufacturing Mission

Once such attitudes and competitive priorities are identified, the task for manufacturing is to arrange its structure and management so as to mesh

How Should You Organize Manufacturing?

with and reinforce this strategy. Manufacturing should be capable of helping the company do what it wants to do without wasting resources in lesser pursuits. This is what we call the company's 'manufacturing mission'.

It is surprising that general managers sometimes tend to lose sight of this concept, since the need for priorities permeates all other arenas of management. For example, marketing managers segment markets and focus product design, promotional and pricing effects around the needs of particular segments, often at the expense of the needs of other segments. And management information systems must be designed to emphasize particular kinds of information at the expense of others.

While it is possible to chalk up to inexperience the belief of many general managers that manufacturing should be capable of doing everything well, it is harder to explain why many manufacturing managers themselves either try to be good at everything at once or focus on the wrong thing. They know that all-purpose tools generally are used only when a specific tool is not available. Perhaps they fall into this trap because of pride, or too little time, or because they are reluctant to say no to their superiors.

All these factors enter into the following scenario. A manufacturing manager has nicely aligned his organization according to corporate priorities when suddenly he is subjected to pressure from marketing because of 'customer complaints' about product quality or delivery times. Under duress, and without sufficient time to examine the trade-offs involved, he attempts to shore up performance along these dimensions. Then he is confronted with pressure from finance to reduce costs or investment or both. Again, in the attempt to respond to the 'corporate will', or at least to oil the squeaky wheel, he reacts. Step by step, priorities and focus disappear, each lagging dimension being brought into line by some function's self-interest.

Falling into such a trap can be devastating, however, because a manufacturing mission that is inconsistent with corporate strategy is just as dangerous as not having any manufacturing mission at all. The more top management delegates key manufacturing decisions to 'manufacturing specialists' (usually engineers), the more likely it is that manufacturing's priorities will be different from corporate priorities. They will reflect engineering priorities, or operating simplicity (often the goal of someone who has worked his way up from the bottom of the organization) – not the needs of the business.

Using Structural Decisions

Translating a set of manufacturing priorities into an appropriate collection of plant, people and policies requires resources, time and management perseverance. As we mentioned earlier, the great bulk of most companies' assets (capital, human and managerial) is found in manufacturing. Moreover, these assets tend to be massive, highly interrelated and long lived – in comparison with marketing and most financial assets. As a result, it is difficult to redirect them, and 'fine-tuning' is almost impossible. Once a change is made, its impact is felt throughout the system and cannot be undone easily.

Such manufacturing inertia is made worse by many manufacturing managers' reluctance to change. And it is further compounded by many top managers' lack of understanding of the kind of changes that are needed, as well as by their unwillingness to commit the resources to effect such changes.

The decisions that implement a set of manufacturing priorities are structural; for a given company or business they are made infrequently and at various intervals. They fall into two broad categories: facilities decisions and infrastructure decisions.

Facilities decisions involve the following considerations:

(1) The total amount of manufacturing and logistics capacity to provide for each product line over time.
(2) How this capacity is broken up into operating units (plants, warehouses, and so on), their size and form (a few large plants versus many small ones), their location, and the degree or manner of their specialization (for example, according to product, process, and so on).
(3) The kind of equipment and production technology used in these plants.
(4) The span of the process – that is, the direction of vertical integration (toward control either of markets or of suppliers), its extent (as reflected roughly by value added as a percentage of sales), and the degree of balance among the capacities of the production stages.

Infrastructure decisions involve the following considerations:

(1) Policies that control the loading of the factory or factories – raw material purchasing, inventory and logistics policies.
(2) Policies that control the movement of goods through the factory or factories – process design, work-force policies and practices, production scheduling, quality control, logistics policies, inventory control.
(3) The manufacturing organizational design that coordinates and directs all of the foregoing.

These two sets of decisions are closely intertwined, of course. A plant's total annual capacity (a facilities decision) depends on whether the production rate is kept as constant as possible over time or, alternatively, changed frequently in an attempt to 'chase demand' (an infrastructure decision). Similarly, work-force policies interact with location and process choices, and purchasing policies interact with vertical integration choices. Decisions regarding organizational design also will be highly dependent on vertical integration decisions, as well as on the company's decisions regarding how various plants are located, specialized and interrelated.

Each of these structural decisions places before the manager a variety of choices, and each choice puts somewhat different weights on the five competitive dimensions. For example, an assembly line is highly interdependent and inflexible but generally promises lower costs and higher predictability than a loosely coupled line or batch-flow operation or a job shop. Similarly, a company that attempts to adjust production rates so as to chase demand will generally have higher costs and lower quality than a company that tries

How Should You Organize Manufacturing?

to maintain more level production and absorb demand fluctuations through inventories.

If consistent priorities are to be maintained, as a company's strategy and manufacturing mission change, then change usually becomes necessary in *all* of these structural categories. Again and again the root of a manufacturing crisis is that a company's manufacturing policies and people – workers, supervisors and managers – become incompatible with its plant and equipment, or both become incompatible with its competitive needs.

Even more subtly, plant may be consistent with policies, but the manufacturing organization that attempts to coordinate them all no longer does its job effectively. For, in a sense, the organization is the glue that keeps manufacturing priorities in place and welds the manufacturing function into a competitive weapon. It also must embody the corporate attitudes and biases already discussed.

In addition, the way manufacturing chooses to organize itself has direct implications for the relative emphasis placed on the five competitive dimensions. Certain types of organizational structures are characterized by high flexibility; others encourage efficiency and tight control; and still others promote dependable promises.

Approaching the Design

How are the appropriate corporate priorities to be maintained in a manufacturing organization that is characterized by a broad mix of products, specifications, process technologies, production volumes, skill levels and customer demand patterns? To answer this question, we must begin by differentiating between the administrative burden on the managements of individual plants and that on the central manufacturing staff. Each alternative approach for organizing a total manufacturing system will place different demands on each of these groups. In a rough sense, the same amount of 'control' must be exercised over the system, no matter how responsibilities are divided between the two.

At one extreme, one could lump all production for all products into a single plant. This makes the job of the central staff relatively easy (in some respects it becomes almost non-existent), but the job of the plant management becomes horrendous. At the other extreme, one could simplify the job of each plant (or operating unit within a given plant), so that each concentrates on a more restricted set of activities (products, processes, volume levels, and so on), in which case the coordinating job of the central organization becomes much more difficult.

Although many companies adopt the first approach, by either design or default, in our experience it becomes increasingly unworkable as more and more complexity is put under one roof. At some point a single large plant, or a contiguous plant complex, breaks down as more products, processes, skill levels and market demands are added to it. Skinner has argued against this approach and for the other extreme in an article in which he advocates dividing up the total manufacturing job into a number of *focused* units, each of which is responsible for a limited set of activities and objectives:

> Each [manufacturing unit should have] its own facilities in which it can concentrate on its particular manufacturing task, using its own workforce management approaches, production control, organization structure, and so forth. Quality and volume levels are not mixed; worker training and incentives have a clear focus; and engineering of processes equipment, and materials handling are specialized as needed. Each [unit] gains experience readily by focusing and concentrating every element of its work on those limited essential objectives which constitute its manufacturing task.[4]

If we adopt this sensible (but radical) approach, we are left with the problem of organizing the central manufacturing staff in such a way that it can effectively manage the resulting diversity of units and tasks. It must somehow maintain the total organization's sense of priorities and manufacturing mission, even though individual units may have quite different tasks and focuses. It carries out this responsibility both directly, by establishing and monitoring the structural policies we mentioned earlier (for example, process design, capacity planning, work-force management, inventory control, logistics, purchasing, and the like), and indirectly, by measuring, evaluating and rewarding individual plants and managers, and through the recruitment and systematic development of those managers.

These basic duties can be performed in a variety of ways, however, and each will communicate a slightly different sense of mission. To illustrate this, let us consider two polar examples – a 'product-focused organization' and a 'process-focused organization'. To clarify this discussion, look at the two highly simplified organizations shown in figure 1 and think about what the tasks of the corporate manufacturing staff and plant managers would be in each.

The corporate staff clearly must play a much more active role in making the second organization work. Logistics movements have to be carefully coordinated, and a change in any of the plants (or the market) can have repercussions throughout the system.

Only at the last stage (Process C), can the plant manager be measured on a profitability basis, and even that measure depends greatly on negotiated transfer prices and the smooth functioning of the rest of the system. He will not have much opportunity to exercise independent decision making, since most variables under his control (capacity, output, specifications, and so on) will affect everybody else. Thus he will probably be regarded as a 'cost centre' and be measured in large part on his ability to work smoothly within this highly interdependent system.

The distinction between such product-focused and process-focused manufacturing organizations should not be confused with the distinction between traditional functional and divisional corporate organizations. In fact, it is entirely possible that two divisions within a divisionally organized company would choose to organize their manufacturing groups differently. The important distinction has less to do with the organization chart than

How Should You Organize Manufacturing?

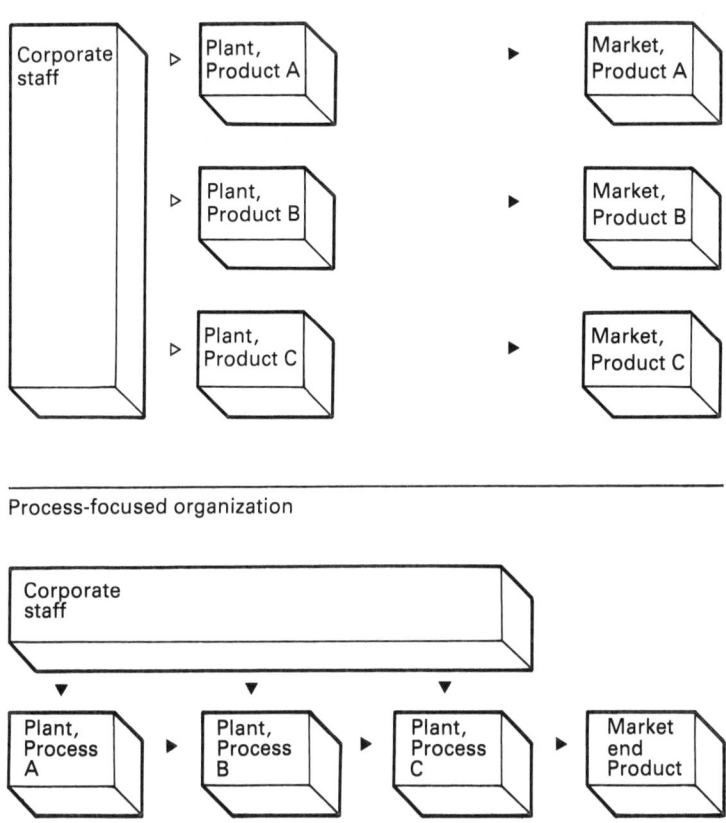

Figure 1 Product-focused and process-focused organizations

with the role and responsibilities of the central manufacturing staff and how far authority is pushed down the organization. In a sense, the distinction is more between centralized control and decentralized control.

With this brief overview, let us turn to more realistic product and process organizations.

Product-focused Organization

Basically, the product-focused organization resembles a traditional plant-with-staff organization, which then replicates itself at higher levels to handle groups of plants and then groups of products and product lines. Authority in the product-focused organization is highly decentralized, which contributes to the flexibility of this type of organization in new product introduction. Each product group is essentially an independent small company, and thus it can react quickly to product development considerations.

A product focus tends to be better suited to less complex, less capital-intensive process technologies, where the capital investment required is generally not high, where economies of scale do not demand large common production facilities, and where flexibility and innovation are more important than careful planning and tight control. A product-focused organization is a 'clean' one, with responsibilities well delineated, and profit or return on investment the primary measures. Such an organization tends to appeal most to companies that have a high need and tolerance for diversity, and whose dominant orientation is to a market or consumer group, as opposed to a technology or a material.

The responsibility for decisions on capital, technology and product development are thrust down from the corporate level to lower levels of management. Plant managers become very important people. This places special burdens on the organization. Product focus demands talented, entrepreneurially minded junior managers and thus much concern for recruiting and managerial development. Junior managers must be tracked carefully through the system, and this implies devoting considerable resources to the company's evaluation and reward system.

And, because staff functions are isolated in individual product lines, the corporate staff must coordinate general policies, goals and personnel across all the product lines. The corporate level central staff is well removed from day-to-day operations, but it is instrumental in communications and co-ordination across groups with regard to such issues as personnel policies, manpower availability, special services (from computer assistance to training programs), capital appropriation requests, and purchasing.

Process-focused Organization

Within a process-focused organization, individual plants are typically dedicated to a variety of different products. Sometimes a product is produced entirely by a single plant in such an organization, but more often the plant is only one of several that add value to the product.

Responsibilities throughout the plant and also throughout the upper management hierarchy are delineated, not by product line, but by segment of the full manufacturing process. Plants tend to be cost centres, not profit centres, and measurement is based on historical or technologically derived standards. An organization with this division of responsibility can properly be called process-focused.

Process focus tends to be better suited to companies with complex (and divisible) processes and with large capital requirements, companies we earlier called material- or technology-oriented companies. Questions of capacity, balance, logistics and technological change and its impact on the process are critical for such companies and absorb much of top management's energies. A process focus is not conducive to the rapid introduction of new products, since it does not assign authority along product lines. Nor is it flexible in altering the output levels of existing products, because of the 'pipeline momentum' in the system. But it can facilitate low-cost production

How Should You Organize Manufacturing? 87

if there are cost advantages deriving from the scale, continuity and technology of the process.

A process-focused organization demands tremendous attention to coordinating functional responsibilities to ensure smooth changes in the product mix. And because control is exercised centrally, young managers must ensure a long and generally a more technical apprenticeship with less decision-making responsibility. This places a burden on upper-level management to keep junior managers motivated and learning.

Despite the strong centralization of control in a process-focused organization, it may not be more efficient (in terms of total manufacturing costs) than a well-managed product-focused organization. The central overhead and logistics costs required by a process focus can sometimes offset any variable cost reductions because of tight control and economies of scale. A product focus, however, is inherently easier to manage because of its small scale and singlemindedness. This usually results in shorter cycle times, less inventories, lower logistics costs and, of course, lower overhead.[5]

The plants in a process organization can be expected to undertake one task that the central staff in a product organization cannot adequately perform, however. Since these plants are technologically based, they tend to be staffed with people who are highly expert and up to date in that technology. They will be aware of technological alternatives and trends, current research, and the operating experience of different technologies at other plants. Operating people in such a plant are more likely to transfer to a similar plant of a competitor's than they are to move to one of the other plants in their own company.

In a product organization, each product-plant complex will involve a number of technologies, and there may not be a sufficient mass of technical expertise to keep abreast of the changing state of the art in that technology. This becomes, then, more a responsibility of the corporate staff or, possibly, of a separate research group in the corporation, which may not even be under the aegis of the manufacturing organization. For this reason, businesses that use highly complex and evolving technologies are often forced to gravitate toward process organizations.

A process organization tends to manage purchasing somewhat better than a product organization does. If purchasing becomes too fragmented because of decentralization, the company as a whole tends to lose economies of scale as well as 'clout' with suppliers. Conversely, centralized purchasing tends to be more bureaucratic and less responsive to local or market needs. The result is usually a combination of both, where through some decision rule the product organizations are given responsibility for certain purchases and a central purchasing department handles the procurement and distribution of the remainder.

Table 2 gives a summary of the important differences between product-focused and process-focused organizations.

Product or Process Focus?
The polar extremes of manufacturing organization – product and process focus – place fundamentally different demands and opportunities on a

TABLE 2   DIFFERENCES BETWEEN PRODUCT-FOCUSED AND PROCESS-FOCUSED MANUFACTURING ORGANIZATIONS

	Product focus	Process focus
Profit or cost responsibility: where located	Product groups	Central organization
Size of corporate staff	Relatively small	Relatively large
Major functions of corporate staff	(a) Review capital appropriation requests (b) Communicate corporate changes and requests (c) Act as clearinghouse for personnel information management recruiting purchasing used equipment management development programs (d) Evaluate and reward plant managers (e) Select plant managers and manage career paths – possibly across product group lines	(a) Coordination with marketing (b) Facilities decisions (c) Personnel policies (d) Purchasing (e) Logistics-inventory management (f) Coordination of production schedules (g) Make versus buy, vertical integration decisions (h) Recruit future plant managers (i) Review plant performance, cost centre basis
Major responsibilities of plant organizations	(a) Coordination with marketing (b) Facilities decisions (subject to marketing) (c) Purchasing and logistics (d) Production scheduling and inventory control (e) Make versus buy (f) Recruit management	(a) Use materials and facilities efficiently (b) Recruit production, clerical, and lower management workers (c) Training and development of future department and plant managers (d) Respond to special requests from marketing within limited ranges

How Should You Organize Manufacturing?

company, and the choice of manufacturing organization should essentially be a choice *between* them. That is, manufacturing confronts a very definite either/or choice of organization – either product-focused or process-focused. Just as individual plants must have a clear focus, so must a central manufacturing organization.

Because the demands of a process-focused organization are so different from those of a product-focused organization – as to policies and practices, measurement and control systems, managerial attitudes, kinds of people, and career paths – it is extremely difficult for a mixed manufacturing organization, with a single central staff, to achieve the kind of policy consistency and organizational stability that can both compete effectively in a given market and cope with growth and change.

A mixed or composite production focus will only invite confusion and a weakening of the corporation's ability to maintain consistency among its manufacturing policies, and between them and its various corporate attitudes. If different manufacturing groups within the same company have different focuses, they should be separated as much as possible – each with its own central staff.

To illustrate, we can examine some mixed organizational focuses and the difficulties they might encounter.

(1) A process-focused factory producing for two distinct product groups would have the organization chart shown in figure 2. Here the corporation is trying to serve two different markets and product lines from the same factory, whose process technology appears to meet the needs of both (it may, in fact, consist of a series of linked process stages operating under tight central control). This kind of organization invites the now-classic problems of Skinner's unfocused factory. The manufacturing mission required by each market may be vastly different, and a plant that tries to carry out both at the same time is likely to do neither well.

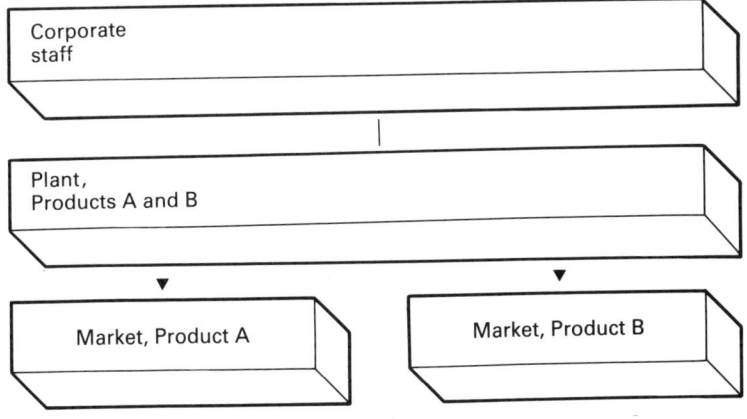

Figure 2   *Process-focused factory serving two different product markets*

Similarly, an organization that uses the manufacturing facilities of one of its product groups to supply a major portion of the needs of another product group market, would be risking the same kind of confusion – that is, a nominally product-focused organization with an organization chart like the one in figure 3.

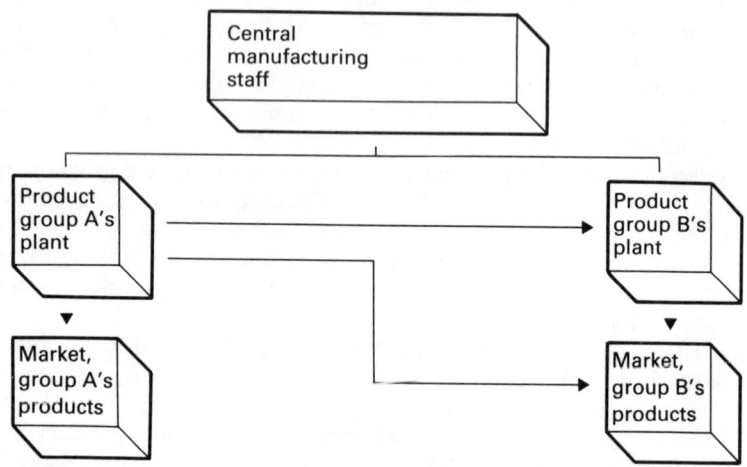

Figure 3   *One product group serving another product group's market*

(2) A process-focused factory supplying parts or materials to two distinct product groups would have the organization chart shown in figure 4. In this instance a corporate staff oversees two independent product groups, which serve two distinct markets, *and* a process-focused plant that supplies both product groups. The usual argument for an independent supplier plant is that economies of scale are possible from combining the requirements of both product groups. No matter what the reason, the supplier plant is coordinated by the same staff that oversees the product groups. One vice president of manufacturing directs a corporate manufacturing staff with one materials manager, one chief of individual engineering, one head of purchasing, one personnel director – all supervising the activities of two product-focused organizations and a process-focused organization.

Another variant of this difficulty is for the captive supplier plant for one product group to supply a major portion of the requirements of another product group's plant. Or a plant belonging to a product-focused division might act as a supplier to one of the plants within a process-focused division.

How else can a company organize around such situations? The important notion is that a plant that attaches certain priorities to different competitive dimensions is likely to prefer suppliers who have the same priorities. This suggests that a company should erect managerial dividing lines between its product- and process-focused manufacturing segments. In particular, transfer of products between product- and process-focused plant groups

How Should You Organize Manufacturing?

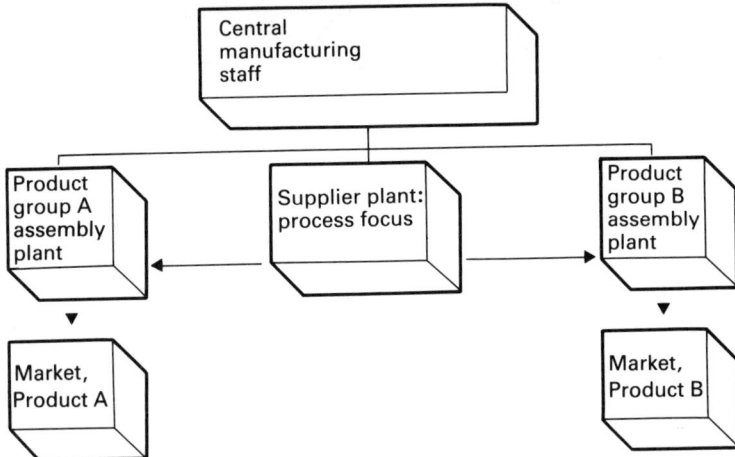

Figure 4   Two product groups and a supplier plant

should not be coordinated by a central staff group but handled through arm's-length bargaining, as if, in effect, they had independent 'subsidiary' relationships within the parent company.

Such an in-house supplier would then be treated like any other supplier, able to resist demands that violate the integrity of its manufacturing mission just as the customer plant is free to select suppliers that are more attuned to its own mission. The organization chart might look something like that shown in figure 5.

Such an arrangement may appear to be needlessly complex and add to the manufacturing's administrative overhead without clear financial benefits. However, combining two dissimilar activities does not reduce complexity; it simply camouflages it and is likely to destroy the focus and distinctiveness of both. Our position is not that both product and process focus cannot exist within the same company but simply that separating them as much as possible will result in less confusion and less danger that different segments of manufacturing will be working at cross purposes.

Test for Organizational Focus

Many companies, consciously or unconsciously, have moved toward precisely this kind of wide separation. In some cases it is explicit, with two or more different staff groups operating relatively autonomously; in others, although a single central staff appears on the organization chart, subgroups within this staff operate independently. One way for a company to test the degree of organizational focus in its manufacturing arm, and whether adequate insulation between product- and process-focused plant groups exists, is to contemplate how it would fragment itself if forced to (by the Antitrust Division of the Department of Justice for example). A segmented and

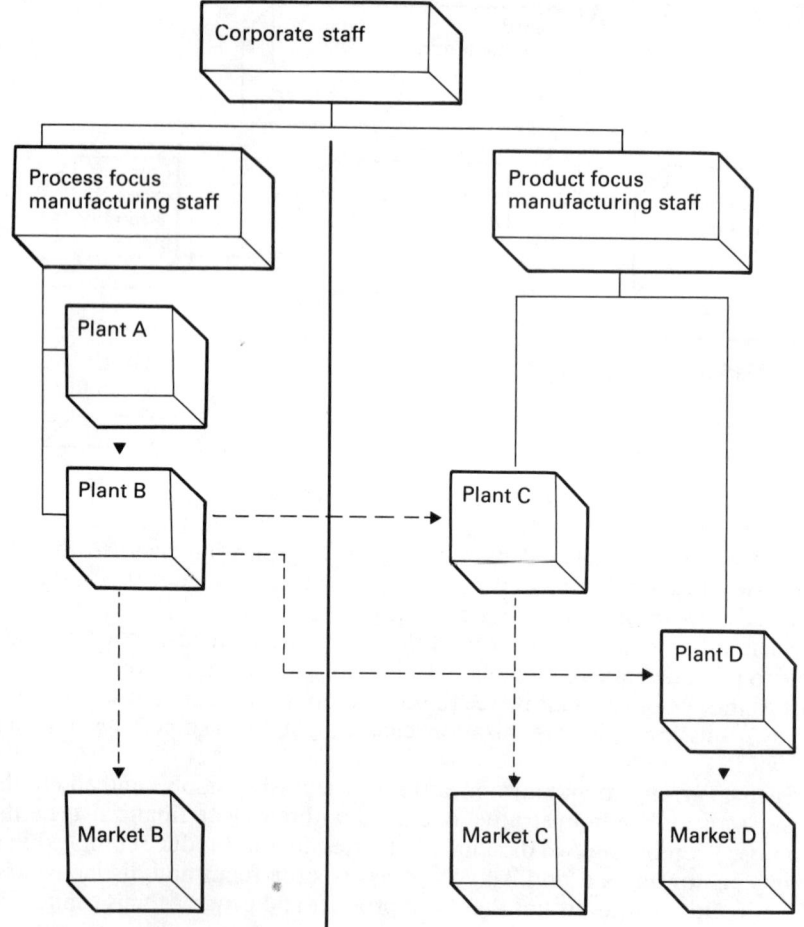

Figure 5   Product-focused division supplying to process-focused division

focused organization should be able to divide itself up cleanly and naturally, with no substantial organizational changes.

Consider the large auto companies. From the point of view of the marketplace, they are organized by product groups (Oldsmobile, Lincoln, Mercury, Chevrolet, and so on), but this organization is essentially cosmetic. In reality, the auto companies are classic examples of large process-focused organizations. Any effort by the Department of Justice to sever these companies by product group is foolish because it cuts across the grain of their manufacturing organization. If the companies had to divest themselves, it could only be by process segment. But the point is that divestiture could be accomplished readily, and this is the acid test of an effective and focused manufacturing organization.

How Should You Organize Manufacturing?

The Impact of Growth

Up to this point we have been arguing that a company's manufacturing function must structure and organize itself so as to conform to the company's priorities for certain competitive dimensions. Moreover, the choice of manufacturing organizational structure – which provides most of the key linkages between the manufacturing group and the company's other people and functions – must also fit with the basic attitudes, the preferences, and the traditions that shape and drive the remainder of the company.

But companies change and grow over time. Unless a manufacturing organization is designed so that it can grow with the company, it will become increasingly unstable and inappropriate to the company's needs. Therefore, simplicity and focus are not sufficient criteria; the organizational design must somehow also incorporate the possibility of growth.

In fact, growth is an enemy of focus and can subvert a healthy manufacturing operation – not all at once, but bit by bit. For example, growth can move a company up against a different set of competitors at the same time as it is acquiring new resources and thus force a change in its competitive strategy. The strategy change may be aggressive and deliberate or unconscious and barely perceived. In either case, however, success for the company may now require different skills from those already mastered – a different manufacturing mission and focus to complement a new corporate strategy.

Even without a change of strategy, growth can diminish a manufacturing organization's ability to maintain its original focus. Especially if growth is rapid, top-level managers will be pressed continually to decide on capital acquisitions and deployment, and to relinquish some authority over operational issues in existing plants. Slowly, focus disintegrates.

To cope with growth, we believe that first one must identify and understand the type of growth being experienced and the demands it will place on the organization. Growth has four important dimensions:

(1) A broadening of the products or product lines being offered.
(2) An extended span of the production process for existing products to increase value added (commonly referred to as vertical integration).
(3) An increased product acceptance within an existing market area.
(4) Expansion of the geographic sales territory serviced by the company.

These types of growth are very different, but it is important to distinguish among them so that the organization design can reflect the *kind* of growth experienced, not simply the fact of growth. This means keeping the organization as stable and focused as possible as growth proceeds.

If growth is predominantly a broadening of product lines, a product-focused organization is probably best suited to the demands for flexibility that such a broadening requires. With such organizations, other aspects of manufacturing, particularly the production of the traditional product lines, need change only little as growth proceeds.

Alternatively, if growth is chiefly toward increasing the span of the process (that is, vertical integration), a process-focused organization can probably best introduce and manage the added segments of the full production process. In this fashion, the separate pieces of the process can be coordinated effectively and confusion can be reduced in the traditional process segments.

Then again, if growth is realized through increased product acceptance, the product becomes more and more a commodity and, as acceptance grows, the company is usually pressed to compete on price. Such pressure generally implies changes in the production process itself: more specialization of equipment and tasks, an increasing ratio of capital to labour expenses, a more standard and rigid flow of the product through the process. The management of such changes in the process is probably best accomplished by an organization that is focused on the process, willing to forsake the flexibilities of a more decentralized product focus.

Growth realized through geographic expansion is more problematic. Sometimes such growth can be met with existing facilities. But frequently, as with many multinational companies, expansion in foreign countries is best met with an entirely separate manufacturing organization that itself can be organized along either a product or a process focus.

Recognizing Common Pitfalls

As we examined a number of manufacturing organizations that had 'lost their way' –become unfocused or whose focus was no longer congruent with corporate needs – it become apparent that in most cases the culprit was growth. Problems due to growth often surface with the apparent breakdown of the relationship between the central manufacturing staff and division or plant management. For example, many companies that have had a strong central manufacturing organization find that as their sales and product offerings grow in size and complexity, the central staff simply cannot continue to perform the same functions as well as before. A tenuous mandate for changing the manufacturing organization surfaces.

Sometimes, product divisions are broken out. But the natural inclination is to strengthen the central staff functions instead, which usually diminishes the decision-making capabilities of plant managers.

As the central staff becomes stronger, it begins to siphon authority and people from the plant organization. Thus the strong tend to get stronger and the weak weaker. At some point this vicious cycle breaks down under the strain of increasing complexity, and then a simple executive order cannot accomplish the profound changes – in people, policies and attitudes –that are necessary to reverse the process and cause decentralization.

We do not mean to imply that decentralizing manufacturing management is always the best path to follow as an organization grows. It may be preferable in some cases to split it apart geographically, with two strong central staffs coordinating the efforts of two independent plant organizations.

How Should You Organize Manufacturing? 95

However, it is sometimes dangerous to delegate too much responsibility for capacity-expansion decisions to a product-oriented manufacturing manager. To keep his own task as simple as possible, he may tend to 'expand in place' – continually expanding current plants or building nearby satellite plants. Over time he may create a set of huge, tightly interconnected plants that exhibit many of the same characteristics as a process organization: tight central control, inflexibility, and constraints on further incremental expansion.

Such a situation could occur in spite of the fact that the corporation as a whole continues to emphasize market flexibility, decentralized responsibility and technological opportunism. The new managers trained in such a complex will have to be different in personality and skills from those in other parts of the company, and a different motivation and compensation system is required. Such a situation can be remedied either by dismembering and reorganizing this product organization or by decoupling it from the rest of the company so that it has more of an independent, subsidiary status, as described earlier.

Product focus can also encroach on an avowed process focus. For example, a company offering several complex products whose manufacture takes these products through very definite process stages, in which the avowed focus is process-oriented, and with separate divisions for stages of the process all subject to strong central direction, must resist the temptation to alter manufacturing so that it can 'get closer to the market'. If the various product lines were allowed to make uncoordinated requests for product-design changes or new-product introductions, the tightly coupled process pipeline could then crumble. Encroaching product focus would subvert it.

Concluding Remarks

Manufacturing functions best when its facilities, technology and policies are consistent with recognized priorities of corporate strategy. Only then can manufacturing gain efficiency without wasting resources by 'improving' operations that do not count.

The manufacturing organization itself must be similarly consistent with corporate priorities. Such organizational focus is aided by simplicity of design. This simplicity in turn requires either a product- or a process-focused form of organization. The proper choice between these two organizational types can smooth a company's growth by lending stability to its operations.

Notes

1. See, for example, Wickham Skinner, 'Manufacturing – Missing Link in Corporate Strategy', *Harvard Business Review*, May–June 1969, p. 136, and 'The Focused Factory', *Harvard Business Review*, May–June 1974, p. 113.
2. Two representative texts are: Kenneth R. Andrews, *The Concept of Corporate Strategy* (Homewood, Ill.: Dow Jones-Irwin, 1971), and H. Igor Ansoff, *Corporate Strategy* (New York: McGraw-Hill, 1965).

3. 'Hewlett-Packard: Where Slower Growth Is Smarter Management', *Business Week*, 9 June 1975, p. 50.
4. See Wickham Skinner, 'The Focused Factory', *Harvard Business Review*, May–June 1974, p. 121.
5. E. F. Schumacher has eloquently argued a similar point in a somewhat different context in his provocative book *Small Is Beautiful* (New York: Harper & Row, 1975).

Part 2

Opportunities for Change in Manufacturing

Introduction

The previous section emphasized the challenges of the 1980s as articulated by the Finniston Report, demonstrated how things have gone wrong in the past and set the strategic context for looking at manufacturing systems today. This section aims to provide examples of the latest developments in manufacturing with some theoretical back-up so that certain applications may be better studied and understood. Broadly speaking the section falls into two blocks, starting with three articles on flexible manufacturing systems, followed by three articles on manufacturing control. A final article opens up some of the issues in computer-aided manufacture. Each article and each block of articles is now introduced in the order in which they are printed in this section.

Flexible Manufacturing Systems

The first article by Shah describes some of the latest developments in Japan. Neither this article, nor those that follow, attempt to cover the whole scene. Rather they give the flavour of some things happening in advanced factories at the time of writing. Shah's particular interest is the hardware (for example, computer-controlled cranes and robots) and how this hardware is laid out and connected on the factory floor. He also alludes to something which is a major topic for this section – flexible manufacturing systems.

The emergence of FMS (flexible manufacturing systems) as a commonly used term in manufacturing has caused confusion. The aim of the introduction at this point is to state a particular point of view about FMS, then to guide the reader through the next two articles, both of which have the word 'flexible' in their titles.

The situation about FMS is confused because the market has been oversold on FMS and undersold on flexibility. Flexibility in manufacturing is a goal about which it is worth putting forward views. To dispute whether a manufacturing system is or is not flexible is also worthwhile. To dispute whether a system is FMS or not FMS is *not* so worthwhile. FMS is something that marketing and academic people sell, and to concentrate the discussion on FMS (rather than on flexibility) is to move away from the heart of the matter. That is the view put forward here, but it is *not* necessarily a view which is generally accepted.

The second article in this block (by Browne *et al.*) provides some useful definitions of flexibility, and confirms the use of FMS as a coordinating term. It is necessary to remember when reading this article that each time the letters FMS occur the argument could be sustained equally well if the letters FMS were not used. Moreover the shiny plastic bag of FMS around the parcel of flexibility may not be as valuable as the authors think, for example they classify a flexible machining cell as 'Type I FMS'. Why not just call it a flexible machining cell? Flexibility is important. FMS are not so important.

However, it is still helpful to use the Browne *et al.* article as a theoretical background for classifying the systems described by Shah in terms of flexibility. For example, figure 5 in Shah is an example of a flexible machining system and so on. The authors assign various characteristics of flexibility to their different types, and that in itself is useful, whatever view is taken of FMS as a classifier.

The next article, by Mallin and Sackett, describes how a small company with minimal experience of advanced manufacturing technology went ahead and designed a flexible assembly system. Their old system suffered from long lead-times, high work-in-progress and poor monitoring performance. It is refreshing to see these authors' concepts of flexibility *not* dominated by FMS. Thus – 'flexibility is to be derived from the good utilization of the human skills available from the existing operators'. A small company requires high system reliability which according to the Browne *et al.* article is more likely to be achieved with a multiline approach. The equivalent of a multiline approach in this small firm is to allow some operators to go on working when others are sick or have gone home. The work-stations in figure 2 in Mallin and Sackett are equivalent to a set of transfer lines. The principle of flexibility is the same.

Control

The next block presents three articles which explore the control aspects of advanced systems. The selection is intended to bring out certain contrasts.

The continued decrease in the physical size of computers and the increase in their processing capabilities have meant that many different kinds of small computers have been installed in factories to control manufacturing. While each computer may be programmed adequately to control its own operations (for example controlling a set of machine tools), problems arise because there may be no links between one computer and another. They may have been bought from different suppliers, so how can the control system of one computer be linked to another, and how can a shared approach be developed?

Introduction

The authors of the first article in this block (Weston *et al.*) see the local area network (LAN) as a practical answer to these questions. While agreeing that the technology of local area networks has advanced since the systems they describe were implemented, nevertheless they believe that the main principle of a LAN remains unchanged. The main principle is that each computer must have its own communications software as well as its applications software. The applications software controls what goes on, for example, in a manufacturing cell or part of a cell. The communications software deals with messages between cells or parts of cells. The value of the Weston *et al.* article is that it gives two examples of how a LAN works in practice. The first example follows what happens in a simple manufacturing cell, and the second example deals with a glass-container production line. One could note in passing that these advanced systems are *not* confined to the area of metal-cutting.

The next article by Greene/Sadowski looks at two activities which a local area network might be expected to perform – cell loading and cell scheduling. The authors begin by asking which is the most appropriate way to manufacture in the first place, i.e. by line layout, function layout or by manufacturing cells. They then describe in some detail the desirable characteristics of manufacturing cells.

The last article in the control block (by Goddard) looks at a totally different type of control system – the system which every manufacturer needs in order to deal with the demands placed on factories by the market. Two systems are contrasted, *kanban* from Japan (which was not touched on by Shah in his article) and *manufacturing resource planning* (MRP II) from the United States of America. This article relates to the other two control articles as follows. Local area networks would in general not be needed under kanban, but they could be a great help to manufacturing resource planning. The concept of a manufacturing cell could be common to both, but the loading and scheduling activities would seem to have more to offer to manufacturing resource planning than to kanban.

Computer-aided Manufacture

The final article in this section (by Hatvany) brings in computer-aided design (CAD) and looks at manufacturing from the perspective of the CAD work-station. The question could perhaps be put as to what is the difference – *is* there any fundamental difference – between the work-station in a flexible assembly system (Mallin/Sackett), the CAD work-station (Hatvany) and a micro (controlling any manufacturing function) plugged in to a local area network (Weston *et al.*)? That is the question which Hatvany is basically addressing, though it is not stated precisely in those terms.

Computer-aided design is mainly used for component or product design, and it can also be used for system design. Hatvany is writing about product design. He approaches the topic through the CAD work-station which he judges correctly can do much more than update drawing designs quickly. CAD as a buzz word has been around far longer than FMS – long enough to create its own subject boundary. This means that Hatvany does not even mention FMS, but the route he takes is a particularly significant one for manufacturing.

Hatvany implies that hardware such as the CAD work-station with its associated software could eventually link up with computer-controlled cranes and the kind of advanced facilities described by Shah at the beginning of this section. The two would eventually come together in a process variously described as computer-aided manufacture or computer-integrated manufacture. The development of appropriate cells (Greene/Sadowski) linked to a control system based on local area networks (Weston) could provide a variety of flexibility (as listed by Browne). The manufacturing systems resulting from these combinations of advanced technology could be commissioned within the philosophy of the focused factory (Skinner, chapter 1.5) and following the strategic considerations set out by Hayes and Schmenner (chapter 1.6). Such configurations could respond effectively to the worries voiced in the Finniston Report (chapter 1.1) so that disasters such as the collapse of the British motorcycle industry (chapter 1.2) do not take place in the future.

2.1

Advanced Manufacturing Systems in Japan

R. Shah

Introduction

Flexible manufacturing systems are being implemented at a fast rate in Japan. The driving force behind this development is the priority given to improving productivity rates in a production and market environment characterized by rising costs, decreasing product life spans, increasing numbers of product variants, and the resulting shift from rigid production lines to adaptable, computer-controlled set-ups.

Leading Japanese machine-tool manufacturers have been quick to realize that the application of the FMS concept in their plants gives them a two-fold return on the high investments involved. The FMS concept is the most efficient method of producing modular components because it enables full, 24 hours per day utilization of expensive production equipment by adding a lightly manned second and an unmanned third shift to a normal day shift.

Secondly, the experience gained with FMS solutions to in-house production problems is essential for the next step, namely to provide the machine-tool user with the hardware and software necessary to implement FMS solutions for his problems. Thus knowhow obtained from pilot systems can be embodied in systems designed to meet customer requirements.

Common Design Factors

The emphasis placed on the two major objectives of ensuring a high productivity rate and facilitating transfer of knowhow to new installations has led to the following common denominator of Japanese FMS solutions: practically

Source: R. Shah, 'Advanced Manufacturing Systems in Japan', from *VDI International Magazine*, January 1983.

all are designed to use standard machine tools and standard cutting parameters. The use of standard machines keeps down investment costs and at the same time provides an easily adaptable basis for modular solutions. And by avoiding forced metal removal rates, system downtime can be minimized because of longer tool life, less frequent mechanical breakdowns and more uniform system operating conditions. The logical consequence of this approach is to operate the system at reduced cutting rates during the unattended night shift.

Unmanned operation of an FMS naturally calls for extensive monitoring devices for checking tools and workpieces as well as machine and transport cycles. Functions such as automatic tool-breakage detection can be solved by relatively simple means, e.g. moving the tool to touch a sensor or a limit switch. Tool-wear monitoring can be effected by measuring spindle torque or, more simply, tool-wear problems can be avoided by automatically replacing tools well before tool wear becomes critical.

Abnormal cutting conditions can be detected by storing cutting torque for different machining processes in a memory and comparing the actual value, computed from motor current, with the stored value (figure 1).

Work-piece transport is effected in the majority of cases by wire-guided pallet trucks, although less flexible arrangements employing rail-guided trucks are used in some installations. Exceptionally, these pallet trucks transport complete tool magazines or special tools.

FMS for Medium-sized Work-pieces

Medium-sized, box-like work-pieces with relatively long machining cycle times – in the order of 1 h or more, so that not more than 8–10 pallets run

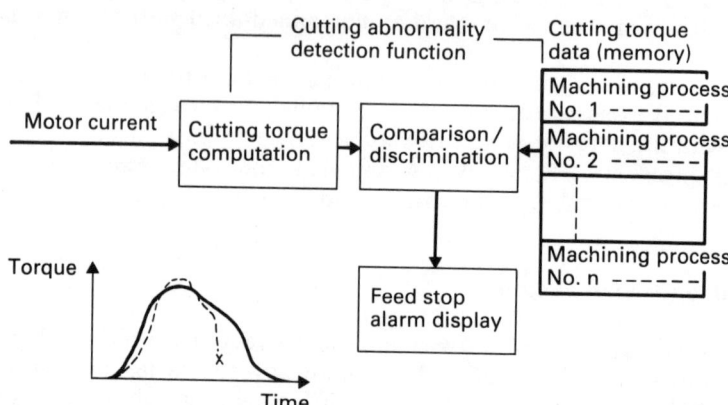

Figure 1 Monitoring abnormal cutting conditions by measuring spindle motor current, calculating cutting torque and comparing the value obtained with that stored in the computer memory for a specific machining process

Advanced Manufacturing Systems in Japan

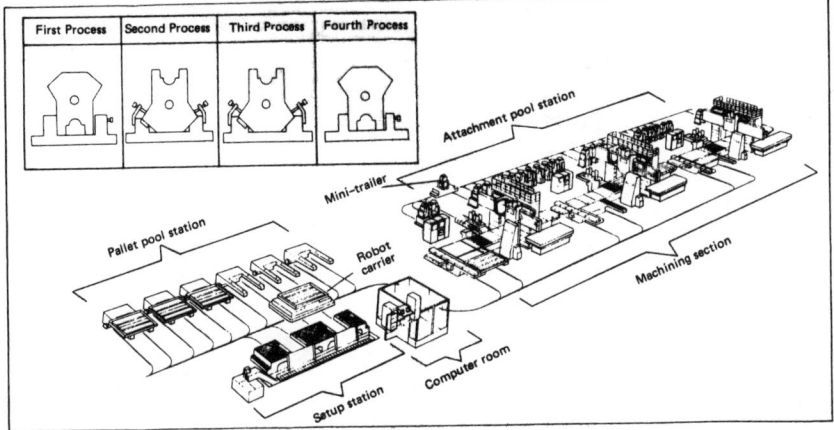

Designed by Shin Nippon Koki of Osaka, the FMS at Mitsubishi's Sagamihara plant comprises three machining centres. As shown in the insert, four different machining processes are carried out. Two different types of wire-guided pallet trucks are employed, one for transporting work-pieces and the other for moving special tools (multispindle and end-milling heads) from the tool buffer store (attachment pool station) to the machines.

These special tools enabled the number of tools required for the four machining processes to be reduced from 180 for conventional machining to 73 (50 standard tools plus 23 attachments). The pallet trucks carrying the attachments travel at a speed of max. 60 m/min and have a positioning accuracy of ±30 mm. Load-carrying capacity is 450 kg. The work-piece pallet trucks travel at a max. speed of 42 m/min, are positioned to within ±10 mm and have a capacity of 5000 kg.

A Mitsubishi MELCOM 70/30 minicomputer controls the following functions:

- Machining processes (via an interface to the Fanuc System 9 numerical control unit on the machining centres)
- Tool life and cutting torque monitoring (with memories storing tool-life data and cutting-torque data for each machining process) as well as automatic measurement function.

All part programs are stored in the memory of the NC units (capacity equivalent to 900 m of punched tape). The computer calls up the appropriate program by specifying the program number.

Monitoring of the machining process as well as automatic compensation of pallet position-ing and work-piece alignment errors are indispensable for unmanned operation of the FMS.

Figure 2 Diesel engine crankcase machining

through the system for a full shift – are ideal for optimum equipment utiliz-ation in an FMS. This is the case with the system installed at the Iga plant of Mori Seiki, Nara (see figure 3). The 13 machining centres (nine vertical spindle and four horizontal spindle machines) have cycle times ranging from 1 to 6 h.

The FMS forms part of a manufacturing set-up comprising a total of 45 machine tools, 35 of which are numerically controlled (see table 1). It is interesting to note that 20 of these NC machines are handled by only 7 oper-ators. Since the 13 FMS machines require only 3 operators per shift and the remaining 12 machines (10 conventional plus 2 NC jig borers) a further 12 operators, the complete set-up necessitates 22 operators per shift.

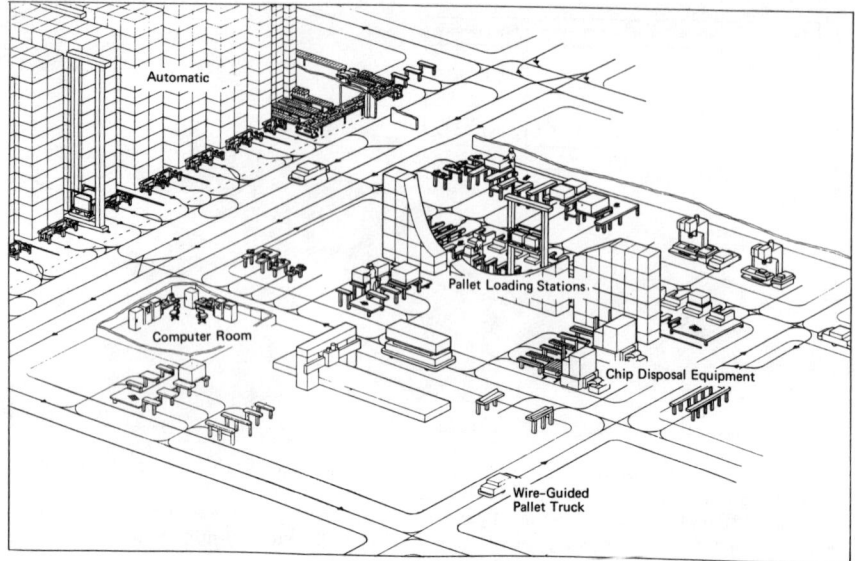

Figure 3 Thirteen machining centres, nine with vertical spindles and four with horizontal spindles, are fed with work-pieces from an automatic warehouse by wire-guided pallet trucks in Mori Seiki's Iga machine tool factory

TABLE 1 MACHINES AND OPERATORS IN MANUFACTURING SET-UP AT MORI SEIKI

	No of machines NC	Conventional	No. of operators NC	Conventional	Total no. of Machines	Operators
FMS	13	-	3	-	13	3
Machines of jig boring accuracy	2	2	2	2	4	4
Remaining machines	20	8	7	8	28	15
Total	35	10	12	10	45	22

Several monitoring devices are fitted to the FMS machines. Tool breakage is detected by moving a sensor to contact the tool nose. If a tool breaks, the machining operation immediately stops and the pallet with the workpiece and the tool are replaced. To avoid machining inaccuracy due to tool wear, tools are replaced according to accumulated data on tool life. After a tool change a built-in sensor automatically compensates for tool length.

Another sensor automatically compensates for alignment errors due to incorrect workpiece positioning on the pallet or due to thermal deformation of the machine. A machined surface or hole is used as reference during alignment error compensation.

Advanced Manufacturing Systems in Japan

One of the features of the pallet system is the use of an easily operated hydraulic clamping device. Depending on the workpiece, either a pull-down or a centre-block clamp is employed. It is claimed that the device has reduced setting-up time from 15 min to less than 3 min. Tools provided in the tool magazines of the nine vertical machining centres suffice for machining up to 117 different workpieces. When additional tools are needed, the pallet truck transfers them from the tool presetting station to the machine. The tool pallet is moved to the machine table, and from there the tool changer takes them up and exchanges them with those no longer required.

Three different wire-guided pallet trucks are employed. Eight units can move loads of up to 1000 kg at speeds of up to 60 m/min, four units handle loads up to 2000 kg at speeds of max. 42 m/min, and the remaining four units handle loads up to 3000 kg at the same top speed.

Table 2 summarizes the benefits obtained with the FMS operation. The number of machines has been reduced by 76 per cent, the production time has been tripled (three shifts instead of one), the efficiency has been increased by nearly 40 per cent, and the number of operators reduced by roughly 90 per cent.

As shown in Fig. 3, the automatic stores are an essential component of the FMS at Mori Seiki's Iga plant. The stores contain a total of 18,780 pallets handled by 13 cranes. Total storage capacity is 7920 t. (There are 12,800 pallets having a load-carrying capacity of 30 kg, 4962 with a capacity of 1000 kg, 736 of 2000 kg, and 282 of 3000 kg.)

A Hitachi E-800 computer together with an IBM S/1 unit controls machining processes, automatic pallet transport and stocking of parts in the automatic stores. Production planning and other functions are effected by a Fujitsu V-850 computer. A total of 45 terminals are installed at various points of the manufacturing plant.

Twelve Operators for Three Shifts

Flexible manufacturing systems can lead to considerable productivity gains. The gains reported by Japanese plants are outstandingly high. A case in point is the FMS installed in the Oguchi plant of Yamazaki. The two-section

TABLE 2 COMPARISON OF FMS WITH CONVENTIONAL SET-UP (Mori Seiki)

	FMS[a]	Conventional	FMS vs Conventional
No. of machines	13	54	− 76%
Production time (22 days/month)	528 h/month	176	+ 200%
Efficiency	93%	67%	+ 38%
No. of operators	3	27	− 89%

Note: [a] 1 manned shift + 2 unmanned shifts.

system comprises 18 machine tools which replace 68 conventional machines (table 3). Labour savings are impressive: only 12 operators are needed for working all three shifts – compared with no less than 215 men for the conventional counterpart.

TABLE 3 COMPARISON OF FMS WITH CONVENTIONAL SET-UP (Yamazaki)

	FMS	Conventional	FMS vs Conventional
Floor area	3000 m^2	9750 m^2	−69%
No. of machines	18	68	−74%
No. of operators	12	215	−94%
Lead time	3 d	80 d	−96%

The first section of the system has 8 horizontal spindle machining centres and is designed to machine 23 different types of medium-sized work-pieces such as spindle heads and others castings. Output of this section is 800 pieces/month. The pallets measuring 1000 × 1000 mm are transported by rail-guided pallet trucks having a load-carrying capacity of 3 t at speeds of up to 60 m/min.

The second section comprises 10 machines (7 vertical spindle and 3 horizontal spindle machining centres) and is capable of machining 51 different work-pieces such as beds, columns and other large parts. Output is 600 pieces/month. The pallets measuring 3000 × 1600 mm are transported by rail-guided pallet trucks having a capacity of 8 t at speeds of up to 40 m/min. 29 pallets can be randomly directed to any of the 10 machines.

Loading and unloading the pallets is effected by two operators per section and per shift (shifts 1 and 2 only). The computer signals the number of the required work-piece to the operator. If this work-piece is not available, an alternative work-piece is selected by the computer. Clamping of the work-piece is effected hydraulically. All pallets needed for the night shift are readied during shifts 1 and 2.

An interesting feature is the use of computer-controlled cranes for changing complete tool magazines. These drum-type magazines contain either 30 or 40 tools. The computer determines when new tools are needed and initiates the magazine changing cycle. Since each machine has a double magazine, the total number of tools immediately available is either 60 or 80. Tool locations not needed are filled with spare tools. Measured values are stored in the computer and then entered directly in the NC units so that no manual tool corrections are needed.

Mechanical probes are used for detecting broken tools. In the case of large tools (exceeding 50 mm diameter), monitoring is effected by measuring the spindle motor current. Further probes are used for detecting work-pieces on the pallets and for measuring work-piece misalignment. Adaptive feedrate control is employed for optimizing roughing operations.

Advanced Manufacturing Systems in Japan

Flexible Machining and Assembly

The concept of flexible automation can be applied to both machining and assembly operations, as exemplified by Fanuc's Fuji complex. One section of the complex is used for machining and assembling electric motors, and the other for similar operations on machine tools and robots. Each FMS is linked via an intermediate store to an automated assembly system.

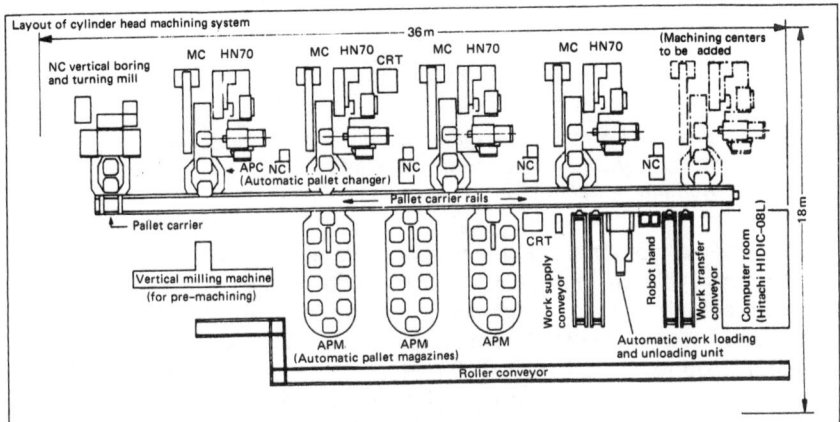

Four machining centres and an NC vertical turning and boring mill (vertical lathe) form the FMS installed at Niigata Engineering's diesel engine plant in Niigata. The work-pieces weigh between 30 and 350 kg and range in size between $280 \times 190 \times 110$ and $870 \times 630 \times 300$ mm. The system processes 30 different cylinder head types in batch sizes between 6 and 30 pieces. Three automatic pallet magazines are provided so that at least one magazine can supply work-pieces when one of the other two is being manually loaded with pallets.

Work-pieces deposited on the left side of the roller conveyor are brought to the automatic work loading and unloading unit. Here a robot places the work-piece on a pallet and initiates hydraulic clamping of the work-piece. After machining, the work-piece is returned to the automatic work loading and unloading unit. The robot unloads the work-piece and transfers it to another conveyor. Together with a vertical milling machine for pre-machining, the system comprises 6 machine tools. These replace 31 machines (including 6 NC units) needed for a coventional set-up. Instead of 31 operators only 4 operators are required. Average operating time of the FMS is 21 h/d compared with 9 h/d for the conventional set-up. Lead time was reduced from 16 to 4 days.

Figure 4   Diesel engine cylinder head machining

Parts machined by the FMS, which is located on the first floor of the building, are temporarily stored in an automatic warehouse. From here they are retrieved when they are needed for assembly in the automatic assembly system on the second floor. The machining cells of Fanuc's FA System consist of NC machines fitted with robots or pallet changers and a monitoring unit (see figure 5), and the assembly cells incorporate one or more robots. The cell robot picks up the parts from the pallet deposited by the wire-guided pallet truck. After assembly, the subassembly is placed on a conveyor and sent to the next assembly cell.

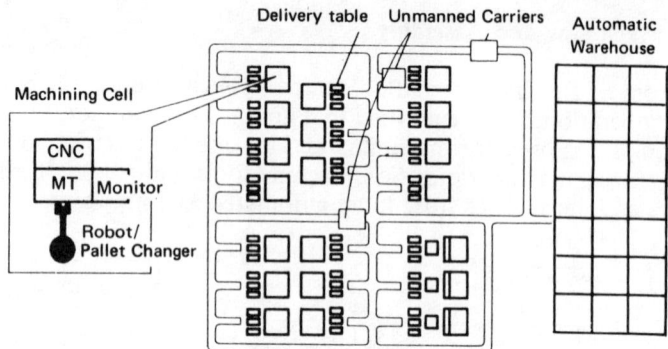

Figure 5 Unmanned carriers (wire-guided pallet trucks) transport work-pieces from the machining cell to delivery tables and from there to the automatic warehouse in Fanuc's 'FA System'

The first FMS comprises 60 machining cells with 52 robots for producing 40 different types of motors. Output is 10,000 motors/month. In all, 900 different components are machined in batch sizes ranging from 20 to 1000. The second FMS is designed to machine parts required for small machine tools and robots. In all, 450 different parts are machined in batch sizes ranging from 5 to 20. Machining and assembly operations are effected by a total permanent staff of 100 persons. Monthly output is 300 robots, 100 EDM cutting machines and 100 small-size machine tools.

Machine utilization rate is increased by taking steps to avoid organizational idle times and providing for 3-shift operation, including an unmanned or lightly manned third shift. This night shift is monitored by fitting two TV cameras to each machining cell. Automatic transport of work-pieces is effected by several means: roller conveyors, wire and rail-guided pallet trucks, as well as robots and computer-controlled cranes.

Since all parts needed for daily assembly are produced on the previous day and stocked in the intermediate store, in-process inventory is minimized. Lead time and capital tied up in stocks are therefore significantly reduced.

2.2

Classification of Flexible Manufacturing Systems

J. Browne, D. Dubois, K. Rathmill, S. Sethi and K. Stecke

A Flexible Manufacturing System (FMS) is an integrated, computer-controlled complex of automated material handling devices and numerically controlled (NC) machine tools that can simultaneously process medium-sized volumes of a variety of part types.[1] This new production technology has been designed to attain the efficiency of well-balanced, machine-paced transfer lines, while utilizing the flexibility that job shops have to simultaneously machine multiple part types.

Recently, many new manufacturing facilities have been labelled FMS. This has caused some confusion about what constitutes an FMS. Flexibility and automation are the key conceptual requirements. However, it is the *extent* of automation and the *diversity* of the parts that are important; some systems are termed FMS just because they contain automated material handling. For example, dedicated, fixed, transfer lines or systems containing only automated storage and retrieval are not FMSs. Other systems only contain several (unintegrated) NC or CNC machines. Still other systems use a computer to control the machines, but often require long set-ups or have no automated parts transfer.

Some systems are called flexible because they produce a variety of parts (of very similar type, using fixed automation). In most of these examples, the operating mode is either transfer line-like or based on producing batches of similar part types.

To help clarify the situation, eight types of flexibilities will be defined and described. Examples or explanations are provided when needed to illustrate a particular flexibility type. Measurement and attainability of each are also discussed.

J. Browne is at University College, Galway; D. Dubois, Centre d'Etudes et de Recherches de Toulouse; K. Rathmill, Cranfield Institute of Technology; S. Sethi, University of Toronto; K. Stecke, The University of Michigan.

Source: J. Browne, D. Dubois, K. Rathmill, S. Sethi and K. Stecke, 'Classification of Flexible Manufacturing Systems', from *The FMS Magazine*, April 1984.

Machine Flexibility

This is the ease of making the changes required to produce a *given* set of part types. *Measurement* of these changes includes, for example, the time to replace worn-out or broken cutting tools, the time to change tools in a tool magazine to produce a different subset of the given part types, and the time to assemble or mount the new fixtures required. The set-up time required for a machine tool to switch from one part type to another includes: cutting tool preparation time; part positioning and releasing time; and NC program changeover time. This flexibility can be *attained* by:

(1) technological progress, such as sophisticated tool-loading and part-loading devices;
(2) Proper operation assignment, so that there is no need to change the cutting tools that are in the tool magazines, or they are changed less often;
(3) having the technological capability of bringing both the part and required cutting tools to the machine tool together.

Process Flexibility

This is the ability to produce a given set of part types, each possibly using different materials, in several ways. Buzacott (1982) calls this 'job flexibility', which 'relates to the mix of jobs which the system can *process*'.[2] Gerwin (1982) calls this 'mix flexibility'.[3] *Process flexibility* increases as machine set-up costs decrease. Each part can be machined individually, and not necessarily in batches. This flexibility can be *measured* by the number of part types that can simultaneously be processed without using batches. This flexibility can be *attained* by having:

(1) *machine flexibility*; and
(2) multi-purpose, adaptable, CNC machining centres.

Product Flexibility

This is the ability to changeover to produce a new (set of) product(s) very economically and quickly. Mandelbaum (1978) calls this 'action flexibility, the capacity for taking new action to meet new circumstances'.[4] Included in this concept is Gerwin's (1982) 'design-change flexibility'. This flexibility heightens a company's potential responsiveness to competitive and/or market changes. *Product flexibility* can be *measured* by the time required to switch from one part mix to another, not necessarily of the same part types. This flexibility can be *attained* by having:

(1) an efficient and automated production planning and control system containing: (i) automatic operation assignment procedures; and (ii) automatic pallet distribution calculation capability.
(2) *machine flexibility*.

Classification of Flexible Manufacturing Systems

Routing Flexibility

This is the ability to handle breakdowns and to continue producing the given set of part types. This ability exists if either a part type can be processed via several routes, or, equivalently, each operation can be performed on more than one machine. Note that this flexibility can be:

(1) *Potential*: part routes are fixed, but parts are automatically rerouted when a breakdown occurs;
(2) *Actual*: identical parts are actually processed through different routes, independent of breakdown situations.

The main, applicable circumstances occur when a system component, such as a machine tool, breaks down. This flexibility can be *measured* by the robustness of the FMS when breakdowns occur: the production rate does not decrease dramatically and parts continue to be processed. This flexibility can be *attained* by allowing for automated and automatic rerouting of parts (*potential routing flexibility*), by pooling machines into machine groups,[5] which also allows machine tool redundancy; and also by duplicating operation assignments.[1] These latter policies provide *actual routing flexibility*. The FMS would then be state-driven by a feedback control policy.

Volume Flexibility

This is the ability to operate an FMS profitably at different production volumes. A higher level of automation increases this flexibility, partly as a result of both lower machine set-up costs and lower variable costs such as direct labour costs. If it is not economical to run a particular system at its usual volume, say during a decrease in market demand or a recession, then there are less personnel problems concerning the idling of labour. Perhaps alternative uses of the FMS could be found. Also, production volumes can vary from week to week, resulting in variable machine and system utilizations. This flexibility can be *measured* by how small the volumes can be for all part types with the system still being run profitably. The lower the volume is, the more *volume-flexible* the system must be. This flexibility can be *attained* by having:

(1) multipurpose machines; and
(2) a layout that is not dedicated to a particular process; and
(3) a sophisticated, automated materials handling system, such as (possibly intelligent) carts, and not fixed-route conveyors; and
(4) *routing flexibility*.

Expansion Flexibility

This is the capability of building a system, and expanding it as needed, easily and *modularly*. This is not possible with most assembly and transfer lines. This flexibility can be *measured* according to how large the FMS can become. This flexibility is *attained* by having:

(1) a non-dedicated, non-process driven layout; and
(2) a flexible materials handling system consisting of, say, wire-guided carts; and
(3) modular, flexible machining cells with pallet changers; and
(4) *routing flexibility.*

Operation Flexibility

This is the ability to interchange the ordering of several operations for each part type. There is usually some required partial precedence structure for a particular part type. However, for some operations, their respective ordering is arbitrary. Some process planner has usually determined a *fixed* ordering of all operations, each on a particular machine (type). However, keeping the routing options open and not pre-determining either the 'next' operation or the 'next' machine increases the flexibility to make these decisions in real-time. These decisions should depend on the current system state (which machine tools are currently idle, busy, or bottleneck).

Production Flexibility

This is the universe of part types that the FMS can produce. This flexibility is measured by the level of existing technology. It is *attained* by increasing the level of technology and the versatility of the machine tools. The capabilities of all the previous flexibilities are required.

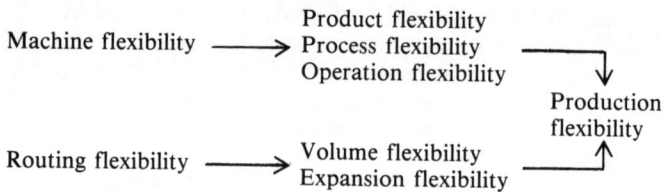

Figure 1 Relationships among flexibility types

Not all of these flexibility types are independent. Figure 1 displays the relationships between the different flexibilities. The arrows signify 'necessary for'. An ideal FMS would possess all of the defined flexibilities. However, the cost of the latest in hardware and the most sophisticated (and at present non-existent!) software to plan and control adequately would be quite high on some of these measures and low on others. For instance, processing a particular group of products may be made possible through the use of head indexers having multiple-spindle heads. However, they hinder both adding new part types to the mix and introducing new part numbers,

Classification of Flexible Manufacturing Systems

since retooling costs are high and changeover time can be a day. Also, some flexible systems (such as the SCAMP system in Colchester, UK) include special-purpose, non-CNC machines, such as hobbing and broaching, which also require (relatively) huge set-up times.

This classification of flexibilities can help categorize different types of FMS.

The *level of automation* helps to determine the amount of available flexibility. Because of the different choices of various flexibility levels, there are different types of FMSs. It is, therefore, useful to classify these systems in terms of their overall flexibility.

Towards a classification of flexible manufacturing systems, Groover (1980) divided FMSs into two distinct types:[6]

(i) dedicated FMS;
(ii) random FMS.

A dedicated system machines a fixed set of part types with well-defined manufacturing requirements over a known time horizon. The 'random FMS', on the other hand, machines a greater variety of parts in random sequence.

In addition to these basic, extreme types of FMSs, all FMSs are different in terms of the amounts of the flexibilities that they utilize. In this section, a classification of FMSs according to their inherent, overall flexibility is provided. Four general *types* of FMS will be defined.

The following standards are provided based on FMS components, which will be used to describe and classify the different types of FMSs:

(1) Machine tools:
- General-purpose or specialized
- Automatic tool changing capabilities (increase flexibility)
- Regarding tool magazines, their capacity, removability, and tool-changing needs (affect the flexibility).

(2) Materials handling system:
- Types include: conveyor or one-way carousel; tow-line with carts; network of wire-guided carts; stand-alone robot carts
- Part movement equipment: palletized and/or fixtured
- Tool transportation system: manual; or, automatically, with parts.

(3) Storage areas for in-process inventory:
- Central buffer storage
- Decentralized buffer at each machine tool
- Local storage

(4) Computer control:
- Distribution of decisions
- Architecture of the information system
- Types of decisions: input sequence; priority rules; part to cart assignment; cart traffic regulation
- Control of part mix: through periodic input; through a feedback-based priority rule.

These 'flexibility' standards for the physical FMS components are used to clarify differences and similarities between the FMS types.

Although not typically considered FMS, this classification scheme will include the flexible assembly system (FAS).

The simplest possible component of an FMS or FAS is a flexible assembly cell (FAC). It consists of one or more robots and peripheral equipment, such as an input/output buffer and automated material handling. To date, only about 6 per cent of robot applications are in assembly.

A flexible assembly system (FAS) consists of two or more FACS. In the future, as the technology develops to allow the interface between manufacturing and assembly, an FAS could also be a component of a flexible system.

The types of FMS described are categorized according to the extent of use of their flexibilities. The classification of a particular FMS usually results basically from its mode of operations as well as the properties of the four components described above.

Type I FMS: Flexible Machining Cell

The simplest, hence most flexible (especially with respect to five of the flexibilities) type of FMS is a flexible machining cell (FMC). It consists of one general-purpose CNC machine tool, interfaced with automated material handling which provides raw castings or semi-finished parts from an input buffer for machining, loads and unloads the machine tool, and transports the finished work-piece to an output buffer for eventual removal to its next destination. An articulated arm, robot, or pallet changer is something used to load and unload. Storage includes the raw castings area, the input and output buffers of the machine tools, and the finished parts area.

Since an FMC contains only one metal-cutting machine tool, one might question its being called a system. However, it has all of the components of an FMS. Also, it is actually an FMS component itself. With one machine tool, it is the smallest, most trivial FMS.

Type II FMS: Flexible Machining System

The second type of FMS can have the following features: it can have real-time, on-line control of part production. It should allow several routes for parts, with small volume production of each, and consists of FMCs of different types of general-purpose, metal-removing machine tools. Real-time control capabilities can *automatically* allow *multiple routes* for parts, which complicate scheduling software. Because of real-time control, however, the actual scheduling might be easier. For example, the scheduling rule might be to route randomly, or route to the nearest free machine tool of the correct machine type. The scheduling rule could be some appropriate, system-dependent, dynamic priority rule with feedback.

Sometimes, dedicated, special-purpose machines tools, such as multiple-spindle head changers, are used in an FMS to increase production. The machine tools are unordered in a process-independent layout. It is the part types that are to be processed by an FMS which define the necessary, required machine tools.

Classification of Flexible Manufacturing Systems

A Type II FMS is highly *machine flexible, process flexible* and *product flexible*. It is also highly *routing flexible*, since it can easily and *automatically* cope with machine tool or other breakdowns if machines are grouped or operation assignments are duplicated.

Within the Type II category, the various kinds of material handling provide a subrange of flexibility. In order of increasing flexibility, various material handling systems include: power roller conveyors, overhead conveyors, shuttle conveyors, in-floor tow line conveyors, and wire-guided carts. Some examples include:

(1) a network of carts and decentralized storage areas, for shorter processing times (Renault Machines Outils, in Boutheon, France);
(2) a tow line with carts and centralized storage areas, for longer processing times (Sundstrand/Caterpillar DNC Line, in Peoria, Illinois, USA).

Type III FMS: Flexible Transfer Line

The third type of FMS has the following features. For all part types, each operation is assigned to, and performed on, only one machine. This results in a *fixed route* for each part through the system. The layout is process-driven and hence ordered. The material handling system is usually a carousel or conveyor. The storage area is local, usually between each machine. In addition to general-purpose machines, it can contain special-purpose machines, robots, and some dedicated equipment. Scheduling, to balance machine workloads, is easier. In fact, a Type III FMS is easier to manage because it operates similarly to a dedicated transfer line. The computer control is more simple and a periodic input of parts is realistic. Once set up, it is easy to run and to be efficient. The difference is that it is set up often and relatively quickly.

A Type III FMS is less *process flexible* and less capable of automatically handling breakdowns. However, the system can adapt by retooling and manually inputting the appropriate command to the computer, to reroute parts to the capable machine tool. This takes more time than the automatic rerouting available to a Type II FMS.

A Type IV FMS: Flexible Transfer Multi-Line

The fourth FMS type of consists of multiple Type III FMSs that are interconnected. This duplication does *not* increase *process flexibility*. Similar to a Type III FMS, scheduling and control are relatively easy, once the system is set up. The main advantage is the redundancy that it provides in a breakdown situation, to increase its *routing flexibility*. It attempts to achieve the best of both FMS Types II and III.

Flexibility Range

All things being equal, a Type II FMS is operated 'flexibly', while a Type III FMS is operated in a much more 'fixed' manner. These types provide the extremes, say, the *bounds* on flexibility. There is, of course, a whole range of flexibilities between the two general types. However, these smaller variations in flexibility are defined by the versatilities and capabilities of the machine tools, which are dictated by the particular FMS application, i.e., the part types to be machined. The types of material handling system also provide subgroups of flexibility. The overall flexibility, however, is defined by an FMS's *mode of operation*.

In general, the FMSs of the United States and the Federal Republic of Germany tend to be more like the Type II FMS, while those of Japan are more similar to Type III. The second floor of Fanuc's Fuji complex, consisting of four flexible transfer lines, is an example of an operating Type IV FMS. It consists of several identical FACs, which are not all identically tooled. Parts do have fixed routes, but if an assembly cell is down, the parts requiring it are automatically able to be routed to another assembly cell, which contains the correct tooling. The first floor of this Fanuc plant, the Motor Manufacturing Division, is a good example of Type II.

All FMSs consist of similar components. The numbers and types of machine tool may differ. What really defines the flexibility of an installation is how it is run. The level of desired flexibility is an important strategic decision in the development and implementation of an FMS. This paper has provided a framework for such strategic decisions.

Acknowledgements

Kathryn E. Stecke's research was supported in part by a summer research grant from the Graduate School of Business Administration at the University of Michigan as well as by a grant by the Ford Motor Company, Dearborn, Michigan.

References

1. Kathryn E. Stecke, 'Formulation and Solution of Nonlinear Integer Production Planning Problems for Flexibile Manufacturing Systems', *Management Science*, vol. 29, no. 3, pp. 273-88 (March 1983).
2. J. A. Buzacott, 'The Fundamental Principles of Flexibility in Manufacturing Systems', *Proceedings of the 1st International Conference on Flexible Manufacturing Systems*. Brighton, UK (20-22 October 1982).
3. Donald Gerwin, 'Do's and Don'ts of Computerized Manufacturing', *Harvard Business Review*, vol. 60, no. 2, pp. 107-16 (March-April 1982).
4. Marvin Mandelbaum, 'Flexibility in Decision-Making: an Exploration and Unification', PhD dissertation, Department of Industrial Engineering, University of Toronto, Ontario, Canada (1978).
5. Kathryn E. Stecke and James J. Solberg, 'The Optimality of Unbalanced Workloads and Machine Group Sizes for Flexible Manufacturing Systems', Working Paper no. 290, Division of Research, Graduate School of Business Administration, University of Michigan, Ann Arbor, MI (January 1982).

6. Mikell P. Groover, *Automation, Production Systems, and Computer-Aided Manufacturing* (Prentice-Hall, Englewood Cliffs, NJ, 1980).
7. D. M. Zelenovic, 'Flexibility–a Condition for Effective Production Systems', *International Journal of Production Research*, vol. 20, no. 3, pp. 319–37 (May–June 1982).

2.3

Design of a Flexible Assembly System for a Small Company

S. J. Mallin and P. J. Sackett

Introduction

In small manufacturing organizations the assembly function remains a labour-intensive area with traditional automated approaches being unsuited to fluctuating product demand. The modular design of a computer-controlled assembly system for the production of a range of transducers in a small company is described. The resultant extendable flexible assembly system accommodates the product diversity of the previous wholly manual set-up whilst offering an increased volume capability. Many features of classical FMS have been realized in this assembly system. Competitiveness in both existing and potential markets is aided by the response characteristics plus quality and reliability of product supply of the flexible assembly system.

The Existing System

Transducer assembly in this company has been a totally manual process requiring a high level of dexterity. Typically six small components are involved, assembled units being 5–7 cm in length. Production is in batches of 25 to 100 with individual operators being responsible for most tasks in a unit process. Build instructions are issued every time a batch is processed as more than 100 variations exist. This situation has arisen because there is a market requirement for customized units in small quantities. The present system is considered to be a maximum capacity for the existing product designs and manufacturing methods; the current annual output of 17,000

S. J. Mallin is from Orbit Controls Ltd; P. J. Sackett is from the University of Bath.
   Source: S. J. Mallin and P. J. Sackett, 'Design of a Flexible Assembly System for a Small Company', from Wilfred B. Heginbotham (ed.) *Programmable Assembly*, IFS (Publications) Ltd., 1984.

Design of a Flexible Assembly System for a Small Company

units is achieved with six operators. However with lead times for new orders running at up to ten weeks the response to customer demand is poor. The lack of sophisticated production equipment means that system performance is wholly labour dependent. Quality levels are more of a problem with sub-contracted components than completed assemblies which have a scrap rate of only 4–7 per cent. There is an attempt to impress quality awareness on operators but in practice this results in a duplication of inspection and test procedures. This 100 per cent inspection policy is costly and by no means infallible.

At an early stage in this project it was established that changes in product design and manufacturing methods could provide a ten-fold increase in capacity without the need to raise the number of operators. However this would amplify the following problems associated with the present methods of production organization:

- Long lead times, due in part to the time taken in preparing schedules, assembly kits and organizing a batch for production. To overcome this, large stocks of finished items are maintained.
- High throughput times and work-in-progress levels; it takes an average of three weeks to process a batch, whereas the unit building time is only 30 min.
- Batch tracking and fault traceability are difficult to the extent that the sources of reject work can rarely be determined.
- Manufacturing data are inconsistent and collection non-real-time.
- High subcontracted components and assembly processes content; this results in a loss of control over key areas of the manufacturing operation.

The working environment can be considered pleasant and benefits from a flexitime attendance basis. The system can accommodate this arrangement due to the independent operation of assembly work-stations. It is likely that any attempt to change this to some rigid flowline-type set-up would be met with opposition and in any case would be undesirable. The standard of work is semiskilled, though interesting, because of the variety of tasks each operator has to perform.

New System Objectives

Traditional automated assembly techniques are not suited to the expected volume demand and product variety at the present time; investigations have shown that less than 10 per cent of the product cost is direct labour and 50 per cent is overheads. These overheads have been identified as the major area for cost savings.

The present system suffers from long lead times, high work-in-progress and poor monitoring of production performance. These problems have all been addressed by flexible manufacturing systems in the batch manufacture of machined items. The problem is how to apply these principles when designing an assembly system for a small manufacturing organization incorporating the following systemal features:

- Adaptable for both expansion and the further automation of individual processes.
- Multi-product capable in high and low volumes.
- The operators' working environment must be maintained.
- No trivialization of the operators' tasks.

The primary requirement is a greatly reduced throughput time and any tooling or process changes must be fast and straightforward. This will in turn reduce work-in-progress and its associated problems. Similarly lead times must be reduced in order to improve response to customer demand and minimize stocks. Flexibility is to be derived through the good utilization of the human skills available from the existing operators, though in order to establish the necessary degree of control, a hierarchical computer facility must be incorporated. This aim for complete control over the manufacturing/assembly process is the key to reducing overheads.

Uncertainty about the future production requirements of the system, and the necessity to learn by experience and gain confidence, demands a modular approach utilizing standard equipment to keep capital investment and risk to a minimum. This ensures that expansion can proceed rapidly when necessary. Real-time data and processed information must be available to management; system status, batch status and production performance all need to be closely monitored. Existing well publicized FMS projects have shown that the application of these techniques benefits from a step-by-step approach, modifying the tactics at each stage yet still working within a predetermined framework. It is important to establish the overall architecture of the system at an early stage in order that future expansion is compatible with other developments in the company.

Realizable flexibility, particularly in the case of small companies without specialist maintenance facilities, demands that system reliability is very high. This requires the use of standard equipment. An additional important face of realizable flexibility in this application is capable operation, in a degraded capacity, with less than the full quota of operators or with isolated overtime working.

System Design

The emphasis has been on designing a system capable of economic operation and flexibility to batch size, product type, working procedures and future demand. The use of human operators greatly aids this flexibility and it is not economically feasible to substitute these assets with automation at present.

The resultant design consists of a number of work-stations linked by a sophisticated work transport capability, and controlled by a hierarchical computer system as in a classical FMS, but there are important differences (see figure 1). Initially these work-stations will be manually operated with the facility to accommodate conversion to a high degree of automation. This requires some component redesign which is being undertaken in

Design of a Flexible Assembly System for a Small Company   123

parallel with the manufacturing programme. Work will have to be processed in small batches, consequently procedures necessary when changing from the assembly of one batch to another must be quick and accurate. This will require a facility for communication between the computer and individual work-stations – a VDU is the obvious choice as it provides a two-way link. The computer will monitor the production process and offer access to real-time information. Physical conveyance of items from one station to another demands an intelligent routing capability as the combination of products to be made require different processes.

There is the added problem of a high variety of products being made at any one time, consequently not all subassemblies in the system will be taking the same route. This requires coded pallets which can be identified at critical stages and distributed to the appropriate work-station.

The company has a minicomputer for handling various administrative tasks including stock control and production scheduling functions. It is intended that the proposed system will eventually be integrated with these.

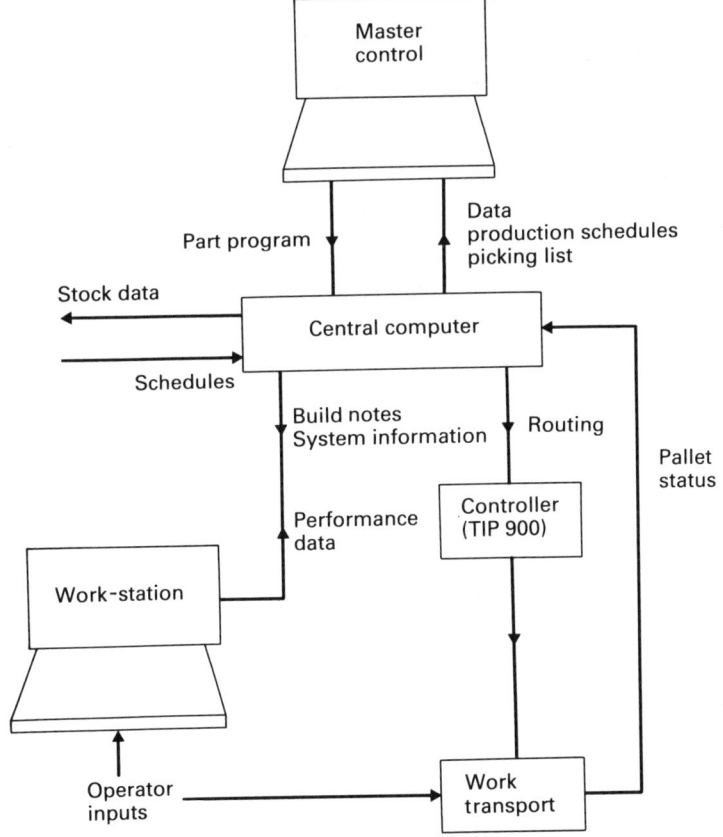

Figure 1   Manufacturing control

Immediate requirements will be for product routing and performance monitoring capability. A lower level of control for repetitive transportation functions will be provided by programmable controllers from the company's own TIP 900 controller range. The transportation system is based on a range of flexible modular assembly units. Typically this equipment is used in stand-alone mode but here the computer provides a much higher level of control. With flexible work-stations the intention is to apply true FMS principles to this small product assembly area at a low capital cost.

Physically the system consists of a number of work-stations as shown in figure 2, the number and layout of these stations being variable for future requirements. A buffer storage facility at each station provides some work-time flexibility and avoids the rigidly enforced discipline of a constantly moving conveyor. Most stations will be flexible in the work that can be done, they simply act as a workplace with the operator performing the necessary assembly function. Variation in the tasks required will maintain the present level of job satisfaction but where the use of certain production equipment is necessary then a station will become dedicated. During operation without a full complement of operators, the buffer stores allow those operators present to work at isolated stations.

In operation, coded pallets containing one or more subassemblies are carried on the conveyor system; code readers monitor their progress and the contents of each pallet are known by the computer (figure 1). Manufacturing routing details, held in the computer memory, divert pallets to the appropriate workplace queue until called for by the operator. Should space not be available in the buffer then the pallet will continue to move around the central rectangle. Once the operator has accepted the pallet, information about assembly/manufacturing details will be displayed on their workplace monitor. On job completion the operator enters information

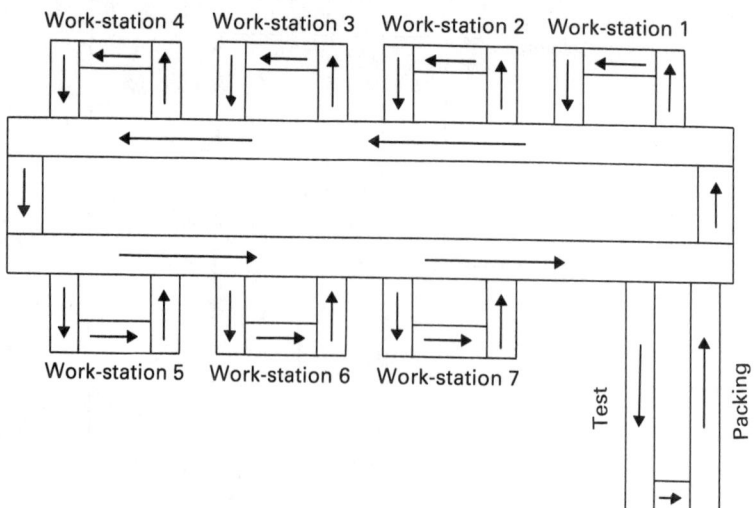

Figure 2 Work transport

requested by the computer. This will include the number of units completed, how many are faulty and reasons for failure. No more pallets can be obtained until the computer is satisfied with the information that it has received.

Monitoring of work-station performance will provide information on processing times and advise on excess deviations. Similarly monitoring of work-station activity will isolate excessive downtime or bottlenecks. Operators will have full access to system status to provide them with the maximum flexibility of work organization consistent with system performance objectives. When a batch is completed, instructions about the next product to be assembled, machine setting changes and components required will be displayed for the operator. This ensures continuity of production as one batch does not have to pass through the system before another can enter. The production scheduling system will already have issued a component picking list and these will have been accessed by the operator. The test and packing stations are common to all products and will have to cope with alternating requirements. By the use of automatic test equipment the test parameters corresponding to the contents of the pallet will be set; this will once again be backed up with displayed instructions. Details of the packed contents will be printed when a pallet arrives; a label to be sent with the work will indicate product type, customer and batch number.

Throughout the system the aim is not to trivialize the operators' tasks by introducing this degree of computer control, but to ensure that system performance is maintained. Indeed it is expected that operators will provide a much higher level of optimization than current mechanistic algorithmic based approaches.

Phased Implementation

Based on current marketing predictions, the company require a fully operational flexible assembly system by early 1986, but the majority of features described here will be available during 1984 in a system capable of rapid capacity expansion. This interim system will not incorporate full integration with the company's existing computer based facilities. It has been established that a staged approach is needed in order to modify the project plan in the light of market requirements and on-going experience. The plan for implementation can be seen in three parts but some concurrent running is taking place:

(1) The installation of a pilot work transport capability, to establish computer interfaces and to develop the communication routines. This provides the opportunity to become acquainted with the system hardware and to make an early start on testing of the computer software which will be the subject of considerable on-going development. It is possible to incorporate the work handling facility into the present manufacturing system from the start, operating as a simple conveyor in the initial stages.

(2) Having established the working pilot system, production engineer and automate selected work-station activities. This will include the introduction of processes which are currently subcontracted, such as plastic injection moulding. It will provide a steady increase in volume capability and spread the normal proving and commissioning procedures as well as the capital requirement.
(3) The integration of other computer based systems, including stock control and production scheduling, once the manufacturing system is on-line. These measures are really refinements and become increasingly valuable as volumes rise. In addition, this requires liaison and input by other areas of the organization.

The use of human inputs underpins this implementation programme and the final set up will still require the existing number of operators although the output will rise substantially. Throughout the development stages it is necessary to prepare the existing manufacturing/assembly system, including the people, for the changeover and to maintain output. This is particularly critical during the initial stage when spare capacity is not available and means gradually changing production methods so that they are organized in a way similar to the new system but still on a manual basis. The changeover will then be a relatively simple process with operators only needing to become acquainted with the new equipment, not a wholly new way of working.

2.4

The Use of Commercial Local Area Network in Distributed Machine and Process Control Systems

R. H. Weston, P. D. Hanlon and A. Salihi

Over the last few years industrial control systems have exhibited a trend away from centralized control towards far greater use of distributed intelligence. However, although numerous advances have been made in automation which, together with the greatly reduced cost and increased reliability of modern computer technology, has made distributed systems an attractive solution, similar advances have not been apparent in the communications techniques employed between these systems.

For office environments a wide range of baseband local area computer communication networks are now available.[1-3] Some of these networks have been designed with reference to emerging international standards[4] and, when appropriate software becomes available will allow computers produced by different manufacturers to be linked together in a convenient manner. However, in applications where unsuitable environmental conditions prevail (with extreme conditions of temperature and/or electrical noise) the suitability of many such local area networks has yet to be demonstrated. Furthermore, in many manufacturing plants there is a need to link a wide range of computer types which may have been installed over many years. A number of manufacturers of process and machine control systems have noted the need for improved communications within manufacturing plants and have adapted the latest developments in local area computer network technology to suit the particular requirements of industrial control.[5-7] Unfortunately, to date, these networks are predominantly 'closed' which limits the user to purchasing equipment from a single supplier. Thus for the industrial user, wishing to utilize a local area network to connect process and machine computer control systems of different

R. H. Weston, P. D. Hanlon and A. Salihi are in the Department of Engineering Production, University of Loughborough, Leicestershire.

Source: R. H. Weston, P. D. Hanlon and A. Salihi, 'The Use of Commercial Local Area Network in Distributed Machine and Process Control Systems', *Electronics & Power*, May 1983.

manufacture, a significant investment is required primarily to develop software both at communications and applications levels. This situation is marginally improved with regard to commercially available broadband systems* which have now been used for some years in industrial control schemes[8,9] but usually such systems will be associated with higher hardware costs.

This article considers the use of a commercially available baseband network which was designed by the manufacturer of a range of industrial programmable controllers to facilitate communication between such controllers operating in industrial environments. Thus, in its commercially available form this network is closed. However, procedures whereby such a network can be 'opened' to facilitate communication between computers of different manufacture are considered in the following.

Control of a Simple Manufacturing Cell

A simple manufacturing cell was constructed to perform drilling, inspection and handling operations on turned components. Commercially available industrial programmable controllers (PCs) were utilized to achieve sequential control of cell elements. Communication between individual PCs was necessary to allow the individual sequencing of elements to be integrated to achieve the complete manufacturing cycle. Such communication was achieved by employing a local area network as supplied by the PC manufacturer. At the time of cell construction the availability of such a network represented a major advance in 'off-the-shelf' technology for use in industrial environments and allowed considerable flexibility when compared with conventional techniques for integrating such control sequences.

The major mechanical elements of the cell are a rotary transfer drilling machine and a pick-and-place robot. The drilling machine is equipped with mechanisms for part feed and eject and has a six-station rotary indexing table with clamps that allow parts to be rigidly held on the table as the various drilling operations are carried out. The entire machine is pneumatically powered and is controlled by a bank of solenoid-operated valves. Pistons have been used to feed the parts onto the table, to clamp the parts before drilling and to unclamp the parts after drilling. A jet of air then blows the parts out of the machine onto a chute leading to the pick-and-place robot. Each of the three simultaneous drilling operations is carried out by a small, pneumatically powered drill. A total of ten digital output lines are required to control this machine and nine signals are fed back into control system digital inputs. Once again, the operating sequences have been programmed into a PC using relay ladder diagrams.

One of the index positions on the rotary table has been reserved for part inspection where an optical probe is used to establish drilling depth. As the inspection station is physically located with the drilling machine, the digital

---

* In baseband systems, each data transmission occupies the complete bandwidth of the transmission medium for a time period agreed by arbitration. In broadband systems a proportion of the complete bandwidth is allocated to each station using frequency division multiplexing.

signal it produces has been fed directly into the same programmable controller.

TABLE 1 COMMUNICATIONS SOFTWARE FOR NETWORK-CONCURRENT TASKS

Hardware driver level
- interrupt-driven character handling

ANSI DEF1 protocol level
- ENCODE • DECODE

Error recovery level
- RETRANS • timing

Applications software message routing level
- message tables for transmission and reception

The pick-and-place robot incorporated in the cell has 'cylindrical' co-ordinate motion and is powered by solenoid-operated pneumatic valves. The manipulator can be moved to predetermined positions which are set up on mechanical end stops. In addition, intermediate stops are provided on the rotary and vertical axis, enabling a total of 18 preset positions to be obtained. The manipulator is free to rotate through 90° and can open and close to pick up parts. A total of seven digital output lines are required to control the robot, each being capable of switching a few hundred milliamps at 24 V. The arm position is fed back to the control system via proximity detectors placed at each end stop, such that a signal is generated once the robot has reached the required position. These signals are fed into six digital inputs to the control system.

In the past, considerable effort has been made to develop interactive programming software for this robot.[10] However, in this instance, the operating sequences were programmed entirely using the relay ladder diagram language common on many programmable control systems.

The technique of using individual control systems, each dedicated to a single task, in a cell of this type, has many advantages which can be summarized as:

- Each item of the cell can be operated independently under its own control system.
- The cell can be quickly reconfigured, should manufacturing requirements alter, without rewiring, as no alterations to the individual systems are required.
- The control program of each element can be modified without disturbing the other elements of the cell.
- An individual control system failure will only affect one element in the cell and so 'fail soft' design techniques can be employed to maintain production if some redundancy has been included.[11]

Features of the Local Area Network

The individual programmable controllers used are Allen Bradley mini PLC 2 devices, each being equipped with a communications adaptor module which is an interface module supplied by the manufacturers to permit information transfer between the manufacturers' programmable controllers and their local area network (the manufacturers refer to this network in their advertising literature as a 'data highway'). The communications adaptor module is located within the input/output rack of the associated programmable controller.

The particular local area network utilizes low-cost twin-axial cable and a bus topology allowing communication between up to 64 interface modules which can be either communications adaptor modules, which provide an interface to programmable controllers, or communications controller modules which facilitate interfacing to computer stations. Generally, the maximum rate at which data 'can be transmitted (50 kbit/s) is not high when compared with that from many commercial systems. However, the network was designed specifically to link programmable controllers operating in industrial environments. A system of floating mastership has been adopted to ensure that only one station attempts to transmit on the highway at a given time. After gaining mastership of the highway, a station is permitted to transmit all messages stored in its buffer, a maximum of 256 bytes. It must then carry out a poll of all active stations to determine which station should then obtain mastership, this poll being carried out in two stages. Initially, a poll is made for stations with high priority messages to send and, secondly, if unsuccessful, a poll of stations with normal priority messages to send. In addition, each station includes procedures for detecting a faulty master station, which will automatically disconnect leaving the highway free to correctly operating stations. As all interface modules are transformer coupled to the cable, it is unlikely that a failure in a single station would result in a total network failure, and indeed steps have been taken to ensure the integrity of the communications system in a variety of failure modes.

The maximum total length of the network cable is approximately 3 km and so provides a reasonable compromise between high-speed local area networks which cover about 1 km typically and long-haul broadband networks based on CATV technology with lengths up to 80 km.

Communication between Programmable Controllers

To achieve control of the manufacturing cell, single-bit data transfers are required to integrate the sequencing of cell elements. Also the results of the inspection must be transmitted and used to determine whether the pick-and-place robot places the component in an 'accept' or 'reject' bin. To achieve such an integration where communication between PCs involves the use of programming instructions which are represented by an extension of the normal set of 'ladder' symbols which are in common use with industrial PCs. By adopting a symbolic approach, a technician should be capable of achieving such communications programming relatively quickly and without the need for extensive specialized training.

Symbolic instructions can be formed to allow block data transfers (up to 256 bytes) between PCs. This allows the transmission and reception of pro-

LANs in Machine and Process Control Systems 131

grams, program reference data and operator messages. One of three levels of remote PC memory protection can be selected for such data transfers; the level determines whether all or some particular section of remote PC memory can be accessed. For the technician programming 'communication rungs', protocol handling is transparent with automatic acknowledgement of commands, automatic transmission retries, and some automatic error detection procedures.

The use of communication ladder rungs is clearly appropriate for small systems where reliable communications between PCs can be quickly established, as many tasks are handled transparently thus reducing the required level of programming expertise. However, this approach to programming will become extremely awkward for large systems with many PCs and complex communications.

Production Control and Monitoring Facility

Production control and monitoring facilities were to be included to serve the manufacturing cell described. A computer station and file server were included to allow the introduction of such facilities. The network interfaces incorporated into these stations (communications controller modules) differ considerably from those used to connect the PCs to the network, but are standard computer communication modules as supplied by the manufacturer. While the communications adaptor modules plug directly into the PC rack and are transparent to the user, the communications controller modules merely provide a standard RS232 interface with ANSI DEF1 protocol to be connected to the computer control station. Each computer station can communicate over the network via this RS232 link using commands which, although PC orientated, can also be employed to transfer data between computer stations on the network. Messages passed over the network in this manner can be one of two types, either commands or replies, and may be assigned either a normal or high priority; however, reply messages may only be initiated in response to the reception of a command message.

TABLE 2 FEATURES OF THE APPLICATIONS SOFTWARE FOR CONTROL OF THE MANUFACTURING CELL

Concurrent tasks utilize the resources of the file server to provide:
- productivity monitoring
- report generation/real-time clock
- downloading of operating sequences
- operator interface for generation of user-defined application tasks

---

To achieve cell supervision, it was necessary to develop two distinct software packages for the supervisory station (which itself consists of a Texas Instruments 9900-based single-board computer (101-M) with expansion memory and two serial RS232 ports, one coupled to a standard terminal, the other to a communications controller module). These software packages were required to provide both a general purpose communications package to handle message transmission over the network and an applications package to provide cell control and monitoring facilities as required by this particular application. Tables 1 and 2 illustrate the features of these software packages. All software for the supervisory station was developed in PASCAL and configured to run under a real-time multitasking environment.

Various versions of applications software have been developed for the manufacturing cell and used with the general purpose communications package to provide a range of supervisory functions and operator facilities. In particular, production control ladder programs can be downloaded, or uploaded, from the file server to allow robot and rotary transfer machine sequences to be altered, or stored, from a remote location. Monitoring facilities have also been included to allow productivity monitoring with applications software configured to generate production efficiency and cell downtime reports either locally, at one of the PCs, or centrally at the supervisory station. Such reports can also be stored at the network file server.

The network file server is based on an Apple microcomputer with dual mini-floppy-disc drives and a serial interface linked to the data highway via a second communications controller module. The file server is designed to provide any system, connected to the data highway via a communications controller module, with the ability to save and recall information from its disc drives, and is sited remotely from the manufacturing cell in a room where the environmental conditions can be more closely controlled. The software for this station is also developed in PASCAL but linked with assembly level input/output routines where speed is essential.

Networks in the Manufacture of Glass Containers

The construction of the manufacturing cell serves to illustrate how software can be configured for a commercially available local area network to allow the linking of computer systems of different manufacture. Such a situation arises in many process plants where control systems have been purchased from many different manufacturers: often a manufacturer will have included particular 'process knowledge' within his system which is not available elsewhere. The glass container manufacturing industry represents a typical example where a range of sequence control, continuous process control and combined sequence and continuous process control systems are required to manufacture a large variety of glass containers from batch (see figure 1).

At Loughborough University over the last few years, university/industrial collaborative research activities have been concerned with a number of stages of glass container production including batch control, furnace modelling, forming-machine controls, and container inspection.[12,13] Work in each separate area of plant has been concerned with the application of digital control systems and will culminate in the integration of these plant functions by utilizing local area networks. To date this integration has been concerned largely with forming and inspection systems, and the Allen Bradley local area network has been used to achieve a link between these areas and some management service functions (see figure 2). Also in the current implementation all computer stations except the file server are 9900 microprocessor-based systems. However, network software is currently being configured to allow the inclusion of computer systems produced by various manufacturers. Such computer systems will be included to provide additional links between shop-floor control systems and various management services as dictated by the requirements of the collaborating companies.

It is of particular interest, in the current implementation, that the use of a local area network has allowed a multiprocessor-based control system to be configured for the control of forming machines. Each forming machine comprises a number of independent sections (usually six or eight). These sections are of complex mechancial structure and perform a sequence of interrelated operations to produce containers from 'globs' of molten glass. Conventionally, each section is sequenced by a mechanical drum timer, although a single electronic or computerized timing unit is sometimes used to control all sections of a machine. Using conventional drum, electronic or computerized timing units provides only open-loop sequential control of machine sections. However, in a study at Loughborough a 9900 microprocessor-based system has been produced for control of a single machine section. This control system provides the usual open-loop sequence timing facilities but also allows closed-loop adaptive control of a critical handling operation to reduce the number of defective containers produced.[13] The software for this section controller has also been developed in PASCAL under a real-time multitasking environment, thus allowing the convenient inclusion of the Allen Bradley network communications package (as configured for the manufacturing cell) and the inclusion of applications software to achieve storage and transfer of timing parameters over the network. Such a scheme has allowed a multiprocessor-based control system to be developed for control of complete forming machines (see figure 2). In this scheme, both local and remote supervisory stations are also served by the Allen Bradley network and associated PASCAL-derived communications package. These stations provide operator access in the immediate location of the forming machine and production manager access at a remote location. PASCAL-derived software has also been included to provide appropriate edit and display facilities at each supervisory station, and access to sequence programs (relating to various container types) as stored on the file server.

A data capture system is also included within the current networking scheme to facilitate data collection from both forming and inspection machines on a single production line. Automatic inspection systems are located at various points along a glass container production line to detect a range of expected faults. Faulty containers are ejected from the line and recycled to the furnace, with optical counting equipment located between

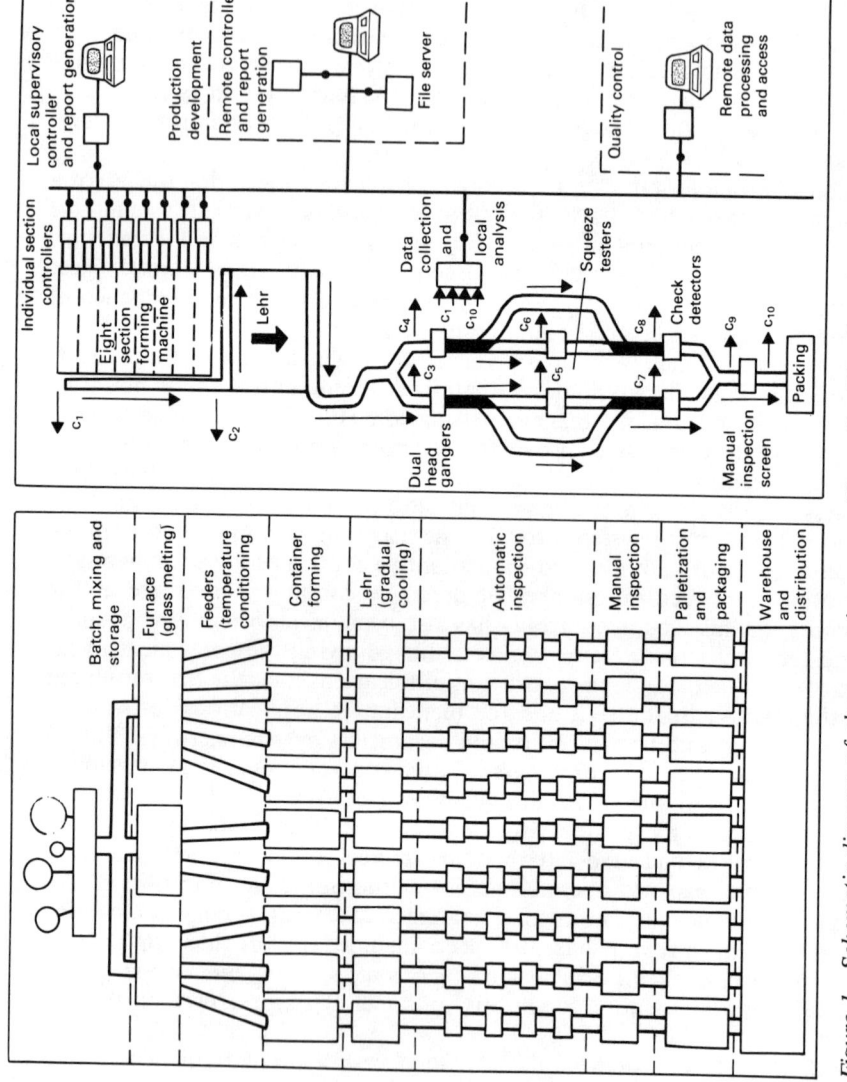

Figure 1 Schematic diagram of glass container production plant

Figure 2 Distributed data capture and control scheme for a glass container production line

inspection machines to monitor the number of rejects at each machine. A 9900-based computer station has been configured to provide online counting and analysis of faults and provides productivity reports on an hourly, shift and daily basis. The software for this station is also PASCAL derived, utilizes the same network communications package, and provides a menu driven operator interface to allow a description of line sensors and counters to be input, or edited, by the production manager. Thus, changes in line characteristics, which occur with some job changes and/or with faulty inspection equipments, can be accounted for with regard to calculations concerning production efficiencies.

Conclusions

Clearly, significant advantages have been gained by using a local area network to link computer systems for both the manufacturing cell and glass container production examples considered. The advantages can be summarized as follows:

- A link between machine control systems can be established to allow online monitoring of productivity and maintenance data.
- Access to network data can be either local or remote from production equipment and can be provided with various levels of security for operators, production managers and research and development personnel.
- File servers, or database computers, can be used to store operating sequences, and process control parameters, for a variety of products.
- Online data collection, storage and analysis can be used as a research tool to provide information concerning each area of plant. Once relationships between separate functional areas can be established, control information can be transmitted between machine controllers and used to improve productivity.
- The facilities described above will promote the future introduction of computer networking schemes which allow the integration of production simulation, planning, scheduling and control functions with those of computer-aided design and shop-floor control.
- Multiprocessor schemes can be configured if data rates between processors are modest. Thus, parallel processing can be achieved with advantages of enhanced processing capabilities and improved reliability.

To install a local area network, it is clear that software must be available to perform both communications tasks and application tasks. At present, in most instances, it is necessary for a user to configure both communications and applications software if there is a requirement to link computer systems, produced by different manufacturers, within an industrial environment. This situation will remain with us until emerging local area network standards become adopted by a range of computer manufacturers and such manufacturers provide appropriate communications software for their computer systems.

The choice of local area network for the applications considered has proved to be appropriate. The availability of this industrial network has allowed the timely realization of a networking scheme for glass container manufacture. It is also fortunate that the hardware is competitively priced (a communications controller module costs approximately £500) and the ability to link industrial programmable controllers with computer stations has and will prove to be extremely useful. Although this network has limited capabilities, when compared with recently introduced local area networks, with regard to maximum data rates, this has not been a limiting factor here.

References

1. 'Local Networks: A Product Review' (Urwick Nexos Ltd., Slough, Berks., 1981).
2. W. P. Sharpe, 'Cambridge Ring: Summary of the Current and Proposed Developments' (SERC, Didcot, Oxon., 1980).
3. R. M. Metcalfe, 'A Strategic Overview of Local Computer Networks', Online Conference on Local Networks and Distributed Office Systems (Online Publications, 1981).
4. C. J. Clancy, 'A Status Report on the IEEE Project 802 Local Network Standard', ibid.
5. A. J. Anderson, 'Distributing Process Control'. *Computer Systems*, May 1982.
6. Allen Bradley, 'Communications Adapter/Communication Controller', (Cleveland, Ohio., Pub. 1771.801/1771.802. January 1981).
7. A. J. Anderson and D. E. Lord, 'Distributing Process Control'. *Computer Systems*, May 1982.
8. G. Harris and D. Wilkins, 'CATV System Speeds Production in Motor Plant', *Commun. Int.*, December 1980.
9. H. Fisher, 'The Computer which Sees the Metro Plant Stays in Fine Tune', *The Engineer*, September 1980.
10. G. P. Charles and R. H. Weston, 'Microprocessor Controls for Limited Function Robots'. *Radio & Electron. Eng.*, vol. 52 (1982).
11. L. D. Burrow, 'The Fail Soft Design of Complex Systems', *IEE Cont. Publ.*, vol. 153 (1977).
12. R. H. Weston and B. Hamilton, 'Microprocessor Control of the I.S. Machine Invert Mechanism', *Glass Technology*, vol. 22, no. 3 (June 1981).
13. R. H. Weston and A. Salihi, 'Adaptive Microprocessor Control of the Cushioning of Pneumatic Cylinders', 13th Int. CIRP Seminar, Levan, Belgium, June 1981.

2.5

Cellular Manufacturing Control

T. J. Greene and R. P. Sadowski

Traditionally, manufacturing systems have been segregated into two categories based on their physical layout. The first category is the line (product) layout where the machines are organized in a serial manner to process a single type of part or a very limited family of parts (figure 1). The second category is the functional layout (process or job shop) where the machines are organized into groups according to capabilities.

A third category for the physical distribution of machines in a manufacturing facility is cellular manufacturing (CM). Cellular manufacturing is a subset and derivative of group technology (GT). Group technology can be defined as the bringing together and organizing (grouping) of common concepts, principles, problems and tasks (technology) to improve productivity[1,2]. Productivity can be defined in a multitude of ways, but generally is thought of as being an increase in output per unit of production time or a decrease in cost per unit produced.

Cellular manufacturing is the physical division of the manufacturing facilities machinery into production cells.[3] Each cell is designed to produce a part family. A part family is defined as a set of parts that require similar machinery, tooling, machine operations, and/or jigs and fixtures.[4] The parts within the family normally will go from raw material to finished parts within a single cell. Usually, the manufacturing facility cannot be completely divided into specialized cells. Rather, a portion of the facility remains as a large functional job shop which has been termed the remainder cell.

T. J. Greene is Assistant Professor in the Department of Industrial Engineering and Operations Research at Virginia Polytechnic Institute and State University, Blacksburg, Virginia; R. P. Sadowski is Associate Professor in the School of Industrial Engineering at Purdue University, West Lafayette, Indiana.

Source: T. J. Greene and R. P. Sadowski, 'Cellular Manufacturing Control', reprinted courtesy of Manufacturing Engineers. Originally published in the *Journal of Manufacturing Systems*, 1983, vol. 2, no. 2, pp. 137–45.

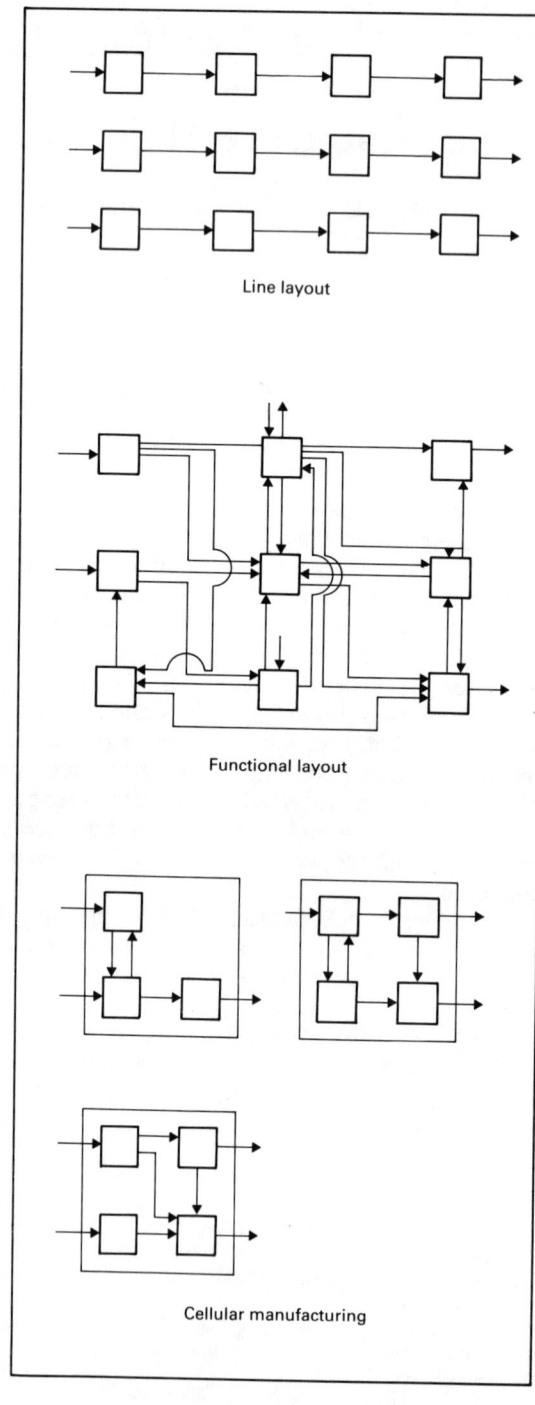

Figure 1 Schematics of three types of manufacturing systems

The overall objective of this paper is to delineate the parameters affecting, and some of the problems associated with, the control of a cellular manufacturing system. Specifically, the paper reviews the advantages and disadvantages of CM, presents basic assumptions, discusses parameters effecting CM control and, finally, discusses available control strategies.

The control of the CM system can be divided into two activities: cell loading and cell scheduling.[5] Cell loading is the determination of which cell, among the feasible cells, the part (job) will be assigned to. Cell scheduling is the internal control of the jobs within each cell. Scheduling, by definition, is the determination of the order of the jobs onto each machine and the determination of the precise start time and completion time of each job on each machine. In reality, most viable control schemes do not perform cell scheduling but rather employ cell sequencing. Sequencing is limited to the determination of the order of the jobs onto each machine, and does not address timing.

Advantages and Disadvantages

It is appropriate to review the advantages and disadvantages associated with a cellular manufacturing system.[6,7]

The advantages of cellular manufacturing control are as follows:

(1) implied reduction of necessary control;
(2) reduced material handling;
(3) reduced set-up time;
(4) reduced tooling;
(5) reduced in-process inventory;
(6) reduced expediting;
(7) increased operator expertise;
(8) improved human relations.

The disadvantages of cellular manufacturing control are as follows:

(1) reduced shop flexibility;
(2) possible reduced machine utilization;
(3) possible extended job flow times;
(4) possible increased job tardiness.

Basic Assumptions

The advantages and disadvantages of CM are based on basic assumptions pertaining to a cellular manufacturing system.[8,9] These assumptions include:

(1) Each cell is a modified flow shop.
(2) The operations of a job should not be split between cells.

(3) For any job there is at least one feasible cell where all operations can be completed.
(4) If there is a specialized cell that a job can be assigned to, it will be assigned to that cell instead of being assigned to the remainder cell.
(5) Jobs can have more than one feasible cell.
(6) Most machines in a cell have some flexibility to perform multiple operations.
(7) The efficiency of a cell and/or machines within the cell to perform the operations on a job is partially correlated to the job's characteristics.
(8) In general, the classic assumptions pertaining to job scheduling.

The maximum benefits of cellular manufacturing (reduced material handling, set-up, tooling, makespan and in-process inventory) can be attained only if all the operations of a job are assigned to only one cell.[4] If even one operation is assigned to another cell, some of the benefits of CM are lost. It should be noted that in reality, it may be infeasible to attain this assumption. But attainment does mean increased productivity, reduced shop congestion, and easier CM control.

Even though a manufacturing facility has a high percentage of cellular division, not all jobs can be completely machined in a specialized cell. These odd jobs are assigned to the remainder cell, and therefore all jobs can be assigned to at least one cell. The jobs that can be machined in one or more specialized cells can usually also be machined in the remainder cell. Therefore, all jobs that can be assigned to a specialized cell can usually be assigned to a minimum of two cells.

In some instances, two or more cells can share a common machine. This can occur when the cells have an adjoining edge or point. Machine sharing can decrease the total number of machines necessary and increase machine utilization. But machine sharing can cause control problems when machine availability conflicts occur.

Besides the basic assumptions regarding CM, there are numerous assumptions pertaining to job scheduling and capacity planning. In particular, many of the developed scheduling techniques are only successful or applicable if the constraining assumptions are adhered to. An understanding of the assumptions and their implications is critical for the successful application of many if not all, of the loading and scheduling techniques. If one or more of these assumptions is violated, the loading or scheduling technique may not be effective.

System Characteristics

There are a large number of variables which could have an effect on the performance of the loading and scheduling techniques.[10,11] These variables are not encompassed by a list of CM assumptions or a list of assumptions for job shop scheduling. The physical CM system and the jobs arriving to the cellular system are defined by these variables. The physical CM system is defined by a set of cellular characteristics. The jobs arriving to the cellular system are defined by a set of job characteristics.

Cell Characteristics

The characteristics of the CM system which partially define the system and have an effect on the control of the system include:

(1) number of cells;
(2) cell size;
(3) total number of machine types;
(4) cell composition;
(5) remainder cell.

Number of Cells

There appears to be no known norm for the number of cells in a CM system. Small job shops might split two or three cells off from the remainder of the shop. A larger facility might have dozens of cells. The published literature adds little information as to the number of cells. In 1975, Shunk indicated that 30-40 per cent of the facility should remain as a job shop and should not be converted into cells.[12]

An objective of cellular manufacturing is to create specialized cells that can process a limited number of different job types. Although a job type should have more than one cell that it can feasibly be assigned to, the job type should not be capable of being processed in all cells. A simplistic example would be all shafts being processed in a shaft type cell and all castings being processed in a casting cell. But a shaft should not be produced in a casting cell and vice versa. Therefore, in some facilities there is no dependence or interaction between groups of cells, thereby allowing for an analysis of a subset of the entire facility. This independence is significant in light of the complexity of the cell loading problem.

Cell Size

The number of machine types per cell defines the cell size. There is a limited amount of published data concerning the number of machine types per cell. The literature indicates that cell size varies from 3 to 15 machines per specialized cell with the mean number of machines per cell being approximately six. It should be noted that cell size is extremely user and industry specific; therefore, the cell size can vary greatly.

As the number of machines in a cell increases beyond six machines, the advantages of cellular manufacturing appear to decrease. The material-handling problem increases rapidly as does the effective control and scheduling problem. As the number of machines in a cell decreases below six, the advantages of cellular manufacturing remain, but the disadvantages become more apparent. The number of job types the cell can accept decreases rapidly with a decrease in cell size. With the decrease in the number of job types the cell can accept, the probability of the cell being extremely underutilized increases. Therefore, the flexibility of both the cell and the entire facility decreases, with a decrease in the cell size.

Total Number of Machine Types

The total number of machine types is the sum total of the number of different types of machines with different capabilities in the facility. The total number of machine types directly effects the cell size and the cell composition. As this number increases, it appears that cell size will increase and/or the composition of each cell will become more individualized. The resultant will then be cells with less flexibility and underutilization.

It should be noted that it appears that CM practitioners rarely consider machine flexibility as an important parameter effecting CM control. Rather, the practitioner accepts the constraints imposed by the CM facility design.

Cell Composition

Cell composition is defined as the specific content of each cell. Cell composition is a characteristic that is very difficult to quantify. A machine-availability matrix, as shown in figure 2, is a matrix quantification of cell composition. This matrix of cell composition can be reduced to a zero-one binary code. But cell composition has yet to be quantified to the degree where a specific cell composition can be assigned a numeric value.

The number of different cell compositions possible for even a small system is quite large. Granted, a number of the cell compositions are in reality identical and can be found by reordering the machine type identities. But there is still a large number of unique cell compositions for a fixed-size facility.

The published body of knowledge provides no direct indication as to what typical cell compositions should be. The literature indirectly suggests that particular sets of cells have similar machine types. For example, all shaft cells have similar machine types as do nearly all casting cells. But there

	\multicolumn{8}{c}{Machine type}
	1	2	3	4				
Cell A	X	X	X					
Cell B		X	X	X				
Cell C		X		X	X	X		
Cell D			X	X	X	X		
Remainder cell	X		X		X	X	X	X

Figure 2 *Machine-availability matrix*

Cellular Manufacturing Control

appears to be little if any similarity of machine types between the shaft cells and the casting cells.

A change in the composition of a specific cell can increase or decrease the number of feasible cells for a number of job types. In addition, a change in the composition of a specific cell can eliminate the only feasible cell for a particular job type or can allow for a new job type. A change in cell composition can easily change the set of possible job types and the job-cell feasibility of the job types.

Remainder Cell

The remainder cell is that portion of the job shop that is not converted into a cellular system. Typically, the remainder cell comprises 30 to 40 per cent of the total facility.[12] But, many of the machine types in the remainder cell are machines which have very low levels of utilization, and/or they are the machines that cannot be moved or require a specific location in the facility. Typically, the few jobs that require these machines are assigned to only the remainder cell. If a job must be diverted from a specialized cell to the remainder cell, then many of the advantages of CM are lost. If the specialized cells have been successfully designed, the number of jobs in proportion to the total number of cells is relatively small.

Job Characteristics

The characteristics which define the jobs that flow through the cellular manufacturing systems are:

(1) job routing;
(2) number of operations per job;
(3) number of different job types;
(4) job mix;
(5) processing time;
(6) due date.

Job Routing

Job routing is defined as the order of machines required to complete the job. Job routing for a cellular system can vary from a flow shop, to a modified flow shop, to a job shop. When designing a cellular manufacturing system, one of the objectives is to design each cell as a small flow shop. Although this is an objective, not all the cells in the system are capable of being a flow shop when initially designed.

As the cellular system progresses in age, the part mix tends to change. With this change in part mix, new parts are introduced to the system which usually will force the cells away from flow shops toward job shops. As a result, control of the cells becomes more difficult and the advantages of cellular manufacturing tend to decrease.

Number of Operations per Job

The ratio of the number of operations per job to the size of the cell directly affects and constrains the size of the cell. As the number of operations per job increases, the number of machines in the cell typically increases. With an increase in cell size, the difficulty of cell loading tends to decrease while the difficulty of cell scheduling increases substantially. The question of an optimal, or even an appropriate ratio has not been addressed at this time.

Number of Different Job Types

A job type is defined as having a unique machine routing. The number of different types is bounded by the job routing, number of operations per job, and the total number of machine types. For a given set of job routings, a given number of operations, and a given total number of machine types, there is a finite number of possible job types. Hopefully, the finite number of possible job types is further constrained to be the set of jobs that can be feasibly assigned to a specialized cell. While a large number of job types does provide flexibility and capability to the facility, it does significantly increase the complexity of the cell scheduling problem.

Job Mix

Job mix is defined as the composition by job type of the jobs in the system. Typically, a CM system is designed for a single job mix or for a very limited range of job mixes. The job mix can and does vary to some degree over time. Whether this variation occurs over a period of weeks, months or years is unknown and is facility specific. But, when the job mix does change, cell utilization, job flow time and job lateness can be severely affected. Obviously, the problems associated with cell loading and cell scheduling are also affected.

Processing Time and Due Date

Both of these variables are of utmost importance to the viability of a CM system. If jobs have unusually large processing times, the ability to provide an acceptable schedule diminishes. If due dates are set unreasonably close to the actual total necessary processing time, then again the ability of the schedule to provide satisfactory completion dates is significantly reduced.

Machine and Job Density

Machine density and job density are two parameters which complete the definition of a CM system.[13] Machine density is defined as the commonality of machine types between cells. Machine density encompasses the cell characteristics, the number of cells, number of machine types per cell, total number of different machine types, and the remainder cell.

Cellular Manufacturing Control

Job density is defined as the proportion of cells the jobs could feasibly be assigned to. Job density encompasses the job characteristics, the number of operations per job, and the number of different job types. Job density also includes the cell characteristics, the number of cells and cell composition.

Machine density and job density, in concert, define the complexity of the CM system. They also provide an indicator as to the difficulty of the cell-loading and cell-scheduling tasks.

Cell Loading

Cell loading is the determination of which cell, among the feasible cells, the job should be assigned to.[14-16] Cell loading is critical because it prescribes the overall balance of the CM system. An improper overall balance can result in poor machine utilization, excessive job tardiness and excessive job flow time. Cell loading is similar to such topics as capacity scheduling, capacity planning, shop loading and workload balancing. There has been a limited amount of published literature detailing applications and research in these areas. With acceptable modifications, several of these techniques are applicable to cellular manufacturing.

Cell loading was addressed by this author in his doctoral dissertation in 1980 and in a subsequent paper.[5, 17] In essence, it was determined that the assignment of a job to a cell requires two tasks; determine which job and determine which cell. The two tasks can be performed in either order. If the job is identified first and then the cell selected, the assignment procedure has job priority. If the cell is identified first and then the job selected, the assignment procedure has machine priority.

It was also determined that there are three pseudo objectives inherent in cell loading. These three pseudo objectives are:

(1) balance the load between cells;
(2) balance the machine loads within each cell;
(3) balance the proportion of jobs with large processing time and jobs with small processing times between and within cells.

The system characteristics, the jobs attributes and the cells attributes were employed in different forms as criteria to identify and select the jobs and cells. Over 30 different assignment techniques were developed and examined. Two assignment techniques, Job-Priority Loading (JPL) and Machine-Priority Loading (MPL) were determined to perform better than the other techniques examined.

Job-Priority Loading and Machine-Priority Loading were evaluated across a wide range of conditions. Random cell assignment and basic cell balancing procedures were used as baselines for comparison. The evaluation was performed using a SLAM simulation model. The performance measures evaluated were mean flow time, mean tardiness and mean machine utilization. Shortest operation time truncated (SOT/T) was employed as the sequencing heuristic.

From the evaluation it was determined that JPL and MPL were significantly better than the two baseline loading techniques for the range of variables examined. In addition, it was determined that several of the variables examined (number of cells, remainder cell job density and preload level) have had an effect on the system but have had no significant effect on the overall performance of JPL and MPL. Finally, four common sequencing heuristics were evaluated in a post test, and it was determined that for JPL and MPL, SOT/T performed as well or better than the other three sequencing heuristics.

There has been little if any other structured research addressing cell loading. In many CM systems, cell loading is not considered because a job is restricted to one and only one feasible cell. While this restriction may be unavoidable in some facilities, it does impose constraints on the system which will limit machine utilization and system flexibility.

Cell Scheduling

If the aforementioned CM assumptions are adhered to, the control of each cell is nothing more than the scheduling of individual, small job shops and/or modified flow shops. There are literally hundreds of published papers dealing with scheduling. In addition, there are thousands of industrial firms which have generated their own scheduling techniques of which there is no published knowledge. Baker, and Conway, Maxwell, and Miller provide excellent textbook surveys of the entire scheduling topic.[18,19] Day and Hottenstein, and Graves provide good surveys of the scheduling problem and the available techniques.[20,21]

Each cell within a cellularly divided manufacturing system can, for simplicity, be considered a modified flow shop. A modified flow shop falls between a job shop and a pure flow shop. By definition, a part in a job shop can enter at any machine, can be routed to any number of machines in any order, and can exit the job shop at any machine. For a pure flow shop, parts can enter at only the first machine, can only follow a single path through the shop, and can exit only at the last machine. For a modified flow shop, parts can enter the shop at one of several machines, can progress through the shop by a limited number of paths, and can exit the shop at one of several machines. There are many levels of modified flow shops depending on the number of entrance and exit machines and the number of paths through the shop.

Much of the published scheduling techniques fail to define accurately the type of shop being studied. Because a modified flow shop employs most of the same characteristics of a job shop, the literature applicable to job-shop scheduling is usually applicable to the modified flow shop.

The job shop can be modelled as either a static or a dynamic system. For a static system, the jobs are pooled and scheduled at fixed time intervals. Once the jobs are scheduled, the schedule is set and fixed. For a dynamic system, the jobs are scheduled as they arrive at the shop or at a machine. With this flexibility, the queues in front of each machine can continually change.

Cellular Manufacturing Control

If the job shop is modelled as a static system, the available scheduling methodologies fall into three categories; combinatorial, mathematical programming and Monte Carlo sampling. Combinatorial methods are based on the changing from one permutation to the next by 'switching around' jobs. Combinatorial methods are best suited for very small problems limited to three or fewer machines. This is due to the factorial increase in permutations making an exhaustive search of all combinations infeasible. Because of the limitations in combinatorial methods, their applicability to the real-world cellular scheduling task is severely limited.

The job-shop scheduling problem has been formulated as an integer program for over 20 years. Since that time, many authors have applied mathematical programming techniques to the problem. The consensus of the scheduling practitioners is that mathematical programming fails to provide real-time control for even small-sized problems, due to excessive computational requirements. In some instances, mathematical programming has been applied with some success in aggregate, long-term planning problems. Tied closely to mathematical programming is enumeration and the associated branch-and-bound techniques. There is a vast array of optimal and sub-optimal seeking branch-and-bound techniques. But for the most part, the results in real-world applications have been the same as for mathematical programming.

If the CM system is modelled as static, then the third control technique available is Monte Carlo sampling and simulation. Monte Carlo sampling and simulation typically refers to the application of heuristic sequencing rules with validation via digital computer simulation. Because nearly all heuristic sequencing rules are applicable for both static and dynamic systems, these rules have been grouped and will be discussed collectively under dynamic systems.

If the cellular manufacturing system is modelled as a dynamic system, the available scheduling methodologies fall into two categories: queuing theory and heuristic sequencing rules. Employing a strict set of assumptions affecting arrival rates, processing times, queue disciplines and routing techniques, the shop with a single machine, the shop with parallel machines and the flow shop have been studied using queuing theory. Because of the added complexity of the job shop, the job shop has received only limited queuing research. In general, queuing theory has found applicability in large aggregate models and in planning models.

Monte Carlo simulation via a digital computer has been the principle tool for analysing heuristic sequencing rules.[22] This has primarily been due to the stochastic nature of the five predominant parameters associated with the job shop. These parameters are:

(1) arrival rate (distribution, mean, variance);
(2) processing rate (distribution, mean, variance);
(3) shop size (number, composition);
(4) job routine (random, uniform, preset);
(5) assignment of due date (distribution, mean, variance).

Sequencing rules are rules which determine the order of jobs to be processed by an individual machine. Most sequencing rules are based on a single characteristic of a job (simple job rules) or a combination of the job's characteristics (complex job rules). Primarily these characteristics are:

(1) processing time;
(2) due date;
(3) number of operations;
(4) cost of job;
(5) set-up time;
(6) arrival time;
(7) next machine(s) or operation(s).

A few sequencing rules are not based on the job's characteristics, but are based on the state of the shop (machine rules). Some machine rules look at alternate routings to balance the shop load. Other machine rules 'look ahead' to determine future shop bottlenecks or underutilization. Some of the machine rules get quite complex and time consuming and begin to approach the problems associated with the static job-shop scheduling methodologies. Because of the large possible variations in job-shop parameters, there has been a considerable amount of job-shop simulation research and applications using a vast array of sequencing rules.[23-6]

The bulk of the simulation research has been carried out using a large set of restrictive assumptions. Only a limited number of simulations have relaxed even a few assumptions. To simulate the real world where most of the research oriented assumptions are non-existent, has received limited attention. This is due to the specialization required to simulate a specific facility, and due to the large increase in complexity required to reflect adequately the real-world facility.

Even with the considerable amount of variation possible within the job-shop parameters, certain priority rules present consistent results. Among simple sequencing rules, Shortest Processing Time (SPT), gives the smallest mean flow time but it also gives a larger flow time variance than First-In-Shop-First-Out (FISFO). Due date, Slack and Slack per operation all give good results for minimizing job lateness.

In general, dispatching rules based on the processing time, operation time, or the operation time multiplied by the total processing time provide better results than FISFO, First-Come-First-Served (FCFS), or Last-In-System-Last-Out (LISLO). Improvements in SPT and Shortest Operation Time (SOT) have been obtained by employing a dual sequencing rule. A dual sequencing rule changes from the primary sequencing rule (SPT, SOT), to a secondary sequencing rule (FISCO, FCFS) at pre-determined time intervals. This change occurs for a fixed period of time to force jobs with large operation times or processsing times through the system, and then returns to the primary sequencing rule. A dual sequencing rule is referred to, in some instances, as truncation. A dual sequencing rule gives a small mean flow time as does SPT or SOT and also reduces the flow time variance.

Concluding Remarks

The control of a group technology cellular manufacturing system is, in fact, a dual problem. The two problems are (1) the loading of the cells, and (2) the scheduling of the individual cells. Cellular manufacturing has a set of inherent advantages and a second, smaller set of inherent disadvantages. The set of advantages are predicated on the adherence to a set of constraining assumptions. The effects of the disadvantages of cellular manufacturing can be minimized by the successful control of the system.

This paper reviews the advantages and disadvantages of cellular manufacturing, and presents some of the implied assumptions. In addition, the variables that could have an effect on cell control are presented. Finally, a discussion of cell loading and cell scheduling methodologies is presented.

References

1. S. P. Mitrofanov, *Scientific Principles of Group Technology* (Boston Spa: National Lending Library) translated from *Nauchnye Osnovy Gruppovoi Tekhnologii* (Leningrad: Lenizdat, 1966).
2. V. A. Petrov, *Flowline Group Production Planning*, English translation by E. Bishop (London: Business Publications, 1968).
3. J. L. Burbidge, *The Introduction of Group Technology* (New York: Wiley and Sons, 1975).
4. J. L. Burbidge, 'Production Flow Analysis', *The Production Engineer*, April/May 1971, pp. 139–52.
5. T. J. Greene and R. P. Sadowski, 'Loading the Cellularly Divided Group Technology Manufacturing Systems', *IL Conference Proceedings*, Fall 1980, pp. 190–5.
6. I. Ham, 'Selected References on Group Technology in English', SME Technical Paper MR 71-284, Society of Manufacturing Engineers, Dearborn, Michigan (1971).
7. I. Ham, 'Introduction to Group Technology', SME Technical Report MMR 76-03, Society of Manufacturing Engineers, Dearborn, Michigan, (1976).
8. F. R. E. Durie, 'A Survey of Group Technology and its Potential for User Application in the United Kingdom', *The Production Engineer*, February 1970, pp. 51–61.
9. T. J. Grayson, 'Some Research Findings on Evaluating the Effectiveness of Group Technology', *International Journal of Production Research*, vol. 16, no. 2 (1978) pp. 89–102.
10. D. Jackson, *Cell System Production* (London: Business Books, 1978) p. 169.
11. H. Opitz and H. P. Wlendahl, 'Group Technology and Manufacturing Systems for Small and Medium Quantity Production', *International Journal of Production Research*, vol. 9, no. 1 (1971) pp. 181–203.
12. D. L. Shunk, 'The Measurements of the Effects of Group Technology by Simulation', doctoral dissertation, Purdue University, West Lafayette, Indiana (December 1976).
13. T. J. Greene, 'Analytical Definition of Cell Composition via Machine Density and Job Density', Working Paper, Department of Industrial Engineering and Operations Research, Virginia Polytechnic Institute and State University, Blacksburg, Virginia (1981).

14. N. Adam and J. Surkis, 'A Comparison of Capacity Planning Techniques in a Job Shop Control System', *Management Science*, vol. 23, no. 9 (May 1977) pp. 1011–15.
15. S. Eilon, 'Five Approaches to Aggregate Production Planning'. *AIIE Transactions*, vol. 7, no. 2 (June 1975) pp. 118–31.
16. S. Khator and C. Moodie, 'A Machine Loading Procedure Which Considers Part Complexity and Machine Capability', *International Journal of Production Research*, vol. 17, no. 1 (1979) pp. 1–10.
17. T. J. Greene, 'Loading Concepts for the Cellular Manufacturing System' doctoral dissertation, Purdue University, West Lafayette, Indiana (August 1980) p. 137.
18. K. R. Baker, *Introduction to Sequencing and Scheduling* (London: John Wiley, 1974).
19. R. W. Conway, W. L. Maxwell and L. W. Miller, *Theory of Scheduling* (Reading, Mass.: Addison-Wesley, 1967).
20. J. E. Day and M. P. Hottenstein, 'Review of Sequencing Research', *Naval Research Logistics Quarterly*, March 1970, pp. 11–39.
21. S. C. Graves, 'A Review of Production Scheduling', *Operations Research*, vol. 29, no. 4 (July–August 1981) pp. 646–75.
22. J. M. Moore and R. G. Wilson, 'A Review of Simulation Research in Job Shop Scheduling'. *Journal of Production and Inventory Management,* vol. 8 (1967) pp. 1–10.
23. D. G. Dannenbring, 'An Evaluation of Flow Shop Sequencing Heuristics', *Management Science*, vol. 23, no. 11 (July 1977) pp. 1174–82.
24. W. S. Gere, Jr. 'Heuristics in Job Shop Scheduling', *Management Science*, vol. 13, no. 3 (November 1966) pp. 167–90.
25. C. H. Jones, 'An Economic Evaluation of Job Shop Dispatching Rules', *Management Science*, vol. 20, no. 3 (November 1973) pp. 293–307.
26. R. Rochette and R. P. Sadowski, 'A Statistical Comparison of the Performance of Simple Dispatching Rules of a Particular Set of Job Shops', *International Journal of Production Research*, vol. 14, no. 1 (January 1976) pp. 63–76.

2.6

Kanban versus MRP II – Which is Best for You?

W. Goddard

There is more than distance separating Japan and America. In the field of production planning and inventory management, the two countries are going in different directions. To the east, it is Kanban; to the west, it is Manufacturing Resource Planning (MRP II).

The goals of each are identical – to aid manufacturing companies in improving customer service, inventory turnover and productivity. Spectacular results can be cited by companies employing each. However, the tools used by Kanban are dramatically different from the tools used by MRP II.

After visiting Japan to compare the pros and cons of Kanban with those of MRP II, I came to two conclusions:

(1) Kanban can succeed only where the user produces highly repetitive products. MRP II, however, works equally well for highly engineered one-of-a-kind environments, make-to-stock products and finished-to-order products.
(2) MRP II has better tools than Kanban, but these tools are more costly. It is very important for a company to evaluate properly not only the costs, but what the paybacks will be. Unless the general manager and his staff can visualize a sizeable return, they will not invest enough of their time and energy to ensure that the company will become a successful user.

Lessons to Learn from Kanban

There are at least three lessons to be learned through understanding the Kanban system.

W. Goddard is President of Oliver Wight Educational Associates Inc.
Source: W. Goddard, 'Kanban versus MRP II – Which is Best for You?', from *Modern Materials Handling*, 5 November 1982.

Lesson number one is apparent to every observer of the Japanese success story. It is called teamwork. The Japanese companies operate with a tremendous amount of team effort. They pull together. They realize that as a team they will be stronger.

The second lesson is that education is the common denominator. This is as true for the successful Toyota Kanban system as it is for all successful MRP II systems. It is better to have a technically imperfect system that the users understand and want to make work, than a technically correct one without user understanding.

The third lesson is that we should not copy their tools. Rather we should continue in the direction of utilizing MRP II to its fullest potential.

The success that Toyota has achieved is not the result of their tools, nor is it how they use them, although they use them very well. *The key is what they do before using their system that permits it to work so well.*

Without a clear distinction between these Kanban tools versus the attitude and philosophy of the Kanban users, we could easily import the wrong message from Japan.

Outstanding Results at Toyota

The successes achieved by several Japanese companies as measured by increased productivity and increased inventory turns border on the unbelievable. One's first reaction is, 'Can they really be that good?'

My visit last year to the Takahama plant of Toyota was with some of this same scepticism. At this facility, Toyota produce their line of forklift trucks. The plant is modern, completed in 1970, and large, over 24 acres under roof. It is a high-volume operation and it uses the Kanban system.

How is it working? In terms of customer service, very well indeed. 'Our on-time delivery performance to the promised date of new trucks is 100 per cent', I was told. 'Our delivery performance for shipping service parts the same day as the orders arrive is 97 per cent.' It is difficult to top that.

How about lead times? What is their cumulative material lead time, top to bottom, including final assembly, subassembly, fabrication and purchasing? American forklift truck manufacturers would reply in the range of 6–9 months. Toyota's response was '1 month!'

How have they accomplished these results? To answer this you have to understand their attitude towards inventory.

Toyota's Philosophy

Inventory, in Toyota's view, is 'a waste'. It is a waste of both space and money. As a result, they have an obsession to eliminate all unnecessary inventory. It is attacked with the same degree of vengeance as their campaign to improve quality by eliminating the causes of defects.

In their desire to achieve the elimination of inventory, they have put together a system that attempts to have every part, be it manufactured or

Kanban versus MRP II

purchased, available 'just in time'. It is a worthy goal. The right part at the right time in the right quantity at the right place is, indeed, what every production planning and inventory management system is striving for.

Toyota supports these words with deeds. They devote great energies to nine fundamentals as each of them contributes greatly to their goals. Our 'typical' approach versus theirs is summarized in table 1.

TABLE 1 HOW TOYOTA'S KANBAN PHILOSOPHY DIFFERS FROM A TYPICAL US COMPANY

Factors	Toyota's Kanban	American philosophy
Inventory	A liability. Every effort must be extended to do away with it.	An asset. It protects against forecast errors, machine problems, late vendor deliveries. More inventory is 'safer'.
Lot sizes	Immediate needs only. A minimum replenishment quantity is desired for both manufactured and purchased parts.	Formulas. We are always revising the optimum lot size with some formula based on the trade-off between the cost of inventories and the cost of set up.
Set-ups	Make them insignificant. This requires either extremely rapid changeover to minimize the impact on production, or the availability of extra machines already set up. Fast changeover permits small lot sizes to be practical, and allows a wide variety of parts to be made frequently.	Low priority. Maximum output is the usual goal. Rarely does similar thought and effort go into achieving quick changeover.
Queues	Eliminate them. When problems occur, identify the causes and correct them. The correction process is aided when queues are small. If the queues are small, it surfaces the need to identify and fix the cause.	Necessary investment. Queues permit succeeding operations to continue in the event of a problem with the feeding operation. Also, by providing a selection of jobs, the factory management has a greater opportunity to match up varying operator skills and machine capabilities, combine set-ups and thus contribute to the efficiency of the operation.
Vendors	Co-workers. They are part of the team. Multiple deliveries for all active items are expected daily. The vendor takes care of the needs of the customer, and the customer treats the vendor as an extension of his factory.	Adversaries. Multiple sources are the rule, and it is typical to play them off against each other.
Quality	Zero defects. If quality is not 100 per cent, production is in jeopardy.	Tolerate some scrap. We usually track what the actual scrap has been and develop formulas for predicting it.
Equipment maintenance	Constant and effective. Machine breakdowns must be minimal.	As required. But not critical because we have queues available.
Lead times	Keep them short. This simplifies the job of marketing, purchasing and manufacturing as it reduces the need for expediting.	The longer the better. Most foremen and purchasing agents want more lead time, not less.
Workers	Management by consensus. Changes are not made until consensus is reached, whether or not a bit of arm twisting is involved. The vital ingredient of 'ownership' is achieved.	Management by edict. New systems are installed in spite of the workers, not thanks to the workers. Then we concentrate on measurements to determine whether or not they're doing it.

These nine – inventory, lot sizes, set-ups, queues, vendors, quality, equipment maintenance, lead times and workers – are the foundations for any manufacturing planning and control system. That is, the system does not dictate these to the users, just the opposite. The user must specify them. It is up to the users to provide this information and maintain it for both the Kanban system and MRP II.

The attitude that Toyota's management and workers bring to each of these issues is not inherent to their 'culture'. In fact, a sizeable number of American firms have both the same philosophy and similar results.

Contrasting one Japanese company's philosophy against a 'typical American company' philosophy may be somewhat unfair. It may not represent your company's approach. However, it is enlightening as it certainly summarizes Toyota's approach.

The important point is that achieving improvements in these fundamentals would help any system to work better.

The Mechanics: Kanban versus MRP II

Every manufacturing company has certain functions that it must perform. Eight of these functions are summarized in table 2, which also lists the tools that both the Kanban system and MRP II use to aid these functions.

TABLE 2 EIGHT MANUFACTURING FUNCTIONS: HOW THEY ARE CONTROLLED BY KANBAN AND MRP II

Functions	Categories	Kanban system	MRP II
Rates of output	Families of products	Levelling	Production Plan
Products to be built	Finished goods for make-to-stock, customer orders for make-to-order	Master Production Schedule	Master Production Schedule
Materials required	Components – both manufactured and purchased	Kanban Cards	Material Requirements Planning (MRP)
Capacity required	Output for key work centres and vendors	Visual	Capacity Requirements Planning (CRP)
Executing capacity plans	Producing enough output to satisfy plans	Visual	Input/Output Controls (I/O)
Executing material plans – manufactured items	Working on right priorities in factory	Kanban Cards	Dispatching Reports
Executing material plans – purchased items	Bringing in right items from vendors	Kanban Cards and unofficial orders	Purchasing Reports
Feedback information	What cannot be executed due to problems	Andon	Anticipated Delay Reports

Note: The same functions are performed by every manufacturing company; however, the tools used by Kanban differ greatly from the MRP II tools. Under Kanban, the tools are manual – Kanban Cards, Andon lights, visual checks and oral orders. Under MRP II, the most important tool is the computer.

Kanban versus MRP II

In reviewing the table, it is important to note that the Kanban Cards – actual paper cards – simply represent one key element within the Kanban system. In a similar manner, MRP (Material Requirements Planning) is simply one key element within MRP II. Neither MRP nor Kanban Cards is a stand-alone system. In both cases, if they were installed by themselves, they would produce few, if any benefits.

Let us review these eight functions that make up the two operating systems and the tools used in both systems.

Establishing Rates of Output

With Toyota's emphasis of 'life-time employment', great care and effort goes into determining the rates of output for their facilities. It is top management's responsibility to determine these rates. The objective is to 'level', to stabilize the labour force. Only with great reluctance would Toyota expand or contract their labour force.

In the US, without debating whether American manufacturing executives put the same amount of emphasis on avoiding layoffs, the process of 'production planning' is exactly the same. The objectives are identical. In companies with MRP II, the top management of the company is establishing rates of output which become their policy for the other resource-planning functions to carry out.

Determining What Products Need To Be Built

The master schedule specifies what products are to be built out through the planning horizon. At Toyota, the master schedule extends three months. The first month is considered firm, and all changes are resisted. The next two months are considered tentative, and very likely will require modifications.

The approach is the same to maintain a good Master Production Schedule in an MRP II system. The planning horizons vary greatly from company to company, as well as the guidelines for managing changes. Yet, a major difference occurs in how the products are lot sized and sequenced within the Kanban Master Schedule.

Determining What Materials Are Required

There are two types of Kanban Cards – a requisition card (authorizing withdrawal of material from the feeding operation) and a production card (authorizing the feeding operation to produce more of what is being withdrawn). It is a non-computer-based system.

With Material Requirements Planning, computer-generated reports advise the material planners what they should order. This process requires a structured bill of material, inventory records (what is on hand in the stockroom plus what is on order), and is driven by a Master Production Schedule. In essence, the analysis compares what is available for inventory to what is needed to advise the planners what is missing, in other words, the need to get more.

With an MRP II system, typically the planner issues a shop order along with a pick list to the stockroom. The pick list authorizes the stockroom to issue the proper material to make the needed item. The shop order is the authorization for the operators to perform the required functions to make the needed item.

With the Kanban system, there is no bill of material explosion on the computer; yet once a component is depleted on the final assembly line, that triggers the replenishment cycle, top to bottom, in a similar manner as would be done with MRP II on the computer.

The two Cards of Kanban perform the same functions as the pick lists and the shop order. But they do it manually.

Determining What Capacity Is Required

With Kanban, it is a non-computer approach. Through knowledge of the daily output volume, the factory foreman and operators determine what they have to do in terms of capacity to support the Master Production Schedule.

There is one other key objective – to do so by having a minimum amount of inventory on the floor. Every operation in the factory is to 'gear-up' to accomplish both missions. They are aided in this task by having multi-skilled operators and sometimes extra machinery. The combination provides great flexibility in responding to the capacity needs.

In the USA, with Capacity Requirements Planning, (CRP) the computer produces reports displaying the time phased loads per key work centre. These reports reflect not only open shop orders that have not passed through the work centre in question, but additionally include all of the planned orders (as calculated by MRP) to gain sufficient planning visibility.

This information is typically reviewed by both the planning department and by the appropriate factory managers. They determine the ability to respond to any predicted upturns or downturns in the capacity required.

Executing the Capacity Plans

At Toyota, if not enough parts are being produced, the final assembly line will shut down shortly. On the other hand, if work is accumulating behind a particular work centre, this queue means that inventory is not at a minimum and steps must be taken to correct it. Thus, the burden is with the factory personnel to plan and to react if adjustments are required to alter the output.

Within MRP II, input/output reports are produced. The objective of these reports is to provide a formal monitoring system. The flow of hours into the key work centres should match the prediction that came from CRP. The flow of hours out of the work centre should reflect the capabilities that the factory agreed to in order to satisfy the capacity plans. If a significant deviation occurs in either, it would signal a problem and cause corrective action to be initiated.

Kanban versus MRP II

Determining What Manufactured Items Should Be Worked On

The Kanban Cards provide this information. The production cards become authorization for the operators to make more. Basically, it is a first come/first serve system – whatever production card arrives first identifies the job that should be worked on next.

Companies using MRP II usually issue a daily dispatch report for each work centre. It lists all of the jobs that are physically there in a priority sequence.

Determining What Purchased Parts Are Required

The actual authorization for a vendor to ship more material is a Kanban Card. The absence of a card means that the vendor is not permitted to deliver material. The objective of their relationship with the vendor is to have a process similar to the relationship within the factory. That is, small lot sizes and frequent replenishments.

Under Kanban, the vendors do get advance notification to permit prior planning to occur. From the master schedule, the customer sends to each of his suppliers a rolling, ninety days projection. The notices to the vendors are treated as 'unofficial orders'. They are used to aid the vendor in material and capacity planning, but do not constitute a firm commitment on the customer's part.

With an MRP II system, computer reports advise purchasing people what items should be bought. The reports also suggest what existing purchase orders should be rescheduled to either arrive earlier or later, based on the changing needs of the company. The planned orders permit purchasing to provide visibility to vendors beyond the lead times.

Feedback Information

In both countries, the notification that execution problems have occurred is manually generated. How this information is communicated, though, differs.

Toyota employs an Andon system, which translates into 'light' or 'lamp'. The Andon is hung over the final assembly line. It is large enough to be seen throughout most of the factory. If an operator is having trouble keeping up with the required production, he signals this potential problem by lighting up his work station in yellow.

If the problem cannot be corrected, this is communicated by lighting up the work station in red. This is a warning that the final assembly line will soon shut down. Obviously, this will generate sufficient activity to either keep that from occurring and/or to minimize the length of the shutdown.

With MRP II, 'anticipated delay reports' are generated by the appropriate people in the factory as well as in purchasing to notify the material planners that delays in achieving schedules will occur. This will lead to a reassessment of the plan.

Limitations of the Kanban System

If a knowledgeable person were to assess the Kanban system by only looking at the tools, his conclusion would be that we have stepped backwards into the 1960s. The big debate then was, what items should be maintained on a reorder point basis versus MRP II.

Kanban Cards operate in much the same manner as a two-bin system, which is a reorder point approach. The two-bin approach has been around for eons. The inventory is separated into two bins or locations. One is used to satisfy the need for that part and as soon as that bin is empty, that is the trigger to replenish this part number. Until it is replenished, the second bin is used to supply the part.

With both the two-bin system and the Kanban system, what has been used is being replenished. The presumption is that if you have used up your inventory you will need more.

The flaws of the reorder point, and the advantages of MRP II, are so well known today that it would be difficult to find an advocate of the reorder point approach. Then how can the Kanban Cards work?

The answer lies not in the cards. Rather, Toyota has done five things to overcome the reorder point flaws:

A Uniquely Structured Master Production Schedule

The master schedule is put together to ensure that the future resembles the past. Great care is made to plan the same products, not only every month, but within each week, and, in turn, every day. This is possible only where a company is making a highly repetitive product. Without this environment, the Kanban Cards would be replenishing the wrong items – the items used would not be the items needed.

The goal is to schedule every product every day, and in a sequence that intermixes all products. If such a plan can be executed, then every day all components are being consumed and all are being replenished. Moreover, all that are being replenished will be needed. It is this sequence that puts the Kanban replenishment system in step with the master schedule.

The typical American manufacturing company schedules products differently. It seeks economies and efficiencies through economical lot sizes, and would batch build these products.

With this approach, the Kanban replenishment system would be out of step with the master schedule. The items being consumed would be replenished prematurely. This is one of the problems with reorder points.

Extremely Small Lot Sizes

Their ultimate goal is to 'use one, make one'. The combination of making products repetitively, as well as in very small quantities, causes a continuous demand on all of the components parts.

Kanban versus MRP II

If the lot sizes are larger, say a month's supply, the demand for the components will be 'lumpy'. The demand at the lower levels will occur twelve times a year, a month apart. Inventory will be increased due to the larger lot size, and due to making it prior to when it is next needed (see figure 1).

Very Short Lead Times

A reorder point system does not identify the need to reschedule. All manufacturing companies are confronted with a steady stream of changes. Forecasts are wrong, bills of material are revised, parts are scrapped, vendors are late, tooling breaks, and so on. However, if the lead times are extremely short, rescheduling is not critical.

With long lead times, if the schedules are not changed to reflect the up-to-date needs, then expediting will replace scheduling. The factory and

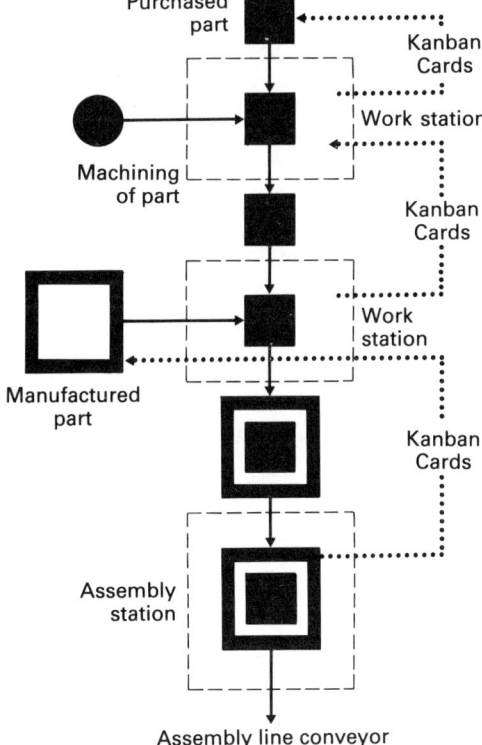

Constant replenishment of materials is achieved in a Kanban system through the use of two types of Kanban Cards. A requisition card authorizes withdrawal of materials from the feeding operation; a production card authorizes the feeding operation to produce more of what is being withdrawn. Once a component is depleted from the final assembly line, that triggers the replenishment cycle, top to bottom. The relationship between the user and a vendor should be the same as the relationship within the factory – small lot sizes, frequent replenishments.

Figure 1 The idea behind Kanban – small lots, frequent replenishments

purchasing will be running to hot lists to answer the question – 'what do you really need?'

Top Down Replenishment

The master schedule and the Kanban Cards are not hooked together as a computer is linked with MRP. Nevertheless, if something is not used in final assembly, no replenishment action will take place underneath it. In essence, Kanban ties everything together via the consumption at the master schedule level.

A conventional order point system does not have these ties. It assumes each item is a stand-alone item, to be replenished independently.

Informal Capacity Planning

The burden is on both the factory as well as vendors to gear up to handle any increased or decreased volume in the master schedule. Because the master schedule generates the need for a steady, repetitive flow of parts, capacity planning at all work centres is fairly straightforward (see figure 2).

Without this feature, the surprises caused by manufacturing a wide variety of parts in a non-repetitive manner would make this job extremely difficult without a computer.

These constitute the constraints for the Kanban system to work well. Remove any one and the Kanban system comes tumbling down. Therefore, unless a company makes highly repetitive products and unless they can accomplish all five points, they should not use the Kanban system.

'Just-in-Time' Deliveries

All of the Kanban tools and all of the Kanban users' efforts are dedicated to the 'just-in-time' and minimum inventory objectives. The goals are highly commendable; attaining them would be extremely desirable.

	Week 1	Week 2
Toyota (Kanban)	A B A B A B A B A B A C A C A C A C A C	A B A B A B A B A B A C A C A C A C A C
US (MRP II)	A A A A A A A A A A A A A A A A A A A A	B B B B B B C C C C B B B B C C C C C C

There is a big difference between the master schedule for a Kanban system and for a typical American manufacturer. Suppose a company has an output of 100 products per day, and that marketing forecasts that 50 per cent of the sales will be Product A, 25 per cent will be Product B, and 25 per cent Product C. The typical US plant might make Product A for five straight days, change over to Product B for two and a half days, then produce Product C for the balance of the week. However, under a Kanban system, a Japanese plant will make Product A, followed by B, followed by A, followed by C. Their goal is to schedule every product, every day, and in a sequence which intermixes all products.

Figure 2   A Kanban Master Production Schedule – the future resembles the past

Kanban versus MRP II

Just picture such a factory where the components required for final assembly arrive just in time and all of the purchased materials show up just in time to support the manufacturing operations. If, in fact, all of this could be achieved, the impact in terms of improved inventory turns and fast response to the marketplace would be spectacular. Additionally, a company would eliminate shortages and thereby gain a tremendous impact on improved productivity.

With MRP II the objectives are the same. Instead of the phrase 'just-in-time' our term is 'drop dead dates'. It means no fat, no lies; it means every schedule lined up to the needs of the company. It means complete honesty to the foreman and to the buyers, valid dates on the factory and purchase orders. It means that if the schedules are executed, the items will come in just when needed. The foreman and the operator know that in the event that a schedule is not met, a shortage will develop.

If a company used the tools of MRP II with the same starting point as Toyota (queues, lot sizes, safety stock, lead times, vendors, and a similar execution of schedules), the results would be as good. But the opposite would not be so. If the Kanban system was used in a company that did not resemble Toyota's environment, the results would not nearly be as good as with an MRP II system.

The Major Advantages of Kanban and MRP II

Kanban System

The tools are less expensive. A number of functions, such as material planning, capacity planning, and dispatching, are done manually. With MRP II, these functions require a computer to keep the vast amount of data up to date. With Kanban, fewer people are required to perform these same functions.

The Kanban system depends heavily on the foreman and operators – the line people. Their job is not to have somebody else tell them whether or not they are performing well, but to make that determination themselves and take whatever corrective action is required. The typical company using MRP II has a number of planners reading output reports, responding to action messages, maintaining data, and the like.

However, if the Kanban tools were employed in an environment different from the conditions that Toyota surrounds itself with, it would simply be an 'order launching and expedite' system. The reorder point approach is a very expensive system to operate. It generates excessive inventories of mismatched parts, while at the same time requiring massive expediting to react to shortages. Inexpensive tools that cannot get the job done are not a bargain.

MRP II

It can plan ahead. All of the functions that make up MRP II are 'forward looking'. For example, MRP advises replenishing material only if it is predicted that more is needed.

A Kanban system is 'backward looking'. It replenishes material when depleted. This is a significant difference. Only when you can make the future resemble the past will they both respond in a similar manner. With a repetitive product, this can be achieved. However, for non-repetitive products, MRP II's approach is far better.

It can plan other activities. Activities such as design engineering and drafting are critical 'upstream functions' that can be planned by MRP II. Predicting what capacity is required and maintaining up-to-date priorities are important for these highly skilled resources. Companies are also using MRP II to predict the need for tooling and maintenance items.

It can coordinate distribution centres. Within an MRP II system, Distribution Resource Planning is the approach that not only plans the resource needs at these remote locations, but, in turn, coordinates their replenishment with the manufacturing facilities. DRP operates in a similar manner to MRP II – it can project the need for material, space, and people at the warehouse, as well as the size of the replenishment shipments in terms of weight, pallets, and cube.

It can aid financial planning. A distinguishing feature of MRP II is that the financial planning system is an extension of the operating system. One set of books for the company is the result. For many companies, this is not the case. Rather, their financial people have developed their own set of books. They have learned the hard way that the data coming out of the factory are not reliable. Much second guessing and reserves are required to protect against potential end-of-the-year financial shrinkage.

It can handle 'what if' questions. Although it costs more to put data in a computer than to handle it manually, a company can do more with the data. For example, one of the most valuable uses of any system is to predict the consequences of alternate plans. The computer doesn't pick the best plan, but it provides information so that management can review the impact of the choices prior to selecting the one that makes the most sense. MRP II can show the consequences in terms of materials, capacity and money. This would be an asset for any manager.

Where Do We Go from Here

The list of American companies utilizing MRP II and achieving spectacular results is far longer than the Kanban users. Because of the excellent track record achieved by MRP II, a number of Japanese firms have decided that this is the proper approach. Makita Electric Works Ltd and Stanley Electric have material requirements planning systems that work well. Additionally, they have put as much time and effort into the fundamentals as Toyota has for Kanban.

The Japanese have studied our approaches and experiences. They have learned from us. We, in turn, should study approaches such as Toyota's Kanban system and profit from this analysis.

But it is not the Kanban System that we should import. Rather it is the 'Kando' of Toyota's Kanban that we need more of. Certainly, it is not

Kanban versus MRP II

simply installing a new MRP II system that will make us better; it's how we use it. But MRP II represents the right direction for manufacturing companies to manage themselves in a more productive manner.

Without a formal scheduling system that works, most American companies will not get all of the players to play team ball. MRP II provides the 'glue' that can bond a team together.

A manufacturing planning and control system is made up of two ingredients – tools and people. The ideal combination would be to have the best possible tools and people using them properly. But in the final analysis, team work is the key. It is Toyota's trump card. It is the same trump card for the successful users of MRP II.

2.7

Computer-aided Manufacture

J. Hatvany

Design, as was pointed out in an earlier survey,[1] is the set of activities leading from the establishment of a product requirement to the generation of all the information necessary for making the product. In the case of the mechanical engineering industries, the main chapters of this process have been formulated[2] as shown in table 1.

By no means all these activities have so far been furnished with computer aids, and certainly no system yet exists which is able to integrate them into one interrelated process of CAD, leading to a snowball-like information enhancement facility from the conceptual phase to the updated maintenance of the complete product and production data. That, however, is the

TABLE 1   SET DESIGN OF ACTIVITIES TO GENERATE ALL THE INFORMATION NECESSARY TO MAKE A PRODUCT ONCE ITS REQUIREMENTS ARE ESTABLISHED

Step 1	Step 2	Step 3
Product Structure definition	Detailing	Process planning
Concept sketching	drafting	Operation planning
Design parameter definition	documentation	Jig, fixture and tool design
Design logic rules definition	(drawings, lists)	NC programming
Dynamic dimensioning		Programming of dimensional and quality controls
3D model building		
Analysis, simulation, optimization		Programming of automated assembly (robots)
Viewing, aesthetic and topological verification		Design and documentation of maintenance procedures

J. Hatvany is Head of the Mechanical Engineering Division at The Computer and Automation Institute, Hungarian Academy of Sciences, Budapest.
  Source: J. Hatvany, 'Computer-aided Manufacture', Computer-aided Design, vol. 16, no. 3 (May 1984).

Computer-aided Manufacture

object of the current work in the area, for the aim of CAD development is not simply to furnish computer programs and hardware for certain of the greater or more demanding calculative and data processing requirements, but to create a coherent system encompassing the entire process.

The creation of an overall CAD system of the type outlined is difficult not only because there are a number of missing links, but also because interconnecting the existing ones is not a simple matter of concatenation. The activities listed need to be accessed and used almost at random, corresponding to the requirements of the many iterative loops between them. It may, for instance, turn out that an assembly task can be much more easily automated if a particular part is slightly redesigned, and this in turn can involve using a different process, different tooling, etc. Another difficulty in linking the design activities is that they may be using entirely different data representations, programming languages (e.g. in the case of a finite element analysis program, or a dynamic simulation), or even different fundamental modelling principles.

With a view to these difficulties, a stepwise approach was adopted and most companies in the mechanical engineering industries started right at the centre of the list by introducing computer-aided drafting and list-generating subsystems. In most countries these are still the most widespread CAD applications.[3] In other areas progress has been made both up and down the list.

In the upward direction, the practical limit has been 'dynamic dimensioning', e.g. of mechanical linkages, rotating components, vehicle and machine tool structures, etc. The highly important techniques of '3D modelling' (of which more will be said later) have permitted internal computer representations of objects to be created in such a way as to permit most types of 'analysis' and 'viewing' to be carried out and also to provide an efficient basis for 'detailing'. As far as the top four items on the list are concerned, they have not yet been incorporated into practical, industrial systems.

In the downward direction a link was established in the early 1970s between drafting systems and NC programming so that the operations involved in the detailing phase (and the data representations generated by them) could be used directly for the preparation of control tapes for machine tools. Although such an arrangement has frequently been called a CADCAM system, it does not really satisfy the criteria of either the design or the manufacturing sides. Ultimately the outcome of the design process outlined in table 1 should yield all the information in table 2. From this type of information it should then be possible to extract all the data required for the CAM, production scheduling, accounting, stock management and other functions involved in CIM (computer-integrated manufacturing).

Much work is now being done on computer-aided process planning and operation planning. Several systems are already in operation. However, there are only a very few pilot systems that have successfully established an organic link between the design activities preceding and including detailing and drafting (see table 1) on the one hand, and NC programming on the

TABLE 2 OUTCOME OF THE DESIGN PROCESS IN TABLE 1

The machining sequences on each machine tool
The sequence of machine tools for machining the parts
Jig, fixture and tooling data
Full toolpath and machining data (feed rates, etc.) for machining a part of the desired shape
Blank material requirement of each part
Machining times/part/machine
Transport routing of materials, parts and tools for the machining operation
Assembly sequence
Parts, materials and tools required for assembly
Full motion and operation data for assembly machines (robots)
Assembly operation times
Full motion, measurement and evaluation data for measuring parts and assemblies
Testing and checking instructions
Maintenance and repair instructions

other. Jig, fixture and tool design and the last three items of step 3 in table 1 are as yet completely separate activities, since no efficient method is available for the automatic extraction and incorporation of the data required. Much work still lies ahead therefore, before we shall be able to talk of truly integrated CADCAM systems.

The enormous complexity and sophistication of the tools required and the cost of the hardware needed to implement them were at first all grossly underestimated and the proliferation of CAD in the mechanical engineering industries was relatively slow in the 1970s. Systems were first introduced in those industries where the new products and technologies made them indispensible. These were the aerospace and related defence industries. The next were those industries – primarily shipbuilding and motor cars – where the competitive situation, and in particular the need to shorten product development cycles, made it imperative to introduce CAD. Lastly, towards the late 1970s and in the early 1980s the second category underwent a very swift expansion due to the changed constraints and possibilities of these years.

The general pattern of CAD systems introduction was that of creating 'islands',[4] e.g. in the automotive industry for car-body design, for structural analysis, for detailing and drafting, and for NC programming. It is only very recently that attempts have been made to link these islands organically.

The initial expectation (fuelled by the primitive types of returns-on-investments calculations required by accountants) that computer-aided drafting would lead to enormous productivity gains in terms of savings on labour costs, has not been justified. The economic benefits of the introduction of CAD systems have been very much more subtle in that they have contributed not so much to the improvement of indices in a falsely perceived technical–economic continuum, as to the *survival* of companies in the real world of a non-linear, discontinuous state-space. In other words they have allowed companies to appear on the market earlier, with products that are of better quality, better engineered (easier to manufacture) and better documented. Thus the catastrophic demise that has overcome many of their

Computer-aided Manufacture

more conservative competitors has been avoided. A 'computerization effect' *per se* exists where the introduction of a computer-aided activity forces the introduction of revitalization, better discipline and more modern management throughout the plant. This effect has been particularly powerful in those countries where great leeway had in any case to be made up in these respects.

Recent Developments

Dominant among recent developments has been the sharp decrease in the cost-effectiveness of CAD systems. It combined with the economic imperatives of the early 1980s to send sales soaring at a rate unparalleled by almost any other product in these lean years. According to a recent estimate,[5] 7330 CAD work-stations were shipped in Western Europe in 1982, with an annual 25.1 per cent projected growth to 1988, leading to 28,100 units sold in that year. (For graphic terminals alone, the corresponding figures are 16,360 for 1982, 58,400 for 1988.) Perhaps even more telling is the fact that although more than half of the 1982 CAD users in the USA had acquired their systems as recently as 1981, more than 70 per cent declared that they were very satisfied.[6] For those familiar with the usual installation and acclimatization problems of new computer systems in industrial organizations, this indicates that the systems bought satisfied a real need and were able to do so in an efficient, congenial and cost-effective way. This has been very much helped by the proliferation of relatively low-cost systems (costing less than $100,000 each). In 1981 about 580 of these were installed in the USA, by 1986 their annual sales are expected to rise to 10,600, accounting for 20 per cent of the total CADCAM market revenues.

The 'effectiveness' component of the cost-effectiveness formula has been enhanced mainly by the tremendous increase in computing power which we have witnessed in recent years. The super computers which are still needed as 'number crunchers' and as database machines in the design of complex products such as air- and spacecraft, ships, nuclear reactors, etc., have not only become much faster and more flexible, but also more easily accessible by a multitude of engineering users through reliable, ubiquitous, high-speed networks. The minicomputer – the work-horse of the medium-to-low cost CAD work-station – has become a 'mega-mini', i.e. a 32-bit machine with 2–8 Mbyte of store, well able to handle all the computing needs of the designers of most of the normal products of the mechanical engineering industry. Fastest, most stunning and most unexpected of all, however, has been the meteoric impact of the microcomputer. While the lower end of the microcomputer spectrum at first raised many false expectations among engineers who thought they could easily implement CAD systems on their sons' home computers, the upper (professional) end of the microcomputer range has swiftly caught up with (and surpassed) the 16-bit mini's abilities and is now moving into the mega-mini range. A recently announced model,[7] with a processor chip running at 10 MHz is said to be 'roughly comparable to DEC's VAX 11/780 running non-floatingpoint applications'. Each processor board of this machine (there can be up to four), supports 2 Mbyte of memory. The machine has an Ethernet board allowing communication with a very high-speed LAN, and an 85 Mbyte Winchester disc. Apart from the super-complex products mentioned above, there can indeed be few mechanical engineering design tasks that cannot be solved with this *low-cost*, micro configuration.

These orders-of-magnitude improvements in the cost-effectiveness of the computer power available for the CAD component of CADCAM, have coincided with a similarly spectacular increase in demand, due to the changes that have come about in the economic climate. As one representative of the West European motor-car industry put it:

> Competition is becoming manifest in the speed of the development of new models and in a variety of types that often confuses the customer. This compulsion to introduce new motor-car models quickly and frequently, leads the manufacturer to search for processes that will shorten the development times and production engineering times of new models.[8]

Similar demands are posed by the sharpened economic climate in most other product lines and in some these are further aggravated by the absolute need to use computer-aids not only to achieve competitive variety and product-cycles, but also competitive technical and ecological parameters, such as minimum-weight structures, high-speed kinematics, automated assembly, low fuel consumption, low waste emission, etc.

From the point of view of the demand caused by the sharpened economic climate and the supply offered by the vastly decreased cost-effectiveness of recent equipment, the conditions were ripe in the early 1980s for the spectacular breakthrough which in fact occurred. A third fortuitous factor must also be taken into account, however: the maturing of both the general-purpose and specific software that permitted the new work-stations to be integrated into the design and manufacturing activities of an industrial plant far more quickly and efficiently. The general-purpose software comprises:

- congenial operating systems;
- ergonomically and aesthetically pleasant computer graphics;[9]
- high-level programming languages;
- versatile and comfortable database management systems;[10]
- easy and transparent network communication facilities, etc.

The specific software is understood to include all those engineering programs which are now available as tools for the designer, e.g.:

- finite-element analysis systems;
- sculptured surface design and manipulation programs;
- volumetric modelling facilities;
- realistic image synthesis;
- computer-aided operation, process- and motion planning;[11]
- kinematic and dynamic simulation and analysis, etc.

Computer-aided Manufacture

Purchasers of CAD systems often used to have great difficulty in acquiring the specific software necessary for their particular design tasks, and particularly in fitting together these pieces of software to run as a single system. It was to overcome these difficulties that turnkey systems became so popular. (Turnkey systems offer the user the integrated hardware and software facilities suited to his industry's specific requirements.) They became popular despite the fact that many of the turnkey systems later tended severely to limit the user's flexibility, his ability to expand his system and to achieve the potential product diversity and flexibility which have increasingly become fundamental conditions for corporate survival. The problem has been tackled in two ways. On the one hand, turnkey systems have recently begun to become more versatile, adapting to the new requirements formulated by a number of CADCAM consultants as *sine qua non* conditions for the purchase of these systems. A typical advice check-list[12] tells the would-be purchaser not only to:

- develop a systematic request for proposals,
- undertake site visits,
- leave the onus of proof on the vendor, and
- mandate the running of benchmarks,

(these should all be obvious steps, though they are frequently neglected), but also advises us to enquire about the facilities the system offers for:

- the entry of micro-based systems,
- connection to extant and future networks, and
- building a common CADCAM database.

On the other hand, there has also been a trend away from turnkey systems, based on the proliferation of both *de facto* and *de jure* standards and of the availability of packages which can be used relatively easily as building blocks by the user, to build his own system. The packages are convenient partly because of the facilities offered by modern operating systems, partly because of their compliance with these standards.

Most of the useful standards have penetrated the CADCAM field from other areas of computer usage. These include:

- operating systems, e.g. UNIX;
- the post-FORTRAN languages, e.g. PASCAL and perhaps ADA;
- networking principles: ISO-OSI;
- LANS: ETHERNET
- computer graphics packages, e.g. GKS.

Others have been born indigenously in the course of CADCAM research and development. These include the VDI guidelines for CAD,[13] the emerging *de facto* input and output standards for finite-element analysis and for geometric modelling programs and also the rather unfortunate IGES standard for transmitting drawings. The power of these standards (even in their nascent stage) is shown by the fact that vendors like to advertise conformity with them[9] as a selling advantage because of the ease with which the user can then employ their product as a building block.

In some cases the specific requirements of the CADCAM process have led to development trends that diverge from the standardization processes in other application fields. Database management systems are a case in point, where the widely accepted CODASYL model (and its ancillary standards) is conceptionally ill-suited to the requirements of a process which demands:[10]

- a flexible, multilayered database architecture,
- dynamic data structure definition facilities,
- an extremely large database control domain, and
- trial and error design process facilities.

It has to be realized, that unlike the business DBMS user, the mechanical engineer is a casual user, for whom the main data is that contained in his geometric model. While efforts are being made to reconcile these requirements with the newer relational databases, it seems quite probable that mechanical engineering CADCAM systems will eventually evolve database management standards of their own.

The Present and the Future

Although CADCAM systems have become much more congenial, serviceable and better value for money in the last few years, they are still alien in many ways to the accustomed style of the mechanical engineering factory. They fall severely short of the expectations that designers and production engineers would like to formulate with respect to their computer aids.

The alien feel of computer systems is, of course, partly due to the fact that they require orderly thought and action, the truthful reporting of events and conditions, rational and swift decisions, well-defined goals and a host of similar characteristics that can be summed up as those of efficient, modern management and engineering practices. As far, therefore, as the introduction (or even the threatened introduction) of computers obliges the company to streamline its procedures and the conduct of its affairs, the effect of their alienation from the old ways can only be considered beneficial. This applies not only to the displacement of outdated business management techniques, but in at least equal measure to that of the old rule-of-thumb secretive instinctive design and production engineering routines that are still to be found in many factories.

Another aspect of the alien feel of computers, however, is due to the fact that they still require the engineer to learn too much about what ought to be their own internal business. This knowledge is sometimes euphemistically described as 'computer science', but is in fact closer to low-level bit-juggling. It covers things like assembler coding, the quirks of file-handling systems, the internal intricacies of graphics packages, job-control languages, etc. When the coming importance of computers was first realized,

Computer-aided Manufacture

children in elementary schools were assiduously taught binary arithmetic, because this knowledge was assumed to be necessary for communication with the new beast. Several big steps have since been taken to teach the beast to understand us, instead of having to teach our children to understand it. Children are now taught (or better still, teach themselves) to think logically, to formulate problems, to play and to learn using the computer as their tool and their toy. Engineers have not been able to get quite so far yet, not only because some of the means for making computers more congenial to them are still lacking, but also because those that do exist are frequently not available to them on the particular commercial product they have purchased.

The biggest disappointment to forward-looking engineers has been that CAD systems are still very far short of the *integrative role* that they are in due course expected to play. This expectation primarily involves the ability to conduct the entire series of activities formulated in table 1 in *a single design and implementation process*. We have said of the top four items (of step 1 in table 1) that they have not yet been incorporated into practical industrial systems. The reason for this is that the mode of thought, the reasoning and retrieval procedures required in these phases are fundamentally different from those used in the implementation of explicit engineering calculations. In these phases the designer is exercising his heuristic talents, trial-and-error procedures, apparently irrelevant excursions into distant knowledge domains and conclusions drawn from ill-formulated and deficient data which is the normal adjunct of his creative activity. The 'classical', algorithmically-based computer techniques are ill-suited to these methods and efforts have therefore been focused on using the new techniques of knowledge engineering, such as problem-solvers and expert system technology to create effective computer aids. Once these are successfully and cost-effectively implemented, it will indeed be possible to carry out 4D design, i.e. 'putting the tools of 3-dimensional modelling and simulation to work earlier in the development process, carrying them all the way through the time sequence of design, production and application'.[14]

Roland Schmitt takes the example of a washing machine in the early stages of design:

> This simulated washing machine will be fully operational; you'll be able to wash a load of simulated wash in it . . . it will display color-coded indications of the mechanical, thermal, or electric performance of each part . . . it will also simulate, on an accelerated time scale, the aging of the system and its parts.

Going further down table 1, we come to some more items that need new knowledge engineering and also database management techniques to be implemented. All the specific information for the programming of dimensional and quality controls, for programming automated assembly and for the design and documentation of maintenance procedure is (or should be, or could be) present *somewhere* in the computer system. This is as a result of the design activities undertaken in the previous phases, and all the general rules for using this specific information can usually be explicitly formulated. The algorithmic procedures presently used and the limitations of the database systems, however, have not permitted these phases to be integrated with the preceding ones and automated. Continuing experiments with problem-solving techniques and expert system approaches[15] hold out hope of relatively fast progress in these areas once the appropriately priced equipment, or, 'fifth-generation technology' is generally available.

In a recent international survey of the CAM scene it was stated that 'technological process planning . . . is assuming a vastly enhanced role, partly in providing automatic links between CAD and CAM, partly as a growing software component of machine tool control units'.[16] This quotation serves to indicate the extent to which the spatial and functional separation of formerly distinct CAD and CAM features is being broken down by the new distributed processing facilities that microcomputers and local-area networking have put at our disposal. In fact the division of the information categories in table 2 into those belonging to the methods or scheduling *office* and others that are related to the *shop floor* are tending to become irrelevant. On the contrary, it is becoming increasingly recognized that such functions as workshop scheduling and process planning need to be optimized *together*. There is no point, for example, in selecting maximum cutting rates (and thus maximal tool wear) for a machine which for higher-level scheduling considerations will not be fully loaded with work in the next period. The end here is once again integration, and the means to it involve an efficient blending of powerful algorithmic, non-algorithmic and data handling techniques.

Evidently CADCAM systems of the complexity which has been outlined (involving all the phases and information categories of tables 1 and 2 in a single dataflow) require not only specific techniques for each phase, but have to be carefully and deliberately designed to operate as an integrated whole. This design task transcends by far the bounds with which 'paper-and-pencil' or *ad hoc* piecing together techniques are able to cope. Not surprisingly, it requires computer-aided systems design technologies. Several appropriate ones have recently been developed and used. Sophisticated systems design techniques are thus one of the new integrative features that have emerged. The other, more fundamental and more specific to CADCAM in the mechanical engineering field, is geometric modelling.[17] Geometric modelling is integrative not because it will change the mechanical engineer's way of visualizing an object within a foreseeable future: it will not. The reason is that the new feasible, practical and available geometric modelling systems which now exist are the biggest step taken in recent years towards an acceptable, unique and unequivocal *internal representation* of the mechanical engineering product and its parts, throughout all the phases of design and manufacture. They are the kernel around which the meat of data from conceptional design to product testing and maintenance can grow in an orderly way.

References

1. J. Hatvany, W. Newman, and M. Sabin, 'World Survey of CAD', *Comput.-Aided Des.*, vol. 9, no. 2 (April 1977) pp. 79-98.
2. F. M. Lillehagen and T. Dokken, 'Towards a Methodology for Constructing Product Modelling Databases in CAD', in J. Encarnacao and F.-L. Krause, (eds), *File Structures and Databases for CAD* (Amsterdam: North-Holland, 1982) p. 70.
3. E. Arnold and P. Senker, 'Computer-aided Design in the UK Engineering Industry', *CAD 82* (Guildford: Butterworth, 1982) pp. 1-7.
4. K. Pasemann, 'Einsatz von CAD-Systemen bei VW', in R. Goebl and F. Pacha (eds), CADCAM – *Rechnergestütztes Konstruieren und Fertigen* (Vienna: R. Oldenbourg, 1982) pp. 284-95.
5. M. Park, 'Graphics' Rise Mushrooms as Users Watch Their Data', *Comput. Weekly*, 15 September 1983, p. 23.
6. T. Scannel, 'CADCAM Features Rated Over Price', *Computerworld*, 28 June 1982, pp. 53-4.
7. S. W. Fields, '$10,000 Buys Graphics Station', *Electronics*, 30 June 1982, pp. 139-40.
8. G. Hartwich, 'Bedeutung der CADCAM Technologie für die Automobilproduktion', *Zeitschr. für Wirtsch. Fertigung*, Supplement vol. 78, no. 10 (October 1983) pp. 58-62.
9. S. Lowenthal and D. Grabel, 'Multiple Processors Equip Terminal for High-level Graphics Functions', *Electronics*, 10 March 1983, pp. 129-32.
10. M. Managaki, 'Database Facilities for Computer-aided Engineering Systems', *NEC Res. & Develop.*, no. 70 (July 1983) pp. 64-70.
11. G. Reinauer, 'Rechnergestützte Variantenkonstruktion im Ingenieurenbereich', in R. Goebl and F. Pacha (eds) CADCAM – *Rechnergestütztes Konstruieren und Fertigen* (Vienna: R. Oldenbourg, 1982) pp. 208-24.
12. E. Teicholz, 'Choosing a Turnkey CADD System', *Datamation*, vol. 28, no. 2 (1982) pp. 118-22.
13. *VDI-Handbuch Konstruktion*, 2 vols. (Düsseldorf: VDI-Verlag 1982).
14. R. W. Schmitt, 'Beyond the Factory of the Future', in *Conference on CAD-CAM Technology in Mechanical Engineering*, MIT (1982) pp. 5-9.
15. M. Horváth and A. Márkus, 'Practical Methods and Techniques, New Ventures in CADCAM', in E. A. Warman (ed.), *Computer Applications in Production and Engineering* (Amsterdam: North-Holland, 1983) pp. 749-64.
16. J. Hatvany, M. E. Merchant, K. Rathmill and H. Yoshikawa, *World Survey of CAM* (Borough Green: Butterworths, 1983).
17. G. Allen, 'Future Trends in Geometric Modelling', *Conference on CADCAM Technology in Mechanical Engineering*, MIT (1982) pp. 339-49.

Part 3

Change: How Techniques Can Be Used

Introduction

In the factory of the future designers are presented with far more choice in what they can do than ever before: there is now the possibility of designing a manufacturing system with the flexibility of a job shop and the efficiency of an automated line. But to take advantage of this opportunity designers need to look at how new techniques can help them in the design of such a system.

No longer can one assume that one machine or cell is suited for just one type of job, nor expect that the job the system was originally designed for will remain unchanged for any length of time. Speed of change is difficult to predict but what is certain is that fast and accurate response to new needs is vital in the present competitive environment. This calls for techniques to be used in designing the initial plant and manufacturing operation that will enable future incremental changes to be made quickly and easily. The designer is also being presented with new forms of technology which will provide both better products and increased productivity. The price to pay is the very much greater capital cost of new technology. This means that the designer must take more care that the correct choice of 'high tech' equipment is made: a 'wrong' choice could have very serious consequences for the firm. These reasons make the use of good analytical techniques in planning and design essential to reduce the risk involved and respond to the need for future changes.

The cost of advanced technology is not the only problem to be considered. The equipment, especially software, itself becomes outdated very soon. Recognizing this fact, accountants are now making the payback requirement a much shorter period than before. Thus it is now even more essential that the potential problems of implementation are sorted out in the design stage. With the use of a CAD layout package one factory was able to move its entire manufacturing set-up to a new factory without stopping production, the only problem being an incorrectly placed white board in the conference room. A second manufacturer discovered that by using geometric simulation methods he could have saved at least six weeks in the implementation stage of a robot cell.

This part of the book looks at some of the modern techniques which help the designer in this task. The aim is to give an insight into how, when and where a given approach can be used in designing a manufacturing system. It is impossible to review all the techniques in the space available, and so the intention is to show how embodying the use of computer simulation and mathematical modelling can aid design. Several different techniques are illustrated and will provide insight into how to approach others, what questions to ask about them so that you use them for appropriate purposes.

Why do we need new techniques? The first paper (by Nicol and Hollier) looks at problems of plant layout and discusses findings of a survey into how often firms made a non-trivial change to their plant layout. They found the average life of a layout to be three years. This showed more than half the firms studied had serious problems with their layout, in spite of a considerable planning effort. Even where the layout was satisfactory originally, within a year it needed to be changed. In one case, increase in production requirement meant that the original layout was no longer appropriate. As it had been planned using a CAD package, the line managers were able to use the same system to replan the new layout quickly.

The second paper (by Black) is about problems arising from not having enough information to plan use of capacity sensibly. This directly affects the fulfilment of orders. The paper looks at the way Westland Helicopters overcame this problem, and the main point made is the need to have the right information in the right place, at the right time and in the correct form. Also there is no point in having a computer database for storing information if you do not have the appropriate software for accessing it. This software is not necessarily a ready written package but may need to be tailored to the firm's requirements as in Westland's case.

Even when it has been designed with the firm's objectives firmly in mind, problems are caused when these objectives are changed. The next paper (by Wild) looks at the business environment within which designs are used. The author examines, through a case-study, the effect that business decisions have on operations management strategy and vice versa. He shows that capacity planning is more than a set of number-crunching techniques. The techniques used must relate to the qualitative business strategy which depends on several factors. If these factors change, the overall strategy may have to be rethought. Though Wild does not go this far, a change of strategy could involve a change of techniques used.

The next four papers form the core group of the section in which the use of mathematical models and simulation is examined. The first two papers of this group show how simulation is used for both complete and incremental change in manufacturing methods. The last two papers examine the problems, advantages and limitations involved in using these techniques.

Warnecke and Vettin give an example of how various computer software packages have been used to help with planning a complex flexible manufacturing system. They use packages to help compare the merits of different systems and simulation to determine the best layout and work flow.

Introduction

Hutchinson shows how simulation can be used to design an automated material handling system in a traditional job shop. This is an example of how simulation can be used at one stage in an incremental development which could eventually lead to a complete FMS.

These papers show that modelling and simulation techniques can be useful in designing a manufacturing system. Like all techniques, they need to be applied properly. The last two papers in this group, by Kay and Tinarelli, deal with mathematical models and computer simulation in general. Both papers give you a deeper insight into the problems, advantages and limitations of modelling and simulation.

Kay describes and compares a mathematical model with event simulation within the context of an FMS. He highlights the strengths and weaknesses of both, and gives an indication of when to use either. After this, Tinarelli reviews the mathematical models used in inventory control. He first examines a classic theoretical inventory model, and he then develops practical models for use in business situations, by relaxing or abandoning some of the assumptions in the theoretical model. Choosing the most suitable model for a particular application is a matter of deciding which assumptions are acceptable. For instance there is little point in using a model containing the assumption that there are no limits to the space and capital invested in inventory if both are constrained.

The next two papers move away from techniques which can be used to help design a manufacturing system to looking at how one of the new tools is designed. The tool is CADCAM. It comprises two techniques: CAD which was introduced in part 2, and CAM which is Computer-aided Manufacture. At the moment the main use of CAD is in product design. This alters the way a traditional drawing-office works. But at the same time CAM has come to the shop floor with NC machines being developed into CNC machines. There is an appreciable research effort going into providing an interface between the design of the product and its manufacture on a CNC machine. At present the interface is more often than not a paper tape produced by the CAD system for a given NC machine.

The paper by Smith and Wellington shows that a step towards interfacing CAD directly with CAM has been made. The US National Bureau of Standards has created Initial Graphics Exchange Specification (IGES) to provide a commonly accepted interface. The paper describes how the specification has been developed with the help of industry in the USA. It remains to be seen if this specification is accepted worldwide. Whether it is or not this paper provides an insight into how this problem is being tackled.

The paper by Hannam and Plummer exemplifies some of the current research into CADCAM computer interfaces. The interesting part is how they are attempting to capture production engineering practice and incorporate it in the planning software to free the planner for concentration on more complex tasks.

The paper by Kilmartin and Hannam looks at technology after it has been implemented and uses a systems approach to discover why the machines are underutilized and how to improve the situation. The paper is important on two counts: it highlights the need to examine the working system and compare it with its design criteria; it shows the need for the use of a systems approach when designing, or in this case redesigning, a manufacturing system. The technology is based on NC machines and could be considered old but the lessons learnt from this paper are even more pertinent today, with the greater expenditure involved. The paper points out that once a decision has been made to install advanced equipment, few companies re-examine the decision they have made. Without an audit of the system there is no feedback as to whether it is achieving its objectives. In the case given in the paper the machines were underutilized. Using a systems approach the authors identify where problems existed and how the system could be changed to improve the utilization. This shows the importance of looking at the system as a whole and not just in parts.

3.1

Plant Layout in Practice

L. M. Nicol and R. H. Hollier

Objectives

The general objective of the research was to determine under what conditions and constraints layout planning decisions are made, and whether the constraints applied by standard methods of solution are relevant to practical applications.

The work was carried out by structural interview and personal inspection of 33 companies selected so as to represent a high recent involvement in layout planning in manufacturing operations. All industrial sectors occurring within the catchment area of the survey were included, but distribution and service activities were excluded. The selection of the sample was made by saturation coverage of companies in, or close to, a number of major industrial estates in Cheshire and Clwyd to the south-west of Manchester.

Characteristics of the Sample

Only three companies were locally based with more than half the sample owned by multinational or UK groups in *The Times* 'Top 1000'. The average age of companies on their present sites was 17 years; 66 per cent had existed for less than 15 years compared with a national average of about 15 per cent.[1] Two-thirds were involved in engineering, including components and vehicles. Manufacturing strategy employed included product layout, process layout, fixed position assembly and group cell techniques (Group Technology in its wider context was not involved). The average floor area

---

L. M. Nicol and R. H. Hollier are in the Department of Management Sciences, UMIST, Manchester.
Source: L. M. Nicol and R. H. Hollier, 'Plant Layout in Practice', from *Material Flow*, 1983, 1, pp. 177–88.

was 271,000 sq ft and the smallest firm occupied 10,000 sq ft, compared with a national average of 2500 sq ft for manufacturing companies.

Stability of the Layout

An attempt was made to measure the rate of change of layout experienced by the respondents. It was felt to be unreasonable to consider every change of manufacturing route, handling method or individual plant item as a measure of rate of change, since in general these are accommodated without significant effect on the other flows or processes. The definition of the effective lifetime of a layout was taken as the elapsed time from installation until action is taken to replace or reposition at least one-third of all key manufacturing operations, or until at least one-third of the products are replaced by new models not compatible in terms of handling or processing with their predecessors. This subjective definition was generally accepted by the majority of those interviewed.

All companies visited were asked to define the number of such major layout changes in the previous 10 years. One firm was omitted from the analysis, a chemical company which makes major new plant installations at least every six months, but frequently retains them for periods of 5 to 20 years. It was not felt that either period gave a fair indication of the rate of change of the layout. An analysis is shown in table 1.

The trend to increasing stability with increasing age and size is to be expected and little significance can be read into the absolute value of the figures quoted below. More significant is the fact that nearly half the companies surveyed (42 per cent) had an average layout stability of two years or less. The mean of all firms was just over three years and was shorter for the engineering companies. Although many of the engineering firms were smaller than average, there were no significant differences in the lists below.

The prime conclusion from this evidence is that radical layout changes occur frequently and that management should therefore take this into account in their forward planning.

TABLE 1 LAYOUT LIFE COMPARED WITH SECTOR, AGE AND SIZE

Sector	Average layout life (yr)
22 Engineering	2.6
10 Other	4.4
All 32 companies	3.2

Age	Sample size	Average life (yr)	Size (K sq ft)	Sample size	Average life (yr)
Pre 1966	11	5.1	Over 400	5	6.6
1966–76	13	3.1	100–400	9	3.4
1976–81	8	2.0	50–100	10	3.1
			Under 50	8	1.9

Plant Layout in Practice

Layout Problems

After discussion of materials handling methods and flows all companies admitted to problems. These have been classified as shown in table 2. Table 2 compares the causes of major and minor problems. For comparison the total frequency in the sample having the same cause is quoted where possible. This cannot, of course, be done for the planning and policies area, nor without considerable study in depth can the effects of technological developments be judged. Several companies specifically refused to discuss research programmes while others had clearly accommodated significant changes in processes and materials. It was not possible to judge who had failed to make such adjustments nor who had done so without leaving signs for the non-technical observer.

Major Problems

The causes of the major problems are now discussed.

TABLE 2 COMPARISON OF CAUSES OF MAJOR AND MINOR PROBLEMS

Cause of layout problem	Frequency	Number of companies with major layout problems	Companies affected with minor layout problems
Buildings			
Obsolete buildings	7	4	2
Split site	2	2	—
Unsuitable buildings by decision	4	4	—
Road access	8	1	1
Planning and policies			
Group or Head Office decisions	N/A	5	4
Local decisions	N/A	5	2
Equipment purchases	N/A	—	3
Technology and market			
Product range	14	5	2
Technology	N/A	2	—
Volume			
Expansion	9	1	3
Recession	6	2	4
Other			
Management style	N/A	—	1
Total causes		31	22
Total companies		16	15

Note: Two companies had only trivial problems

Buildings and Site Problems

In four instances the buildings were obsolete and unsuitable for the production processes being carried out. Naturally this occurred only with firms which had been established some time (all were over 15 years old), but in only four out of sixteen in this age group was it a major problem. In two other instances the age of the site and buildings gave some concern, but for the other ten long-established firms this was not a restraining factor.

Two companies had been forced, through growth, to operate on two separate sites. In both there was an uneasy relationship between principal and satellite sites. The underlying cause of this problem was the expansion of their businesses which required the acquisition of additional premises. Both were on modern industrial estates with adjacent vacant plots, so it was disappointing that they were unable to make arrangements with the developers for contiguous extensions.

Resulting from decisions of management, four companies had occupied premises which were unsuitable in significant respects for their purposes. Of these, one had made a recent decision to occupy an existing factory in preference to commissioning a new building. This was clearly a sound short-term financial judgement, but the initial advantage may be negated when proposals for investment in alterations and mechanical handling are considered later. Another had on two occasions (initial acquisition and extension) for reasons of expediency made decisions which conflicted with its real needs. The clear heights of the advance factory and its extension were too low for some of the plant installed and layout compromises had to be made. Justification for the decisions was that if the opportunity had not been taken quickly the work would have returned to the parent company in the Midlands or have been subcontracted elsewhere. This approach had since been used for the layout of a second extension. In the other two cases, the growth of the firms had outstripped the ability of the premises to accommodate them. One occupied a long narrow factory to assemble machines which took up half the width. This created a bottleneck in the central gangway. Expansion space was created by a further extension and load-bearing wall and creating another bottleneck. The other had accommodated production, development and welfare premises in one block and had now found that the welfare and laboratory accommodation which was built to a different specification was obstructing the growth of production facilities as well as creating a safety hazard at times.

On no fewer than eight occasions it was found that access for goods vechicles to loading or unloading points restrained the ability to make the best use of space. Although this had a major impact on layout in only one instance, it is an indictment of estate developers that this should be so.

Layout Planning Methods and Policies

The standard of professionalism of management interviewed was high. This was not surprising for a group consisting largely of subsidiaries of national or international companies. Because the respondents varied from Managing

Plant Layout in Practice

Director to Engineering/Works/Plant Manager, a fair comparison of individuals was not possible. It was disappointing to note that only four individuals had heard of Muther's Systematic Layout Planning[2] or any other formal approach. All, however, had a clear understanding of the difference between product and process layouts and the concept of a job shop. About three-quarters of the managers knew about Group Technology,[3] although only six had made a conscious decision about its use in their layouts. In five instances company policy decisions generally made at a higher level than the most senior local manager had adversely affected the layout in a major way. Two companies were referred to in the previous section. Group policy had resulted in the acquisition of buildings which were not properly suited to their needs. In addition, one of these was forced by delivery deadlines on a new product range to install additional equipment in the easiest, not the best location. It then had a considerable amount of backtracking and cross-flow of work. Another was forced to accommodate additional finished goods storage within a year of full production start-up and to alter much of their use of space as a result. A fourth transferred to new premises on the promise of a 100 per cent increase in output and was faced with a greater than 50 per cent drop. The failure of markets and marketing to meet these forecasts invalidated many of the layout decisions. Although the fifth company's problem with premises was exaggerated by its initial conservative attitude to expansion, the policy decision to combine production and other facilities in one building appears to have been the real cause.

In five instances local planning policies gave rise to major problems. One committed considerable resources to specialized containers to be drawn on a floor-mounted railway. After installation it was discovered that the product produced loose fibres and fragments which blocked the track, the drive mechanism and the trailers. This was an avoidable local error. Another had a progressive policy about plant modernization and replacement but treated each case individually. This was probably correct from the point of view of financial control, but it was also used to restrict production management's layout planning. No consideration was given to the location of subsequent anticipated, but unapproved machines when each new item of plant was received and installed. Two others had solvable problems whose existence was due almost entirely to not having adapted their layouts to changes in product. In both cases it was necessary to re-allocate certain machines and to dedicate them to the production of what had become the major volume product. The fifth had produced a layout with inherent housekeeping and environmental problems. Although it could be argued that the amount of cross-flow of work was difficult to control, its implementation could certainly have been improved.

Technology and Market Developments

One aspect of flexibility is the ability to accommodate major extensions to the product range in size or materials. Although many companies had to overcome such challenges it is significant that only five were left with problems which they associated with their new product ranges. Of these companies, three have been referred to earlier as having defective local planning or policies and occupied premises which were partially or wholly obsolete. One company had found that the length of some of its new products, which was comparable to stanchion spacing, and the bulkiness of others (motorcar chassis assemblies), made them difficult to manoeuvre in the restricted space available.

Two other companies were overtaken by technological developments. One, in textiles, lost part of its process to foreign suppliers, and another found that new ranges of plastics were not suitable for the machinery and methods already installed.

Recession or Expansion

All companies had been affected to some degree by the economic recession which began to take effect fully in 1979. Apart from one company which had suffered some redundancies at its previous location but which was in the process of consolidating and expanding its new labour force, only three companies had neither declared redundancies nor allowed their personnel to decline in numbers in the preceding four or five years. They included a manufacturer of mechanical parts for construction vehicles who was protected by parent company policy and by exports. Part of the price of this protection was the speed of response to new orders which led to the layout problems discussed earlier. Also in the growth sector were a small independent company with a large share of a specialized market for food-processing machinery, and another which had obtained a share of a long-term (15-year) programme of collaboration with a European consortium. Neither had generated major layout problems as a result of their expansion.

Many other companies had absorbed cycles of decline and expansion. In the two significant cases the companies had run out of space during their recent growth and had been forced over a second site. One had been trapped by the combination of expansionist management policies and recession among its customers into a major rundown of production. Another appeared to have been in the wrong market and in spite of switching several times in order to save jobs had also reduced its staff by more than 50 per cent. A third, with expansion in some markets, hit the recession in specialist motorcars and this contributed substantially to its difficulties.

Summary of Major Layout Problems

Although no single cause accounted for more than five (or about 15 per cent) of the occasions on which major layout problems resulted, the most significant can be ranked as follows:

- Group or Head Office planning or policy decisions;
- local planning or policy decisions;
- extension of product range to meet market needs;
- obsolete buildings;

Plant Layout in Practice

- unsuitable buildings not obsolete;
- split site;
- technology changes;
- recession;
- expansion;
- road access.

From this analysis of the characteristics of these 16 companies it can be seen that those with major layout problems were slightly less likely to be old, very large or very small and slightly more likely to be about 10 years old and about 100,000 sq ft in area.

Minor Problems

The underlying causes of minor problems with the layout were not so easy to identify as the major problems. Care had to be taken to ensure that the layout and associated activities were not being used as scapegoats or symptoms of difficulties elsewhere in the organization.

From this analysis of the major and minor problems the following conclusions can be drawn:

(1) All companies who had been deeply affected by the recession showed signs of this in the quality of their layout. In contrast, less than half of those who had undertaken expansions into new products had inadequate layout as a result. This may well be because expansion tends to be managed and planned, whereas recession is often not recognized until it has happened. It is nevertheless disappointing that so many had problems arising out of their expansion programmes.

(2) Half of those who had increased their product ranges by extension of size, capacity or variety, excluding those who expanded into new products, had generated layout problems by so doing. In most cases there were major problems.

(3) Eight companies had difficulty with access, but in only two cases did this affect the layout.

(4) Seven companies were located in obsolete buildings (about 20 per cent) and almost all were paying a price for this in terms of layout effectiveness.

General Operating Characteristics

Influences on the Layout Plan

The use of the term 'influence' was described in the interview as an incidental factor which affected the layout decision but was not a major objective or dominating criterion. Examples of the extent of influence come from two mass production companies. For one company, the building was a shell designed round the processing and handling equipment which therefore dominated the layout design. For the other, although the plant and equipment influenced the layout, the development of a minimum materials handling operation was paramount and the plant was located after handling systems had been decided. These influences are not exclusive and are duplicated in some cases:

External
- Architect, consulting engineer   2
- Parent company   11
- Design of process equipment   6
- Systematic layout planning   1

Company Policy
- Prejudice or directors' view   3
- Buildings and previous layout   3
- R&D direction   2
- Cash limits   2

Company Management
- Organization structure   1
- Methods/quality   2
- Sales function   2
- Consensus of staff   2

Objectives

None of the respondents had based its layout planning on a specific and quantified measure of any kind. Those who used minimum handling as an objective thought about it in purely qualitative terms, usually dominated by the concept of 'flow'. This applied whether or not there was a conventional product flow line. With few exceptions one or more objectives were clearly understood and brought forward in answer to the appropriate question. Even those who had to stop to consider were quite clear in their minds as to their layout objectives. Respondents were urged to quote objectives relevant to their own particular businesses and not to advance general theories which they had learnt from textbooks, or which they felt should apply in a perfect operation. The result is again a wide diversity of view which is summarized in table 3.

Flexibility

The amount of flexibility demanded from a layout is never easy to define. It is frequently possible to increase total production or the volume of a single product or group of products by the acquisition of a relatively small amount of plant or equipment. If this is done then the layout is in fact changed and it cannot be said to have been truly flexible enough to cope with the altered business situation. However, this is felt to be an unrealistic restraint. Pro-

Plant Layout in Practice

TABLE 3 LAYOUT OBJECTIVES USED BY RESPONDENTS

Factors	Occurrences	Group totals
Plant and handling		30
Flow	13	
Ease of handling	6	
Minimum materials handling cost	1	
Quality of handling	1	
Plant availability/utilization	2	
Space utilization	7	
Manufacturing		19
Capacity	1	
Productivity	6	
Quality of production	3	
Production cost	2	
Minimum WIP	1	
Ease of supervision	5	
Minimum indirects	1	
Personnel		5
Safety	4	
Appearance	1	
Finance		Nil
General		13
Flexibility	3	
Expansion	2	
Practical	1	
Minimum change	1	
Speed of Installation	2	
Process layout	1	
Cell layout	1	
Work station layout	1	
Line balance	1	

vided that only minor rearrangement of local work-stations or the introduction of low-cost standard equipment is necessary, it is fair to say that the original layout had sufficient flexibility for its business needs.

However, if major plant purchases are required, total departmental relayouts are necessary or significant equipment moves between departments have to be undertaken, then it is postulated that the original layout did not have sufficient flexibility.

With these conditions in mind, all respondents were asked to specify, based on recent production experience, what amount of flexibility in output they were expected to be able to achieve. Specifically they were asked if the volume of product A doubled and that of product B halved would they still be able to meet production requirements. Similarly, if the number of products in the range doubled or halved, could production requirements be met. Thus, the answer to the flexibility question was stated in terms of a factor to be applied over the range, but not to imply a total volume expansion or contraction. The results are set out in table 4.

TABLE 4 FLEXIBILITY FACTORS OF THE RESPONDENTS

Flexibility factor	No. of companies
Greater than ×2	18
Approx. ×1.5	8
Less than ×1.1	7
Total	33

Number of Departments

There is often no definitive count of the number of departments in a factory. It is a subjective decision as to whether two physically similar or adjacent units performing slightly different functions or operations should be regarded as one department or two. It is therefore only possible to assess a range of complexity. This was done based on factory layout plans, descriptions of the operations and conducted tours of the plant.

A further attempt was made to assess the effective number of departments assuming relationship diagrams were to be drawn. The following assumptions were made:

(1) Short, continuous manufacturing processes in one building were treated as one department, even if several processes were involved (e.g. assemble, test and pack).
(2) Compatible service or subsidiary operations were combined if they were currently adjacent, has some commonality of staff or supervision and clearly had a similar or identical relationship with other processes (e.g. purchasing and production control in a general office or quality control, inspection and test).

The analysis of the number of departments in the sample companies is given in table 5.

A number of significant observations can be made from this analysis:

(1) Even though the size of the companies concerned placed them well above average for UK manufacturing units, the technical complexity of the departmental relationships from the point of view of layout planning was relatively low. Almost all companies had 15 or fewer effectively different departments. It should be noted that this statement assumes that the departmental organization structure and relationships apply homogeneously throughout each department. There were undoubtedly sections within departments which had anomalous relationships with other sections in another or a number of other departments. However, it should be noted

Plant Layout in Practice

TABLE 5 NUMBER OF DEPARTMENTS IN COMPANIES STUDIED

	\multicolumn{6}{c}{Number of companies}
	Total	0–10 depts	11–15 depts	16–20 depts	21–40 depts	Over 40 depts
All departments included						
Total sample	32	6	11	10	3	2
Companies with major problems	16	0	8	5	2	1
Others	16	6	3	5	1	1
Production depts only						
Total sample	32	19	8	3	2	1
Companies with major problems	16	9	4	2	1	0
Others	16	10	4	1	1	1
Effective number of depts for planning purposes						
Total sample	32	24	8	0	1	0
Companies with major problems	16	9	7	0	0	0
Others	16	15	1	0	1	0

Note: One company omitted.

that if Burbidge's system of Production Flow Analysis[3] is applied, it would generally result in re-allocating the individual section to an existing department where it would be more appropriate, rather than creating additional departments which would complicate the flow relationships. It is certain that the responsible managers interviewed did not conceive their layout problems to embrace a relationship matrix of greater dimension than about $n = 15$.

(2) A significantly higher proportion of those companies which were classified as having major layout problems had more than ten significant departments for planning purposes. As the reasons for their major layout problems were more frequently connected with the buildings and with company policies than with the complexity of the manufacturing operation, it is not believed that this is a causal relationship. It is more likely that the external constraints which produced the problems with layout also restricted management's ability so to structure its organization as to reduce the complexity of the department relationships.

(3) There was only one unit in which n was greater than 15. This company was the largest in the sample producing three major products, one on a very slow moving line and the other two in fixed position assemblies. There was a large number of feeder departments generally in string or star formations, some jointly feeding all the assembly lines and some specifically feeding one or other of the lines. Each of the departments utilized a significant amount of plant and space requiring specialized operators and supervision. In fact, of the 23 work centres, the effective planning decisions were restricted to 10 groups. From a practical point of view the principal problems which the managers had to overcome were all at the points at which the material moved between these 10 groups.

Comparison with Previous Studies

Although minimization of materials handling cost dominates the thinking of theoretical layout analysts, there have been few studies of actual costs and their relationship to other costs incurred by industry. Williams[4] and Carrie[5] have both reported small studies. A rigorous examination was carried out by the Department of Industry[6] which included surveys and case-studies of 30 companies, and advice on how to carry out cost method audits. During the present research it was not possible to obtain sufficient financial information to repeat this work, but one of the major components of materials handling was examined in some detail.

All respondents specified the number of personnel who were employed full time on handling, storage or transport duties and estimated the number and commitment of those who included handling as part of their task (e.g. supervisors and operators), and this was compared with the total number of factory personnel. The distribution of responses is shown in figure 1, with the comparable chart from the Department of Industry report[6] superimposed for comparison. As can be seen, the apparent cost in the present survey is slightly less than was reported in 1976, but is clearly of approximately the same magnitude.

In spite of the fact that these costs amount to about 12 per cent of total works labour cost, and therefore over 10 per cent of the works payroll, no company was aware of either percentage until questioned. In fact, there was in some cases an exaggerated degree of complacency. One company reported: 'Materials handling costs must be very small because the total overhead burden is only 9 per cent.' In this case a ratio of 5.5 per cent of handling to total works labour cost was calculated. Even this was hard to believe as the handling methods left considerable room for improvement.

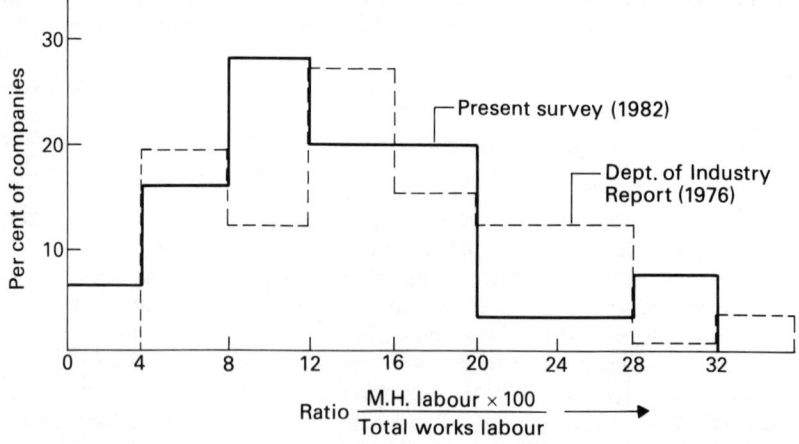

Figure 1   Frequency distribution of materials handling cost

Plant Layout in Practice

The impression gained on the factory tour was that this company was no better than the average of those visited.

Five principal causes of high costs were identified in the Department of Industry report.[6] They are discussed below:

Lack of Awareness of Costs

This survey absolutely confirms the conclusion that firms are unaware of their materials handling costs.

Lack of a Site Development Plan

While this was true for many companies, it was not a valid general criticism. All the largest companies had detailed and comprehensive plans. In total, 13 out of 33 (39 per cent) had clear plans involving more than an outline sketch of possible extensions superimposed on the existing layout. In spite of this, three of the thirteen still had major layout problems. The other ten perhaps owe their relative success to the planning which had been undertaken. It should, however, be noted that in several cases the plans which were inevitably based on projected space expansion were clearly obsolete as considerable growth had been achieved by reducing the size of product or plant. In only three cases did the development plan meet the criteria which it is believed the Department of Industry investigators envisaged.

Organizational Weakness

No information was collected on the identity of staff responsible for materials handling. A wide diversity was apparent in responsibility for plant layout with considerable confusion existing. For instance, on 11 occasions the layout was influenced by the parent company, yet in only one of these did the parent take full responsibility. Generally, the local manager was held responsible for operating a system which he was often told to implement. On only three occasions was the layout delegated to a planner who did not have the status of membership of the local executive board or management team. On only one occasion was the layout and handling problem perceived as a major duty of a senior manager. Generally it was an additional task to many others and was handled personally in times of crisis or by working late.

Lack of Systems Approach to Materials Handling

Most of the companies visited used an *ad hoc* approach to layout and materials handling. There was evidence of a considerable amount of effort and professionalism at the stage of implementation and in a few cases with evaluation, solution and design of layouts. None of the companies visited had a relationship diagram and those that had prepared flow charts had done so on the basis of operational processes rather than handling requirements. The lack of awareness of costs also meant that no company had a detailed materials handling cost matrix.

This practical approach resulted in some of the problems mentioned not being exposed until after implementation.

Lack of Finance

As with the Department of Industry study,[6] lack of funds was frequently assumed to be a constraint but less often proved to be so. Lack of financial planning caused major problems for one company, but its overall lack of profitability, affecting all those in recession, did not directly contribute to excessive handling costs.

Conclusions

(1) No company was directly aware of its materials handling costs.
(2) The median rate of materials handling labour cost to total works labour costs was 0.12.
(3) Nearly half the companies had encountered major problems with their layouts.
(4) The life-span of the average plant layout was about three years and nearly half of the layouts could be expected to be radically altered within two years.
(5) Companies that had been affected by the recession generally had problems with their layout and handling.
(6) Companies that had expanded were unlikely to have major problems with their layouts.
(7) Companies that had increased the number of products in their range were more likely to have problems than those that had expanded in volume or had introduced new ranges.
(8) More than half the companies contributed directly to their layout problems by policy decisions made either locally or at Group or Head Office, and about a third of the companies had major problems as a result.
(9) Most of those occupying old or obsolete buildings had layout or handling problems.
(10) Building factors were more likely to create major problems, whereas volume factors were more likely to create minor problems.
(11) There was no general consensus about layout objectives. The only recurring themes were flow (about half of the companies) and space utilization and productivity (less than one quarter each). The way in which these objectives were treated was also inconsistent and frequently unsystematic.
(12) While many layouts were designed for a predetermined fixed volume level which could be only marginally exceeded, in over half the cases, particularly those nearer to the job shop operating system, companies had experienced, or currently anticipated, volume changes in individual products or groups of products by a factor of two or more.

Plant Layout in Practice

(13) Most companies used a variety of handling systems as appropriate or available with consequent effects on the cost-distance relationship. In addition, several had taken localized action on handling between adjacent departments, effectively creating a minimum handling cost relationship.

(14) Practical expediency was always allowed to over-ride predetermined relationship constraints, resulting in traffic routes being established through departments with variable numbers of direct adjacencies being created, ranging from one to eight.

(15) The number of departments for which planning decisions on a flow or relationship basis had to be made individually was never greater than 15.

References

1. *Regional Statistics* (London: Central Statistical Office. HMSO, 1980).
2. R. Muther, *Systematic Layout Planning* (Maidenhead: McGraw-Hill, 1961).
3. J. L. Burbidge, *The Introduction of Group Technology* (London: Heinemann, 1975).
4. J. M. Williams, 'Material Handling: Special Report', *Industrial Management*, April 1981.
5. A. S. Carrie, *Estimation of Handling Cost Reductions due to Layout Changes: Proceedings of 19th MTDR Conference, London*, 1978.
6. Department of Industry, *Committee for Materials Handling: Material Handling Costs: A New Look at Manufacture* (London: HMSO, 1976).

3.2

Capacity Planning System

J. Black

Introduction

Westland Helicopters, Yeovil, is investing about £9 million over the next five years in its gear shop in an attempt to increase capacity and reduce lead times, thus leading to better delivery performance and increased competitivity.

However, there were two problems to be solved first before the investment plan could begin. One was to find out exactly what plant needed to be bought to meet future demand and the other was to gain better control over production.

As a consequence, Westland has spent over a year in developing its own computerized finite capacity loading system in an attempt to solve these two problems. The result is a system comprising over one million lines of COBOL code that can now be run either nightly or fortnightly.

The gear shop at Westland Helicopters manufactures high-quality gears for the Westland Lynx and Sea King and for the Aerospatiale Gazelle and Super Puma helicopters. Other products are rotor-blade pins for the Boeing Vertol CH47D Chinook helicopter and gears of up to 2 m diameter for rock crushing machinery and cranes.

The gear shop contains 113 cutting machines between 5 and 45 years old. There is a heat treatment facility and limited crack detection and anodic facilities, but most operations requiring this treatment are performed in a separate department or even subcontracted. There are currently 141 direct workers who operate these machines on a two-shift system. One group of machines is manned on three shifts.

J. Black, at the time of writing, was a manufacturing systems engineer at Westland Helicopters, Yeovil, Somerset, England.

Source: J. Black, 'Developing Your Own Capacity Planning System', from *The Production Engineer*, March 1984.

Capacity Planning System

The lead time on the manufacturing of a gear is between 6 and 18 months depending on the gear. Gears are issued to the shop in batches of between 1 and 30 gears, with an average batch size of 17, and there are generally around 1500 live batches in the shop. This represents over 200 distinct part numbers. Finally, there are between 20 and 100 operations to be completed on each gear, depending on the gear; up to half of these can be inspection operations.

Discounting the operations performed outside the department and taking the mix of work into account, there can be around 20,000 operations outstanding in the shop. Most machining operations can be performed on a variety of different machines. In some cases, this is as many as five similar machines.

There is already a computerized system in the gearshop and throughout Westland for tracking and recording each job and each man. This Open Shop Order System (oso) will show the current operation, location and quantity of the batch, the operations outstanding and, if the job is delayed, the reason.

A Time and Attendance System (T&A) is used for real-time monitoring of job costs. Operators clock on to a job on the system and also record their sickness and holidays on it.

An MRP program is run fortnightly which, based on the required date of each finished gear, backstages seven days per cutting operation to produce a theoretical start date for each operation. This takes no account of capacity.

There is also a manual list that is used to progress jobs in the shop. This list is inevitably in conflict with the computer-based list and is based on experience and feel for the jobs.

The last part in the jigsaw is the fact that the gearshop output is about one year in arrears, although no one knows the exact figure. This leads to outside customers' orders being delayed to ensure that delivery to Westland's own production line is on target.

Having examined the environment and the requirements, Westland looked at the commercially available systems. In all, 94 systems were examined ranging from IBM's CAPOSS-E to tiny systems running on microcomputers. From a shortlist of 12, only one came close and after visits and detailed examination, not even this one was suitable. The main deficiencies of these systems were:

- alternative machines for operations were not available;
- some systems were not fast enough to cope with 20 to 100 thousand operations within two hours processing time (which Westland already used).
- some systems could not run on an IBM mainframe;
- the suppliers of some systems were inexperienced;
- many systems did not load to finite capacity.

Most suppliers offered to modify their systems to accommodate these extra requirements but there was no guarantee of their ability to achieve this. Also by the time the extra work had been done, the cost of the systems was rising past £100,000. This would be in addition to any work necessary to join the system to the existing in-house systems.

It had been hoped that an outside package would provide 80 per cent of the system at 20 per cent of the cost of developing Westland's own. In the end it appeared that a package would provide 50 per cent of the system at 200 per cent of the cost. Therefore, Westland decided to write its own system.

The system rests on a foundation of five major input sources of information, which are:

- the Machine File, which contains every machine to be loaded, whether it is available or broken down and, if the latter, the earliest date it can be loaded
- the Manning File, which holds every direct worker and inspector which is to be loaded, whether they are on holiday over the next fortnight, and which section of machines they work on.

These two together form the basis for the Capacity File.

- the OSO File. This holds a record for every batch from which are selected all the batches passing through the gearshop
- the Routing File. This is accessed to determine which machine, and which alternative machines if available, can be loaded to perform an operation
- the Time and Attendance System. This is interrogated to determine whether any job has started and if so how much time has been spent on it to date.

These three files, taken together, form the Load File. All except the Routing File are updated in real time. The Routing File is updated twice weekly. The capacity planning system takes new versions of all of the files each night and therefore includes any changes to the availability or number of machines or men, the jobs available, the quantity and position and the time spent on each job. Except for the Machine File, all the files existed before the introduction of the capacity planning system, as did the responsibility for their maintenance. Therefore the additional work involved in keeping the data accurate for the new system is low.

However, even though the responsibility is known, the accuracy is not always 100 per cent. The capacity planning system will highlight the inaccuracy and make more people aware of it even though the older systems always required accurate data. In other words, the new system is not imposing any new requirements for data accuracy.

Scratch

Once the files are acceptably accurate, the system can run in two modes: fortnightly and nightly. Fortnightly the system starts from scratch and loads all the work available to the predicted capacity available. In the gearshop

Capacity Planning System

the work can stretch up to two years into the future. Nightly the system loads only the first 10 per cent or so of the work in order to update the work-to lists and other daily expediting lists. The system runs at around 4am, in time to produce the lists for 7.30am. However, if the lists are not available then, the previous day's list can be used because each list displays the work for the next three working days.

The system starts by preparing the work-load data from the OSO and T&A systems. Having determined the operations and outstanding times for jobs which are available it reads the Routing File (in the fortnightly mode) to pick up which machines can do the job. It also finds the set and run time for the job from the Routing File. If no times are available it consults an extensive list of defaults supplied by the cost engineers. Batches of the same part number and operation which will be processed within a few days of each other are 'bulked' together.

The next stage is to optimize the machine usage. Given a set of jobs for the same group of machines, some jobs will be able to go on any of the machines whilst others may go only on one or two of them. In order to maximize utilization of machines, a routine in the system makes a choice of which machine to use for each job by directing those with many alternatives away from the machines that will be wanted by those jobs with few alternatives (see figure 1). The routine is only simulating what the shop supervision would do on an *ad hoc* basis.

Once the machine has been selected, the capacity database is created from the Machine and Manning Files. Breakdowns and holidays are accounted for and coverage and efficiency factors are also used to determine how much time is available on each machine and man for each day for the next few years. Then, each operation is loaded to a machine and a man, taking

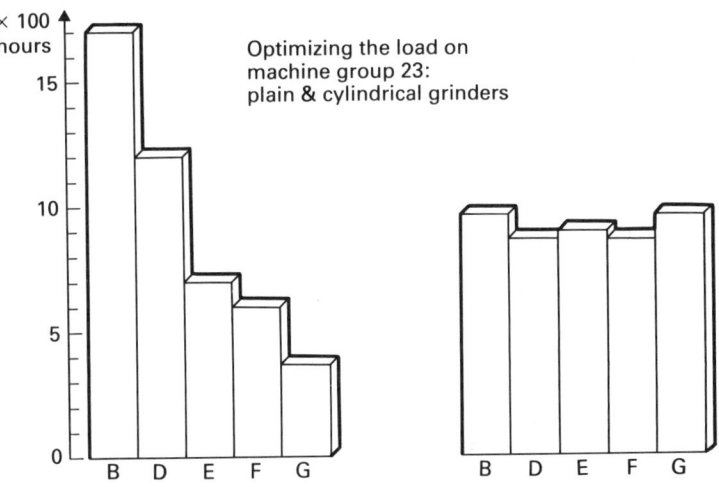

Figure 1 The effect of the system's routine for allocating loads to alternative machines compared with using only the first-choice machines

into account all the requirements set out above. The system assumes any man in a section can work any machine, that a job is to be completed before another can be started, that a transit time is needed and that the jobs are processed in order of descending required lead time compression.

The system produces around 20 types of report. A forward load report for example shows the hours work that has been loaded by the system to finite capacity and the hours work that is available, and required to be done in each week to infinite capacity. A graph of deviation from required delivery date against number of batches can also be produced (see figure 2). The desired shape is a tall thin spike situated on the origin. A similar graph is also printed of the change in delivery prediction from that of two weeks ago. This illustrates the speed of movement of the deliveries – whether the shop is slipping or advancing. These graphs are a one-sheet view of the whole manufacturing shop and form a clear picture for the directors downwards of the state of the shop.

A simulation system has also been written which works in exactly the same way using most of the same programs. In addition, there is the facility to alter the machines, the men, the parameters and the Routing File inputs to the system. For example, the user can propose to buy certain machines, remove others, add men to work them and maybe route some high-cost jobs to these machines. The system will amend the relevant files and process the

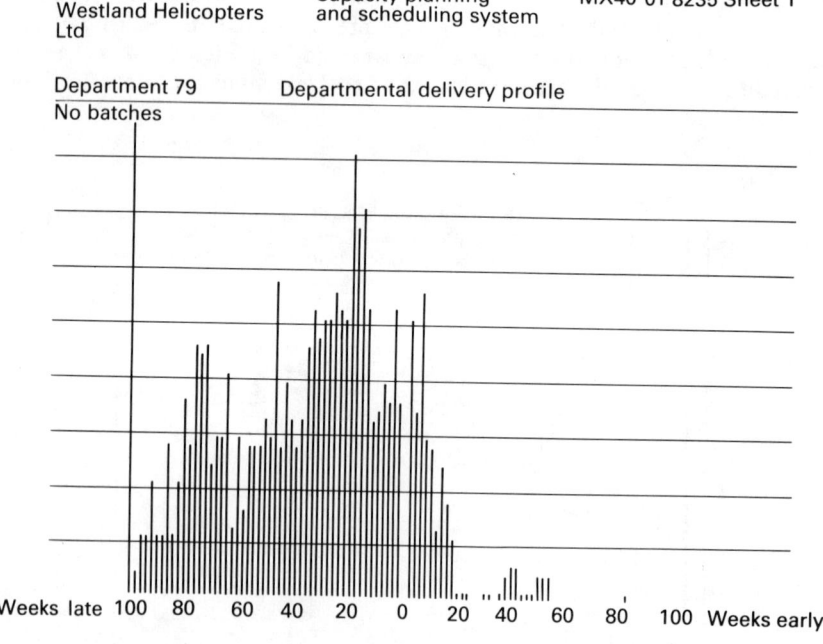

Figure 2   A typical graph report showing required delivery date plotted against the number of batches

Capacity Planning System

workload. The reports produced can then be compared to those of the last live run to determine what effect the proposals will have.

This data is usually required for cost justifying new machines, but traditionally takes months to collect, is generally based on hypothesis and experience and never contemplates any knock-on effect to other machines. The new system will make a big change to the method of choosing and justifying machines and should save many hours of clerical work.

The main departments and people who discussed the development of the system included shop supervision, production engineering, production control, production systems control, inspection and cost control. Their experience of computer systems varied from nil to very conversant. Problems arose sometimes because of some people who had put their own system in 15 years before and others who had bought a home computer: both had different and inaccurate views of the method of systems design prevailing at Westland.

However, even though it was often tedious and slow to get these 20 or 30 people to agree to what frequently seemed trivial matters, it paid off in the long run. By having everyone on board from the beginning, implementation and acceptance were made much easier. All users were involved right from the start to avoid any fear of a system that was not fully understood.

All the users described above were keen to participate because of the outputs that they would get. These fall into four categories:

- daily work-to lists for production control and shop supervision,
- load graphs against machines, sections and the department for production control and production engineering,
- predictions of batch finish dates for progress, and predictions of batch positions for production engineering,
- and all the loads and predictions from the modelling system for production control and production engineering.

The reports also point the user towards exception reporting. They are to highlight jobs that haven't moved according to plan, so that instead of progressing every job, only those jobs that actually require effort are reported. This may seem obvious, but in a factory where the exception philosophy is not present, this system seems a good opportunity to introduce it.

The layouts of the reports and screens were discussed in theory and with mock-ups before the programs were written. However, many had to be amended once the users had started testing the system. They could not grasp enough detail from mock-ups and had to have the paper in their hands in order to assess it properly.

When the system was performing all that was required, it was presented to the users. This meeting was held six months after the system specification had been agreed and a year from the start of the whole project. In that time many ideas had been proposed and some discarded but the system performed as the specification had described. However after three hours' discussion a list of around a dozen amendments was established; these were necessary before the system was acceptable.

Within three weeks the new system was ready for their perusal: nearly all the major programs had been changed slightly. This time the system was agreed to be acceptable but could still not be implemented because of the problem of incorrect data.

A lot of effort went into preparing the base data at the same time as the system was being written. The new information required was the exact machine, and any alternatives, that each operation could be performed on. A set of programs was written that would list all the operations requiring information. These lists were sent to the shopfloor where the shop supervision inserted the letter codes of the machines against each operation. In the gear shop about 7000 operations were updated over a period of four or five months. Each month the supervision's lists were removed for updating a master file, and new shortened lists sent back. Unfortunately the information generated was not complete. The progress in clearing up the base data followed a classic pareto curve: the last 5 per cent taking four or five weeks.

Until people are using the system live, they will not appreciate the effect of data inaccuracies. But they will not use the system until it is accurate.

In order to accept the system, the users attempted to compare its results with those of existing systems. The work-to lists seemed to tie up well with the first records on the old sequence tab system produced by oso. The total workload on the shop agreed with the existing figures. The load on the machines was not available anywhere else but was felt to be right. On the whole the content did not conflict with any other pre-existing system. The presentation of the information was also felt to be acceptable, once it had been extensively modified following the first presentation.

There have been some major spin-offs from a system that was originally intended for capacity planning and scheduling. First, the Routing File underwent an extensive and thorough purge. Many years of inconsistencies required a lot of work to correct.

Secondly, in order to clear up the Routing File, new standards were drawn up, machine groups rationalized and many operations previously brushed under the carpet had to be allocated a specific machine group.

Thirdly, a centralized Machine File was created. This can now list all the machines on site and can be interrogated live or by keyword. There was neither the need nor the inclination to have such a file before this system was developed.

Fourthly, with a centralized Machine File available, on-line information on machine breakdowns and their duration is now visible company wide. With a small degree of extra work, the live machine database and the on-line breakdown facility could be extended to provide extensive information on such subjects as speeds and feeds, breakdown causes and so on.

Fifthly, production engineers now use the system to determine when work is going to be at certain machines so as to order new tooling for delivery at that time. This should reduce the incidence of new jobs not being worked on due to lack of tools.

Although the system has been running for less than a year, there are already some lessons which can be learnt. Computer systems have been introduced to manufacturing areas before, but this was one of the first in this company that was sought by all levels of user. Involving a large number of users was no real problem, except when trying to organize meetings and get agreement on necessary preliminary points.

3.3

Decision-making in Operations Management

R. Wild

An operating system utilizes resources to convert inputs into outputs in the form of goods or services. Conventionally, operations management is defined as the task of designing, establishing, planning, running, controlling, maintaining and improving such systems. As the output of such systems constitutes both goods and services this establishes operations management as a field of activity somewhat broader than production (or manufacturing) management which solely provides goods or artefacts. However the distinction between goods and services is unclear and the latter category is broad and heterogeneous. It may therefore be worthwhile to have a more detailed definition:

> *An operating system is a combination of resources combined for the purposes of manufacture, transport, supply and service.*[1]

These four functions are defined as below:

(1) *Manufacture*, where the main characteristic is that something is physically created, i.e. the output consists of goods which differ physically in form, content, etc, from those materials input to the system. (A change in *form* utility of input resources.)

(2) *Transport*, where the main characteristic is that someone or something is moved, i.e. the location of someone or something is changed. (A change in *place* utility of an input resource.)

(3) *Supply*, where the main characteristic is that the ownership of goods is changed. (A change in *possession* utility of an input resource.)

R. Wild is Head of the Departments of Engineering and Management Systems and Production Technology at Brunel University and senior member of staff at Henley Management Centre.
 Source: R. Wild, 'Decision-making in Operations Management', from *Management Decisions*, 1983, vol. 21, no. 1.

Decision-making in Operations Management

(4) *Service*, where the main characteristic is the treatment or accommodation of something or someone. (A change in *state* utility of an input resource.)

This identifies the principal components of the operating system as physical resources, e.g. materials, machines and labour. It suggests that the main activity of operations managers is the use of such resources to serve the function(s) of the system, i.e. to satisfy the system's customers, and also to achieve adequate resource utilization. Thus operations management can be seen as concerned with the design and planning, operation and control of systems for manufacture, transport, supply and service to satisfy customers' needs and achieve acceptable levels of resource utilization.

Operations management, then, is a central function within most organizations whether business, industrial, commercial, etc. It could be argued that those who manage operations, whatever their actual title, will be responsible for the management of the principal physical resources of the organization and the development of these resources in such ways as to ensure adequate utilization, and the acquisition or retention of sufficient customers. This view suggests that effectiveness in the management of operations is essential to the effectiveness of the organization, i.e. operations management is an area of fundamental importance, where effectiveness is a prerequisite to overall business effectiveness.

Operations Management Decision-making

The above comments aim to identify operations management as an area worthy of consideration, and also to suggest that some decisions of operations managers are of importance to those with decision-making responsibilities in other functions in the organization. In this article we shall consider the manner in which these decisions of operations managers are made. We shall consider this *operations management decision-making process* within the broader business context and, in particular, the relationships with decision-making in other functions and at a policy level in the business.

Paradoxically whilst much of what is written about operations management is concerned with a form of decision-making – solving of particular problems – relatively little attention has been given to the wider decision-making process. We define the operations management decision-making process at this level, as the formulation of overall strategies for operations, typically involving interrelated areas of responsibility with operations management, and the taking of decisions in those areas in the pursuit of these strategies, all within the broader business context.

Textbooks have in the past viewed operations management in terms of the occasional or repetitive solving of specific problems in areas such as scheduling, inventories, planning, control, etc. They have emphasized the analytical solution of such problems, and other approaches involving the manipulation of variables in the pursuit of some given objective function, e.g. duration, utilization, throughput, cost, etc.

Certainly the importance of taking such decisions in conjunction with those in other business functions (especially marketing) has been demonstrated, although specifically in connection with manufacturing management.[2-6] Deriving from this some authors have suggested approaches for manufacturing management policy-making.[7-11] However in so much as a body of knowledge exists relating specifically to the broad field of operations management it is still *largely* of a 'problem solving' nature. It might be argued that this body of knowledge is essentially theoretically oriented, that relatively little of such an approach is employed in practice, and that the role of the operations manager within the business is (or should be) something greater than the occasional solution of defined and specific problems with established procedures.

Our objective is to consider the manner in which the operations management decision-making process takes place within the context of business decision-making, and to suggest a simple framework for the further examination of this process. For simplicity we shall focus on one area of operations management, namely the management of capacity. This is chosen because of its importance and relevance in the management of all types of operating systems. Additionally it would seem to be a policy-related decision area,[11] and one in which traditional textbook type treatments tend to rely heavily upon quantitative problem-solving techniques. For illustration we shall refer to the brief (factual) case-study given in the Appendix, which illustrates many of the issues we wish to raise. It has the additional advantages of showing a 'change' situation, and one in which the role of the operations manager is readily identifiable.

Capacity Management Decisions

Basically, the objective of capacity management is to balance the level of operations with the level of demand. This involves the consideration of likely medium- to long-term demand patterns, to permit the determination of the capacity required to meet such demand, and the development of strategies for the deployment of resources, in particular for accommodating changes in the demand levels. Two basic capacity management strategies exist, namely:

(1) to provide for efficient adjustment or variation of system capacity, to match demand level changes;
(2) to eliminate or reduce the need for such adjustments in system capacity.

In more detail[1] the strategies may be seen to offer operations managers the following for use individually or in combination:

Strategy 1: provide for efficient adjustment of system capacity (e.g. through subcontracting, changes in make/buy balance, reducing material content, work-hour changes, work-force size changes, resource transfers, etc.)

Decision-making in Operations Management

Strategy 2: eliminate or reduce the need for adjustments in system capacity, through:
    (a) maintaining excess capacity, i.e. sufficient to meet all future demand;
    (b) reducing or smoothing the effect of demand-level fluctuations by:
        (i) fixing an upper-capacity limit, and beyond that expecting either loss of trade or customer queueing and reduced service;
        (ii) using output stocks to absorb demand level fluctuations.

A Case Example

The case (see Appendix) is a 'before and after' situation. The principal features of the 'before' situation may be summarized as follows:

- the importance of providing high customer service, to ensure market share retention and increase market penetration;
- the forecasting and 'anticipation' of future demand to the extent of creating imaginary customers, giving a situation in which the nature of future demand, i.e. the type of items required by future customers, is assumed to be known, even if the level of demand is not known for the same future period;
- a low resource utilization situation apparently established as the norm (at least during parts of the trade cycle) and apparently tolerated by TMD Ltd and the group, hence:
- the existence of excess capacity;
- the existence of output stocks of finished products;
- the existence of all the above as the conventional, i.e. customary, situation under an established factory manager.

The above can be seen as the use of capacity management strategy (2bii), with the suggestion that in times of increased demand the norm would be the use of strategy (2bi). This is an appropriate approach given the dominant objective of the factory manager (high customer service) and the expectation and tolerance of low resource utilization at certain times. Thus the 'pipeline' system creates a situation in which the nature of demand is predictable which in turn permits the use of output stocks of goods.

Following the business policy decision substantial changes must result. Primarily, the decision changes the predictability of demand. This in turn prevents the use of output stocks of finished goods which in turn necessitates the adoption of a different capacity management strategy. This is reinforced by the suggestion that adequate resource utilization is desirable alongside the need to provide adequate levels of customer service. Thus the operations manager (i.e. the Factory A manager) has to adopt a different approach to the management of capacity, and with this perhaps also a different approach to production scheduling and the management of inventories.

This 'before' and 'after' case illustrates several factors of relevance in our consideration of the operations manager's capacity management decision-making process. This may be summarized as follows:

(1) The existence of *feasibility* factors. A particular strategy for the solution of problems, e.g. capacity management problems, may be feasible in certain situations and infeasible in others. In the 'before' situation a particular capacity management strategy was feasible (2bii) whilst the policy change eliminated that feasibility.
(2) The existence of certain *desirability* factors. Both 'before' and 'after', the provision of a high level of customer service was desirable, whereas in the 'after' situation the pursuit of both customer service and resource utilization in some acceptable balance is seen to be desirable. In both situations this 'desirability' factor is seen to derive from a set of business objectives interpreted to the operations function.

Alongside these two factors, and influencing the operations manager's decision-making, one might speculate on the existence of a set of *'preference'* considerations. Whilst feasibility may be considered to be the 'what can be done' consideration and desirability the 'what must be achieved' consideration, 'preference' factors might be seen to be the 'what the operations manager would like to do' consideration. Here the operations manager seeks to create a situation which he prefers in order, for example, to minimize his risks, etc. In this case his preferred situation is entirely compatible with the 'before' situation, if one sees an entirely 'buffered' situation, i.e. where the operating system has both inputs from sources, and outputs to customers buffered through the existence of stocks, as being preferential.[12] However in the 'after' situation, in considering preferred outcomes, the operations manager has a more difficult task. He must provide an adequate level of performance on two basically conflicting objectives whilst having his available capacity management strategies reduced through feasibility constraints. Given the information in the case, the operations manager will probably prefer not to adopt capacity strategy (1) if only because of social and community considerations. Strategy (2a) will be undesirable from productivity considerations and, we must speculate therefore, that a mixed strategy will be adopted depending upon (2bi) with appropriate aspects of strategy (1).

This situation highlights a further relevant factor – the relative *power* of the operations manager. In this case the previously high power of the operations manager is reduced, thus given the increased constraints (feasibility) and the increased complexity of objectives (desirability), he must inevitably compromise his own preferences. The situation is redeemed only by the fact that the operations manager is dealing with an established situation in which there is considerable custom and practice, from which changes may be required. This perhaps permits the retention of some options (i.e. some power is retained), which would not have existed were the situation that of establishing a new factor to deal from the outset with the 'after' situation described in the case.

Contingent Factors

The capacity management decisions referred to in the case were seen to be contingent upon three factors – feasibility, desirability and preference.

Decision-making in Operations Management

Whilst such factors may influence decision-making in most situations, they will have a particular form and derivation for the operations manager.

Feasibility

The feasibility of a particular course of action for the principal decision-making areas of operations management, e.g. capacity management, scheduling, inventory, etc., will largely be influenced by the nature of the operating system, which in turn will be a function of the demand situation, the processes and outputs involved, and the system's function.

It has been seen that the predictability of the *nature of demand*, i.e. whether or not it is known what future customers will want, will influence the feasibility of the existence of output stocks created in anticipation of demand, and ultimately the use of input stocks of particular resources. For example, an operating system established to satisfy a totally unpredictable demand will neither contain output stocks of finished (unsold) goods nor stocks of specialized input resources, e.g. specialist materials, equipment etc.

The types of *process* and the *outputs* involved may well influence the nature of the system. For example, in electrical power generation, even though the nature of future demand is known (i.e. for electricity of a particular voltage etc.), it will not normally be possible to provide substantial output stocks. The *function of the system* will also influence its nature; transport and service systems differ from service and manufacturing systems, as in both cases the customer, or some physical item provided by the customer, will be a direct input resource to the treatment/conversion process. In the case of service and transport systems, queues of customers or items provided by customers may exist awaiting treatment, thus giving an input resource queue, whilst in other circumstances such queuing will be infeasible or undesirable, e.g. in the case of emergency systems etc.

Thus the nature of demand, process and outputs, system function, and the relationship with the customer will influence the nature of the system, which in turn will have a major feasibility influence upon the approaches adopted by operations managers in managing such systems.

Desirability

The desirability of pursuing a particular approach in managing the system will largely be influenced by the operations manager's perceptions of desired outcomes which in turn will be associated with explicit or implicit business objectives. Thus, considering the twin objectives of providing customers service and achieving high resource utilization, an emphasis upon the former (as in the TMD 'before' situation) will possibly encourage the adoption of particular strategies in capacity management, scheduling etc., whilst an emphasis on resource utilization and productivity may encourage a different approach. For example, given feasibility, an emphasis on customer service will encourage the use of output stocks and possibly the maintenance of excess capacity, whilst an emphasis upon resource utilization may mitigate against the use of output stocks and lead to a reduction in capacity and thus the need to depend upon variations in system capacity as the principal capacity management strategy (strategy 1), or customer queuing and loss of trade (strategy 2a). Whilst in general the operations manager's basic strategies may be seen as a function of the given or required balance between customer service and productivity, other objectives will have a 'desirability' influence, e.g. labour policies, pricing policies etc. All such factors will be beyond the direct control of the operations manager. We can consider them to be policy level decisions to which the operations manager will make some contribution.

Preference

Given feasibility and desirability we would expect operations managers to have certain preferences. For example he/she may prefer a 'buffered' situation as in the 'before' situation in the case. This through the use of inventories, permits the decoupling of the 'core' of the operating system, i.e. the transformation system, from changes in supply and/or demand levels. Such an arrangement will provide the maximum choice of strategies for the management of capacity, scheduling etc., at the expense, however, of the need for inventory management, and the commitment of capital to inventories. In a labour-intensive system the operations manager may prefer a capacity management strategy which minimizes the amount of change in the labour force, hours worked etc., thus minimizing the risk of labour/industrial relations problems. The operations manager may prefer a scheduling procedure which avoids the need to schedule all internal activities directly in response to individual customers' due dates. The adoption of a more 'internally' oriented scheduling strategy may permit higher resource utilization. It may be preferred to retain existing practices and procedures and avoid the complexity of the adoption of mixed strategies, e.g. the simultaneous use of a particular approach to capacity management, scheduling, inventory management etc., for different products or services, or different approaches at different times – i.e. a preference to achieve and retain stability.

The concept of the *power* of the operations manager, as described above, may be seen to relate to the extent that he can exercise preference considerations. Such power may be informal or formal. It may have been acquired, have evolved, or simply exist because of the broader circumstances, e.g. the existence of minimum feasibility and desirability constraints. This view associates 'power' with the scope, freedom of action, and breadth of choice of the operations manager, given feasibility and desirability constraints. Thus the 'power' of the operations manager may be the means by which he/she seeks to achieve some balance between the three contingent factors. This, however, is largely an internal perspective. We must recognize that such power, perhaps rather more broadly defined, may be exercised by the operations manager in seeking to influence both the feasibility and desirability constraints which operate on him. Thus, in certain circumstances, an operations manager may be able to influence product design and/or marketing policy in order to make feasible the provision of output stocks of uncommitted goods. For example, in the TMD case the operations manager

Decision-making in Operations Management

may seek to encourage the redesign of the equipment in order to permit part assembly of finished goods in anticipation of receipt of order. Further he may seek to retain an overriding commitment to customer service, and a tolerance of low resource utilization. Thus the extent to which the operations manager contributes to and influences these policy-level decisions will at least ensure that such decision-making takes account of the needs, constraints and abilities of the operations function, and at best ensure that such constraints are minimized thus maximizing preference.

This means that operations managers who are unable, or unwilling, to influence policy-level decisions within the organization may have to operate in highly undesirable situations, seemingly being required to meet conflicting objectives whilst using resources in a diverse range of activities in a continually changing situation, etc. In such circumstances the power of the operations manager approaches zero, no preference is exercised, and the operations manager's decision-making process is entirely constrained by 'external' factors.

The Decision-making Process

Summarizing, we have viewed operations management decision-making as a process where outcomes are influenced by feasibility, desirability and preference factors. This can be shown as a simple model, as in figure 1. This

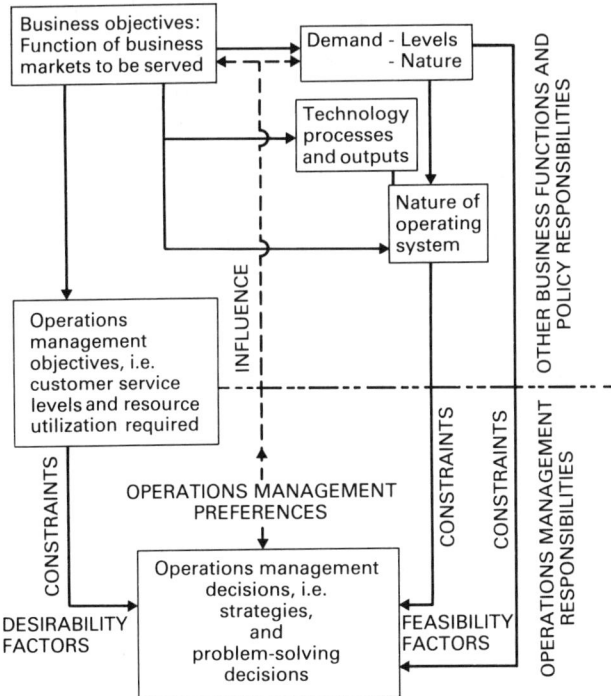

Figure 1   The context of the operations management decision-making process

supports the contention that the operations manager's decision-making process has clear cause and effect relationships with policy decision-making and the decisions in other business functions. The recognition of these relationships and the adoption of a suitable decision-making process is a principal requirement for effective operations management, and the solution of particular problems must be seen as a subsidiary part of this decision-making process. The operations manager's responsibility within the broad business context must include the recognition of the fact that decisions in other functions will limit his own decisions; but, equally important, he must also seek to influence those factors which give rise to feasibility and desirability constraints on his decisions in order to exercise his own preferences.

APPENDIX

TMD Ltd – Factory 'A'

TMD Ltd is a part of a large engineering group whose products range through mechanical engineering, electrical engineering and specialist metal goods. It has one factory in each of four towns in the northern part of the United Kingdom. It also manufactures in the USA and one other European country. The principal UK factory (Factory 'A') employs approximately 800 personnel of whom 400 are direct 'shopfloor employees'. These numbers have changed little in recent years. It is the only large employer in the town.

Products

Factory 'A' makes only one product – a machine for the manufacture of items in a specialist process industry. These are electro-mechanical and the design is a direct development of similar machines made on this site over the past 100 years. The machines cost about £20,000. The manufacture of the product involves machining, assembly, test, disassembly, packaging and despatch.

Markets

The products of the factory are marketed worldwide. There are no major UK competitors, but very substantial foreign competition exists. Throughout the world there are approximately 20 competing companies. Demand for these products has an approximate four-year cycle. This is an established-pattern in the industry. Much of TMD's demand comes from existing customers. Approximately 85 per cent of items sold go to such customers to replace existing machinery, to expand existing plants, or for the establishment of new plants. Price and customer service is a major factor in winning orders, and most companies are prepared to buy equipment from a variety of manufacturers, thus supplier loyalty is low.

Decision-making in Operations Management

Marketing

The factory's worldwide sales team are backed up by a group of technical sales personnel located at the factory. They tend to deal eventually with all prospective customers, since customers in general require their machines to have specific features. Often customers have direct contact with company research/development and manufacturing personnel for this reason. Sales personnel tend to quote a delivery time which has been previously agreed within the company by all key personnel. Currently that delivery time is 23 weeks from receipt of order. Sales personnel quote a price based on a 'cost plus' procedure with a known minimum acceptable price for each product.

Production Planning/Control

In general, orders are scheduled for manufacture on a 'first come, first served' basis, with some exceptions – e.g. for major companies placing initial orders with the prospect of bulk orders to follow. For production planning and control the factory operates a form of order 'pipeline' or order book. The pipeline contains all orders which have been released to manufacture at a given time. When demand is high the pipeline contains firm, committed orders only – i.e. orders against specific customer requirements for delivery at agreed times at an agreed cost. When demand is low certain speculative orders are released into this 'pipeline'. Relevant information is scrutinized at senior management meetings and decisions are made as to which items to release speculatively, into the order pipeline for manufacture. Available information includes the orders placed plus the possible orders anticipated by sales personnel, i.e. the potential orders currently under discussion with potential customers. Given knowledge of customers from previous orders, and the general level of demand in the industry etc., management will decide which of these orders to release speculatively into the order pipeline when the flow of firm orders onto the manufacturing shops is inadequate fully to occupy sufficient available manufacturing capacity.

Approximately 20 per cent of the manufactured content of the machines is common, i.e. is required irrespective of the product specification required by the customer. Thus in manufacturing to speculative orders for the product, the factory must in effect manufacture entire machines to the anticipated requirements of an expected customer. Because of the design of such machines it is not possible to manufacture say 80 per cent of the machine and leave the remaining 20 per cent to be completed when firm orders are received. For the past ten years the factory has been required to manufacture against a pipeline of orders comprising firm orders plus speculative orders for the products. The balance between firm and speculative orders has varied depending upon the general level of demand experienced by the factory.

Last year following a period of bad company and group performance a new Managing Director was appointed to TMD and is now located at Factory 'A'. Several changes were then introduced, one of which affected Factory 'A'. Because of a substantial build up in the capital tied up in finished but unsold products and the substantial overdraft required to fund such a stock, the Board made a policy decision not to manufacture goods of a particular specification against future anticipated orders, i.e. not to build products to the specification required by customers with whom negotiations are currently proceeding but from whom firm orders have not yet been received.

A redesign of the products has now begun, the intention being that the old machine be assembled in 'modular' form such that up to 80 per cent of the items to be manufactured are common to all possible customer requirements leaving only 20 per cent of the content being made/assembled against specific customer needs.

Factory Organization

The company operates on a two-shift system. Recently there has been no overtime work, and factory output has been approximately 70 per cent of full capacity. Overall responsibility for the factory lies with the Factory Manager who has held the job for 10 years. Reporting to him are the Personnel, Facilities, Departmental, Finance Management, Services, Quality and Sales Managers. The Factory Manager is on the main TMD Ltd Board.

References

1. R. Wild, *Concepts for Operations Management* (New York: John Wiley, 1977).
2. W. Skinner, 'Manufacturing – Missing Link in Corporate Strategy', *Harvard Business Review*, vol. 47 (May–June 1969), pp. 136–45.
3. W. Skinner, 'The Focused Factory', *Harvard Business Review*, vol. 52 (May–June 1974) pp. 113–21.
4. K. G. Lockyer, 'Production Management: the Unaccepted Challenge', Inaugural Lecture, University of Bradford, 28 October 1975.
5. C. C. New, 'What We Need is a Manufacturing and Marketing Strategy', *Sunday Times*, 5 November 1978.
6. R. H. Hayes and S. C. Wheelwright, 'Link Manufacturing Process and Product Life Cycles', *Harvard Business Review*, vol 57 (January–February 1979) pp. 133–40.
7. W. Skinner, *Manufacturing in the Corporate Strategy* (New York: Wiley-Interscience, 1978).
8. S. S. Miller and D. C. D. Rogers, *Manufacturing Policy* (Homewood, Ill.: Irwin, 1964).
9. R. H. Hayes and R. W. Schmenner, 'How Should You Organise Manufacturing?' *Harvard Business Review*, vol. 56 (January–February 1978) pp. 105–18.
10. B. C. Twiss, 'Strategy and Planning for Production', in B. Taylor and J. R. Sparkes (eds), *Corporate Strategy and Planning* (London: Heinemann, 1977) pp. 197–214.
11. T. A. Faulhaber, *Manufacturing: Strategy for Growth and Change*, American Management Association (1967); T. D. Weinshall and B. C. Twiss *Organisational Problems in European Manufacture*, vols 1 and 2 (London: Longmans, 1973).
12. J. D. Thompson, *Organizations in Action* (Maidenhead: McGraw-Hill, 1967).

3.4

Technical Investment Planning of Flexible Manufacturing Systems – the Applications of Practice-oriented Methods

H. J. Warnecke and G. Vettin

Many production enterprises are currently being affected by structural changes which are caused by factors both internal and external to the company. The market demands an increasing variety of products and of product variants. For the manufacturer, the life of many products has a tendency to decrease. A steady rise in the cost of personnel, material and plants can be seen, as well as the declining cost of electronic controls and auxiliary electronic data processing (EDP) equipment.

Therefore, the main aim in the planning of new manufacturing concepts is to find technical/organizational system solutions that satisfy overall company aims. More frequent product changes and smaller batch quantities, in conjunction with the desire for shorter order throughput times, require a higher level of organization of order processing.

Flexible manufacturing systems are a suitable means of accounting for these trends in manufacturing engineering, with the aid of new machine concepts, automated work-pieces and information flow.

Requirements of Technical Investment Planning

The technical investment planning of flexible manufacturing systems has four main aims as shown in figure 1.

The definition of the machining tasks necessitates the analysis of the work-piece spectrum and the recording of all machining requirements. The

---

H. J. Warnecke is Professor of Industrial Production and Factory Management at Stuttgart University. G. Vettin is Head of Manufacturing Systems at the Frauenhofer Institute of Production and Automation in Stuttgart.

Source: H. J. Warnecke and G. Vettin, 'Technical Investment Planning of Flexible Manufacturing Systems – the Applications of Practice-oriented Methods', reprinted courtesy of the Society of Manufacturing Engineers. Originally published in the *Journal of Manufacturing Systems*, 1982, vol. 1, no. 1.

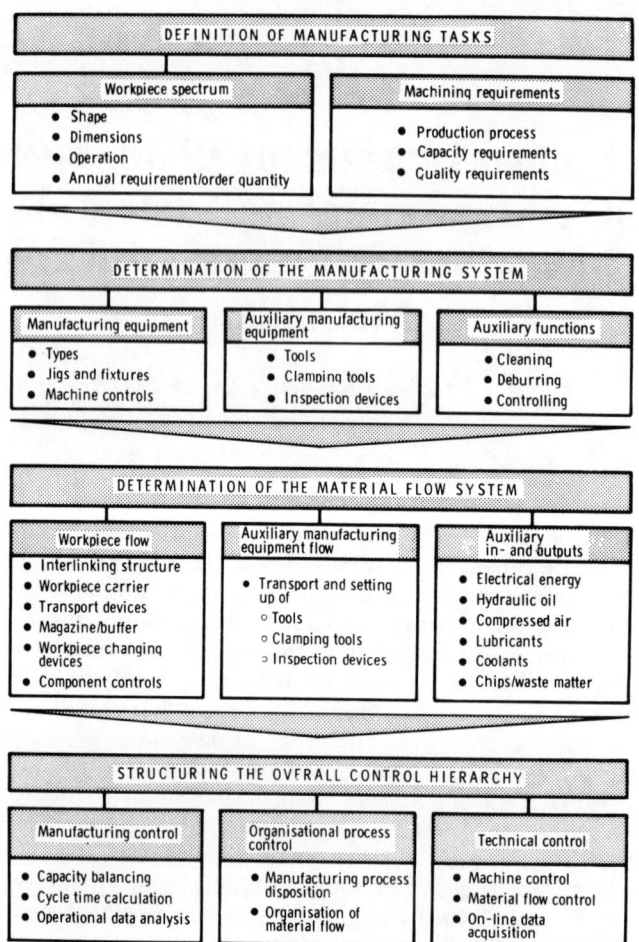

Figure 1 Requirements of technical investment planning

data obtained in this way form the basis for determining the machining system. The work-stations have to be interconnected by the material flow system. Suitable means must be determined for the transport, storage and presetting of the work-pieces, the auxiliary manufacturing equipment, and supporting materials. The interaction of the components of the machining and the material flow-systems is governed by the overall control system. The latter has the task of coordinating the time requirements of the manufacturing orders with the capacities of the manufacturing system, and of distributing, collecting and evaluating the information necessary for the running of the plant.

Definition and Layout

The term flexibility describes the ability of a manufacturing plant to perform different production tasks. The larger the variety of production tasks that can be performed with the minimal resetting effort needed between orders, the higher the level of flexibility. The following definition is used as a prerequisite for the consideration of flexibility, within the scope of technical investment planning:

(1) 'Short-term flexibility' designates the effort necessary for the resetting between known production tasks within the scope of the current production program.
(2) 'Long-term flexibility' describes the effort required for the resetting for new production tasks because of changes in the production program, and the changes in the qualitative and quantitative capacity requirements associated with this.

The criteria for short-term flexibility are mainly the effort needed for setting up and resetting, those for long-term flexibility are the costs of new investments and reconstructions.

A flexible manufacturing system contains several automated machine tools of a universal or special nature, and where necessary, of further workstations which are interconnected by an automated work-piece flow system such that different work-pieces can be machined at the same time within the system. The various work-pieces can pass through the system along different routes. In this way, automated multistep, multiple-product manufacturing is possible within a flexible manufacturing system. Set-up times for the system components are arranged so that an uninterrupted operation of the other components is possible during the setting up process.

In a flexible transfer line the work-stations are interconnected by an automated work-piece flow system according to the line principle. A flexible transfer line is capable of simultaneously or sequentially machining different work-pieces passing through the system along the same route. In between the stations, buffers may be located to balance differences in cycle times, set-up times, or short-term breakdowns. These buffers are provided to minimize the effects of these variables on the other system components.

Planning of the Machining System

The machining system includes those components of the manufacturing system which directly take part in the production process (manufacturing equipment and auxiliary manufacturing equipment). The largest part of the property investment of the company lies in the machining system. The planning of the machining system is therefore a central task of technical investment planning. Realization of the machining system should follow the four main steps of the sequence shown in figure 2.

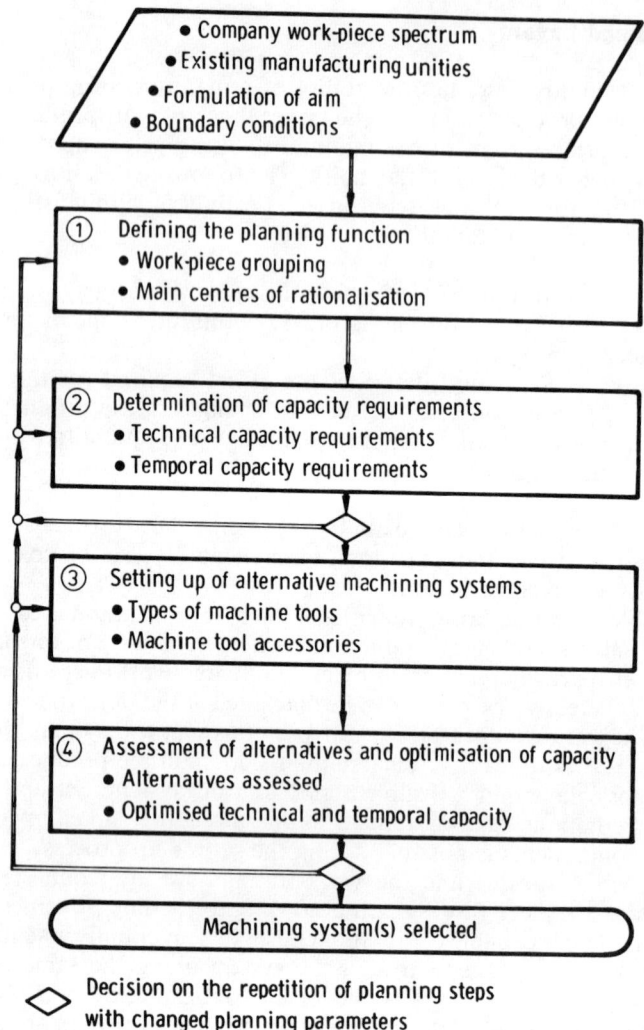

Figure 2 Schematic sequence of the planning of the machining system

The multitude of planning parameters and their expression necessitates a strategic procedure in order to keep the planning effort within acceptable limits. After the second stage of the planning process, an intermediate assessment is therefore carried out with a view to the expected technical and temporal degree of capacity utilization, the result of which may well necessitate a repetition of steps 1 and/or 2 with changed planning parameters. In a similar way, an assessment of the alternative machining systems is carried out after Step 4, on the result of which hinges the decision of whether an iterative optimization of the technical and temporal capacity should be used.

Technical Investment Planning of FMSS

In the case of large work-piece spectra and the voluminous data associated therewith, a precise limitation and definition of the planning task is indicated in step 1. The work-piece spectrum, in a two-stage data-reduction process, is initially sorted into groups with the aid of a classification system and a parts list analysis. This, amongst other things, is done by sorting out the individual parts of product families into rotational and non-rotational parts, and, within these main groups, into functional families. The number of work-pieces to be expected for the main groups is determined by way of a requirements prognosis. With the aid of the product-quantum-analysis, one then orders the work-pieces according to quantity, with respect to the parameter considered in each case. A common form of presentation of the product-quantum-analysis is the ABC-analysis, in which the cumulative frequency of the parameter variables is plotted against the number of individual work-piece codes. For further planning steps, study of the A and B parts is usually sufficient, since the highest rationalization effects can be obtained by proper investment measures.

For the selected work-piece spectrum and the now defined planning task, the technical and temporal capacity requirements must be defined in the following planning step. The technical capacity requirements are the result of the production and machining requirements, and must be transformed into alternative qualitative tool and machine concepts. These must then be quantified according to the machining time requirements. Auxiliary aids for this planning stage are: (1) systems for recording standardized machining elements, (2) coordination matrices for interconnecting the machining operations, (3) tool planning concept and machine tool planning concept, and (4) EDP programs for the calculation of production times.

For this step, one can also refer back to various systems of computer-aided production planning as developed at the technical universities Aachen, Berlin and Stuttgart. However, only systems according to the generating principle are suitable for this since it, unlike the variant principle, enables the determination of the most suitable production concept independent of previous production.

The results of the capacity determination are alternative machine concepts and their associated tool concepts. From this the requirements for machine tools on the market, or capability lists for special-purpose machines can be written. The multitude of market offers for numerically controlled machine tools, and the multitude of selection criteria to be considered, were good cause for producing an EDP supported method for the selection of NC machine tools. This auxiliary planning aid includes a data bank and EDP programs for the selection of different types and for the alteration of machine accessories. The multiple step selection process takes place in dialogue mode with the computer, and is explained in figure 3.

The preselection criteria, which can be selected at random according to type, quantity and expression, make up the input variables for the program FILTER, which filters out from the data bank those machine types that partly or fully satisfy the requirements. During the second selection stage the intermediate file of the PWZMA program is processed further. With its help the data of a certain machine type are assembled into the best-suited machine

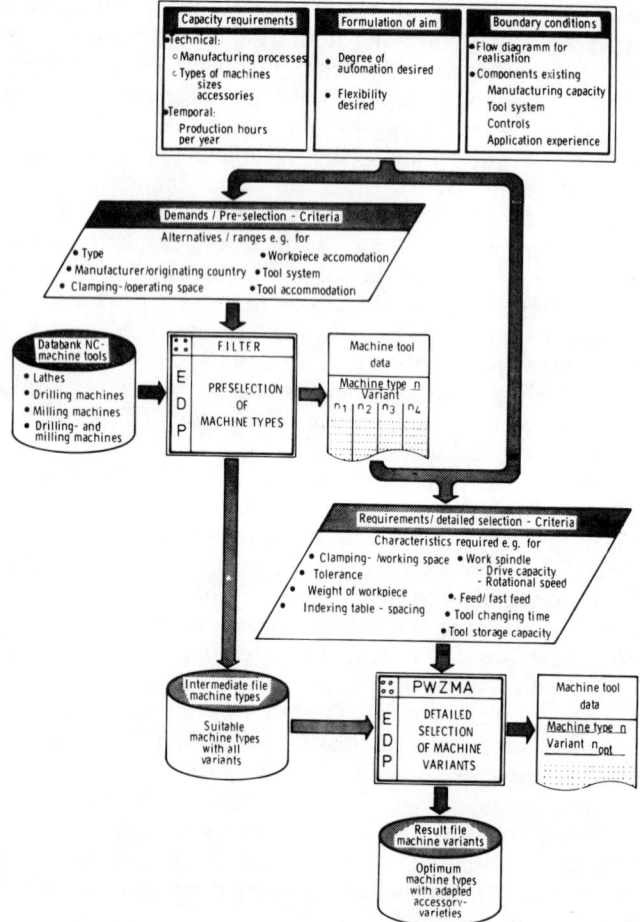

Figure 3   Principle of EDP-supported machine selection

variant, with due consideration of the peculiarities of features and of modular building block systems.

The setting up and evaluation of the machining system will be illustrated by the example of the planned flexible production of gearboxes as shown in figure 4.

Originating from the capacity requirements, suitable machine types available on the market were determined with the aid of the data bank. The analysis of manufacturers' offers for these machine types, and for single and multispindle, type-related tools, formed the basis for the evaluation of the alternatives. Starting from the investment costs for special-purpose tools and the hourly rate of the machining system, the necessary yearly savings in time are determined for a specified ammortization period for the special-purpose tools.

Technical Investment Planning of FMSS

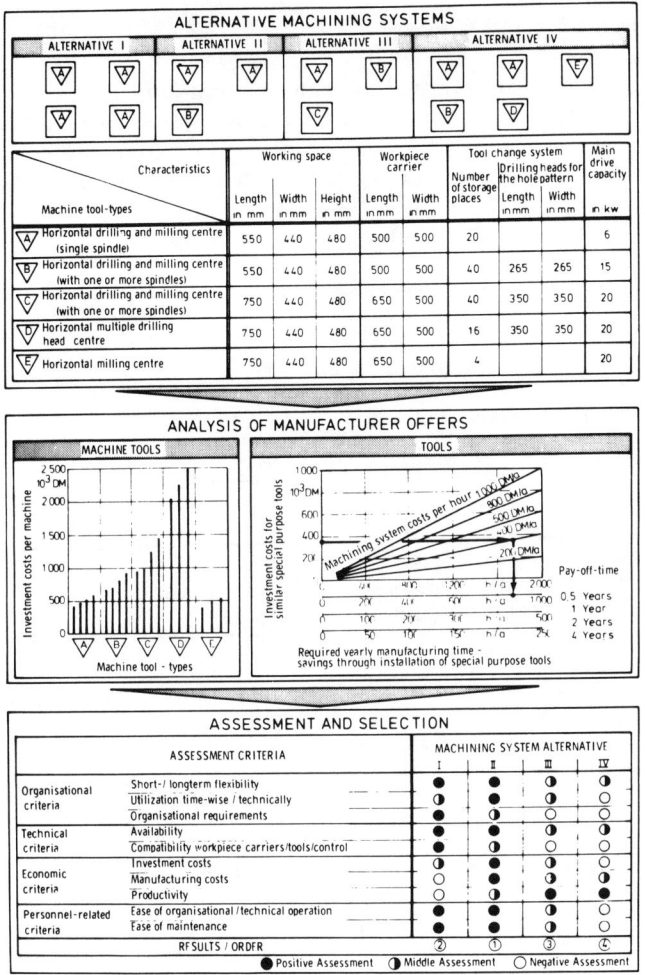

Figure 4   Machining system for the flexible manufacture of gear boxes

An economic use of special-purpose tools results if the effective time saving is higher than the limiting value thus established. The result of the evaluation shows a clear advantage of Alternative II over Alternative I, and especially over Alternatives III and IV. Reasons for this are the high flexibility and good temporal utilization of Alternative II, at comparatively low costs and good serviceability. Therefore, the decision went in favour of Alternative II, with three drilling and milling centres of the same size, of which at least one would have to be equipped for use with larger multiple drilling heads.

Planning the Overall Concept

The technical/organizational overall concept integrates the three subsystems: machining system, material flow system and overall control system. The main task of technical investment planning thereby is the structuring of the layout and of the work-piece flow system. Because of the multitude of parameters to be considered, a strategic procedure is recommended, as show in the planning sequence in figure 5.

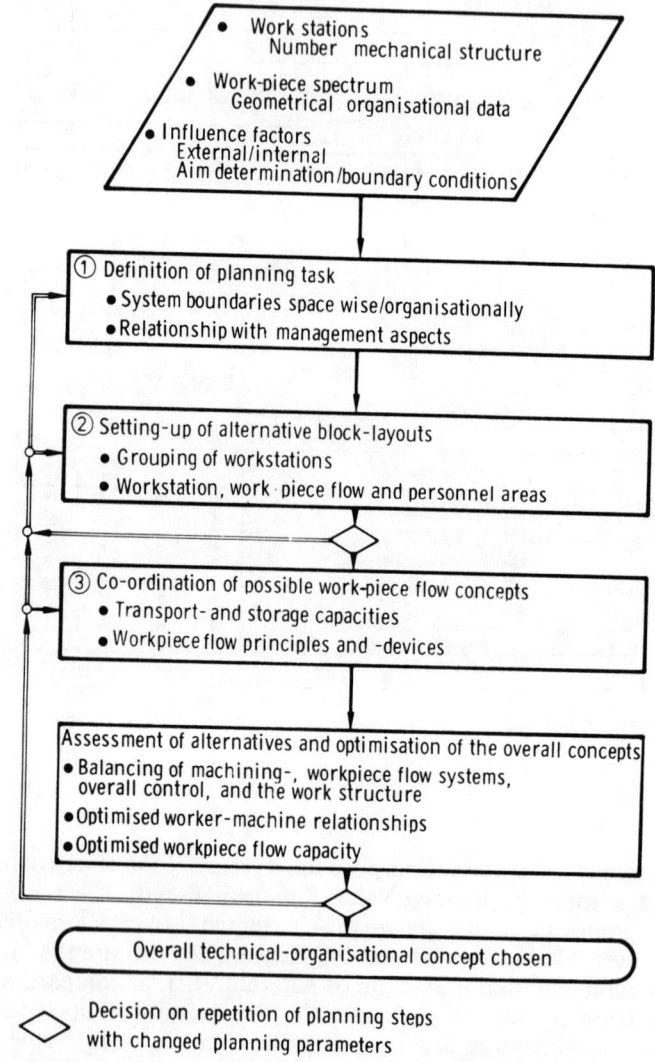

Figure 5 *Schematic sequence of the planning of overall technical/organizational concepts*

Technical Investment Planning of FMSS

Numerous methods exist for solving the factory-planning type problems of the optimum arrangement of work-stations. Their main aim is usually to minimize transport costs. As another important boundary condition, the requirement of human work-places must be borne in mind, whereby ergonomic criteria such as safeguarding against noxious emissions must be considered.

As a prerequisite for the determination of suitable work-piece flow principles and devices, the approximate transport and storage capacities must be determined. The transitional relationships between the work-stations, and their spatial layout are the basis of this calculation. In the selection and formation of the principles and technical components of the work-piece flow system, the following basic requirements must be observed, whose realization will positively influence the practicability of overall concepts for flexible manufacturing systems:

(1) The work-stations must be laid out in the form of flexible manufacturing cells which have standardized transition points with regard to the work-piece flow system and the overall control system.
(2) Work-piece transport and storage must be performed by means of standardized work-piece carriers possessing a minimum number of work-piece-related parts.
(3) The formation of work-piece carriers, set-up and changing devices must take place so that the overall expense for the work-piece flow system is kept to a minimum.
(4) Conventionally mechanized or automated transport and storage of the work-piece carriers should be possible, and the work-pieces in the work-piece carrier should also be manually accessible.

For easier selection of one or several initial solutions for the work-piece flow system, the basic types of work-piece flow for flexible manufacturing systems sketched in figure 6 have been defined:

1. Basic type A—Shuttle transport with exactly one trolley.
2. Basic type B—Loop transport with several trolleys.
3. Basic type C—Loop transport with continuous conveyors.
4. Variation 1—Decentralized storage.
5. Variation 2—Decentralized and central storage.

In the formation of larger manufacturing installations, their layout is made possible through various subsystems according to the basic types. Thereby it is best to interconnect the subsystems via a common central store.

The procedure for establishing technical/organizational overall concepts for flexible manufacturing systems will be illustrated by the planning of new manufacturing structures for precision tools. The task consisted of the total restructuring of the company by an overall concept in which the manufacturing areas of the production stations were joined via an overall EDP organization.

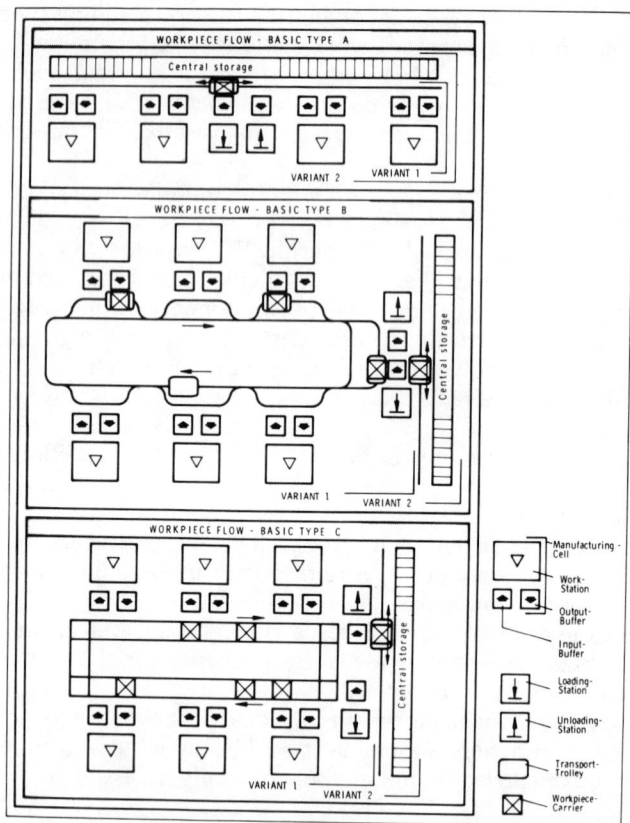

Figure 6   Basic types of work-piece flow

Planning of the machining system resulted in 26 work-stations for one manufacturing area. Based on this magnitude of the system, a grouping of the work-stations into subsystems had to be performed. To begin with, block layouts were made for the three organization types: (1) routing principle, (2) flow principle, and (3) cell principle. To each of these layout alternatives, alternative work-piece flow concepts were allocated.

The alternative overall concepts sketched in figure 7, distinguish themselves apart from their machines and work-piece flow layouts mainly with respect to work organization and degree of automation of the work-piece and information flow systems. The higher the number of the organization interconnected work-stations, and the lower the intermediate storage capacity within a production area, the higher this degree of automation must be and the degree of centralization of the work and of the production organization. According to this, Alternative II exhibits the highest degree of automation, followed by Alternatives I and IV, and then Alternatives III and V. This subdivision applies because of the requirement of being able to produce economically large, medium and small batches within each alternative, and

Technical Investment Planning of FMSS

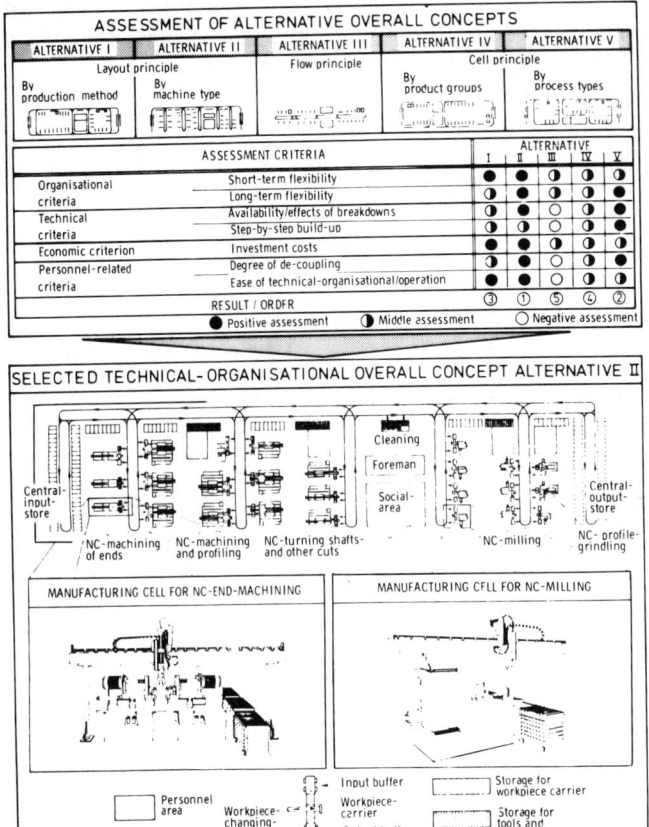

Figure 7   Assessment of alternative concepts

of satisfying the aims of low throughput times on high capacity utilization in particular cases.

The evaluation of the alternative overall concepts lead to the selection of Alternative II, since this principle with its small machine groups of equal or similar type, meets both the technical and economic, as well as the organizational and personnel related requirements. The principle of standardized work-piece carriers and work-piece set-up and changing devices is illustrated by the sample presentation of the two manufacturing cells. The off-the-floor arrangement of the handling devices facilitates manual accessibility of the machine during resetting, and maintenance and operation for small series, for which the resetting of the handling device would be uneconomical.

Layout with the Aid of Simulation

The application of a simulation procedure in the technical investment planning of automated manufacturing systems takes place by obtaining information about the overall concept and components of the plant from an analysis of the time characteristics of the planned installation, which enables evaluative optimization of the works. Hence, the main task exists not in a system analysis, but rather in a system synthesis.

To comply with this task, the overall concept with its components layout and processing, structure and organization of a planned installation, must be represented by a model (figure 8). Because of the alternating effect of the layout and processing structures, those manufacturing and work-piece flow organizations must be considered which have parameters which affect the constructional layout structure.

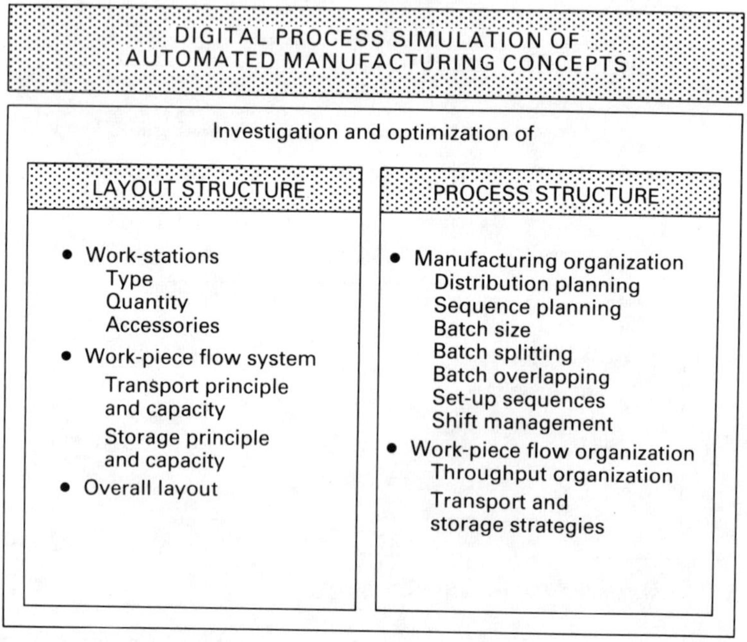

DIGITAL PROCESS SIMULATION OF AUTOMATED MANUFACTURING CONCEPTS

Investigation and optimization of

LAYOUT STRUCTURE

- Work-stations
  Type
  Quantity
  Accessories
- Work-piece flow system
  Transport principle and capacity
  Storage principle and capacity
- Overall layout

PROCESS STRUCTURE

- Manufacturing organization
  Distribution planning
  Sequence planning
  Batch size
  Batch splitting
  Batch overlapping
  Set-up sequences
  Shift management
- Work-piece flow organization
  Throughput organization
  Transport and storage strategies

Figure 8   Requirements for a method for digital process simulation

The requirements shown in figure 8 are fulfilled by the problem- and user-oriented modular program MUSIK for the simulation of automated flexible manufacturing concepts. The program operates on the basis of the event-oriented simulation language GPSS, and was written in FORTRAN IV. Substantial parts of the FORTRAN-GPSS subprograms were modified and complemented by further subprograms. The most important subprograms serve the purpose of:

(1) control by time and event;
(2) representation of the layout structure and its components;
(3) calculation of changes of state of the components;
(4) throughput organization of movable elements;
(5) organization and control of the work-piece flow system;
(6) input and preparation of data for the layout structure, processing structure and the simulation runs;

Technical Investment Planning of FMSS

(7) output of simulation run and the results;
(8) statistical evaluation and preparation of simulation results;
(9) graphical representation illustrating the layout structure and the present condition of the system.

Simulation models for the basic types of work-piece flow of flexible manufacturing systems were granted with the help of this simulation program (figure 6). With the completed simulation analyses, layout guidelines and application boundaries for manufacturing systems were derived which are sufficiently similar to the underlying basic model structures. From the results of the simulation, the application ranges for the basic work-piece flow types as shown in figure 9 were derived in order to compare these three basic layouts. These results are valid for the ranges of the work-station and work-piece flow systems parameters that apply to flexible manufacturing systems. The layout of a flexible manufacturing system should fall into the application ranges seen from figure 9, considering that investment costs are lower for Basic Type A than for Basic Type B, and these in turn are lower than those for Basic Type C.

Simulation investigations had to be carried out within the scope of such technical investment planning for an FMS for the machining of approximately 200 different work-pieces for commercial vehicle gear boxes. The results of the simulation are given in the following extracts.

The work-piece flow alternatives considered were systems with shuttle transport (rack loader or stacker crane, Basic Type A) and with logs (electrical overhead crane, Basic Type C). Centralized and decentralized storage was planned to be the storage principle.

In a series of tests, the influence of batch size on various system parameters, the temporal utilization of work-stations, the length of queues before the work-stations, and the throughput times were, among other things, investigated. The results in figure 10 illustrate the relationship between the number of work-pieces carriers and the utilization of the bottle-neck machine determining productivity, as well as the mean throughput time. Clearly, machine utilization and therefore productive performance, cannot be raised any higher by an increase in the number of work-piece carriers, than a bottom limit which is unrelated to batch size. A further increase in the number of work-piece carriers will only bring about an increase in the size of the intermediate storage stock, and therefore higher throughput times.

Among other things which could be carried out with the simulation calculations, are an optimization of parameters – batch size, intermediate storage capacity and number of work-piece carriers. From these calculations, the optimum batch size with a supply of 75–100 work-piece carriers, lies between 180–240 pieces. The performance of the machining and the work-piece flow system was analysed by further simulation, and was optimized with respect to organization. These investigations could prove that the transport capacity of a stacker crane is sufficient to cope with any operating conditions of the work-stations that could be expected. The decision was therefore made in favour of this, the most economic, work-piece flow alternative (figure 11).

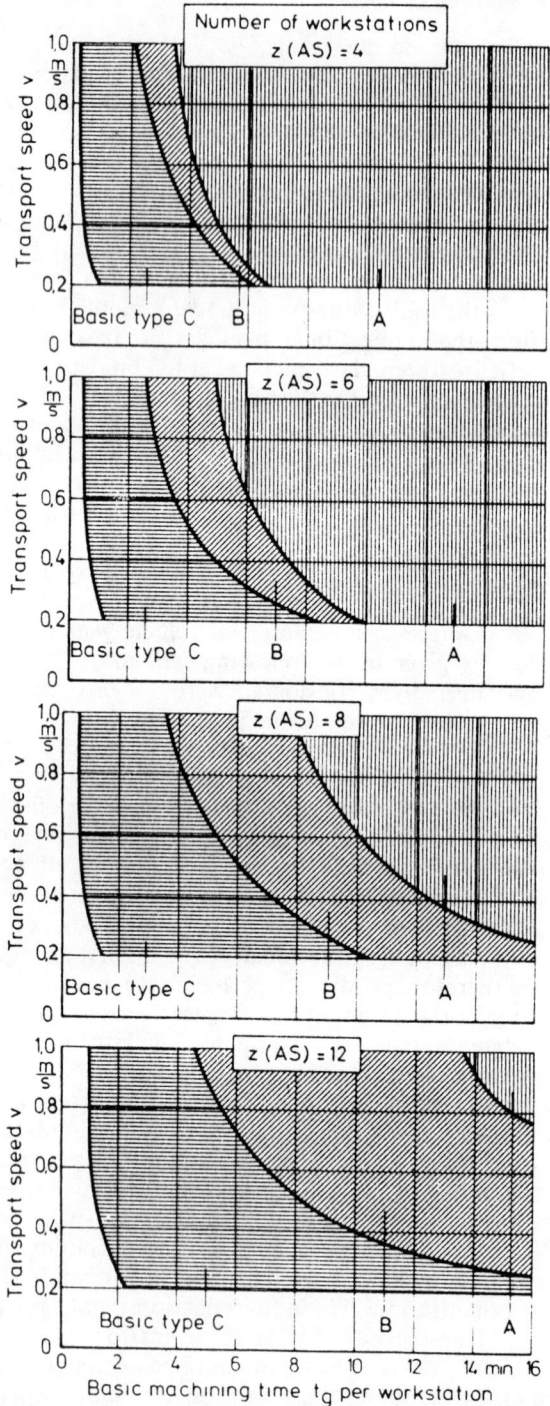

Figure 9   Areas of application of the basic work-piece flow types A, B and C

Technical Investment Planning of FMSS

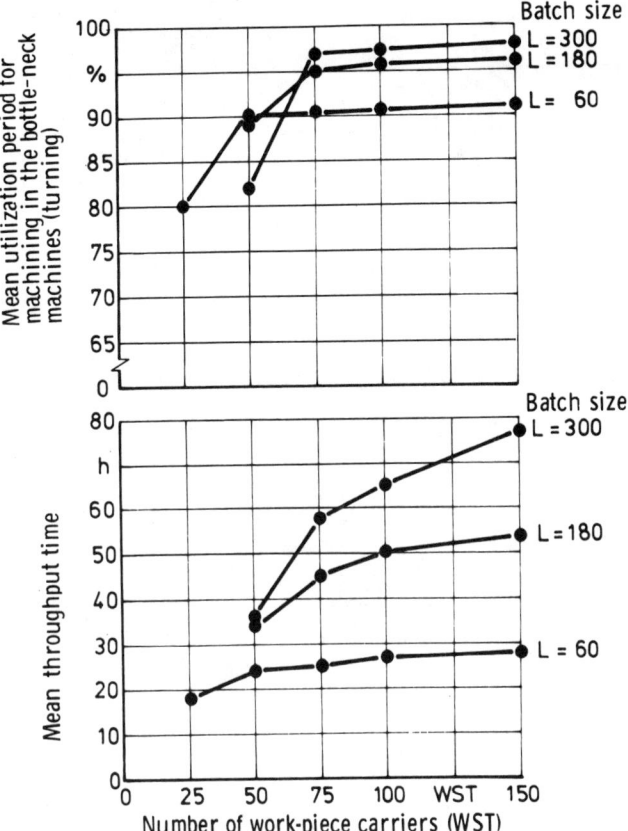

Figure 10 Influence of the number of work-piece carriers on system characteristics

Evaluation of the Economics

The economic advantages of a flexible manufacturing plant result from the degree of long- and short-term flexibility. To evaluate the short-term flexibility, it is practical to establish the optimum batch size for the alternative concepts, and the limiting batch size, where costs are equal for the flexible and the conventional solutions. Depending on a batch size which is sensible from an overall company viewpoint, the decision as to the most suitable alternative is then made.

The economic advantages of long-term flexibility consist in the more economic adaptability of the qualitative and quantitative capacity to changing manufacturing tasks, and in the longer useful life of the plant or of part of its components. The application of dynamic procedures of economic assessment, allowing for cost and return factors per certain time period, is especially desirable in the evaluation of long-term flexibility. However, the data needed for this are only available in rare cases with sufficient accuracy.

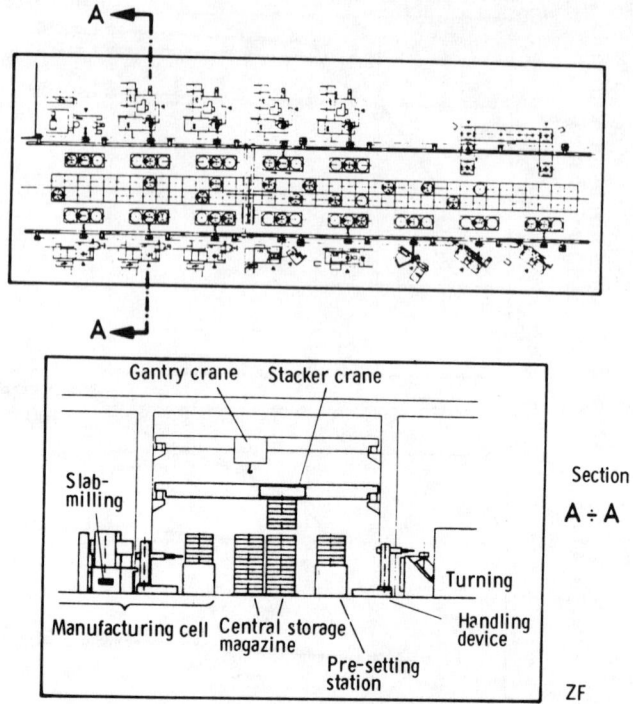

Figure 11 Manufacturing system for disc-shaped gear box components

The economic evaluation of flexible manufacturing systems in investment planning comparative cost calculations, in conjunction with the principle of sensitivity analysis, are therefore suitable auxiliary aids. One thereby determines the manufacturing costs for the alternative concepts by using an estimated span of possibilities for uncertain or changing parameters. By repeated calculation of the manufacturing cost with average, optimistic and pessimistic values for the uncertain parameters and for various time periods, the influence on the manufacturing costs can be shown. This procedure was also used in the planning of the flexible manufacturing system shown in figure 11.

A significant difference exists between conventional manufacturing and the manufacturing system in terms of manufacturing costs, in the decrease of variable costs, and (amongst other things), the diminished expenditure necessary for the set up of the manufacturing system. Due to higher hourly rates, the fixed costs are, however, higher than in the conventional system. For this reason, limiting batch sizes may be determined below which lower-cost production is guaranteed for the manufacturing system. A substantial task in the cost comparison calculation was the determination of the boundary batch sizes as a function of the variable system parameters.

The manufacturing costs for a representative work-piece at maximum and minimum investment cost for the manufacturing system are shown in figure 12 as a function of batch size. Depending on the magnitude of the investment costs for the manufacturing system, the boundary batch size for the wheels mentioned in the example will lie between 200 and 500 pieces. A value of 270 pieces was finally established as a probable mean value for the boundary batch size.

The economic advantages of the flexible manufacturing system are brought out all the more by decreasing batch sizes. On the one hand, this is favoured by the overall trend towards a larger number of types and variants in production. On the other hand, even larger orders can be completed in smaller batches if it is possible to execute the areas immediately before and after production with more flexibility, thus approaching the aim of 'storage-free' production.

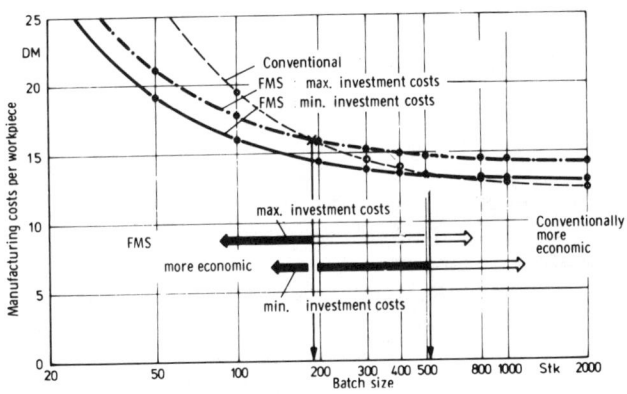

Figure 12 Influence of investment costs on the limiting batch size

Concluding Remarks

The complexity of manufacturing systems, which increases with increasing automation and flexibility, necessitates the application of procedures for the technical investment planning which enables accurate planning at justifiable planning expense. With these procedures the investment decision can be prepared on a sound basis, and the investment can be decreased.

A strategic procedure is necessary and the application of EDP is advisable for the planning of the machining system and for the setting up, evaluation and optimization of the technical organizational overall concepts. Computer support is sensible for the determination of capacity requirements, the selection of machine tools, and in the simulation of the operational process sequence of the planned installation.

The sample application of the planning methods by way of different problem types arising from industrial production companies illustrates the procedure, and supports the usefulness of such auxiliary means for industrial practice.

3.5

The Design of an Automated Material Handling System for a Job Shop

G. K. Hutchinson

Introduction

The automation of batch production system is of great current interest because of its potential improvements in productivity. In most systems, the key to automation is the design of the material handling system. This paper describes the design of an automated material handling system for an eleven-machine, sheet-metal shop. The design included the transport system, choice of buffer sizes, dispatching rules and scheduling procedures. The design was tested by simulation using a model developed using an interactive simulation system, CAPS. The operating environment is described and the development of the scheduling procedures given in detail. Of particular interest is a procedure based on downstream pull, which includes the use of a measure of the desirability of getting a job to subsequent machines in scheduling its current operation. The important factors in the design are investigated by simulation and the results discussed. The final design showed an improvement of over 73 per cent as compared with the manual material handling system. It is concluded that interactive model development and simulation provides a desirable approach to batch manufacturing system design.

The Operating Environment

The company is a large manufacturer of electrical and mechanical components, selling to a worldwide market. Most of the sales of interest are of

---

G. K. Hutchinson is Professor of Management Information Systems in the School of Business Administration, The University of Wisconsin, Milwaukee.
    Source: G. K. Hutchinson, 'The Design of an Automated Material Handling System for a Job Shop', from *Computers in Industry*, 1983, vol. 4, pp. 139–45.

The Design of an Automated Material Handling System

customized units made of unique parts and/or standard components. The subject facility functions as a large, complex job shop producing sheet-metal parts. It consisted of eleven machines working two shifts per day. The orders were processed in batches, ranging in size from 1 to 10,000, with most in the 10 to 100 range. The orders followed a routing consisting of operations which could vary from 1 to 13 with the average being 4½. Each operation specified the required machine group and the standard time for the operation. The work load variety was large, and the company maintains over 20,000 routings. During a single day about 300 operations, or 68 orders on the average, were completed. The average time for an order to be processed through the shop was 10 days, giving an average backlog of 680 orders. Machine utilization was in the 60–70 per cent range.

The original dispatching function was based upon a computer algorithm which assumed infinite capacity of the machine groups and was driven primarily by the due date of the order. The result was a daily dispatch list for each of the machines in the group. When a new task was needed at a machine, the next order listed on the dispatch list was chosen. In actuality, high-priority jobs were frequently processed without use of a dispatch list, through supervisor intervention.

The computer algorithm which generated the dispatch list operated upon the backlog of orders as defined by its shop status file. Each transaction involving the physical orders was recorded and entered into the shop status update file. The dispatching algorithm was run each night after updating the shop status file. The major transactions of interest were the assignment of an operation to a machine group (removal of the order from the file) and completion of an operation (entry into the file if subsequent operations required). This procedure guaranteed that the flow time of a job, measured in days, could not be less than its number of operations, regardless of priority or work load. In addition to this known delay of one day per operation, additional delays were often experienced due to recording, order entry or computer processing backlogs.

The physical work flow centred around work storage racks, which served as a work-in-process buffer for all machine groups. When a machine completed the processing of an operation, a fork lift was sent to the machine to pick up the order, move it to a rack and unload it, find the next order from the dispatch list, pick it up and return it to the machine. The machine operator would then set up the machine and process the operation. Upon completion of the operation, the operator would enter that fact on an operation completion card for future update of the shop status file. The eleven machines were future organized into eight machine groups with three machines in the first, two in the second, and one in each of the others.

The above served as the basis of operation although frequently modified by management to achieve higher machine utilization, labour economics or priority performance. The most frequent modification was the processing of high-priority jobs out of sequence, often causing congestion, confusion, consternation, added labour costs, lower machine utilization and higher indirect labour. Within the constraints of priority performance, the implicit objective of management was to minimize direct labour cost. Management could pull operators from other areas to improve machine utilization, schedule overtime on a machine by machine basis, and schedule multishift operations. All of these alternatives were used as deemed appropriate by the supervisor. His basis for decisions was the dispatch list – which summarized backlog for each machine group, the status of the machines, availability of labour, and knowledge about the backlog of work which was not included in the dispatch list, such as long operations and 'super hot' priority jobs.

Automation of Material Handling

The initial study objective was to determine the feasibility of automating the material handling in the shop. The plan was to develop a simulation of the shop as it currently operated and to modify the model to reflect how it was anticipated that the shop would operate with automated material handling. The routings for 300 orders were chosen and assumed to be typical of the shop's work load. An analysis of priorities showed them to be rather uniform in distribution. Management's perception was that there were five priority classes ranging from 'super hot' to 'no hurry'. The distribution of orders into these classes was determined and used in all subsequent models. From the 300 routings, a subgroup of 50 was randomly selected and became the basis for generation of the workload.

Validity of the model was checked at the micro-level by detailed analysis of men, work-piece and machine status change. At the macro-level, machine utilization and system output measures were matched against actual system performance. Basic run conditions were established. A simulation period of 10 days was chosen with an initial backlog of 100 orders and an arrival rate of 35 orders per day. Under these conditions, 26 orders per day were processed with machine utilization in the 60–5 per cent days range. Although basic statistical tests were applied, the validity of the model was really established by the agreement among the researcher and shop management that the model performed as the shop would under the same conditions with respect to all major factors.

The shop backlog (the rack) exhibited an interesting behaviour pattern in these early runs. Typically, the backlog decreased over the first 2–3 days, then grew as the incoming rate exceeded the completion rate. The cause of this behaviour pattern was not initially obvious as the system was processing more than 35 jobs per day at the start. Several experiments were run including a higher beginning backlog (the low point occurred at a later time) and increased arrival rate (the dip was less and the build-up more rapid). Upon detailed analysis it was concluded that the observed behaviour was the result of the workload per machine group not being as evenly balanced in incoming orders as in the beginning backlog. During the early part of the run there was a higher probability of a machine group whose average utilization was expected to be low finding a job it could process, leading directly to increased production. As the jobs for the lightly loaded machine groups were processed, the probability of finding additional jobs decreased, with the observed consequences.

The Design of an Automated Material Handling System

The early runs characterized the material handling system by the number of fork lifts available and their delivery time, i.e. the actual time to perform the required service. A detailed analysis of the runs indicated that, although the fork lifts lists were not overloaded, they caused losses in machine utilization due to both the structure of their operating procedure and the delays caused by their unavailability.

To investigate the automation of material handling, the changes necessary to reflect the intended automation were incorporated in the model. The same procedure was used but travel times were reduced to reflect management's best estimate of how the system should operate. A slight improvement, to 27.5 orders per day on average, resulted with the consequent higher machine utilization.

The next model modification was done to reflect a change in the structure of the material handling operation. Local queues were placed at the machine groups. This eliminated the necessity to return orders which had just completed an operation to the rack; they could be sent directly to the next group. This also reduced the delay from the completion of one job to the start of the next. It also removed the requirement to wait at least one day before a subsequent operation could begin. With this system, orders could be moved directly to the queue of the next machine group if another operation were required and there was a position in the group's queue. If not, the order was returned to the rack. This model used the dispatching rationale of the existing system for the entry of orders onto the shop floor. With these changes, the backlog was reduced rapidly to a low point of 49 jobs, an average of 33.5 jobs were completed per day, and machine utilization was in the 70–80 per cent range. An analysis of the individual machines suggested that improvements could be made by a better dispatching procedure.

Dispatching Algorithm Development

Up to this point, the performance improvements, from 26 to 33.5 orders per day (28.8 per cent), were a result of automating the material handling and providing local buffers for the machine groups. The next logical step was investigation of dispatching algorithms for bringing orders into the shop. It should be clear that long-run improvement in average order turnaround time (from order entry into the shop to its completion) with a stable workload mix can only be achieved by improved machine utilization. To capitalize on this the following procedure was programmed:

(1) The most heavily loaded machine group was determined on the basis of the total work for all remaining operations on those orders available in the backlog.
(2) In priority order, all orders to be processed on the most heavily loaded machine group were scheduled for their next operation.
(3) After all orders destined for the most heavily loaded machine group were scheduled, steps 1 and 2 were repeated for the next most heavily loaded machine group and this process repeated until all orders were scheduled.

The schedule thus generated served as the dispatch list for choosing the next order to be sent to a machine group when that decision was invoked. The schedule was generated at the start of each day and was not subsequently updated. This reflected the anticipated implementation of overnight batch processing rather than on-line implementation.

Early runs of this procedure showed that processing capacity was greater than the input rate of 35 orders per day. The incoming order rate was raised to 40, giving a completion average of 38.0 orders per day with machine utilizations over 78 per cent. Analysis of these runs indicated that the procedure performed to its intended objective well, i.e. the most heavily loaded machine groups achieved high utilization. Priority performance did not appear to deteriorate significantly but there were indications that improvement could be made in the utilization of the light loaded machine groups.

A second procedure, called Downstream Pull, was developed. The basic contention was that heavily loaded machines didn't really need special scheduling consideration as they would have work, with high probability, and that emphasis in scheduling should be on (1) making work available to lightly loaded machines and (2) providing good priority service. Previous research on Flexible Manufacturing Systems (FMSs) suggested that a procedure could be developed that would put more emphasis on scheduling the lightly loaded machines, thus improving their utilization, without hurting the performance of the heavily loaded machines. The reasoning was that heavily loaded machines, by definition, would have a higher probability of work availability, so they should provide management with alternatives as to the sequence in which work could be processed. From these alternatives, one should choose the sequence to achieve higher utilization of the lightly loaded machines, to emphasize production, or to minimize the turnaround time of priority jobs. The result could be the same utilization of the heavily loaded machines and improved performance of the other criteria.

Essentially, the problem is one of the simultaneous optimization of a multi-dimensional objective function in a stochastic, dynamic environment. The basic problem is analogous to that of the control of flexible manufacturing systems,[1] where simulation has proven to be a viable method of studying and improving the scheduling and control functions.[2] The approach in FMS scheduling and control has been to build a model of the system, test scheduling and control algorithms through simulation, choose the algorithms which best meet management's objectives, and incorporate those algorithms in the actual system. Often it has proven useful to design the algorithms in a manner that allows management to alter easily the relative emphasis to be placed on each of its multiple objectives. A method for accomplishing this has been outlined in earlier work.[1]

A major difference between FMSs and the sheet shop was that all operational decisions were under computer control in the FMS. In the sheet shop the preliminary design anticipated a system where:

(1) shop floor control, the sequencing of the orders at a machine group, would be done by a procedure that was sufficiently simple that any machine operator could implement it;

The Design of an Automated Material Handling System

(2) there would be no on-line devices at the work stations;
(3) the algorithms which processed the preference ranking of the orders would be run each night on a remote batch computer.

The anticipated design made it clear that it would be impossible to use the computer to support the decision making at the work stations on a real-time basis. The result that evolved was to operate each machine group first-come first-serve. System control was implemented by the choice of the algorithm which preference ranked the orders by machine group. The decisions were implemented by the supervisor who used the preference listing to dispatch work to the machine groups based on their physical backlogs.

There were four factors which determined the preference ranking using Downstream Pull:

(1) desirability of running a job at the current machine group;
(2) 'pull' of downstream machine groups;
(3) priority class of the job's order;
(4) time of the order in the shop.

The preference ranking for the order was calculated as:

$$P_i = \sum_{j=1}^{4} w_j f_{ji}$$

where:
P_i is the preference ranking index for order i,
w_j is the weight applied to factor j,
f_{ji} is the value of factor j for order i.

The desirability of running a particular job at a machine group was taken from sequencing theory. Many criteria for measuring the performance of a job shop are optimized by the shortest-job-first rule. The first factor was simply the expected processing time of the job's operation on that machine group.

The 'pull' factor accessed the desirability of having the job processed at its current machine group so that it would be available for the processing of its subsequent operations at other machine groups, including its current group, if the routing dictated its future return. This was done by first attempting to measure each machine group's need for work. The backlog of uncompleted operations was used to calculate for each machine group:

(1) TWA_i, the total hours of work in the backlog for group i;
(2) FOA_i, the total hours of work on the current (next operation) group i.

For instance, if all of the operations to be done on a group were the next operations for their respective orders, TWA would equal FOA, if there were no current operations for a group. FOA would be zero. Both TWA and FOA were divided by the hours available during the next 24 hours at the group to give a measure of the total load for the group that was immediately available, PFO, and totally available, PTW. Various algorithms were tested to combine PFO and PTW to give an index of the desirability of 'pulling' work, MDGS, for each machine group. The characteristics desired were:

(1) groups that were heavily loaded with current operations, PFO close to 100 per cent, should have a very low index;
(2) groups that were overloaded with current operations, PFO greater than 100 per cent, should have a zero or negative index;
(3) the index should (a) increase as PFO decreased, and (b) increase as the total work available, PTW, increased;
(4) the highest indexes should be for those groups with a great deal of work in the backlog, high PTW, but little of it available as the current operation, low PFO.

Several algorithms were tested. The choice between them was an arbitrary judgement, but the chosen one was parameterized so that its mapping function could be easily changed. The remaining step in calculating the order's 'pull' factor was to, for each operation subsequent to the current, determine the expected value of pull for the machine groups remaining on its routing. This was done as the product of the pull of the group times the probability of getting to that operation. The latter was an arbitrary (but parameterized), single valued, vector of probabilities for reaching subsequent operations. Clearly, more sophisticated methods could have been used, but did not appear warranted. The pull factor for the job was the summation of these expected values.

The third factor was based upon the priority class. The only problem encountered was to determine the range of values and the relative value of each of the five priority classes. A cubic function gave a transformation that had management's approval and was used.

The final factor was the length of time the order had been in the shop. This was included to prevent orders from 'getting stuck' because of their relative lack of desirability as measured by the first three factors. It was simply the number of days since arrival in the shop.

An important point was the manner in which these factors were developed was parameterized so that they could be easily altered. This was also true of the weights w_i used in combining the factors to give the order's preference ranking index P_j.

Two sets of parameters were tested. Both were able to achieve production rates of 40–6 orders per day (after increasing the input rate) with most machine utilizations in the 85–90 per cent range, a considerable improvement over the other alternatives. Both provided rapid flow times for orders. In a typical run, the top four (of five) priority classes had more orders processed in under one day than in any other single number of days, and even in the lowest priority class 21 of 38 orders completed were done in under two days. With this reduction in order flow times, work-in-process was also substantially reduced, by a factor of 5. It was clear that, based on simulation runs, the use of an automated MHS together with either of the preference

The Design of an Automated Material Handling System

ranking procedures for scheduling would provide substantial improvements over current operations and the other alternatives considered.

The system design was 'fine tuned' by studies to determine (1) number of local work-station queue positions, (2) number of transporters, (3) the sensitivity of the system to transport times, and (4) the dispatching procedure. One of the major advantages of automated material handling was having a local queue of orders at the machine groups. The design envisioned a limited number of local queue positions. Too many positions would waste valuable floor space and too few would result in machine delays and extra movement of orders within the system. Previous simulations had been based on a maximum of eight positions for each machine. The number of positions is closely related to both the variance in the work load on the system and the dispatching policy. In any system, variance is the enemy of efficiency; the greater the variance the greater the resources required will be to achieve a given level of performance. In this case, queue positions were the obvious resources to reduce variance problems. It was concluded that five were sufficient when used in conjunction with adequate transport and reasonable dispatching.

The automated material handling system was characterized for the simulation studies as the technological time to pick up and deliver a job and the number of transporters available. The technological time was the result of an estimate of transporter speed and expected travel distance. No provision was made for delays due to congestion of the transport system. The issue was the total capacity of the transport system to fulfill the machine requirements. As in most material handling situations, one can overcome long transport times with the addition of transporters. This was the case in this design. Doubling estimated transport times required less than twice the number of transporters to maintain production levels. These results were not independent of local queue sizes, dispatch procedures, and queue reservation policy. The general result of these runs was the feeling that any errors in estimation of transport times could easily be corrected by the use of additional transporters and it was concluded that the design was robust.

The procedure to be used by the supervisor in dispatching jobs to machine groups was also of concern. The first approach tried was to keep the queue at each machine group full, i.e. dispatch a job to a machine whenever there was a place for it. This approach produced a high utilization of the machines, as there was work in the queue whenever there was work within the system. It created problems of flow-time increases, excess transporter usage, poor priority performance, and increased work-in-process. All of these were a direct result of an increase in the number of times an order that had finished an operation was not able to join the queue at its next machine and had to be returned to the storage rack. The orders forced to do this were independent of order priority and were often delayed for long periods in the rack. To overcome these excess moves, a procedure was adopted that reserved a number of the queue positions at each machine for orders already in the shop and thereby limited the entry of new orders. Increasing this number reduced the number of times that orders had to be returned to the rack while increasing the probability that a machine would be temporarily idle when there were orders in the system for it. The basic operating rule for the supervisor was much like the inventory order policy, 'When the queue is down to four, that's the time to send some more.' The impact on the system can be most easily visualized in figure 1 where the moves back to rack and the total machine-wait-time-when-work-available are plotted against per cent reservations for three runs with other factors held constant. In all runs there were five positions. With 80 per cent reservations there was often only one job available at the machine with the consequence that it was frequently completed before the next job became available. With 60 per cent reservations, there could be two jobs available and the problem was practically eliminated.

As the per cent reservation was reduced, more jobs could be dispatched into the system. Since the total production capacity was increased only slightly, more jobs had to be returned to the rack. The moves to back-to-rack increased but not as dramatically as the machine wait time was decreased. The final design was based upon five positions with three reserved for orders within the system.

The Simulation

The model was specified using activity cycles[3] and the Computer-aided Programming for Simulation – CAPS. CAPS accepts activity cycles as inputs from a user dialog and writes the simulation program specified by the user in Extended Control and Simulation Language – ECSL.[4] The basic CAPS model was producing output within two hours of approaching the computer terminal. Modifications at subsequent stages were done by editing the ECSL code.[5]

Conclusions

Simulation was shown to be a valuable method for investigating the design and control of manufacturing systems. Over a period of six weeks two basic

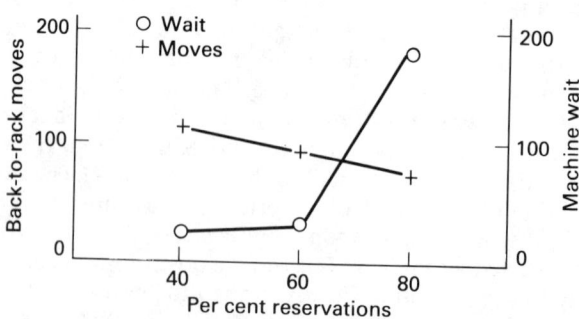

Figure 1 The impact of queue reservations

The Design of an Automated Material Handling System

models and three scheduling procedures were developed, validated and evaluated in the design of an automated material handling system for a job shop. Sensitivity testing showed the system to be robust and control procedures appear to be simple enough to be easily implemented. System production was estimated to increase from 26.0 to 45.0 orders per day, an improvement of 73 per cent. Turnaround time for orders decreased from ten days to two days with the corresponding five-to-one reduction in work-in-process. A dispatching procedure, downstream pull, was found to be particularly effective by assigning work to heavily loaded machines so that it will be available for processing on lightly loaded machines. Interactive simulation model development using activity cycles was shown to be a useful method to reduce model development time.

References

1. G. K. Hutchinson, 'The Control of Flexible Manufacturing Systems: Required Information and Algorithm Structures', in *Information Control Problems in Manufacturing Technology*, International Federation of Automatic Control, Pergamon Press (October 1977).
2. G. K. Hutchinson, 'Simulation: an Aid to FMS Design', *Proceedings Internationaler Kongress Metallbearbeitung 1978*, Karl-Marx-Stadt (March 1978).
3. G. K. Hutchinson, 'The Automation of Simulation', *Proceedings of the Winter Simulation Conference* (December 1980).
4. A. T. Clementson, 'Extended Control and Simulation Language: User's Manual', University of Birmingham, Birmingham, England (March 1978).
5. A. T. Clementson, 'ECSL-CAPS', University of Birmingham, Birmingham, England (1977).

3.6

The Use of Modelling and Simulation Techniques in the Design of Manufacturing Systems

J. M. Kay

Introduction

The use of hard automation in the manufacturing industries has been accepted for many years. The design problem has been one of developing and implementing the appropriate technology and perhaps ensuring a balanced line, i.e. no bottlenecks. Automotive vehicle production lines are an example. There is some variety in the vehicles produced but they are essentially the same model. In recent years, when product life-cycles have shortened and there is an increasing reluctance to manufacture for stock, the interest in flexible automation is growing rapidly. The development of the microprocessor and the consequent availability of cheap computing power means that computer control of a manufacturing system is no longer a prohibitively expensive overhead. The technology required to develop Flexible Manufacturing Systems (FMS) is generally available. The major problems with the design of a manufacturing system is in the organization and integration of the various sections. For high-volume production such as the motorcar, the hard automation approach will probably remain. In medium- and small-volume products there is a need to be able to switch from product to product without losing productivity. This flexibility was always available in the traditional manually operated job shop but the productivity was low and due to the lack of integration between each manufacturing stage a part could spend most of its time in the factory waiting for the next process stage to be available.

The aim of an FMS is to keep some of this flexibility but also to maintain the production rates expected for high-volume products. By integrating the

J. M. Kay is a Senior Research Officer in the College of Manufacturing, Cranfield Institute of Technology.

Source: J. M. Kay, 'The Use of Modelling and Simulation Techniques in the Design of Manufacturing Systems', *International Conference on the Development of Flexible Automation Systems IEE 10–12 July 1984 Conference Publication 237*, published by the Institution of Electrical Engineers.

Modelling and Simulation in System Design 243

various production processes by use of the controlling computer, the throughput time and hence the work-in-progress levels should be minimized. This desire for flexibility or versatility greatly increases the complexity of the system designer's task. He no longer has to design a system to manufacture only one or a very limited range of parts, but a system which will be able to manufacture a large range of products. The system will also be expected to manufacture products which have yet to be designed. Because of the complexity involved it is necessary that the system designer is able to vigorously test his ideas. This is where the use of modelling and simulation techniques become essential. They provide the only method of proving that the system will perform in the expected manner, save for actually implementing the design which could be a very expensive method of finding some design error.

What Do We Mean by Modelling and Simulation?

The terms 'modelling' and 'simulation' can mean very different things in different areas of technology. The aircraft industries use simulators for training aircrew. The electronic industry use simulators for testing circuits. Scientists and social scientists develop models to test their theoretical predictions. Many industries use physical scale models in the development of products or for testing purposes, e.g. wind tunnel models. For the purpose of this paper the terms 'modelling' and 'simulation' imply a computer program which, given sufficient information to describe the operation and initial conditions of a manufacturing system, will provide numerical and/or graphical information on the performance of the proposed system. Any simulator or model should allow a thorough assessment of the system's capabilities, its deficiencies and any possible bottlenecks.

What Information Are We Looking For?

The most obvious answer is the production rate, what the system will produce per shift, per day or whatever time period we choose to consider, under varying conditions. The production figures should not be thought of as fixed values but should be considered as a function of the various system parameters. The production rate will vary with initial conditions, work schedule and product mix, machine reliability and the number of parts in the system. Some idea of how the production rate varies with these parameters can greatly influence any design modifications and how the system should be operated.

We should also be able to predict throughput-times as a function of the various system parameters for any given part. The time a product has to spend in the system is often as important as the production rate. This is especially true in made-to-order industries and when it is desired to minimize stock and work-in-progress levels. Other important areas in which a model or simulation should be useful is in providing machine utilization values and queue length information. The machine utilization is the fraction of time a machine is in use. If a machine or group of machines is heavily utilized compared to the other machines in a randomly routed FMS, queues of parts will develop. Depending on the particular system design, allowance must be made for these queues. Some sort of buffer store may be necessary or a new operating code developed.

Types of Models and Simulations

There are many different types of models and simulations possible, each having its own advantages and disadvantages. They range from very simple mathematical models to comprehensive simulations known as emulators. This paper will consider four categories. They are closed queuing network mathematical models, detailed discrete simulations, simulators with graphical or animation capabilities, and specific simulators for looking at problem sections of the overall system.

Mathematical Models

The most commonly used mathematical models are based on CAN-Q (Computer Analysis of Networks of Queues). The theory behind this closed-loop queuing network was developed by Jackson[1] and enhanced by Solberg,[2] Gordon and Newell,[3] and by Buzen[4]. Their ideas were incorporated in the development at Cranfield of a Generalized Modelling System (GMS).[5] This model sees FMS as a number of work-stations, each containing one or more machines which are linked by some transport mechanism. There is a fixed number of parts in the system. This may be considered as the same parts recirculating or a new part entering as soon as one leaves. The model requires the following information as input data:

(1) the number of work-stations and the number of servers (machines) at each work-station;
(2) number of different work-pieces in the system and the mix ratio;
(3) the work-in-process level;
(4) the route and process times for each work-piece;
(5) the number of servers and average time taken by the transport system.

The model does not proceed through a step-by-step evaluation of the operations in a given system, but makes predictions based on the above-mentioned theory, about the long-term average performance of the system.

The model produces the following system performance measures:

(1) production rates,
(2) machine utilizations,
(3) throughput times,
(4) work-in-progress,
(5) machine bottleneck and buffer queue data,
(6) design curves,
(7) sensitivity analysis.

Modelling and Simulation in System Design

The buffer queue data is a prediction of the probabilities of queue lengths at each work-station. This data tells us what fraction of time the queue will exceed a given value. The average value is also given. For a highly utilized work-station, the queue lengths will generally be longer than for a low utilization work-station.

The sensitivity analysis tells us what is the effect on the production rates of varying the process times at the various work-stations, e.g. a one per cent decrease in the process times at work-station 3 gives a 0.3 per cent increase in production.

The above information is provided in numerical form, but graphical representation of some sections is possible. Machine utilization and queue length histograms together with the design curves, i.e. plots of production rate and throughput time against work-in-progress level, may be obtained. An example of a machine utilization histogram is shown in figure 1. This shows the percentage utilizations for a 5-work-station system, station number 6 being the transport system. Work-station number 1 has a utilization of 83 per cent whereas the transport system only has a utilization of 32 per cent.

The major advantage of using mathematical models is the ease and speed of use. They are normally data driven, i.e. new models may be created by a change of input data, and hence no software modifications are necessary. The input data requirements are simple and no detailed knowledge of system interaction is required.

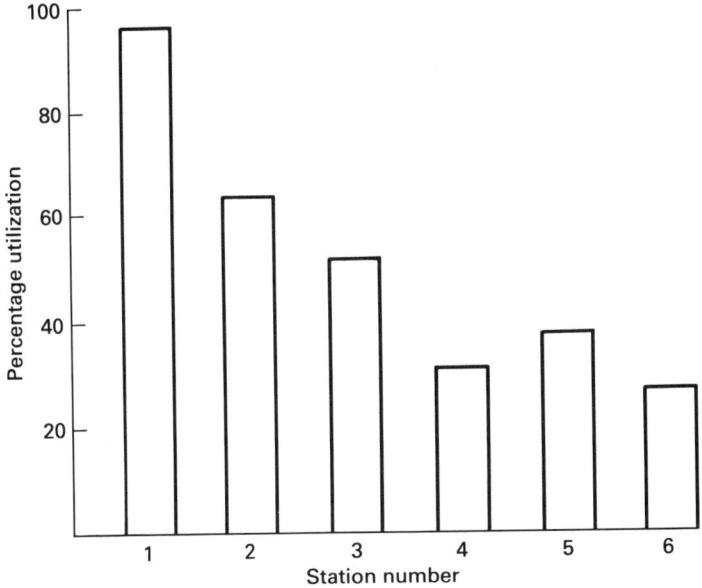

Figure 1   Output example for GMS

The major disadvantage is that the model only gives long-term average results. It assumes that the system is in a state of equilibrium with a fixed number of parts in a fixed mix ratio. Certain unrealistic assumptions have to be made. It is assumed that each work-station has unlimited buffer store. The model does inform the user of the size of the queues so decisions may be made on how to allow for the queues. The disadvantage is that the problem of blocking cannot be studied. An example of blocking is when a part is due to be moved to a work-station whose available buffer store is occupied. This often means that the second buffer store becomes full and processed parts cannot be unloaded. In a real FMS some sort of decision mechanism must be incorporated to overcome this problem. Unfortunately this strategy cannot be tested by the mathematical model.

Although GMS requires a route around the system for each part this information is not actually used. The theory assumes a random routing and uses the information provided to calculate the visit frequencies and durations. The order of work-station visits is unimportant as far as the model is concerned. Again this assumption leads to an overlooking of the blocking problem. Because the results are long-term averages it is not possible to perform experiments that involve time-dependent properties. Events such as machine breakdowns, rescheduling, shift start-up and varying the number of parts in the system cannot be studied. For example, it is possible to consider a system with and without a certain machine and obtain two sets of results. What is not available is the transition between the two steady states.

To summarize, the mathematical models such as CAN-Q and GMS, provide a quick, easy-to-use design aid for a manufacturing system designer. Care must be taken in the interpretation of the results because of the averaging effect and neglect of interactions.

Detailed Discrete Simulators

The terms 'model' and 'simulation' are often used interchangeably but here we shall restrict the term 'model' to be a mathematical model and a 'simulator' to refer to a step-by-step calculation of how a proposed system will perform. Because every event is considered in as much detail as required, it is possible to build into a model all the decision-making logic that the final system will use. This enables much more realistic predictions to be made about a system's performance. The basis of the normal type of simulation is that each activity currently active is checked for its finishing time. The next activity or activities to be completed define the next time step. At the end of this time step, the appropriate activities are stopped and the appropriate totals updated. The next stage is probably the most complex. It has to decide which activities may be started. It is in this section that the proposed system's decision-making philosophy must be incorporated. Once the new activities, if any, have been allocated the appropriate times, the cycle is repeated. These new activities together with those already active are considered to decide the next time step. This is essentially the three-phase approach favoured in the UK. A variation of this is the two-phase approach in which the stopping and starting sections or phases are combined. This is the approach favoured in the USA.

It is possible to construct a simulation using any computer language, but it is usual to use a high-level language such as FORTRAN. This means starting each simulation task afresh and producing a new program each time. Because many of the systems under consideration have similar properties and they are essentially being considered by the same simulation method, it is possible to use previously developed software. This use of a library of subroutines or a package is the most commonly used method. The first package was the General Simulation Program (GSP) written by Tocker[6] and there has been considerable development since then. A brief history of the development of these packages and a discussion of the different types of simulation is given by Mills.[7] These packages now form the basis of most simulation work. They have the ability to perform most of the procedures the user will want to use. Rather than create new software, the existing package subroutines may be used. It is not possible to implement every task or decision-making process using the packages facilities, but because they are usually written in a high-level language, it is possible to include user-written software into the package-based program.

Because the proposed system is represented by the software construction, considerable effort is needed in collecting information on how the system is to be operated. This must be done before the simulation work proceeds. It is also advisable to build into the simulation program the ability to perform the experiments needed to analyse the system's characteristics. If they are not available, new software will have to be produced every time some system parameter is varied. This means that considerable problem definition, program planning and data collection is necessary. The creation of the simulation program has been greatly simplified by the availability of simulation packages and may be accomplished relatively easily by experienced users. The time scale involved is a function of the system complexity and the level of detail involved.

Once the simulation program has been produced it is necessary to prove or validate it. This is difficult when considering a proposed system and there is nothing with which to compare the results. Nevertheless care should be taken to ensure that the program accurately reflects the desired system. It is now possible to perform the necessary 'What If?' experiments. This stage is used to find how the system will perform under various conditions and control philosophies. Because this simulation is a step-by-step, event driven representation, it is possible to perform time-dependent experiments. The best procedures for system start-up and how to cope with breakdowns may be investigated under various conditions. This leads to refinements of the operating philosophy. The different experiments possible are only limited by the user's imagination but one of the first things to discover from the simulation are the system properties that have the greatest effect on performance. The system designer may then concentrate on these areas. It is so much easier, quicker and less expensive to perform experiments using simulation than on a real system.

A recent development is the use of code generators as an aid to the use of simulation packages. Normally by the use of a series of questions, the code generator extracts information from the user in such a way as to allow it to call up its own library subroutines to construct a simulation program. This speeds up the procedure and perhaps allows a less experienced user to produce quickly a usable program. The code may be less efficient than that created by an experienced user, but the reduced development time balances this drawback. If it is not possible to include some detailed procedure by using the code generator, additional software may be included.

Simulators with Animation

The development of low-cost colour graphic terminals with local intelligence has allowed simulation to include animation facilities. The animation is normally a scaled map of the system which allows parts, robotrucks etc., to be shown moving from machine to machine. The colour facility makes comprehension of display much easier. The animation system is an extension of the discrete simulation described above. It is essential that it is able to provide the numerical information as well as the display. This permits the system to be actually seen in action, especially useful in considering bottlenecks and any possible blocking. The simulator, in stepping through the actions of the system, not only updates the running totals but must also update the animated display. The actual display is controlled by a local processor, but it is still a considerable overhead on the program. It is usually possible to switch off the display.

There are some drawbacks and limitations in using one of these systems. There is a limit to the amount of detail that may be displayed on a terminal screen. This may be inconvenient for large systems, but it is sometimes possible to have two or more display 'pages' which may be continually updated and switched back and forth as required. Another drawback is the problem of time-scaling. In a non-animated simulation it is desirable to have the ratio of real time to simulated time to be high as possible. This gives the results in the shortest possible computer time. When using an animated simulation, however, this ratio must be chosen with care. If it is too high the effect is like a speeded-up film and there is little benefit to the user. If it is too low, the animation becomes much clearer but results in very long run times. It is necessary to balance the need for numerical information with the desire for a sensible visualization.

One of the major advantages of the animation is the selling or justifying a proposed system. Any presentation of a proposal is much more convincing if the system may be seen 'in action' and the effect of various decisions demonstrated. When a design exercise is completed the animated simulation may be used for training operating personnel. The effects of decisions are shown clearly by the display and reflected in the numerical information. Any mistakes made are easily rectified. Because in this case the need is to visualize the system in operation the time ratio may be kept low to make the display reflect the actual system.

Specific Simulation

In a manufacturing system there are several areas where very detailed investigation may be required. Where such an area may be considered in total

Modelling and Simulation in System Design 249

or partial isolation, the simulation may be performed separately. The three categories considered above looked at the total system, but it is possible to obtain results for a problem area and use them as inputs to the main simulation.

One such area that may be considered in partial isolation is a single or multirobot assembly cell. Collision avoidance and synchronization are problems which have to be considered in more than just availability and time variables. The actual physical movements must be considered in great detail. Robot simulation packages are now available which assist in this task. The design of the work cell and the robot programming may also be performed using these packages. They usually employ a dynamic, 3-D CAD-like display which means that the hardware needed to run the packages is expensive. Hopefully as the technology is developed the price will fall. This form of simulation produces time values for the various tasks to be undertaken, which may be fed into the main system simulation. The particular work-cell need not be considered in detail but considered as a black box within the program. The principle use of these packages is the cell design and robot program, but if they are available they can simplify the task of system simulation.

When an FMS is being considered, the flexibility is limited by several factors. Obviously the mass, volume and maching capabilities of the machine tools or work-stations may have severe limitations, and the capacity of any transport system restricts the range of parts which may be produced. Another major factor affecting the flexibility or versatility of a system is the availability of the cutting tools at the correct work-station, at the correct time.

Machining centres and especially lathes have a limited tool-storage capacity, and when a system is being designed for limited manual intervention it is essential to consider the tool-storage and tool-transport facilities. To aid the design of the tooling system, two simulation programs have been written at Cranfield. The first model, TOOLSIM1 allows the interactions between a machine, its primary or machine-based tool store, a secondary tool store and the associated tool-transfer mechanisms to be investigated. A schematic diagram of this system is shown in figure 2. The second model, TOOLSIM2, permits an extension of this system to include several machines and their associated primary stores which may be linked to a common secondary store. A three-machine version of this type of system is shown in figure 3. The models have been made as general as possible by allowing the primary-exhange mechanism, between the primary store and the machine spindle, and secondary-exchange mechanism, between the two stores, to be selected from a list of four possible options. Currently the tool stores are

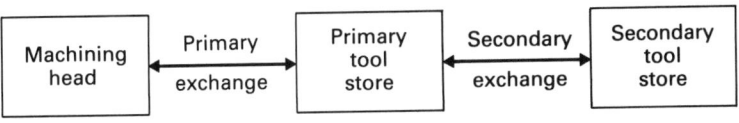

Figure 2   Schematic of TOOLSIM1

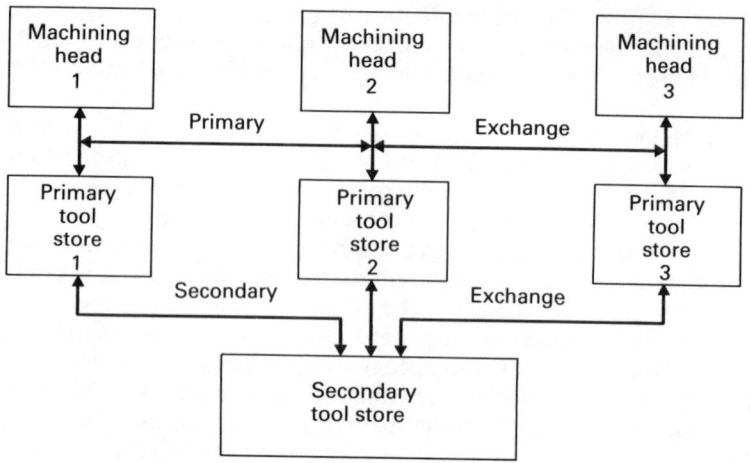

Figure 3 Schematic example of TOOLSIM2

assumed to be of a closed-loop form which may be rotated in either direction to minimize tool-selection times. It is possible to include routines to allow for other types of stores. Because special exchange procedures are required by some types of tool changer, it is necessary to specify the oversize tools which require three empty pockets.

These programs may be used to calculate the time taken by a machine or a group of machines to perform a set of machining operations. This time will depend on the type of tool changer, the initial positions of the tools and the speed of the store rotation. These times may be used as inputs to the total system simulation. The second model TOOLSIM2 is more likely to be used to test a proposed operating philosophy. When unmanned operation is planned, allowance must be made for the replacement of broken or worn tools. The effect of varying the number of duplicate or sister tools and the criteria used to decide priorities may be investigated. The secondary store may be used only to provide replacement tools or it may hold all the tools with the primary store acting as a buffer for tools being transferred into the spindle. The first method minimizes the tool changes but may need many more duplicates or limit the system flexibility. The second method minimizes the number of tools but will require many more tool movements. The optimum is likely to be somewhere between these extremes. The operating philosophy that the simulation indicates to be preferable may then be used as the basis for controlling the tool storage and transport system. A fuller description is given by Kay and Walmsley.[5]

The Use of Simulation and Modelling Techniques

In order to make the best use of the design aids available we must consider their advantages and disadvantages. Mathematical models are generally

Modelling and Simulation in System Design

quick and easy to use due to their limited data input requirements. Unfortunately they only predict the long-term average performance of the proposed manufacturing system. A discrete simulation is much more time consuming, and hence, costly, to develop. Considerably more detail may be built into the program which leads to a requirement for comprehensive information on the proposed system and how it is to be used. Consequently the output may also be very detailed and a wide range of system parameters may be considered.

This suggests the use of a mathematical model as a method to perform a quick if limited analysis of a proposed system. It will indicate to the designer the expected production rates, throughput times, machine utilizations, etc., for a given product mix. It is also possible to perform experiments to investigate variations in system design. This is especially important when a particular work-station appears to be a bottleneck, i.e. its utilization is much higher than the other machines. The sort of questions that may be asked are: What if an extra identical machine is added? What if the process times at the machine may be reduced? What if some tasks are transferred to other machines?

Because the models may be developed quickly and cheaply, this type of analysis may be undertaken for several possible solutions to the production problem. This type of exercise provides production predictions but economic investigations must be undertaken in parallel. The production rates and work-in-progress levels will play a part in the economic considerations but the costs of the machines, tooling, transport mechanisms, control software, installation and running costs are also necessary. When all the information is available, comparisons may be made and a nominally 'best' solution selected.

We are now at the stage when we want to refine our system design and to understand in greater detail how the system will operate. Particular problem areas may be simulated to find optimum solutions but eventually it is necessary to 'prove' that the proposed system will provide the benefits required. Comprehensive data about the parts to be produced, the machine and transport capabilities and reliabilities, how many pallets and fixtures are available etc., must be obtained to test fully the design. The input variables may be varied to see if a better solution exists. This simulation in greater detail is performed at this later stage because of the time and hence the cost involved. To undertake this work for a range of possible systems would be very time consuming and expensive.

When the design is finalized it is necessary to convince someone to spend the money. This may mean justifying the scheme to a board of directors or selling the idea to a client company. If the discrete simulation has been performed using a system which includes animation facilities this task is made much easier. The actual operation of the system may be seen on a VDU screen with parts moving about on conveyors or robotrucks. Obviously the financial implications will be carefully considered but a realistic demonstration of a system in operation will carry considerable weight.

To summarize this procedure we may use a mathematical model to obtain a quick comparison of the various options. The 'best' proposal is then considered in detail by the use of discrete simulation methods, with or without animation facilities. Any problem areas may be considered in greater detail by using specific simulators.

When the design has been completed we will have a mathematical model and a simulation program which may now be used for other purposes. During the implementation there could be changes to the design. These may be tested by using the already established software and data. It is possible to use the simulation as an aid to scheduling. It could predict the results of selecting the various schedule options and also indicate the state of the manufacturing system at the end of the period under consideration. If the simulation is integrated with a system-monitoring scheme, valuable management information could be provided. As mentioned above, a simulation especially in conjunction with an animated display is a valuable aid to personnel training. This may be undertaken before the system is operational or for the training of new personnel after commissioning without interfering with production. The introduction of new parts into the system may also be tested.

Future Developments

The most important possible development is the introduction of Artificial Intelligence techniques into the design of FMS or manufacturing systems in general. The concept of an expert system with built-in 'experience' could lead to a considerable shortening of the design time. It could be used to help specify the system's hardware components such as machine tools or be used to help the financial justification. Expert systems which construct a mathematical model or a simulation program could enable untrained personnel to reap their benefits directly. Perhaps a more realistic development is the enhancement to the code generators which construct simulation programs. These could be made more user friendly and oriented towards the engineer rather than the simulation exponent. An interesting proposal suggested by Mills[7] is the inclusion of control and scheduling statements into the simulation in a form which would allow direct implementation into the actual control software. This would save a duplication of effort and lead to a greater confidence that the control software will work.

Acknowledgements

The author would like to acknowledge the continuing support of the Department of Industry and the National Engineering Laboratory in the development of the FMS simulation and modelling tools at Cranfield.

References

1. J. R. Jackson, *Management Science*, vol. 10 (1963).
2. J. J. Solberg, 'Optimal Design and Control of Computerised Manufacturing Systems', *Proc. AIEE*, Systems engineering Conference (1976).

3. W. J. Gordon and G. F. Newell, *Oper. Res., vol. 15* (1967) pp. 254–65.
4. J. P. Buzen, *Comm. ACM*, vol. 16 (1973) pp. 527–31.
5. J. M. Kay and A. J. Walmsley, *Proc. FMSI* (1982) pp. 463–80.
6. K. D. Tocher et al., *J.R. Stat. Soc., A122 no. 4* (1958) pp. 484–510.
7. R. I. Mills, *Proc. FM2* (1983) pp. 185–96.

3.7

Inventory Control: Models and Problems

G. Urgeletti Tinarelli

Introduction

The problem of inventory control today represents one of the most important areas of Operational Research (OR) and much has already been written on the subject. It would therefore be impossible to review all the ideas discussed under this heading.

Our purpose is less ambitious particularly since important reviews have already been published that are useful for an overview of the subject (see e.g. the works of Whitin,[64] Hanssmann,[19] Veinott,[59] Clark[7]).

Let us begin our discussion of inventory problems with Wilson's classical model which, in spite of its characteristically wide range of assumptions that render it unsuitable for a treatment of concrete problems, brings together all the aspects which we believe to be essential to the majority of inventory control problems. We would like to insist that an accurate study of Wilson's model is important not only from the historical point of view but also because from this model it is possible to extrapolate more general models on the one hand, and more particular models on the other.

From this position we will be able to link various problems and establish a classification that, we think, provides a useful guide to what has already been written on the most famous models. The reader will forgive us if this review tends more to a discussion of the problems than of the mathematical techniques used to solve them: the author is convinced that today – as in its origins – the main task of OR is to suggest solutions to real problems; it is a factor in the business of survival. We shall also present a selective list of articles on the subject, which have appeared in the last few years.

G. Urgeletti Tinarelli is Associate Professor of Operations Research at the Faculty of Economics, University of Parma, Italy.

Source: G. Urgeletti Tinarelli, 'Inventory Control: Models and Problems', from *European Journal of Operational Research*, 1983, vol. 14, pp. 1–12.

Inventory Control: Models and Problems

It is well known that problems of inventory control, especially in manufacturing industry, are linked to problems of production programming and often are resolved along with these, if not actually as a subordinate problem. We shall try not to treat such problems in this work. For an accurate review of these problems, see the work of Gelders and Van Wassenhove.[13]

Historical Outline

The first mathematical model for inventory control which we know about is generally referred to as *Wilson's model* and was obtained by Harris in 1915 while he was working on a system of production planning and inventory control on behalf of the Westinghouse Co.

Several years later Wilson[63] presented the same formula and all its possible applications in a model for inventory control conceived for commercial enterprises.

The first probabilistic model, now known as 'newsboy problem', was obtained during World War II and after during the 1950s, rigorous and systematic analyses began to appear.

One of the first texts which deal with probabilistic models in inventory control was Whitin's,[65] the same author that produced along with Wagner[61] the dynamic version of the economic lot size model.

In 1958 one of the first rigorous analyses of this problem that came from an economist's pen appeared;[1] during this period research into inventory problems multiplied at both the practical and the theoretical levels. An interesting text that surveys all the problems studied up to 1962 is Hanssmann;[20] Hadley and Whitin's[18] work is also excellent for its clarity and depth.

After 1957 and the appearance of Belmann's 'Dynamic Programming' many real dynamic problems were resolved using this method.

In the last few years, with the greater diffusion of computers, research has been based more on simulation, which allows the relatively easy solution for problems which would otherwise be impossible to solve.

Problems of Inventory Control

Any resource that is left in storage awaiting use is called inventory. Examples of this are: raw materials, unfinished and finished goods, goods awaiting sale to commercial enterprises or even spare part and consumer material that is used during normal activity of a company.

Controlling inventory means assuring its accessibility, its quality, the time and place of its storage, and all this at the lowest possible cost. The state of the inventory is a result of a process of entry and exit of goods; however, since we can only control entry of goods – and, moreover, only partially – inventory control consists, in practice, in asking and answering the question '*How much and when to order*'. These are the fundamental problems that a controller of inventory must seek to answer and mathematical models are designed to propose a rational solution.

Presented in this way inventory control problems may seem quite simple but in fact their complexity comes from the diversity of real situations to which different basic suppositions suggest different solutions.

Since in every company every decision is taken for economic reasons and therefore in these problems the objective function can be seen as a cost to be minimized, let us list the main costs in an inventory system.

These are:

(1) *cost of buying the goods that are to be conserved.* This is of special significance when the price changes according to the size of the lot, or with time or by seasons, with economic trends, etc.;

(2) *ordering cost for an order placed from a supplier or else set up cost.* Often this is considered constant, that is to say independent of the size of the lot ordered or produced;

(3) *conservation cost of the goods in inventory* (*holding cost*). This includes costs of the following types: storage, insurance, handling but, above all, the cost of interest on the capital tied up in stock. The latter can represent a real drain that must be sustained with loans from a third party, or can also be considered as capital diverted from other profitable ends. This cost is generally considered as a percentage of the average value of the inventory. Other costs hitherto considered as conservation costs are: (*a*) obsolence, (*b*) loss through shrinkage or deterioration;

(4) *shortage costs*: this situation occurs when a real, or more often supposed, loss results from a demand that is greater than stock in hand. To express this quantitatively, although approximately, it would be necessary to consider all the immediate and future effects of an '*out of stock*' situation. The result differs markedly when different factors are taken into consideration (type of client, product, company, market) and it is very difficult to value the nature and size of these costs.

Now follows a list of the symbols we shall be using in our paper, and their meaning:

$S(t)$ inventory on hand at time t;
$\bar{S}(t)$ available inventory or '*inventory position*'; that is to say inventory on hand plus inventory on order minus any backorders;
λ demand in one unit of time;
T time between two successive orders;
τ time between the decision to issue an order and the time of its arrival in storage (lead time);
rt time between two successive surveys of stock levels;
r reorder point; that is to say the point of $\bar{S}(t)$ at which it is necessary to issue a new order;
s safety stock; that is to say the average portion of $S(t)$ that is on hand at the arrival of the new lot;
R the maximum value of $\bar{S}(t)$;
Q the reordered lot;
A the fixed cost of placing an order;

Inventory Control: Models and Problems 257

C   cost of every unit procured;
I   conservation cost per unit of capital and unit of time;
π   shortage cost; that is to say the cost per unit of demand when the system is in stock-out.

Wilson's Model and its Basic Assumptions

Wilson's model is a reference point for nearly all inventory control, not so much because it really represents many real situations but because by modifying its basic assumptions where necessary, many real models can be extrapolated.

These assumptions are:

(0)   one single product is stored in one single stocking location.

Concerning arrival of stock:
(1)   the product is delivered all at the same time (or the replenishment rate is infinite);
(2)   unit cost of purchasing (C) is known, constant through time and independent of the number of units acquired with every order;
(3)   any quantity can be ordered even if this is not a whole figure;
(4)   order cost (A) is constant and independent of the size of the order;
(5)   the product is ordered autonomously; that is to say that it is ordered alone and does not depend on the order of the other products;
(6)   lead time is known and constant.

Concerning exits:
(7)   demand is known, continuous and constant through time (d is the quantity of demand in one unit of time);
(8)   demand of product doesn't affect the demand of other products;
(9)   'stock-out' situations are unacceptable because the cost of this situation is extremly high.

Concerning the control and conservation of the product:
(10)   the product is indefinitely conservable;
(11)   the unit cost of conservation is calculated as a fixed percentage proportionate to the value of the stock and the time it must be conserved;
(12)   planning horizons are infinite;
(13)   there are no limits to space and capital invested in inventory.

In these conditions the optimum lot to be ordered, which we shall indicate by Q_w, is obtained simply by minimizing annual ordering and conservation costs. This is expressed in the following function:

$$y(Q) = A\frac{\lambda}{Q} + IC\frac{Q}{2} \quad (Q > 0).$$

The minimum value is then

$$Q = \sqrt{\left(\frac{2A\lambda}{IC}\right)} = Q_w,$$

where it results:

$y(Q_w) = \sqrt{(2AIC\lambda)} = y_w.$

The optimum recycling period is therefore constant:

$$T_w = \frac{Q_w}{\lambda} = \sqrt{\left(\frac{2A}{IC\lambda}\right)}.$$

The reordering point coincides with lead time demand because since all the factors are known beforehand, it is better not to have stock on hand when the new lot arrives.

Therefore we have: $r = \lambda\tau$ and $s = 0$.

Modifications to Wilson's Model

As we have already said, Wilson's model was already being adapted and generalized soon after its first appearance, to include assumptions that are closer to real management situations. A few of these generalizations have become classics in themselves and form the basis for deterministic models.

Let us examine the variations that seem most important: these are obtained by relaxing or abandoning the assumptions listed in the previous section.

The result is a primary classification that we shall present briefly in figure 1.

(a) *If we abandon assumption (1)*, we have an EOQ model with a finite production rate: this brings to consideration the problem of production's lot selection balancing equipment costs and conservation cost. This we shall call PLS.

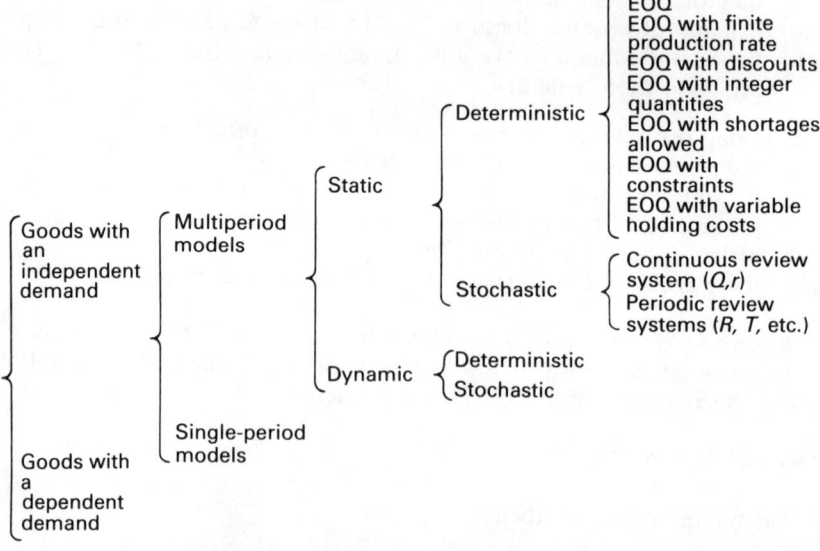

Figure 1 Primary classification of models

Inventory Control: Models and Problems 259

If we say that p is the quantity produced in one unit of time (*production rate*) and we preserve the meaning of all the above symbols, we can easily see that the best PLS (Q_p) is

$$Q_p = \sqrt{\left(\frac{2\lambda A}{IC}\right)} \quad \sqrt{\left(\frac{p}{p-\lambda}\right)} = Q_w \sqrt{\left(\frac{p}{p-\lambda}\right)}$$

and has the value

$$y_p = y_w \sqrt{\left(\frac{p-\lambda}{p}\right)}$$

Therefore, in general it is true that

$Q_p > Q_w$ and $y_p < y_w$.

However, when, as often happens in practice, $p \gg d$, we find that

$Q_p \approx Q_w$ and $y_p \approx y_w$.

(b) *If we abandon assumption (2)*, that is to say, we accept that the price of the goods depends on the quantity acquired by one order ($C = C(Q)$) we have another model called EOQ with discounts (depending on the quantity ordered).

The objective function should include the annual cost of orders, the annual conservation cost and the annual cost of acquisition. In practice variations in price are due to discounts made by the supplier for purchases of certain size. If we suppose that we have only two prices: C_1 and C_2 ($C_1 < C_2$) respectively for $Q < Q_1$ and for $Q \geq Q_1$ the objective function is as follows:

$$y = \begin{cases} A\frac{\lambda}{Q} + IC_1 \frac{Q}{2} + C_1\lambda, & 0 < Q < Q_1, \\ A\frac{\lambda}{Q} + IC_2 \frac{Q}{2} + C_2\lambda, & Q \geq Q_1 \end{cases}$$

and the minimum value is found using well-known analytical techniques. The above case is true when the reduced price is applied to the whole lot; if we assume that C_2 is applied only to an excess part of the same lot, the objective function becomes more complex but it becomes easier to find the minimum value, in that now we have a continuous function.

(c) *If we abandon assumption (3)*, that is to say that we can only order whole quantities or multiples of fixed lots, as is often true in practice, we have a very similar model to Wilson's, in which variables are only whole and positive numbers and the results are not very different from those of EOQ.

(d) *If we abandon assumption (9)*, that is to say that we accept that we can be out of stock (even if we have access to all the necessary information beforehand), we have an EOQ model with shortage allowed. Usually in this situation we identify two possible cases:

backorders: that is to say that the clients are prepared to wait and to accept a late delivery;

lost sales: that is to say that clients are not prepared to wait and take their custom elsewhere.

In the first case the total of annual ordering, holding and stock-out costs is a function of two variables, Q and b, which indicate respectively the lot and the maximum lack of stock. The minimum value for these is indicated by Q^* and b^*:

$$Q^* = Q_w \sqrt{\left(\frac{\pi + IC}{\pi}\right)} \quad (Q^* > Q_w),$$

$$b^* = \sqrt{\left(\frac{2AIC\lambda}{\pi(IC+\pi)}\right)}$$

and has the value

$$y^* = y_w \sqrt{\left(\frac{\pi}{\pi + IC}\right)} < y_w.$$

π represents the shortage cost per unit of lacking merchandise and unit of time.

In the second case the optimal solution is given by

$$Q = Q_w, \quad b = 0.$$

We conclude that if shortage costs are not considered infinite and that if the client concerned is prepared to accept a late delivery of the goods (as in a monopoly situation), then it is better to make him wait; if, on the other hand, the client is not prepared to wait then it is always better not to go out of stock.

(e) *If we abandon assumption (13)*, we have a management example in which the size of the lots acquired are conditioned by capital restraints and/or space. The problem becomes interesting if we consider the case of two or more articles of merchandise and a constraint active (see figure 2).

In this situation, given that v is the limit of volume (or capital), v_i is the volume (or capital) required by the ith item ($i = 1, 2, \ldots, n$), the problem can be set out as the search for the minimum value of the function of n variables:

$$y(Q_1, Q_2, \ldots, Q_n) = \sum_{i=1}^{n} \left(A_i \frac{\lambda_i}{Q_i} + IC_i \frac{Q_i}{2}\right)$$

with the constraints

$$\sum_{i=1}^{n} v_i Q_i \leq v,$$

$$Q_i > 0 \quad (i = 1, 2, \ldots, n).$$

The solution can be found using Lagrange's multiplier technique. However, since the unknowns (Q_i) are not found explicitly as a function of

Inventory Control: Models and Problems

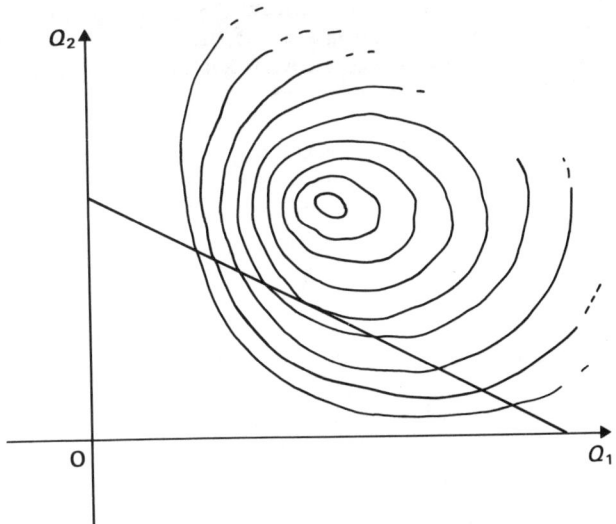

Figure 2 Two or more articles of merchandise and a constraint

their parameters, the system of partial derivatives equalized to zero is normally resolved by an iterative method.

The problem of two contemporaneous constraints (capital and space etc.) is more complex but the framework is the same.

(f) *If we abandon assumption (11)* (constant unit costs of conservation), we can accept that I is a step function of Q to suggest the case of renting extra storage space when the inventory is greater than a certain volume: a situation that is quite common in reality.

This assumption has been examined by Hanssmann,[19] for example, and its pattern is similar to the EOQ with discounts.

(g) *If we abandon assumption (7)* (constant rate of demand), we can suppose that demand varies for various reasons as for example, a result of publicity, and other processes that have a bearing on demand. More simply we can envisage that this is a decreasing function of price (this assumption has also been treated by Hanssmann[20]).

(h) *If we accept that demand or time for placing a new order (lead time) or both are not known beforehand and are governed by chance* (assumptions (6) and (7)), we arrive at the most interesting variation of the many that can be generalized from Wilson's model. These new assumptions give us a wide range of new models (stochastic models) that are numerous because they must represent many different real situations. The distinctions that are normally made, following Hadley and Whitin,[18] are the following:

(1) *reorder point models*. In these models we assume that constant volumes (Q) are to be ordered every time that the inventory reaches the reorder point (r). They are referred to as (Q, r) systems.

This type of inventory management, if we are to take its definition literally, is carried out by a continuous review system (for example using real-time accountancy) that allows a constant checking of the level of inventory and an immediate perception of the passing of the reorder point. In fact this can be achieved also using periodic review systems if the interval between two revisions (rt) is sufficiently short with respect to the assumed demand of the item;

(2) *models assuming a periodic revision of inventory*. In these models we assume that orders are made only at fixed periods usually at equal intervals and coinciding with revision times. Note that the difference between this and the previous models is that here the reorder cycles are constant and the size of the lot variable, whereas in the previous pattern it is the size of the lot that is constant and cycles variable.

We would also like to remind the reader that this kind of check can be carried out using manual accountacy systems as well as automatic batch accountancy.

The most common types of periodic revisions are:

- (T, R) – with constant intervals, length in time T, we must reorder what is necessary to bring the inventory position to level R;
- (T, R, r) – as in the above case, except that a new order is made only when the inventory stock is below a fixed level r;
- (T, r, nQ) – as in the previous case except that the order quantity must be a multiple of a predetermined lot (Q).

(Symbols and model terminology are extracted from Hadley and Whitin,[18] even though we know that many authors prefer to indicate with S and s the values which we indicate using R and r.)

Whilst in the (T, R) rule a new order is made whenever a review is made, in the other cases this is not necessarily true: in these cases a new order is placed only when the inventory position is below a pre-established level (r).

The decision to choose one of the above solutions – reorder point system or periodic review systems (and in the latter case one of the three systems) – depends on the comparison between reordering costs, revision costs and holding costs. Apart from the fact that the inventory manager is often conditioned by factors outside his control (type of accountancy used in the warehouse, reordering rules set down by the supplier, etc.) it seems obvious that we should limit the use of the reorder point systems, which are by nature more expensive, to articles that have a higher value on the market; that is to say those which in an ABC analysis would be considered in class A. On the other hand slow-moving articles – that is to say those in class C – could be reviewed and reordered at longer intervals. (This was truer some years ago than it is today even if in theory it still holds for the present time. In fact the widespread use of computers allows us to use reorder point systems for all types of goods, whatever their value.)

The value of the unknowns ((Q, r) in the first model, (T, R, r, nQ) in the others) are fixed in an exact way by minimizing the total ordering, holding and shortage costs as a function of these variables.

Even in this case, as in the deterministic case, we must distinguish two situations:

Inventory Control: Models and Problems

- backorders,
- lost sales,

in that these indicate different situations and therefore require different solutions.

However we must say that, even simplifying the basic assumptions, the resulting models are extremely complex and their solutions laborious. In fact in all the stochastic models of this kind, by equalizing to zero the partial derivatives we obtain systems that do not have closed form solutions.

These should, therefore, be resolved with an iterative approach, giving one of the unknowns a hypothetical value (usually we suggest that $Q = Q_w$ in the first step).

However, a current doctrine suggests another solution to these problems.

We fix the value of the unknowns to minimize the total reordering and holding costs – and sometimes, review costs – by subjecting them to the constraint that the probability of no shortfall should not be less than a pre-established L, called *service level*.

L is usually fixed at the outset on the basis of an estimated necessity for the individual product.

Using this second method we can avoid the complicated calculations of the previously stated method and we do not have to give numerical value to the shortage cost, which operators usually refuse to do anyway.

(i) *If we abandon assumption (10)*, that is to say we accept that the product has a limited durability, we enter into the single-period models. The first of them is called *'Newsboy problem'* or also the *'Christmas tree problem'* because it is adapted to perishable goods, which are subject to fashion or other obsolescence or, in any case, products that lose their usefulness at the end of one period in stocks.

In this case the unknown is the amount to be ordered at the beginning of the period: the optimum solution is that which maximizes profits. We must consider that any goods left at the end of the period must be cleared out (and therefore must be considered as *left-over stock* with the appropriate cost); if, on the other hand, demand is greater than the quantity on hand we have a shortfall cost. We do not consider holding costs because the period is very short.

A simplified version of this model is that dealing with goods to be consumed and not with goods to be sold; a more complicated version is that in which we accept that shortage costs are proportionate to the size of the shortage and the length of time the product is out of stock and that holding costs in the warehouse do in fact exist (this model has been examined by Hadley and Whitin[18]).

(j) *If we abandon assumptions (2) and (7)* and we accept that prices, production capacity and, above all, demand vary through time, the resulting models are called dynamic.

Demand can vary as a result of a variety of factors; we shall list only a few:

- seasonality,
- trends.

Generally we distinguish between increasing trends for new products and decreasing trends for goods that are destined to depletion because, for example, they are at the end of their normal life cycle.

Many studies have been made in this field, but in practice only the most simple dynamic problems can be resolved easily. When the number of products is high, even dynamic programming, which is usually suggested as a useful approach, cedes place to heuristics and simulation.

We can bring under this dynamic model also those in which *inflation* has an impact on stock management. It is a subject in itself, a very current and interesting problem. How should one behave in a market with constantly changing prices? The answer is not very easy; however some studies have been made on this problem and a few answers given.

(k) *If we abandon assumption (8)*, we must consider products that have a dependent demand for some reason. Dependence can be of various kinds. We shall list a few examples:

(i) if a product is made up of two or more parts, demand for the final product produces a demand for the component parts;
(ii) some products are complementary (car/petrol, cigarettes/matches) and their demand is necessarily linked;
(iii) certain products are succedanea, that is to say that – within certain limits – they are interchangeable. In this case the demand for one is a function of that of another and their control is therefore interdependent;
(iv) some products supplied by the same commercial source are usually ordered together. Even though there are different articles, they are linked in the acquisition phase.

Types of dependence that we have not identified are studied using different models. The first type is treated using an MRP model (*Material Requirement Planning*). The second could usefully be treated using an MRP model with reordering point.

The last type of interdependence is treated with jointly reordering systems or batch systems.

Finally a further generalization can be achieved by abandoning the assumption (0), that is to say considering the managed goods as being located in more than one point. If the output of one inventory becomes the input of another, then it is called a *series of stations*; if there are several storage points all on the same level, and they supply a storage point downstream or are supplied by a point upstream, they are called *parallel stations*.

These systems of inventory control, which are quite complex, have been explored using heuristics or simulation.

Recent Contributions to the Theory of Inventory Control

We shall now present some of the most recent publications seeking to refer to these in a systematic manner.

Inventory Control: Models and Problems

The classification that we present – which is by definition subjective – will be based on the problems treated in the individual works; it is not within the scope of this review to give a detailed description of the contents of each publication. On the other hand we consider that the criteria used in compiling this list can be useful to both the operational researcher who seeks to improve his own performance and to the academic who wants to be acquainted with the state of the art in this field.

Our classification consist of six groups:

(1) stochastic models,
(2) dynamic demand models,
(3) models for perishables,
(4) joint-ordering systems,
(5) capital and/or volume constraints,
(6) inventory control and devaluation.

Stochastic Models

We shall suggest a few articles that treat in various ways particular stochastic models.

It is well known that the pressing problem in 'reorder point' systems is not so much the choice of the *size* of the lot (Q) but the fixing of the *reorder point* (r) or, alternatively, the *safety stock* (s); the latter problem is common in all stochastic models.

Now there are two factors which play an important role in fixing r:

• handling costs and shortage costs, or alternatively service level;
• the distribution function of lead time demand (which in the most complex case is the product of two random variables: τ and λ).

Examining this problem, some authors seek to determine the distribution function most appropriate in representing demand (see the works by Kottas and Lau,[26] Mumford,[37] Tadikamalla[51]). Others attempt to fix decision variables (r, R, etc.) assuming that demand and/or lead time have a standard distribution (e.g. normal, Poisson, lognormal, binomial, etc.) (Erhardt,[11] Freeland and Porteus,[12] Magson,[33] Kruse,[27] Das,[8] Liberatore[32]).

Gupta[17] considers the relation between the variance of lead time demand and reorder point.

A particularly complex case, in which we admit that demands in successive periods are correlated, is considered by Ray.[43,44]

Different from those already discussed, but still in the stochastic group, is Lau's work[29] which considers an interesting variation on the 'newsboy problem' in which he proposes, as an alternative objective, the maximization of expected utility and the probability of attaining budget goals.

Dynamic Demand Models

As we have already said, when we suppose that demand is not stationary we usually differentiate between an increasing and a decreasing trend. In this article we propose to follow this custom while presenting the papers that come under this heading. More precisely we shall distinguish between articles that treat cases of:

(a) growing demand,
(b) diminishing demand,
(c) demand generally varying due to trend and seasonality.

In group (a) we find the works of Resh, Friedman and Barbosa[45] which consider the classical EOQ model with the assumption that the demand rate is deterministic and increases linearly with time; Kicks and Donaldson[23] propose an approximation method for determining the level for inventory replenishment in the case of variable discrete demand. This method yields satisfactory results when there is a growing demand, but it produces significant errors when demand is diminishing.

Still in this group we include the works of Buchanan,[3] Henery[21] and Silver,[49] of which the first proposes two different approaches and two alternative solution methods for the inventory replenishment problem in the assumption of growing demand, and the second a variation on Donaldson's model, still in a growing demand situation.

Jaiswal and Shah[22] consider then the cases of demand variable in arithmetic and geometric progression.

In group (b) we find the work of Barbosa and Friedman[2] which examines a product with vanishing market demand.

In group (c) are the works of Ritchie,[46] Phelps,[42] Silver[48] and Levary[31] that consider optimal rules for the replenishment of stocks that are subject to trends, seasonality and linear trend followed by a period of steady demand.

Models for Perishables

Among the authors that have recently treated these problems, we call to the reader's attention the following: Nahimias,[38] who presents a series of models that allow us to find the best ordering policy for goods with a pre-established life-time; again Nahimias[39] returns to the subject comparing two dynamic models; and finally Nahimias and Wang[40] present a heuristic for the choice of the optimal lot size and reorder point policy for products that are subject to exponential decay.

On the same subject are the works of Upendra,[53] Duermeyer,[10] Dave and Patel,[9] Weiss[62] and Tadikamalla.[52] Whilst Weiss examines an inventory control model for products under continuous review and for perishables, Tadikamalla suggests an EOQ model for products in which deterioration occurs with a gamma distribution.

Joint-Ordering Systems

It often happens, and this especially in commercial enterprises, that many products — for example those that are usually supplied by the same source — can or must be ordered at the same time. If it is not obligatory, the inventory controller might actually consider the possibility that a policy of joint ordering of stock can be more profitable than one of separate ordering, and in the case that this is found to be true, he should find the optimum interval between two successive replenishments.

There are also other interesting problems:

(a) what should the total value of the lot be and how should this be distributed among the individual items;
(b) how should the same problem be resolved when the supplier concedes a discount relative to the total value of the order.

Can inventory control using joint-ordering systems be realized only with a periodic review policy or also with continuous review policy? If we accept, as seems logical, a periodic review system with fixed intervals, how do we decide on the best out of the many alternative intervals? Finally we may ask in what conditions is a partially joint-reorder system preferable to others.

To some of these questions some answers have already been given: see the work of Urgeletti Tinarelli,[54] Chakravarty,[6] and for analogous problems in the production of joint lots: Korgaonker,[25] Goyal,[14,16] Koa.[24]

Other works solve the problem of inventory control when there are some constraints suggesting the bringing together of lots. These are discussed in the next section.

However, many of the problems in this sector are still without solution especially those that are more strictly operative. It is however probable that in the more complex cases only heuristics or simulation can be used successfully.

Capital and/or Volume Constraints

The control of several articles under some constraints, originally treated by Hanssmann,[20] and by Hadley and Whitin,[18] has been taken up again by Page and Paul in the past few years.[41] The latter suggest that, to overcome the difficulties imposed by constraints, orders should be made at equal intervals, which leads to a more economic solution and overcomes some of the more critical aspects of the Lagrange's multiplier approach. Goyal[15] suggests a further extension to the method of the grouping of orders that is suggested by Page and Paul which he claims improves its efficiency.

Van Nunen and Wessels[58] propose solution methods for dynamics problems; Schrady and Choe[47] present models for several goods under some constraints and controlled by a constant review system.

In one of my papers[56] I show that when only capital constraint is present, with a few specific assumptions, it is possible to find the closed form for optimum lot size and for total inventory control costs. In the same work I also examined the problem under the assumption that some items – the profitable – can be eliminated.

Problems of productivity restriction, space and capital constraints are often considered in papers that use dynamic programming as a method for finding the optimum inventory situation. We would like to remind the reader of Castellani's paper[5] that considers the problem of distributing the limited capacity of a warehouse among various articles with variable parameters (costs, returns, storage and shortage costs).

Inventory Control and Devaluation

As we have already said the problems that currency devaluation causes to inventory controllers are considerable. This is particularly true in certain countries that have suffered a high rate of devaluation in the past years.

For articles that have a constant demand rate, a common and intuitive solution suggests to subtract from the unit cost of storage the rate of revaluation of the article: is this a rational response? We note that the optimum lot size calculated according to this theory is greater than that obtained without considering devaluation. (In fact this second lot is very small because where money depreciates its cost is very high.) However this is logical because if an item is revalued, its conservation cost is less than it is if we consider its holding cost alone; sometimes in this situation we can even make a profit!

The following question is also interesting: what is the optimum lot size if a sporadic increase in price is known beforehand? An expert material manager refuses to indulge in such speculation because he knows how many problems of space, capital and conservation costs this implies, even if the prediction were to be correct. However, at least from a theoretical point of view, it seems very interesting to answer such questions. A few speculative problems have been treated by Buzacott,[4] Urgeletti Tinarelli,[55] Misra[34,35] and Lev and Soyster.[30] In less than recent times, problems by speculation have been treated fully and substantially resolved – by using dynamic programming – by a few Italian authors whose works are all to be found in Volpato.[60]

Final Conclusions

In presenting this review we remarked how difficult it is to unite in a few homogeneous groups so many works of such varied content. It is obvious because every paper is a work in itself, not necessarily linked with its predecessors nor with its successors, even if in some cases this does occur.

A few works could belong to two or more groups, others cannot be included in any of the above groups. We would like to remind the reader that in the latter case are two works that have in common that they are variations on Wilson's classical model. These are: the publication by Subramanyan[50] that proposes a variant of the EOQ formula to consider the case in which demand varies as a result of publicity or, more generally, of a variation in price; and an article by Muhlemann and Valtis Spanopoulos[36] that supposes a holding cost rate that is an increasing function of the average value of the stock. This is quite an elegant way of taking into account the increase in the cost of money with a rise in investment and in practice to consider possible restrictions on maximum capital investment.

References

1. K. J. Arrow, S. Karlin and H. E. Scarf, *Studies in the Mathematical Theory of Inventory and Production* (Stanford: Stanford University Press, 1958).
2. L. C. Barbosa and M. Friedman, 'Inventory Lot Size Models with Vanishing Market', *J. Operational Res. Soc.*, vol. 30 (1979) pp. 1129–32.
3. J. T. Buchanan, 'Alternative Solution Methods for the Inventory Replenishment Problem under Increasing Demands', *J. Operational Res. Soc.*, vol. 31 (7) (1980) pp. 615–20.
4. J. A. Buzacott, 'Economic Order Quantities with Inflation', *Operational Res. Quart.*, vol. 26 (31) (1975) pp. 553–8.
5. G. Castellani, 'Sulla Gestione di un Magazzino nel Caso di Piu Articoli', in M. Volpato, (ed.), *Studi e Modelli di Ricerca Operativa* (Turin: UTET, 1971).
6. A. K. Chakravarty, 'Multi-item Inventory Aggregation into Groups', *J. Operational Res. Soc.*, vol. 32 (1) (1981) pp. 19–26.
7. A. J. Clark, 'An Informal Survey of Multi-echelon Inventory Theory', *Naval Res. Logist. Quart.*, vol. 19 (1972) pp. 621–50.
8. C. Das, 'Some Aids for Lot-size Inventory Control Under Normal Lead Time Demand', *AIIE Trans.*, vol. 7 (1) (1975) pp. 77–9.
9. U. Dave and L. K. Patel, '(T, Sl) Policy Inventory Model for Deteriorating Items with Time Proportional Demand', *J. Operational Res. Soc.*, vol. 32 (2) (1981) pp. 137–42.
10. B. L. Duermeyer, 'A Multi-type Production System for Perishable Inventories', *Operations Res.*, vol. 27 (5) (1979) pp. 935–43.
11. R. Erhardt, 'The Power Approximation for Computing (s, S) Inventory Policies', *Management Sci.*, vol. 25 (1979) pp. 777–86.
12. J. R. Freeland and E. L. Porteus, 'Evaluating the Effectiveness of a New Method for Computing Approximately Optimal (s, S) Inventory Policies', *Operations Res.* vol. 28 (2) (1980) pp. 353–64.
13. L. F. Gelders and L. N. Van Wassenhove, 'Production Planning: a Review', *European J. Operational Res.*, vol. 7 (1981) pp. 101–10.
14. S. K. Goyal, 'Determination of Economic Packaging Frequency in a Multi-brand Joint Replenishment Inventory System', *European J. Operational Res.*, vol. 4 (3) (1980) pp. 185–8.
15. S. K. Goyal, 'A Note on Multi-product Inventory Situations with One Restriction', *Operational Res. Quart.*, vol. 29 (3) (1978) pp. 269–71.
16. S. K. Goyal, 'Economic Packaging Frequency of Perishable Jointly Replenished Items', *Operational Res. Quart.*, vol. 28 (1) (1977) pp. 215–19.
17. N. K. Gupta, 'Effect of the Lead Time on Inventory: a Working Result', *J. Operational Res. Soc.*, vol. 30 (5) (1979) pp. 477–81.
18. G. Hadley and T. M. Whitin, *Analysis of Inventory System* (Englewood Cliffs, NJ: Prentice-Hall, 1963).
19. F. Hanssmann, 'A Survey of Inventory Theory from Operations Research Viewpoint', in R. L. Ackoff (ed.), *Progress in Operations Research*, vol. 1 (New York: Wiley, 1961) pp. 65–104.
20. F. Hanssmann, *Operations Research in Production and Inventory Control* (New York: Wiley, 1962).
21. R. J. Henery, 'Inventory Replenishment Policy for Increasing Demand', *J. Operational Res. Soc.*, vol. 30 (7) (1980) pp. 611–17.
22. M. C. Jaiswal and Y. K. Shah, 'On a Discrete Deterministic Inventory Model with Demand Varying in Progression', *AIIE Trans.*, vol. 8 (4) (1976) pp. 456–60.

23. P. Kicks and W. S. Donaldson, 'Irregular Demand: Assessing a Rough and Ready Lot-size Formula', *J. Operational Res. Soc.*, vol. 31 (8) (1980) pp. 725–32.
24. P. C. Koa, 'A Multi-product Dynamic Lot-size Model with Individual and Joint Set-up Costs', *Operations Res.*, vol. 27 (2) (1979) pp. 279–89.
25. M. G. Korgaonker, 'Integrated Production Inventory Policies for Multistage Multiproduct Batch Production System', *J. Operational Res. Soc.*, vol. 30 (4) (1979) pp. 355–62.
26. J. F. Kottas and H. Lau, 'The Use of Versatile Distribution Families in Some Stochastic Inventory Calculation', *J. Operational Res. Soc.*, vol. 30 (5) (1980) pp. 393–403.
27. W. K. Kruse, 'Waiting Time in an $S-I$, S Inventory System with Arbitrarily Distributed Lead Time', *Operations Res.*, vol. 28 (2) (1980) pp. 348–52.
28. S. Kumaraswamy and E. Sankarasubramanian, 'A Continuous Review of (S, s) Inventory System in which Depletion is Due to Demand and Failure of Units', *J. Operational Res. Soc.*, vol. 32 (11) (1981) pp. 997–1001.
29. H. Lau, 'The Newsboy Problem under Alternative Optimization Objectives', *J. Operational Res. Soc.*, vol. 31 (6) (1980) pp. 525–35.
30. B. Lev and A. L. Soyster, 'An Inventory Model with Finite Horizon and Price Changes', *J. Operational Res. Soc.*, vol. 30 (1) (1979) pp. 43–53.
31. R. R. Levary, 'A Sequential Inventory Control Model with Seasonal Demand', *Omega*, vol. 8 (2) (1979) pp. 243–7.
32. M. J. Liberatore, 'The EOQ Model under Stochastic Lead Time', *Operations Res.*, vol. 27 (2) (1979) pp. 391–6.
33. D. W. Magson, 'Stock Control when the Lead Time Cannot be Considered Constant', *J. Operational Res. Soc.*, vol. 30 (4) (1979) pp. 317–22.
34. R. B. Misra and A. W. Wortham, 'EOQ Model with Continuous Compounding', *Omega*, vol. 5 (1) (1977) pp. 98–9.
35. R. B. Misra, 'A Note on Optimal Inventory Management under Inflation', *Naval Res. Logist. Quart.*, vol. 26 (1) (1979) pp. 161–5.
36. A. P. Muhlemann and N. P. Valtis Spanopoulos, 'A Variable Holding Cost Rate EOQ Model', *European J. Operational Res.*, vol. 4 (2) (1980) pp. 132–5.
37. R. J. Mumford, 'The Numerical Generation of Lead Time Demand Distributions for Inventory Models', *Operational Res. Quart.*, vol. 28 (1) (1977) pp. 79–85.
38. S. Nahimias, 'Optimal Ordering Policies for Perishable Inventory – II', *Operations Res.*, vol. 23 (4) (1975) pp. 735–49.
39. S. Nahimias, 'Comparison Between Two Dynamic Perishable Inventory Models', *Operations Res.*, vol. 25 (1) (1977) pp. 168–72.
40. S. Nahimias and S. S. Wang, 'A Heuristic Lot Size Reorder Point Model for Decaying Inventories', *Management Sci.*, vol. 25 (1) (1979) pp. 90–7.
41. E. Page and R. J. Paul, 'Multi-product Inventory Situation with One Restriction', *Operational Res. Quart.*, vol. 27 (41) (1976) pp. 815–34.
42. R. I. Phelps, 'Optimal Inventory Rule for a Linear Trend in Demand with a Constant Replenishment Period', *J. Operational Res. Soc.*, vol. 31 (5) (1980) pp. 439–42.
43. W. D. Ray, 'Computation of Reorder Levels when the Demands are Correlated and the Lead Time Random', *J. Operational Res. Soc.*, vol. 32 (1) (1981) pp. 27–34.
44. W. D. Ray, 'The Significance of Correlated Demands and Variables Lead Time for Stock Control Policies', *J. Operational Res. Soc.*, vol. 31 (2) (1980) pp. 187–90.

Inventory Control: Models and Problems

45. M. Resh, M. Friedman and L. C. Barbosa, 'On a General Solution of the Deterministic Lot Size Problem with Time-proportional Demand', *Operations Res.*, vol. 24 (4) (1976) pp. 718–25.
46. E. Ritchie, 'Practical Inventory Replenishment Policies for a Linear Trend in Demand Followed by a Period of Steady Demand', *J. Operational Res. Soc.*, vol. 31 (7) (1980) pp. 605–13.
47. D. A. Schrady and U. C. Choe, 'Models for Multi-item Continuous Review Inventory Policies Subject to Constraints', *Naval Res. Logist. Quart.*, vol. 18 (4) (1971) pp. 451–63.
48. E. Silver, 'Inventory Control under a Probabilities Time-varying Demand Pattern', *AIIE Trans.*, vol. 10 (4) (1978) pp. 371–9.
49. E. A. Silver, 'A Simple Inventory Replenishment Decision Rule for a Linear Trend in Demand', *J. Operational Res. Soc.*, vol. 30 (1) (1979) pp. 71–5.
50. E. S. Subramanyan, 'EOQ Formula under Varying Marketing Policies and Conditions', *AIIE Trans.*, vol. 13 (4) (1981) pp. 312–14.
51. P. R. Tadikamalla, 'The Lognormal Approximation to the Lead Time Demand Inventory Control', *Omega* vol. 7 (6) (1979) pp. 553–6.
52. P. R. Tadikamalla, 'An EOQ Inventory Model for Items with Gamma Distributed Deterioration', *AIIE Trans.*, vol. 10 (1) (1978) pp. 100–3.
53. D. Upendra, 'On a Discrete-in-time Order Level Inventory Model for Deteriorating Items', *J. Operational Res. Soc.*, vol. 30 (4) (1979) pp. 349–54.
54. G. Urgeletti Tinarelli, 'A Proposito di Riordini Congiunti', *Atti delle Giornate di Lavoro AIRO*, Torino (1980) pp. 103–17.
55. G. Urgeletti Tinarelli, 'Sulla Determinaziona della Quantità Ottima da Ordinare in Ipotesi di Aumenti dei Prezzi', *Atti delle Giornate di Lavoro AIRO*, Taranto (1976) pp. 165–79.
56. G. Urgeletti Tinarelli, 'Politiche di Gestione a Scorta di Più Articoli in Presenza di un Vincolo di Capitale', *Atti delle Giornate di Lavoro AIRO*, Bologna (1979) pp. 147–61.
57. G. Urgeletti Tinarelli, *La Gestione delle Scorte, Organizzazione, Contabilità ed Automazione* (Milan: ETAS libri, 1981).
58. J. A. E. E. van Nunen and J. Wessels, 'Multi-item Lot Size Determination and Scheduling under Capacity Constraints', *European J. Operational Res.*, vol. 2 (1) (1978) pp. 36–41.
59. A. F. Veinott Jr, 'The Status of Mathematical Inventory Theory', *Management Sci.*, vol. 12 (1966) pp. 745–77.
60. M. Volpato, *Studi e Modelli di Ricerca Operativa* (Turin: UTET, 1971).
61. H. Wagner and T. M. Whitin, 'Dynamic Version of the Economic Lot Size Model', *Management Sci.*, vol. 5 (1) (1958) pp. 89–96.
62. H. J. Weiss, 'Optimal Ordering Policies for Continuous Perishable Inventory Models', *Operations Res.*, vol. 28 (2) (1980) pp. 365–74.
63. R. H. Wilson, 'A Scientific Routine for Stock Control', *Harvard Business Rev.*, vol. 13 (1) (1934) pp. 194–201.
64. T. M. Whitin, 'Inventory Control Research: a Survey', *Management Sci.*, vol. 1 (1954) pp. 32–40.
65. T. M. Whitin, *The Theory of Inventory Management* (Princeton: Princeton University Press, 1953).

3.8

IGES: a Key to CADCAM Systems Integration

B. Smith and J. Wellington

In September 1979, representatives from government and industry joined under the Air Force/CAM program to develop a method for data exchange between different CADCAM systems. The result of this effort, coordinated by the National Bureau of Standards (NBS), was the creation of the Initial Graphics Exchange Specification (IGES), published in January 1980 as an NBS report.

What is IGES?

Recognized as a tool to enhance an organization's productivity, IGES is a data format for describing product design and manufacturing information which has been created and stored in a CADCAM system in computer-readable form. With this common communication format, users should be able to transfer product definition data within the corporate system, as well as between the company and its suppliers and customers.

The immediate benefit of this common format is that a user does not have to develop special translators for each different piece of equipment that is used. The only requirement is to have a translator to and from the IGES format. These translators, called pre- and postprocessors, are generally available from the equipment vendor. An IGES file can be stored on magnetic tape or disk memory for future use and can also be transmitted between systems via telecommunications.

Vendor Involvement

The goal of the IGES project is to achieve portability of data among various CADCAM systems. Certainly the adoption of IGES as a national standard (ANSI

B. Smith is Chairman, and J. Wellington Coordinator of IGES at the National Bureau of Standards, Washington, DC.
Source: B. Smith and J. Wellington, 'IGES: a Key to CADCAM Systems Integration', reprinted from CAD/CAM Technology, Spring, 1984.

IGES: a Key to CADCAM Systems Integration

document Y14.26M, including IGES Version 1.0, adopted September 1981) is a major step toward that goal. But portability will not be realized until quality translator implementations are in widespread use. Recent events have contributed much toward this goal from both a user and a vendor standpoint. Users are now actively writing translators to their in-house developed CADCAM software packages, and vendors in the graphics community are now supplying or are publicly committing themselves to supply IGES translators. Finally, an increasing amount of testing of IGES translator capability has begun between different graphics systems.

In December 1981, the first publicly documented intersystem transfer of IGES information in an actual working environment occurred between two operating facilities of the Department of Energy (DOE). A mechanical part was designed and detailed on a Computervision CADDS4 system located at Sandia National Laboratories in Livermore, California. Three-dimensional model data describing the geometry of the part was expressed in the IGES format on magnetic tape and transported to the Bendix Corp. in Kansas City, Missouri. There it was interpreted on the Control Data Corp. CD 2000 system where data was added to define a cutter path for subsequent NC machining. A production print from Sandia was used during final inspection to verify part accuracy. The IGES translators used were commercially available, vendor-supplied, standard pre- and postprocessors. (The results of this transfer of product data using IGES are fully documented in a report published by Bendix.)

Later, in June 1982 at the NCGA Exposition, Anaheim, California, several tests were performed between Applicon, CALMA, Computervision, Gerber, and Manufacturing and Consulting Services systems. Two other vendors, Control Data and McAuto Unigraphics, supported the walk-through demonstration by providing previously recorded magnetic tapes with sample part geometries in IGES format. The demonstration started with sample model geometry being read into the first vendor's system. The 3-D geometry of the mechanical part from DOE appeared on the screen. Additional geometry was added to the part with the resulting file being written out on an IGES tape. This tape was carried to the next vendor where it was read in and displayed on the screen. The tests proceeded on two different days among the participating vendors. Changes to the model geometry were made at each site and could be seen at all successive locations. In this way, the demonstration vividly showed the excellent progress being made in the vendor implementations.

Other Testing

The AUTOFACT 4 conference and exposition held in Philadelphia from 29 November to 2 December, 1982 provided still another opportunity for testing and public demonstration of IGES capability. Starting with part geometry developed by the IGES Test, Evaluate, and Support Committee, IGES processors handled a test part containing the following entity information: 6 points, 6 lines, 4 arcs, 1 conic, 14 linear/ordinate dimensions,

1 angular dimension, 1 radial dimension and 1 label. Figure 1 illustrates a test part which was successfully loaded, displayed and transferred on CAD-CAM systems from five different vendors in a demonstration at AUTOFACT 4.

This data, which describes the full range of dimensioning needed for communicating engineering drawings, was taken, in turn, to each manufacturer's booth, loaded into a CADCAM system, displayed and then recorded again on a new IGES tape to be carried to the next system.

A more complex test took place at the AUTOFACT 5 conference 14–17 November 1983. Figure 2 shows the 3-D model geometry which was transmitted in addition to three orthogonal views containing major dimensions. (For details, see section on 'IGES Update'.)

Response to this exchange format has been outstanding. In the first two years after publication, over 1200 copies of the specification were provided in answer to requests from industry, the Federal Government, and the academic community – and additional requests are received daily. Representatives from over 56 companies including all major vendors of CAD-CAM equipment currently serve on committees which have been established to aid in the implementation of the specification.

Version 2.0 of IGES, approved in July 1982, represents both a refinement and an extension of the earlier published work. Clarity and precision of the specification have been dramatically improved as the result of wider public review and comment plus feedback from an ever-increasing amount of implementation and testing. In addition, many extensions and enhancements have been incorporated in the specification to expand its capability to communicate a wider range of product data developed and used by computer-aided design and manufacturing systems.

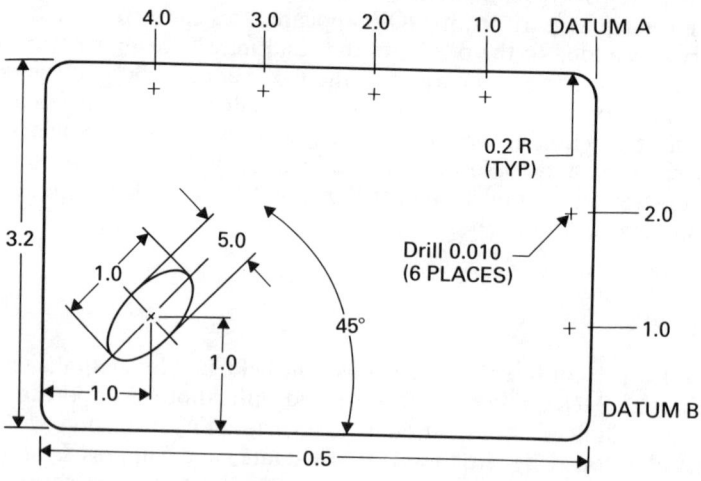

Figure 1   *Test part used at* AUTOFACT 4

IGES: a Key to CADCAM Systems Integration

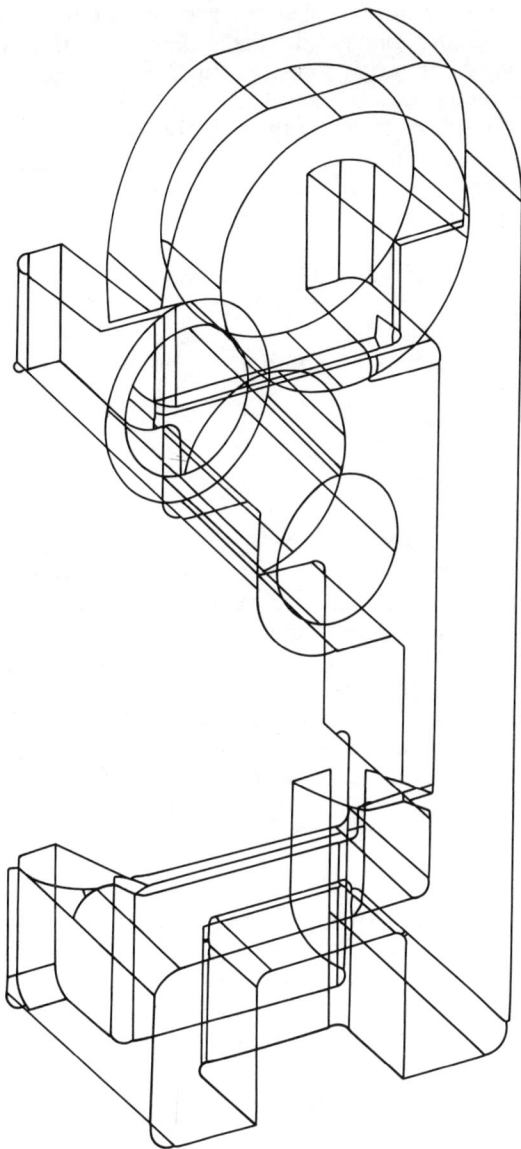

Figure 2   Test part used at AUTOFACT 5

Changes in Version 2.0

Responding to discussions of over 98 change requests, the IGES Extensions and Repairs Committee has expanded the scope of the original specification to make it more generally applicable. Some changes in geometry entities include: parameterization in the Ruled Surface entity, a more general form of the Tabulated Cylinder entity, and the means of relating the Surface of Revolution entity to common geometrical surfaces like spheres and cones.

Two new geometry entities, a Rational B-Spline Surface entity and a related Rational B-Spline Curve entity, have also been added in Version 2.0 in order to provide a much more general approach for surface and curve representation. Other changes include the development and documentation of new structural entities for both rectangular and circular arrays of geometric entities.

In the annotation area, Version 2.0 improves on the earlier work by specifying a much larger set of text fonts, although additional work remains to be done here. Improvements have been made in the clarity of intent for positioning and scaling of text material in a more clearly defined Angular Dimension entity.

New Application Areas

Two major application areas have been addressed by Version 2.0: finite element modeling data and electronics printed wiring board product data. The earlier IGES documentation contained no means of handling this data, yet both are widely used applications on CADCAM systems.

A frequent criticism of the IGES format has been the anticipated large file lengths due primarily to the ASCII (American Standard Code for Information Interchange) character representation. Included in Version 2.0 are the details of an optional or alternate binary format representation which addresses the problems of file size and processing speed. While efficiency improvements vary with word length and other variables, analysis of 20 IGES production files has estimated the savings in file size of 50–68 per cent.

IGES UPDATE *Bruce Krauskopf*

As part of the AUTOFACT 5 conference and exposition, NBS organized a demonstration of the transfer of CADCAM part files using the IGES format. The systems of 12 CADCAM exhibitors at AUTOFACT – Applicon, Autotrol, Bausch & Lomb, CALMA, Control Data Corp., Computervision, Gerber, Graftek, Mantra Datavision, McAuto Unigraphics, MSC, Inc., and Prime Medusa – were used to demonstrate the ability of IGES to standardize data of part programs.

The test part file used in the IGES format represents three-dimensional part geometry for three typical part views with sample dimensioning and annotation. The AUTOFACT demonstration was the largest IGES file transfer to date; a total of 15 CADCAM companies have now successfully shown IGES compatibility. Because of the number of participating vendors at AUTOFACT, a linear data transfer was impractical. Rather, the participants were organ-

---

B. Krauskopf is associate editor of *Manufacturing Engineering*.

IGES: a Key to CADCAM Systems Integration

ized into three groups; the part file was transferred within each group. The Mantra solids modeling system was not included in the test groups; the company produced a boundary file calculation from the solid model part file and produced an IGES file as their output. However, since this file contains only geometry without annotation, the Mantra file was not transferred in the test sequence.

Two tests were planned. The first involved part file transfer between participating companies, and the second test was a backup that required direct input of the IGES benchmark file into each system. The backup was to be used if an erroneous output file was transferred from one vendor to another. This strategy was only required for one group because CALMA experienced hardware difficulties on the day of the test. Vendors that were to receive the input from CALMA thus obtained the IGES file input directly and created a compatible output file.

Output from each vendor included plots of each view suitable for 8½ × 11 in (203 × 279 mm) trimming, a fourth isometric view at the vendor's discretion without annotation, and the IGES output file tape. Only minor errors, such as a misplaced leader line or other element, occurred during the test. These problems are currently under examination by the appropriate IGES committees.

3.9

Capturing Production Engineering within a CADCAM System

R. G. Hannam and J. C. S. Plummer

Introduction

Computer-aided design (CAD) and computer-aided manufacture (CAM) have existed separately for a number of years. The activities within CAD have been centred around analysing and optimizing particular designs. Finite element analysis is an example of this. Within CAM, the data-processing capabilities of computers have been exploited for production scheduling and inventory control, and the mathematical capabilities have been exploited for aiding the production of NC tapes. Until fairly recently, CAD and CAM have been developed separately within the design and production functions of companies, each function seeking to exploit computers in its own way.

The coming of CADCAM systems has been heralded as a significant turning point for industry because such systems will permit the integration of CAD and CAM which should lead to considerable productivity gains. If used effectively, the systems will also give companies the benefit of much shorter lead times which will improve market response. The integration of CAD and CAM takes place through using the stored geometry of components and the CADCAM system at many other stages in the production cycle. While 'integration' sounds straightforward enough in theory, the practical realities for any particular company are not always so clear or easy. Many companies see how to use CADCAM systems for carrying out design, for the automatic production of drawings, and for the preparation of NC tapes. Companies are not, however, so aware or able to appreciate how to exploit or develop the design – manufacturing link. For many, it is still a missing link.

R. G. Hannam is in the Department of Mechanical Engineering, UMIST, Manchester; J. C. S. Plummer is in the Department of Mechanical Engineering, Heriot-Watt University, Edinburgh.

Source: R. G. Hannam and J. C. S. Plummer, 'Capturing Production Engineering within a CADCAM System', from *International Journal of Production Research*, 1984, vol. 22, no. 2, pp. 267–80.

Production Engineering within a CADCAM System

This paper reports on part of a programme being carried out to develop approaches to integrating design and manufacture through CADCAM systems. The paper describes how, within a CADCAM-based process planning system, it is possible to capture production engineering practice and how, once captured, it can be exploited either by production engineers or by draftsmen. The software described was developed on the Computervision CADCAM system at UMIST but is capable of being implemented on most CADCAM systems and is currently being developed for use on the Ferranti Cetec system at Heriot–Watt University.

It will be assumed readers are familiar with the main features of the hardware and software of CADCAM systems: those who are not should refer to Smith (1983) or Hannam et al. (1982).

The Production–Design Link

The production engineer has the task of taking a new design, generally in the form of detail and assembly drawings, and deciding how best to manufacture it. The task involves the detailed planning of the methods of manufacture together with the design of tools and fixtures. In carrying out these tasks, the production engineer will draw on his own experience and knowledge of previous practice and will endeavour to use standard production engineering procedures and his own company standards. However, his ability to do this will depend on his ability to recall what the standards are, what tooling exists, and on his memory of how any similar parts have been made before. Referring to previous practices and looking up data in books and standards can be a time-consuming task and an individual's memory span is limited. Due to time pressures, there will be many occasions when the engineer is more likely to plan from scratch, calling up new tooling if necessary, because this is going to be a quicker planning method than delving into past practice.

A further problem can exist for companies, which can lead to greater diversity of planning. This results from most companies having more than one planner. The planning variation produced by one planner will be increased with every additional planner. The problems resulting from all these factors are:

(1) no consistency of planning within a company;
(2) an increasing diversity of tooling (giving poor standardization); and
(3) an appreciable time delay in being prepared to start manufacture. This is because, although the planner may have completed his task in a reasonable time, new tools may have to be ordered as a result of his work with a delay in consequence.

Many aspects of planning lend themselves to computerization, particularly those associated with storing and recalling standards and previous practice. Various approaches to computerizing planning are in existence (for example Eskiciogla and Davies (1981), Lewis et al. (1982)) but these have not generally been developed to exploit the capabilities of CADCAM systems nor do they provide a design–manufacture link as achieved by the approach described in this paper. As companies increasingly move to using CADCAM systems in design and drawing offices, it will become increasingly important to have standard production engineering practices available in a suitable form to support planning or design. As will be seen, once the production engineering practice has been captured within the process planning software, much of the routine planning can be handled fairly automatically, leaving the planner free to concentrate on more complex tasks and on improving the methods used. The approach described has been implemented for turned parts.

The Component Geometry Foundation

In simple terms, a designer usually specifies the shapes of components, together with their dimensions and material, whilst the production engineer specifies the machines, tooling and all the other details required to manufacture them. The shape comes first but once the shape exists, then, in many instances, the tooling required to produce the shape follows directly from the shape. Immediate examples of this are a drilled hole and an external groove which will respectively require a given diameter drill and a certain width grooving tool. Further, the shape of the workpiece is also used to select which types of lathe can or should be used to turn it. For example, a shaft component will be turned on a centre lathe. Relationships such as these have been brought together in a computer program package called 'Shapes', which not only relates tooling, machine, and component geometry in the software but also simultaneously builds in good production practice. This will be illustrated as 'Shapes' is explained.

Figure 1 illustrates what 'Shapes' does and how it can be viewed by the production engineer. Component information starts from the design office (box 1.1) and has to be entered into the CADCAM system in terms of shape elements (box 1.2). The shape elements are defined in terms of machined features (such as bores, internal and external threads) and raw material forms (such as hexagonal bar). Figure 2 shows a component exploded into its individual shape elements (which can be 'external' or 'internal' shape elements) and the Appendix lists the types of internal and external shape elements available within 'Shapes '. The dimensions of the shape elements also have to be entered (box 1.4) and for some features, such as drilled holes and threads, these have to conform to a standard size. The draughting routines for the construction of the shape elements have been programmed into the CADCAM software and are called up by using the CADCAM system tablet menu and electronic pen. Thus shape elements only require selecting, dimensions entered and positioning. The element is then drawn on the screen automatically and can be visually checked and amended if necessary. The software details of 'Shapes' are explained in Plummer and Hannam (1983).

The following sections deal with the production engineering aspects of 'Shapes' and show how the routines within 'Shapes' which select the tooling and machines have as much good practice built into them as is feasible.

Production Engineering within a CADCAM System

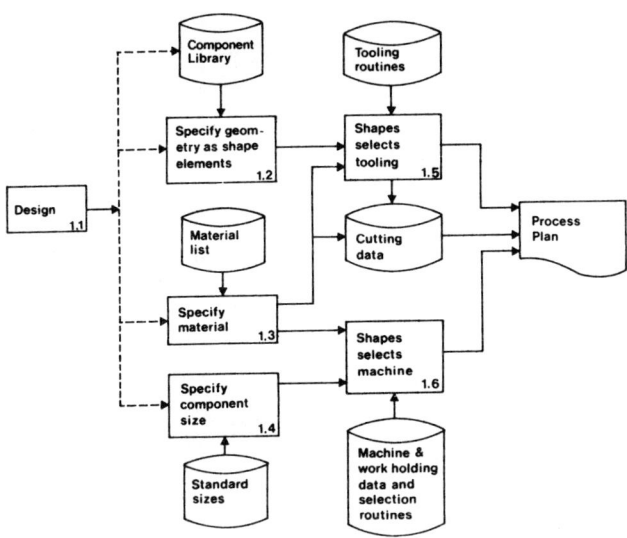

Figure 1 Block diagram showing user inputs and 'Shapes' actions

Machine Selection

Figure 1 shows that 'Shapes' needs information on the material and component size to enable it to select a suitable lathe to machine a component. The material information to be entered includes not only the material specification but also its form (e.g. bright bar, black bar, casting). The constraints and specification of each machine tool available for production have to be written into the selection routines in terms of machine type and capacity. In selecting a machine, 'Shapes' also selects the necessary collets, chucks and centres to hold the workpiece.

In the present implementation of 'Shapes', three types of lathe have been specified. Their specifications are based upon typical CNC turning centres, manufactured and marketed by a well-known company. General machine features include a disc turret, slant bed, swarf conveyor, programmable tailstock, steady attachment and a parts catcher.

The three turning centres differ primarily by their mode of work holding, whether collet chuck, three-jaw chuck or face plate. The turning centre with the collet chuck is specified to be limited to machining 'smooth' extruded bars, since the surface of other material forms may cause gripping problems for the collets. This machine has a bar feeder attachment so that suitably sized hexagonal, round and square-sectioned bars can be fed through the spindle. Only the machining of first operation work is permitted on the collet chuck machine since all work is parted-off.

The turning centre with the three-jaw chuck is front loaded and is specified either for second operation work which has been previously turned or centred, or for bright round bar which is too large for the collet chuck

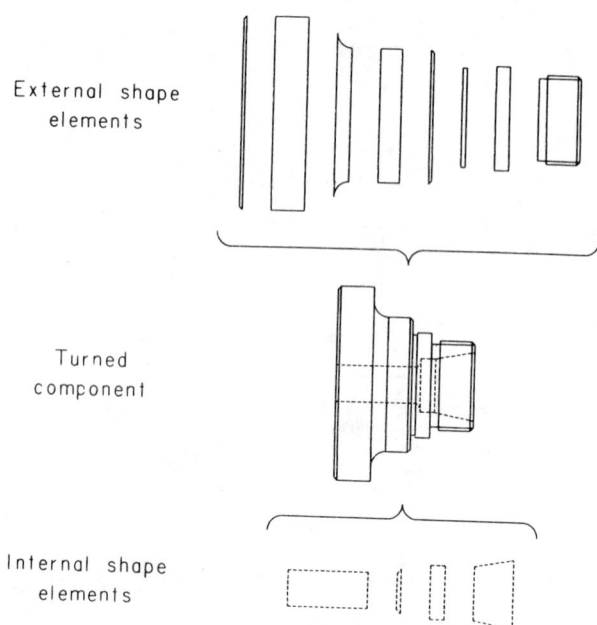

Figure 2 The 'explosion' of a component into its shape elements

machine. Black or cast bar is not permitted since a three-jaw chuck cannot be guaranteed to hold this form of work securely (a four-jaw chuck should be used). Turning between centres can also be performed on this machine by using the tailstock centre and inserting a centre through the chuck into the spindle. A three-jaw chuck is not called up to grip the headstock centre since the self-centring mechanism of such a chuck is unlikely to find the true centre of rotation. This in turn would cause the headstock centre and hence the workpiece to rotate eccentrically, so that second operation machining would not be concentric with the first operation machining.

The third turning centre specified has a variety of face plates for clamping castings, fabrications and forgings. The work is mounted, set and balanced on a suitable face plate, away from the machine, and then loaded with its fixture on to the spindle when required.

Each machine has a disc turret which can hold fourteen tool assemblies, seven outer and seven inner positioned tools. The outer positioned tools are used to machine the external features of a component and are attached to the disc turret using slide-mating tool blocks. The inner positioned tools are required to produce the internal features of a component.

During entry of the component data, the software routines constantly monitor the construction of a component to ensure that at least one of the machines with appropriate work holding can be employed. If an occasion arose where a component could not be produced by the machines available, then the software is programmed to halt the design process and inform the engineer.

Production Engineering within a CADCAM System

To summarize, the software routines select a turning centre according to the raw material form and the overall dimensions of the part to be machined. The form of raw material dictates the mode of work holding and hence the *type* of turning centre. The overall dimensions of the finished part dictate the *size* of machine to be employed. Since three types of turning centre are available and one size for each type, the selection in the current version is limited to ensuring that the component size is within the working capacity of the machine type chosen. To increase the number of lathes available, the constraints of the additional machines will have to be built into the selection procedure of the software. The modular nature of 'Shapes' permits this to be done easily, and in this manner, 'Shapes' can be tailored for a specific manufacturing environment.

Tools and Tool-assembly Selection

'Shapes' selects the cutting tools and also the non-cutting tools which complement the cutting tools in a ready-to-use package. Thus, the selection of a 12.5 mm diameter centre drill also entails the automatic selection of the collet and collet chuck to hold the centre drill. The resulting assembly is illustrated in figure 3. To enhance interchangeability, this particular type of chuck and collet is also specified for gripping other tools of the same diameter, such as standard length and extra long jobber drills. Moreover, given a series of collets, this chuck can accommodate a whole range of such tools.

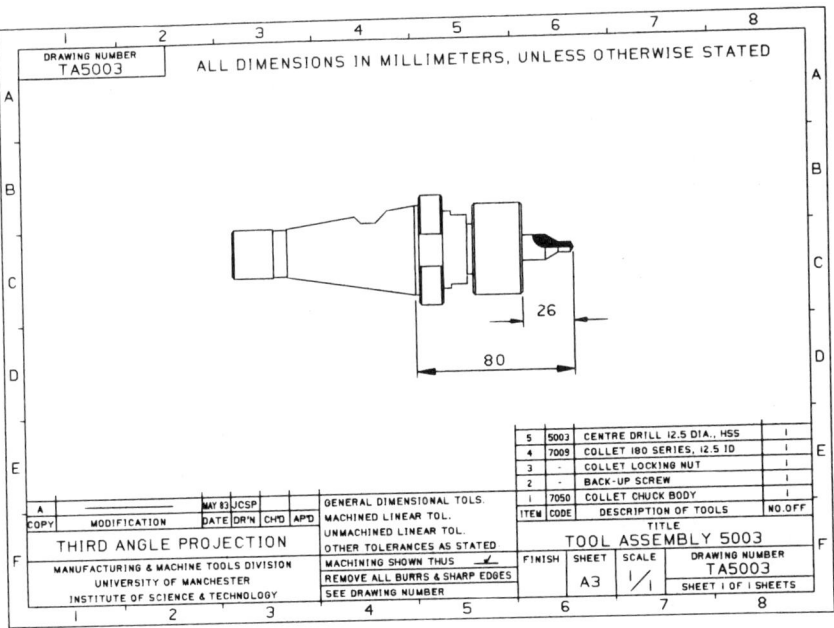

Figure 3 A tool assembly

All tools deemed necessary to carry out machining on the specified turning centres have been compiled into a 'tool library'. Each tool in the library is given a unique tool code consisting of four numbers. This is so each tool can be identified and subsequently allocated by its individual tool code. The first number of the code denotes the type of tool, whilst the remaining digits represent the membership number within that particular tool classification. Tool assemblies such as that shown in figure 3 are referred to by a six-digit code consisting of the prefix TA5003 (for Tool Assembly) followed by the tool code belonging to the most prominent member for the assembly which in this case is the centre drill.

The selection of tools and tool assemblies is performed automatically by reference to the type of work-piece material and one of the following factors:

(1) the form of individual shape elements,
(2) the size and form of raw material,
(3) the requirements of 'assembled' shape elements.

Each of these three factors has been chosen because it allows certain parts of standard production engineering practice to be built into the software to produce a complete tooling package. The link between tooling and shape elements is implicit in the description and specification of many of the shape elements so the selection of tooling to produce such shape elements is relatively straightforward. For example, a blind, tapped hole may require a centre drill, tapping drill, taper tap, second cut tap, and plug tap. In this instance not only are the tool assemblies identified but also the logical machining sequence to produce the shape element. The succession of tool assemblies employed to perform specific operations during manufacture, whereby the next tool in the machining sequence is totally dependent upon its predecessor, gives rise to the use of 'tool hierarchies'. Hence, on selecting the tool code for the plug tap assembly, the choice of the other tools in this hierarchy is automatically made. This is illustrated in figure 4 which shows the information printed out following the selection of the tool assemblies to produce a counterbored hole. The interactive procedure for specifying the counterbored hole is shown in figure 5 and will be discussed later.

The size and form of raw material is the second factor leading to the selection of certain tools. For example, one of the manufacturing conditions built into the software is that bright round bar can be fed through the spindle of the collet chuck machine. This entails gripping the material, positioning it and eventually parting-off and catching the resulting work-piece. In this case, the size and form of raw material causes 'Shapes' to specify an appropriate size and shape of collet, a bar stop mounted in the turret, an appropriately sized parting-off tool and a parts catcher.

A related feature built into the software is the standardization of the width of parting-off tools. Table 1 shows how the swing of the bar stock is linked to the width of parting-off tool. The term 'swing' is used to include the across-corners dimensions of hexagonal and square bar as well as the diameter of round bar. The tool width is also used in a routine which

Production Engineering within a CADCAM System

```
                    20-06-83    13:53:18
        == TOOL ASSEMBLY ALLOCATION : COMPONENT 12345MA1 ==
        SHAPE ELEMENT : 2 COUNTERBORED HOLES, 12MM NOMINAL DIA.*30MM LONG
        HOLE TYPE     : THROUGH
        CODE    DESCRIPTION OF TOOLING
        5005    CENTRE DRILL, HSS, 25MM BODY DIA.
        5017    JOBBER DRILL, HSS, 6.8MM DIA. (PILOT)
        5025    JOBBER DRILL, HSS, 12.2MM DIA. (CLEARANCE)
        5109    SLOT DRILL, HSS, 24MM DIA.
        == SPEED & FEED ALLOCATION : COMPONENT 12345MA1 ==
        TOOL ASSEMBLY : TA5005
        CUTTING TOOL  : CENTRE DRILL, HSS, 25MM BODY DIA.
           NOMINAL CUTTING SPEED = 636REV/MIN
           NOMINAL CUTTING FEED  = 79MM/MIN
        TOOL ASSEMBLY : TA5017
        CUTTING TOOL  : JOBBER DRILL, HSS, 6.8MM DIA. (PILOT)
           NOMINAL CUTTING SPEED = 1169REV/MIN
           NOMINAL CUTTING FEED  = 146MM/MIN
        TOOL ASSEMBLY : TA5025
        CUTTING TOOL  : JOBBER DRILL, HSS, 12.2MM DIA. (CLEARANCE)
           NOMINAL CUTTING SPEED = 652REV/MIN
           NOMINAL CUTTING FEED  = 81MM/MIN
        TOOL ASSEMBLY : TA5109
        CUTTING TOOL  : SLOT DRILL, HSS, 24MM DIA.
           NOMINAL CUTTING SPEED = 331REV/MIN
           NOMINAL CUTTING FEED  = 41MM/MIN
```

Figure 4 A typical Tool Assembly Allocation print-out illustrating the hierarchy of tools

```
            WHAT SIZE IS THE NOMINAL COUNTERBORE DIAMETER ?
            DIAMETER=13 )
            NOTE  -  13MM IS NOT A RECOMMENDED NOMINAL DIAMETER
            THE FOLLOWING NOMINAL DIAMETERS ARE SUPPORTED:-
                ==   3  ==   4  ==   5  ==   6  ==   8  ==
                ==  10  ==  12  ==  16  ==  20  ==  24  ==
                ==  30  ==  36  ==  45  ==  52  ==  60  ==
                   OMITTED NOMINAL DIAMETERS MAY BE INCLUDED
                       PENDING SUFFICIENT JUSTIFICATION
            WHAT SIZE IS THE NOMINAL COUNTERBORE DIAMETER ?
            DIAMETER=12 )
            WHAT SIZE IS THE OVERALL COUNTERBORE LENGTH ?
            LENGTH=10 )
            NOTE  -  10MM IS TOO SHORT IN PROPORTION TO DEPTH OF HEAD
                  -  MINIMUM OVERALL LENGTH IS 1.5*NOM. DIA.=18MM
            WHAT SIZE IS THE OVERALL COUNTERBORE LENGTH ?
            LENGTH=65 )
            NOTE  -  65MM EXCEEDS USABLE LENGTH OF DRILL
                  -  MAXIMUM OVERALL LENGTH IS 5*NOM. DIA.=60MM
            WHAT SIZE IS THE OVERALL COUNTERBORE LENGTH ?
            LENGTH=30 )
            HOW MANY 12MM NOMINAL DIA.*30MM LONG COUNTERBORED HOLES ARE THERE ?
            NUMBER OF COUNTERBORED HOLES=2 )
            2 HOLES  -  ARE YOU SURE ?
            YES=Y; NO=N; REPLY=Y
            DIGITIZE DATUM POINT TO POSITION 1ST. COUNTERBORED HOLE
            DIG X50Y50 )
```

Figure 5 The interactive procedures for specifying a counterbored hole
(user responses are underlined)

calculates the total length of bar stock required to complete a given batch order by using the known width as a machining allowance.

TABLE 1 STANDARD WIDTHS OF PARTING-OFF TOOLS

Range of bar stock swing (mm)	Width of parting-off tool (mm)
$10 \leq \text{swing} \leq 15$	3
$15 < \text{swing} \leq 25$	4
$25 < \text{swing} \leq 20$	6
$50 < \text{swing} \leq 65$	8

The third way of selecting tools is through programmed interactions which occur when individual shape elements are 'assembled' together to form a complete component. This leads to the selection of roughing and/or finishing tools and the choice of whether these tools are to be left or right handed. The principle behind the selection of these turning tools is shown in figure 6. The component illustrated comprises three plain circular elements, with the central element having the largest diameter. Hence, to machine this component in one setting, several roughing cuts and a finishing cut have to be performed by both left- and right-hand tools. This is a case where the selection of tools can only occur once the geometry of the component has been completely specified. The software is programmed to select left- and/or right-hand tools by ascertaining the positions of elements with respect to the element with the largest diameter. (Rechucking of the component is also taken into account.) For example, the component shown in figure 6 can be machined in one setting, so all elements to the right of the largest element will need to be machined by left-hand tools, and vice versa for right-hand tools. The choice whether to use roughing and/or finishing tools is determined by the amount of material to be removed, which in turn is determined by the work-piece–tool material relationship. A typical depth of finishing cut when using a tungsten carbide tool to machine mild steel is 0.5 mm; likewise, a typical roughing cut is 4 mm deep. Therefore, knowing the original size and final size of the work-piece material, and using standard depth of cuts, the software can work out the need for roughing and/or finishing tools, as well as calculating the number of tool passes required.

Figure 7 shows the complete print-out for the machine and tooling selections for the component shown in figure 8. The shape elements which are entered to construct the component are those shown in figure 2.

Additional Good Practice

CADCAM computers have the same storage ability as other computers and this can be exploited while taking advantage of their graphics capabilities. Within the routines of 'Shapes' there are many examples of how good production engineering practice has been incorporated through exploiting the graphics

Production Engineering within a CADCAM System

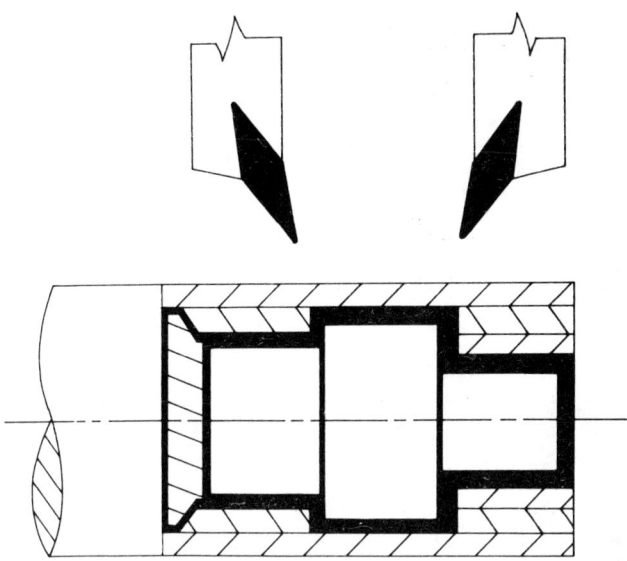

Figure 6 A typical geometry which is analysed to determine hand of tools and use of roughing and/or finishing tools

and storage abilities of CADCAM systems. Four further examples will be described.

The first example relates to the provision of tool setting data. Such data may be used by a tool setter or by a planner. Good practice requires that tools are set with the minimum amount of projection possible. This practice ensures maximum tool rigidity which enhances workpiece accuracy, improves tool life and increases productivity by allowing faster feed rates. Tooling data and its associated pictorial representation (as, for example, shown in figure 3) can be stored in a CADCAM system and it can show a best set-up condition. The drawing can easily be referenced by the production engineer so that good practice is automatically presented to him and copies can be easily supplied to a tool setter. Should the production engineer wish to use a non-standard set-up, then this will take time and effort on his part to create. Human nature is such that he will probably take the easiest route and thus use the standard and follow good practice.

The second example of good practice relates to when the component geometry is being entered into the system. At this stage, all holes and bores are automatically shown within their shape elements as starting with a small chamfer. The purpose of these chamfers is to act as a location aid or 'lead-in' for subsequent machining and/or assembly operations. Apart from breaking the edge, a chamfer also reduces the problems of drill wander and premature tool wear. At the tooling stage, the chamfer can be provided without extra tooling by 'over using' a centre drill or by including the feature in the programmed path of a boring bar. Including this feature as a standard in the geometry displayed reminds the engineer of its importance.

288   *Change: How Techniques Can Be Used*

```
                  14-06-83      19:17 ;33
       == MACHINE TOOL ALLOCATION : COMPONENT  12345CA8 ==

       CODE    DESCRIPTION OF MACHINE
       T002    TURNING CENTRE WITH 3-JAW CHUCK


                    14-06-83      19-17-33
       == TOOL ASSEMBLY ALLOCATION : COMPONENT 12345CA8 ==
          ** 1ST. OPERATION WORK **
       COMPOSITE      : 2 EXTERNAL ELEMENTS
       OVERALL SIZE   : 130MM DIA.*25MM LONG
       CODE    DESCRIPTION OF TOOLING
       8030    LATHE 3-JAW CHUCK
       6006    RENISHAW TOUCH TRIGGER PROBE
       2030    ROUGHING TOOL, WC, LH
       2032    SLIDING & FACING TOOL, WC, LH

          ** 2ND. OPERATION WORK **
       COMPOSITE      : 6 EXTERNAL ELEMENTS
       OVERALL SIZE   : 110MM DIA.*70MM LONG
       CODE    DESCRIPTION OF TOOLING
       8030    LATHE 3-JAW CHUCK
       2030    ROUGHING TOOL, WC, LH
       2032    SLIDING & FACING TOOL, WC, LH
       SHAPE ELEMENT  : 1 EXTERNAL GROOVE, 70MM NOM. DIA.*3MM WIDE*1.5MM DEEP
       GROOVE TYPE    : RECTANGULAR
       CODE    DESCRIPTION OF TOOLING
       2042    EXTERNAL RECESSING TOOL, HSS, 3MM WIDE, LH
       SHAPE ELEMENT  : 1 SCREW THREAD, M60*3MM PITCH*30MM LONG, RH
       THREAD TYPE    : EXTERNAL; 1 END CHAMFERED, 1 END UNDERCUT
       CODE    DESCRIPTION OF TOOLING
       2060    EXTERNAL RECESSING TOOL, WC, 6MM WIDE, LH
       2003    EXTERNAL SCREW CUTTING TOOL, WC, 60DEGREE*0.36MM TIP RADIUS
       COMPOSITE      : 4 INTERNAL ELEMENTS
       OVERALL SIZE   : 46MM DIA.*95MM LONG
       CODE    DESCRIPTION OF TOOLING
       5005    CENTRE DRILL, HSS, 25MM BODY DIA.
       5022    JOBBER DRILL, HSS, 10.2MM DIA. (PILOT)
       5032    JOBBER DRILL, HSS, 19.5MM DIA. (PILOT)
       4000    BORING TOOL, WC, LH


                    14-06-83      19:17:33
       == RAW MATERIAL ALLOCATION : COMPONENT 12345CA8 ==
       BATCH SIZE       = 5 OFF
       DELIVERY DATE    = WEEK 27

       RAW MATERIAL TYPE=CARBON STEEL : ALLOY A
       RAW MATERIAL FORM=BRIGHT ROUND BAR
       RAW MATERIAL SIZE=150MM DIA.*99MM LONG, EACH
```

Figure 7   The process plan for the component shown in Figure 8

The third example is one of a number which could be quoted. It comes from the interactive part of 'Shapes' where the shape element geometry is being specified. An interactive routine is shown in figure 5 and relates to the specification of a shape element for a counterbored hole(s). The figures underlined are the responses the CADCAM system user makes to the questions posed by the 'Shapes' software. The remainder of the print-out is all information presented to the user and illustrates a process by which the user is informed of the standards. Other aspects of good practice can be seen from reading the text of the figure. If the engineer using the system is aware of the standards and uses them, the text sections which start with 'NOTE –' are not displayed and the geometry is entered more quickly as a result.

Production Engineering within a CADCAM *System* 289

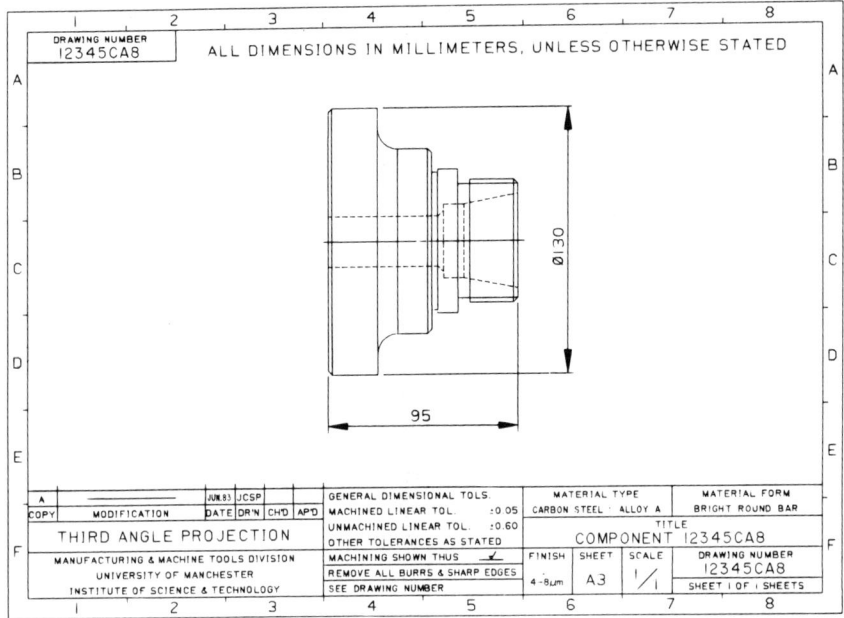

Figure 8   Component 12345CA8 in an automatically generated drawing frame

It has already been explained how 'Shapes' uses information on the form and type of material in selecting suitable tools. The fourth example relates to how 'Shapes' facilitates the use of company standards for material and how it checks that the form and type of material are compatible. As the component geometry is entered, 'Shapes' monitors the maximum diameter entered to check that the working capacity of the machines available is not exceeded. It also monitors the form of the component and checks that:

(1) any square or hexagonal section sizes specified can be met from the standard sections available,
(2) only one size of hexagonal or square section is called for, and
(3) the diameter of any circular elements are less than or equal to the size across flats of hexagonal or square-sectioned bar.

The last two checks are carried out because it is assumed provisions are not made for producing square or hexagonal sections on the lathes. These have to be provided simply by using appropriately sectioned raw material.

When entering data on circular sectioned components, the production engineer is offered a choice by the software of entering bright round bar, a casting, a fabrication or a forging. 'Shapes' then checks with the type of material entered to check that the type and form are compatible. The type of material entered can be selected only from a standard list which has been programmed into the software. Thus a check is automatically performed on the use of company standards by the drawing office.

Discussion

To be competitive and survive, industry has to keep its manufacturing costs down. One of the prime methods of doing this is through reducing product lead times. This reduces work-in-progress and gives a quicker turnover of working capital. All departments have a part to play in reducing product lead times and this paper has highlighted how the procedures in the production engineering office can be improved, resulting in shorter lead times, through the use of suitable software on a CADCAM system.

The foundation of the approach described is standardization through exploiting the storage capabilities of CADCAM systems, and actually standardizing on good production engineering practice. The approach also exploits the graphics capabilities of CADCAM systems by using component geometry as a starting point. Component geometry is not only the starting point for production planning; if parts are to be made on CNC machines, then the component geometry entered can also be used for automatically generating machining programs.

How far companies wish to standardize is up to them, as are the actual standards they wish to use. 'Shapes' is not a straitjacket but a framework. One enhancement to the basic software is shown at the bottom part of figure 4. This shows the provision of cutting data, in terms of speeds and feed-rates, for the various drills involved in producing the counterbored holes previously referred to. The modular nature of 'Shapes' allows enhancements of this form to be incorporated relatively easily.

The introduction to this paper referred to links between design and manufacture and the part CADCAM systems can ideally play in this. This paper has described 'Shapes' as a tool for production engineers, but there is no reason why it could not be used in the drawing office. A company's production engineers can specify within the software the production standards that they wish to be used and these can then be made available to the draughtsmen. In the first part of 'Shapes', where component geometry is being entered, 'Shapes' can be used as a high-speed draughting aid, but with appropriate standards built in to ensure tooling and machines available within the company are used. If a draughtsman found 'Shapes' would not accept his component, then he would be prompted to liaise with a production engineer and discuss how they might proceed. Thus the use of 'Shapes' and a CADCAM system not only provides a computerized design–manufacture link but can also improve the human communication link, which unfortunately is not always well established. To facilitate the use of 'Shapes' by draughtsmen, a routine for generating a framed drawing of the component entered is built into 'Shapes' and an example of the output from this routine is shown in figure 8. The drawing frame is one of four standard-sized frames which 'Shapes' can select and then fits around the component depending on the component size.

Production Engineering within a CADCAM System 291

Concluding Remarks

Manufacturing companies must increasingly exploit CADCAM systems if they are to stay competitive. CADCAM systems are only tools and, like many tools, they have to be developed and optimized before they are really effective. This paper has described a way forward in exploiting CADCAM systems. While the software has been developed and proved in an academic environment, the tooling and machine data incorporated are all real. Discussions are now under way to develop the implementation within an engineering company.

Acknowledgements

The work described in this paper has been carried out in the Manufacturing and Machine Tools Division of the Department of Mechanical Engineering at UMIST. The assistance of colleagues in the Division's CADCAM Unit is gratefully acknowledged. The support of Mr Plummer by the Science and Engineering Research Council is also acknowledged.

APPENDIX

Groups of Shape Elements and the Types within the Group

(1) *Bores, Holes and Recesses: Circular*
    Clearance hole: straight, blind
    Clearance hole: straight, blind with one end chamfered
    Clearance hole: straight, through
    Clearance hole: straight, through with one end chamfered
    Precision bore: straight, blind
    Precision bore: straight, blind with one end chamfered
    Precision bore: straight, through
    Precision bore: straight, through with one end chamfered
    Tapered bore
    Curved bore: (lengthwise)
    Radiused bore: (lengthwise)
    Recess: rectangular (side face)
    Recess: rectangular (circumferential)
    Recess: semi-circular
    Recess: 90 degree vee-angle

(2) *Centre Drilled Holes*
    Centre drilled hole: blind

(3) *Circular Sections/Turned Diameters: External Lengths*
    Plain section: straight
    Plain section: tapered

Plain section: curved (lengthwise)
Plain section: radiused (lengthwise)
Groove: rectangular (circumferential)
Groove: semi-circular
Groove: 90 degree vee-angle

(4) *Counterbored Holes*
Countered hole: through

(5) *Countersunk Holes*
Countersunk hole: through

(6) *Hexagonal Sections: External Lengths*
No ends chamfered
One end chamfered
Both ends chamfered

(7) *Knurls*
Knurl: diamond pattern with both ends chamfered
Knurl: straight pattern with both ends chamfered

(8) *Screw Threads: ISO Metric*
Internal thread: through
Internal thread: blind
External thread: both ends chamfered
External thread: one end chamfered, one end undercut
External thread: both ends undercut

(9) *Spot Faced Holes*
Spot faced hole: through

(10) *Square Sections: External Lengths*
No ends chamfered
One end chamfered
Both ends chamfered

References

H. Eskicioglu and B. J. Davies, 'Interactive Process Planning System for Prismatic Parts (ICAPP)', *International Journal of Machine Tool Design and Research* vol. 21 (1981) 193.

R. G. Hannam, M. Harrison-Lowe, S. Hinduja and J. C. Welch, 'The Appraisal, Selection and Implementation of a CADCAM system', *Proceedings of Summit on Automated Manufacturing Conference* (London: Engineers' Digest and Automation, 1982).

W. C. Lewis, E. Bartlet, I. I. Finfter and M. M. Barash, 'Tool-oriented Automatic Process Planning', *Proceedings of 23rd International Machine Tool Design and Research Conference* (London: Macmillan, 1982).

J. C. S. Plummer and R. G. Hannam, 'Programming Towards a Flexible Unmanned Factory using a CADCAM System', *Proceedings of Second European Users Conference, Brussels* (Basingstoke, U.K.: ComputerVision (Europe) Inc., 1983).

W. A. Smith (ed.), *A Guide to CADCAM* (London: The Institution of Production Engineers, 1983).

3.10

An In-company Study of NC Machine Utilization and its Improvement by a Systems Approach

B. R. Kilmartin and R. G. Hannam

Introduction

When NC machines first appeared on the market, a great effort was needed and was made to show the potential economic advantages of using them in comparison with conventional machine tools (for example, Dodgson, 1972). This was necessary because of the large price difference between NC and conventional machines. Even though the costs of NC machines are falling in real terms, helped by the fall in the costs of the control systems, NC machines are still generally considerably more expensive than conventional machines. The price difference is likely to remain as manufacturers tend to be continually enhancing the specifications of their machines.

The large cost difference beween NC and conventional machines means that every purchase of a NC machine still requires a detailed financial justification in most companies.

Investment decisions taken by companies are always well scrutinized and the larger the capital cost of any machine, the higher up the corporate management structure will the decision to purchase be made. Once a decision has been made, however, and a machine has been delivered and is working, few companies reexamine the decision they made. One of the main reasons for this is that there are generally far more urgent problems requiring attention which may well include other new investment decisions.

The work reported in this paper is about a company which did carry out a re-examination of their investment decisions and found that the machines they had purchased over a number of years were not as productive as had

---

B. R. Kilmartin is in the Department of Mechanical, Marine and Production Engineering, Liverpool Polytechnic; R. G. Hannam is in the Manufacturing and Machine Tools Division, Mechanical Engineering Department, UMIST, Manchester.

Source: B. R. Kilmartin and R. G. Hannam, 'An In-Company Study of NC Machine Utilization and its Improvement by a Systems Approach', from *International Journal of Production Research*, 1981, vol. 19, no. 3, pp. 289–301.

been assumed. The reasons for this were investigated, and they turned out to be many and diverse.

Having examined all the relevant operational parameters, new methods of working were developed to improve and enhance the productive utilization of the machines. There have been a number of studies of machine-tool utilization both in the UK and overseas (e.g. Dudley, 1975; Becker, 1978). The work of Becker is a good example of the most common approach in that it reports the results of a broad-based survey which well documents the problems of NC machines in general terms. It also compares the survey findings with results from other German studies. However, it only presents limited solutions to the problem of poor utilization and it concentrates on technological problems. The work reported in this paper, in contrast, analyses a specific company situation (which is likely to be typical of many companies) and sets out a comprehensive approach to improving utilization.

The work reported was undertaken as part of the UMIST Platt Saco Lowell Teaching Company Scheme as one of a series being undertaken to investigate and improve existing levels of manufacturing efficiency within the company. The typical arrangements of teaching company schemes have been previously explained by Sury (1979). This investigation was undertaken in a plant manufacturing a variety of parts for textile machinery.

The NC Machines

Since the introduction of NC machine tools in the UK, the company concerned has seen numerical control as being particularly suitable for many of its machining requirements. In 1968, the company purchased its first NC machine, a 2-axis Cintimatic. It followed this over the following six years with the purchase of two more first generation machining centres and five Batchmatic lathes. Details of the machines are given in tables 1 and 2 together with their estimated replacement cost at September 1980 prices. The machines were located within a functionally organized shop. The shop had a turning section which included the NC lathes as a group within the section and a non-turning machine area which included the machining centres. Each NC machine was set and operated by one setter operator.

As part of an on-going investment programme, capital justifications for further NC lathes were regularly prepared by the Production Engineering Department with claims that utilization levels of up to 80 per cent could

TABLE 1 DETAILS OF NC LATHES INVOLVED IN UTILIZATION STUDY

Machine	Control	Bar/ chuck	Year purchased	Cost (£)	Replacement cost (Sept. 1980) (£)
A and B Batchmatic 50/1	NC	Bar	1972	28,000	85,000
C Batchmatic 50/2	CNC	Bar	1974	33,000	85,000
D Batchmatic 75–250	CNC	Chuck	1974	25,000	96,000
E Batchmatic 75–350	CNC	Chuck	1974	35,000	96,000

TABLE 2 DETAILS OF MACHINING CENTRES INVOLVED IN UTILIZATION STUDY

Machine	Control	Year purchased	Cost (£)	Replacement cost (Sept. 1980)[a] (£)
F Cintimatic 220	2-axis NC	1968	28,000	96,000
G Cintimatic 330	3-axis NC	1970	35,000	98,000
H Cim-X	4-axis NC	1971	40,000	120,000

Note: [a] Estimate based on equivalent modern machines.

readily be achieved. These claims were based on the general indications given by machine tool suppliers that in-process presetting, standard tooling and fast change-over times would indeed enable such a figure to be achieved. However, it was known within the company that it was unlikely that a figure of 80 per cent was being achieved on the existing machines. Before committing further capital resources to NC machine tools, the company decided that the performance and utilization of their existing NC machines should be thoroughly examined.

Definition of Machine Utilization

The first problem which presented itself was to determine how the company had defined the term 'machine utilization' because part of the brief of the work was to examine existing assumptions of 80 per cent utilization. When the definition was investigated, it was discovered that two definitions of utilization had actually been used without this being realized within the company and that neither definition was adequately defined for use in a further investigation.

Utilization is usually expressed as a percentage ratio of the form

$$\text{Utilization} = \frac{\sum \text{Productive time}}{\text{Total available time}}$$

Productive use can be considered in terms of tape run times, of component floor-to-floor times or in terms of the number of components produced to the right quality per shift. It can be argued that set-up times and tape proving times should also be included in productive use as these are essential preparations prior to machining. It has been pointed out (Hagan and Leonard, 1973) that there is an additional element to utilization which can be termed 'cost effective utilization'. This looks at how components suitable for NC are actually machined, and whether optimum machining parameters have been used. To be added to this must be that parts have been programmed efficiently.

It was eventually decided to use two definitions, one for management purposes and one for shop-floor purposes. Both would use component floor-to-floor time as a measure of machine productive time as management and

NC Machine Utilization and a Systems Approach

shop-floor personnel considered component handling as an integral part of the machining process. Also, as component floor-to-floor times had been established by the Rate Fixing Department for payment purposes, there were likely to be problems in moving away from this base. The shop-floor definition was also to include set-up times, as shop-floor supervision considered any definition which excluded set-up did not reflect the 'man–machine system'. The two definitions used can therefore be expressed in equation forms as:

$$Ut_1 = \frac{\Sigma (T_f N)}{T} \times 100$$

$$Ut_2 = \frac{\Sigma (T_f N) + \Sigma T_s}{T} \times 100$$

where

Ut_1 = machine utilization (management definition),
Ut_2 = machine utilization (shop-floor definition),
T_f = floor-to-floor time for a component of a batch,
N = number of components of a batch produced successfully,
T_s = set-up time,
T = time-span of utilization evaluation.

Machine Performance Analysis

In examining details of utilization and preparing for the planning of methods to improve it, it was necessary to consider all aspects of machine operation and in particular all those parts of a machine's day when it is not being used productively. NC machines, in common with most other machine tools, are part of a larger system and it is the operation of this system which controls the utilization of the machine and which has to be analysed. To help in this task, the elements of the total system which influence the machine usage were established and these are shown schematically in figure 1.

The performance of all eight NC machines was analysed by monitoring the activities of the machines and the related production–machine system over a period of 16 weeks. The monitoring was carried out using the machine shop's own reporting system and by the machine operators maintaining a log. Daily reviews of the data so obtained were carried out by one of the authors in discussion with the machines' supervisors and operators. Before the start of the monitoring, the operators were concerned that participation in the monitoring would mean that they were being excessively scrutinized by the survey. However, the co-operation of the operators was obtained eventually by stressing that it was the machines' performance that was primarily under investigation.

The average results of the monitoring over the 16 weeks are shown for all the machines in figure 2. These show that it was possible to account definitely for between 82 and 90 per cent of the machines' activities. The

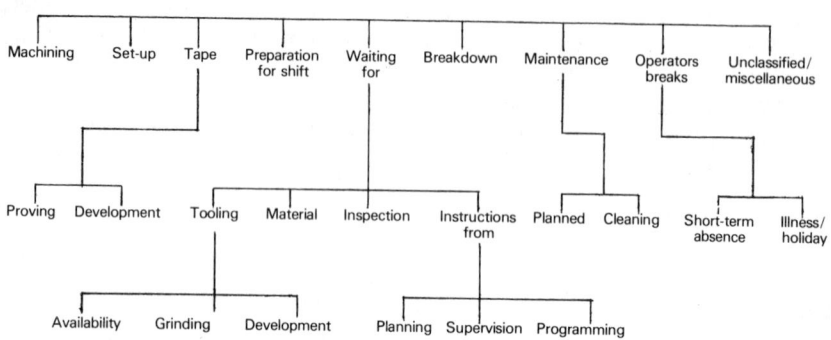

Figure 1   Elements of NC machine utilization

unaccounted non-productive times are likely to be made up of many small items or short delays which inevitably occur when production is as interrupted as it turned out to be. No attempt was made to ensure that the operators accounted for every minute of his or the machines' times as it was felt that this would encourage him to distort his results, rather than report as accurately as possible what he considered had happened. Tea breaks and other absences will certainly be included under the unclassified heading but it was not considered sensible to investigate whether breaks were shorter or longer than authorized. It was found impracticable to expect the operators to classify the time under all the headings of figure 1, due to the small magnitude of some of the times and their number. The elements shown in figure 2 were found to be the major ones which operators reported but useful information on the importance of some of the others was found during discussions with the operators.

Over the period of the 16-weeks survey the average machine utilization (Ut_1) for the lathes was 39 per cent and for the machining centres 53 per cent, with setting up accounting for an additional 8 and 13 per cent respectively.

Discussion of the Performance Analysis

Utilization on the NC lathes was found to be low for a number of reasons. It was adversely affected by breakdowns due to mechanical and electrical faults (an average of 16 per cent), tooling and fixturing problems (6 per cent) and tape proving (8 per cent). Random electronic failure of the NC control systems was the main cause of breakdown during the survey. Efforts by both the suppliers' service engineers and company personnel to diagnose the faults often proved ineffective due to inadequate diagnostic facilities on the

NC *Machine Utilization and a Systems Approach*

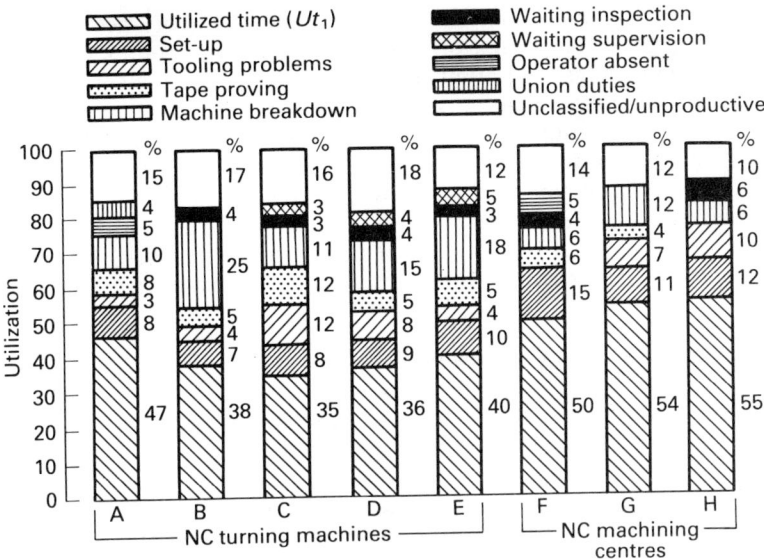

Figure 2 Average results of machine utilization survey

control systems. This was particularly true of lathe 'B' which experienced an intermittent fault throughout the monitoring period which helped to account for the 25 per cent breakdown on this machine. The absence of effective diagnostic facilities on the older types of control was particularly highlighted by the results. Other typical failures logged on the lathes included oil leaks and hydraulic failures, malfunctions of the tape reader and problems with the spindle and turret due to electrical failures.

Tooling, fixturing and tape proving problems were often related and accounted together for an average of 14 per cent of machine usage, which is a significant percentage. The majority of new shaft type components were initially scheduled to lathe 'C' because of the CNC facilities available which eased programme development. This explains why lathe 'C' had a higher percentage of tape proving. Some of the time spent on tooling, fixturing and tape proving resulted from their lack of availability. Procedures were failing which had been specifically designed to ensure documentation, tooling and gauging were all available at the machine prior to component manufacture.

The machining centres proved to be far more reliable than the lathes, with breakdowns only averaging 8 per cent. These were mainly due to electrical faults. Repeated tape reader faults on all three machines during the early weeks of the monitoring period resulted in a thorough service by the control system's suppliers and this improved subsequent reliability. The proving of new tooling, fixturing and tapes averaged 11 per cent and problems in this area were generally caused by the first time set-up and machining of newly designed gearbox housings. Complex tooling and fixturing were required to machine these components and it was anticipated that tape and tool proving might take time. To minimize first-off inspection time, a Maxi-check 3-axis computerized inspection machine was used and company personnel considered that this reduced first-off inspection time by about a half and thus released the machines more quickly for subsequent components.

The unavailability of suitably trained setter operators was found to be the cause of delays on a number of occasions. This was due to the policy of having one setter operator per machine and the lack of reserve operators. The one operator policy had been adopted with the installation of the early NC machines and had been maintained by union pressure. Reserve operators had not been recruited because of a general recruiting difficulty which was exacerbated by a restriction on earnings resulting from a wage agreement.

Performance Analysis Conclusions

From the monitoring and associated discussions, the following main reasons for the poor utilization were identified.

(1) Set-up times were a significant proportion of cutting time. Average set-up times on the lathes were between 25 and 50 per cent greater than originally estimated.
(2) Machine reliability was poor with excessive mechanical and electrical problems.
(3) Existing control procedures did not guarantee the availability of tooling, gauges and documentation at a machine when required.
(4) Tape and tooling proving and development on the machine took a significant time.
(5) Operator absences from the machine always resulted in a break in machine use.
(6) Payment of the operators provided very little incentive to them to maintain high utilization.
(7) Periodic failures of organizational and control procedures occurred resulting in delays.
(8) Supervision of the NC machines was only a partial responsibility for the section foreman and at times this caused problems. The foreman had little experience of NC operation and the resulting lack of appreciation of how they should be used or how they should be supervised.

On the positive side, quality problems did not occur with the machines but this might reflect back on the long set-up times. Material availability was not a problem because more jobs were scheduled (on the basis of a higher utilization) than were actually produced on the machines. Liaison between operators and programmers was good but the programmers probably spent too long at the machines sorting out problems.

Cost Effective Utilization

It has been previously pointed out that the evaluation of utilization Ut_1 only provides a numerical value which indicates a percentage of the time a

NC Machine Utilization and a Systems Approach

machine tool is producing components. The utilization figure so obtained fails, however, to show whether it is 'cost effective utilization' (that is whether the components are sufficiently complex to justify their production by NC) and whether the machines' features such as power, capacity, speed and feed ranges, attachment available, etc. are adequately used. Dodgson (1972) shows by examples that production by NC is only justified for more complex components because the production time savings that can be achieved are much greater than with simpler components.

Complexity Analysis

Whilst simple and complex components are easily recognized, it was considered desirable to quantify component complexity by some means so that the components scheduled to the NC machines could be evaluated for NC production. This was important for the turned components as the lathes machined a large number of components of varying complexity. One method adopted was to use the work-piece complexity factor analysis of Brunn (1975). However, this by itself does not give any guide as to a level of complexity suitable for NC and no other work was found which suggested means of establishing suitable levels. It was decided therefore to analyse component complexity additionally in terms of the number of turret stations used in machining the component. A large sample of the components scheduled to be machined on lathes A and B and C was analysed in this way for both turrets ('X' and 'W'). Typical results of the analysis are shown in figure 3, the case shown being for machine 'C'; the results for the other machines were very similar. Average turret station use was as shown in table 3.

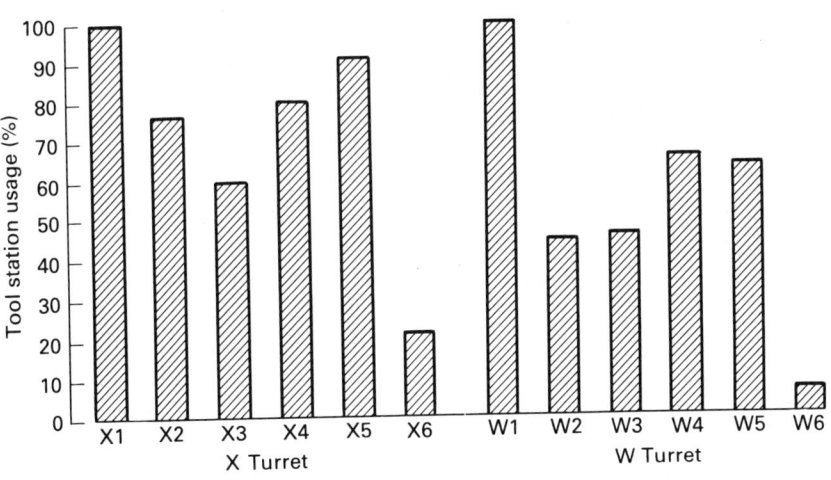

Figure 3 Tool station usage against tool station number (Machine C)

TABLE 3

Machine	Turret	Station use (%)	Sample size
A,B	X	69	78
	W	50	
C	X	72	75
	W	54	
D	X	85	19
	W	36	
E	X	60	10
	W	51	

W turrets both on the bar machines (A, B and C) and the lathes D and E are used only for drilling and other internal operations and therefore lower use is to be expected.

A standard of complexity of 50 per cent combined average turret station utilization was set which resulted in approximately 20 per cent of the components for each of the lathes being classified as not adequately complex and these were earmarked to be scheduled to other machines. There was a generally poor correlation between the complexity factor analysis (of Brunn) and the tool station usage figure but this was not unexpected as Brunn's factor is primarily an aid to estimating production times. It was found however that good correlation did exist at the 50 per cent turret station use figure which corresponds with a complexity factor of about 30. Those components which were rejected all had a factor below 30 and those which were retained were above. The correlation would not have existed had a different usage value been chosen.

Efficient Programming

The method adopted to assess whether the power and capabilities of the machines were being properly exploited was to check the cutting speeds and feed-rates selected by company programmers with those recommended by the machine tool manufacturers. It was considered that these would be fairly near to the optimum.

To check that components had been effectively programmed required a subjective judgement in that it is difficult to determine an optimum program sequence. However, the method adopted was to have a small number of the turned and milled components which have previously been programmed by various company programmers re-programmed by an experienced programmer. Both these checks showed that existing company practice was generally efficient.

A Systems Approach to Utilization Improvement

The approach adopted in the analysis of utilization was to list every aspect of the production situation and to try to account for the total time available

NC Machine Utilization and a Systems Approach

for production in terms of this list. While this method was effective in analysing the problem, it was not considered to be an effective framework for communicating to company management the total problem found, nor was it adequate for proposing methods for its improvement. It became apparent that the only really effective way to consider, develop and implement improvements in machine utilization was to use a systems approach.

The approach has the advantage that it stresses the interdependence of the many factors which affect utilization and it emphasizes the fact that it is the total system which must be efficient if utilization is to be high. The approach helps to give company managers a perspective of what is wrong and at the same time assists them in using their own experience in identifying further potential improvements.

Engineering systems can be illustrated in a number of ways and the purpose of systems analysis is to define the logic of a system and hence lead on to the construction of a suitable diagrammatic representation of the system. Flow charts, block diagrams and circuit diagrams are often used. The system associated with the use of an NC machine proved difficult to define as a single circuit diagram or flow chart because of the complex interaction of the engineering and management influence within the system. The diagrammatic representation eventually used was to split the system representation into two parts, the first being in the form of a circuit diagram and the second a modified Venn diagram of the form shown in figure 4.

The circuit diagram illustrates that for components to be machined they have to pass through the stages of setting, machining and inspection although setting and inspection may only concern the first one or two components. Each stage is illustrated as having a resistance to component flow as well as switches which can inhibit component flow completely. The elements which may act as resistances slowing the speed of production or as off-switches, completely stopping production, are shown in the Venn diagram. The relationship between the elements which primarily influence the machine and those which primarily influence the operator are indicated by their position in the diagram. It should be noted that the operator and the machine are shown in the centre of the diagram as the functioning elements which are to speed production or inhibit it. It should be noted that the operator is not shown as being in charge of the system. He can do much to get the system to operate well but only once the system is functioning in other ways. The only element that the operator controls is the machine, and this message is fundamental to production management.

The responsibility for all the other elements in the diagram belongs to management. Examples of what this can mean in practice will now be given. The examples are selected from the proposals made to the management of the company under investigation. Many of these proposals have been implemented. In all the areas discussed, the operator was kept informed of and involved in the schemes and ideas as they developed.

Planned Maintenance

Machine breakdown is a 'switch off' type of disturbance and the performance analysis found a significant proportion of breakdowns. This was

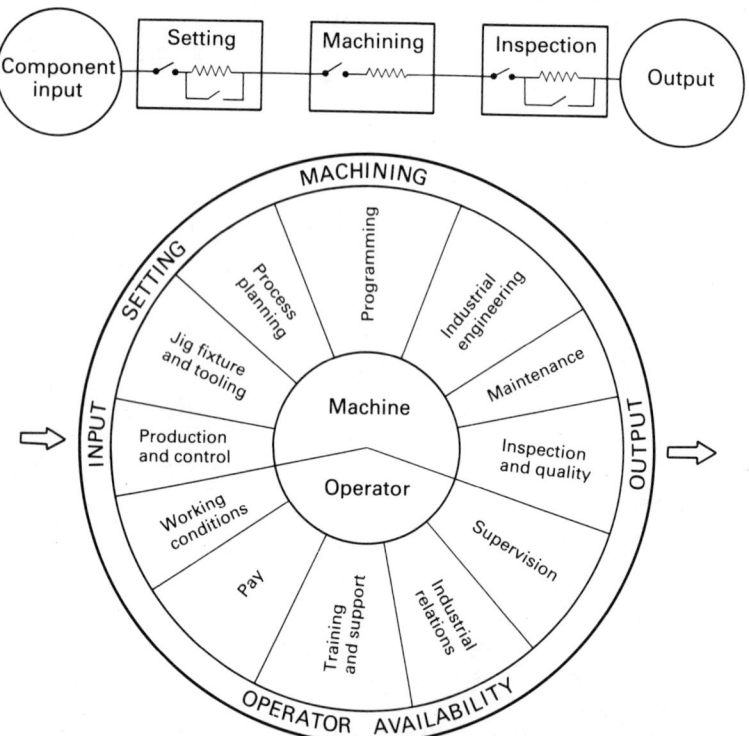

Figure 4 The systems associated with component manufacture by NC

tackled by developing a planned maintenance policy and by setting up suitable procedures both externally and internally in collaboration with the machine tool suppliers and service organizations. Such procedures and policies are not uncommon and the details need not be discussed here. The implementation of the scheme cost money but the machine availability was found to have increased by between 7 and 10 per cent in a follow-up survey. Also, the responsibility of the operator and his chargehand in the early stages of a breakdown problem have been spelt out and this increased their identity with the total machine system and enhanced their motivation to ensure production continuity.

Operator Support

Two major factors affecting utilization of the lathes were the duration of setting-up and the lack of availability of necessary tooling, fixturing or gauging when required. These problems were related in that set-up was often delayed by the operator having to search for equipment as well as carry out a number of indirect functions during the setting process which took him from the machine. These functions included the collection of tools from stores: grinding tools and chuck jaws: collecting NC documentation

NC Machine Utilization and a Systems Approach

from the programming department and solving queries which arose with the documentation. There were also problems caused by other operator absences from the machine and these were accentuated by the lack of reserve operators to take over during holiday or sick periods. These problems were tackled together by developing a support system for the operator. The elements of this system completely illustrate the philosophy of adopting a systems approach to improving utilization.

The new support system consisted of three related changes in working practice. These involved (i) a new machine layout, (ii) the setting up of a service centre for the NC lathes, and (iii) the adoption of multi-manning with the introduction of suitable financial incentives for the operators. The philosophy behind these changes was to remove the requirement for an operator to leave a machine during its set-up by having all the services required provided from a 'service centre' by an 'in-process worker'. The in-process worker is based in the service centre where he prepares kits for each new set-up for each NC machine. The kits are prepared in advance of each set-up, loaded on to a setting trolley, and supplied to operators when required. The operator thus knows that all tapes, tooling, gauges, setting equipment, drawings, tool layouts and material have been assembled and checked in advance. The trolley is also used to off-load the previous set-up and the 'in-process worker' re-stores the tooling in the service area, arranging for regrinding of tooling as required. The 'in-process' worker is also available to follow up programming enquiries with the programming department, leaving the operator to continue production if this is possible.

The layout of the machines within the shop was arranged in a way that the service centre had the machines grouped immediately adjacent to it. This not only enhanced communication between the operators and the in-process worker but enabled all operators to see the machines in the group reasonably well. This requirement was to assist a multi-manning arrangement. It was important that the new arrangement required no extra workers initially and therefore the operation of the machines and the duties of the in-process worker had all to be carried out by the present operators. This meant that the principle of one operator to one machine was to be abandoned but it did not mean a reduction in the number of operators. A weekly turn in the service centre was proposed for the operators so that their work was varied and so that they would always be using some of the kits they had themselves prepared. Sufficient trolleys were specified so that kits for a complete week's production could be prepared.

Estimates for the time required by the in-process worker to complete his task showed that initially he would have time to spare and could assist the operators. However, as utilization improved, which it should, the in-process worker would be kept continuously busy with the batch sizes currently specified.

Supervision

Improved supervision of the new layout of machines and service centre was required to ensure its smooth launch and satisfactory reporting of its problems to management. Under the old layout, the supervision of the NC machines had only been part of the responsibility of a foreman looking after all the lathes and this had been reflected in the lack of push on operators to overcome machine problems quickly. One of the existing operators of the machines was therefore selected to become a charge-hand on the section so that the section had a definite leader, who was fully familiar with all aspects of NC machine operation.

Discussion

These three examples illustrate aspects of the systems approach which were developed to improve the utilization problem. Other actions, such as improved training, the provision and training of a reserve operator, the negotiations of an incentive scheme, were also put in hand.

It was calculated that an 8 to 10 per cent improvement in utilization would be required to pay off the capital investment required for the service centre over two years. There was more than adequate scope for this.

As utilization improved, new limitations on the system utilization would occur but these would be more easily identified with the benefits of the system approach.

The support system for the NC lathes proposed in this paper has a number of noteworthy aspects. Firstly, it emphasizes that NC machines do not automatically have low set-up times. Just as programming and tape preparation can be carried out off-line, so must other opportunities be identified to prepare for set-up off-line if set-up times are to be short. Operators need additional support to achieve this end. Secondly, improved operator efficiency and multi-manning schemes need not simply lead to redundant operators. Improved efficiency of the total operation may mean more is required of the existing operators, not less operators. Thirdly, there are ways in which the involvement and motivation of the operators towards their jobs can be enhanced. If management recognizes its total responsibility to achieving high utilization in the first place, then it is able to delegate some of this responsibility to those operating the machines. This will enhance the commitment of the operators. Fourthly, if changes in operating procedure are to be made, there are advantages in making a number at the same time, ensuring operator consultation and involvement during the development of the schemes. This can then be coupled with the negotiation of an incentive scheme to ensure the operator sees a benefit from the changes as well as management. Fifthly, when adopting the systems approach to improving utilization, it is important to keep as short as possible the lines of communication which must be associated with any procedure. This has been achieved in this instance by enlarging the scope of the operator's work and by avoiding an interface in the operating procedure occurring at the machine. Delays which may occur have been moved to a possible delay at the service support centre, rather than at the machine. Here they are more tolerable.

Conclusion

This paper has illustrated the need for, and advantages of, adopting a systems approach to tackling the problem of low NC machine utilization. It has illustrated that NC machines in many cases need additional investment in supporting services to ensure their reliability and the realization of a high utilization. This is particularly true on NC turning machines where cycle times are lower and changes of batch are likely to be more frequent than on machine centres. Lathe operations which require frequent operator involvement and frequent starting and stopping are the source of most problems and where a systems approach is essential.

The systems approach is important because it emphasizes management responsibility for high utilization rather than the operators' responsibility. Only when management has accepted its responsibilities and acted to ensure high utilization can some of their responsibility be delegated to the operator. The systems approach has been shown to be able to analyse and integrate the assessment of the combined engineering and management systems associated with the operation of NC machine tools.

Acknowledgements

The authors would like to thank the staff of Platt Saco Lowell who co-operated in this project, particularly Mr W. Sutcliffe, and the Science Research Council for financial support.

References

G. Becker, 'Ausfallzeiten an NC-Maschinen', *Werkstaft Betrieb*, vol. 111 (1978) p. 12.
P. J. Brunn, 'The Output Utilisation and Selection of Lathes', Ph.D. thesis, UMIST Manchester, 1975.
F. Dodgson, 'Economic Justification of NC Lathes', *Machinery Prod. Engng.*, 10 May 1972.
N. A. Dudley, *Industrial Productivity: Scope for Improvement* (West Midlands Economic Planning Council, 1972).
P. C. Hagan and R. Leonard, 'Strategies for Increasing the Utilization and Output of Machine Tools', *14th M.T.D.R. Conference* (Oxford: Pergamon Press, 1973).
R. Sury, 'A Perspective of a Teaching Company Programme' (The Institution of Production Engineers; E. W. Hancock Paper, 27 March 1979).

Index

Aachen University, 219
ABC analysis, 219, 262
action flexibility, 112
activity cycles, 240
adaptation policy, 8, 43–50 *passim*
advanced economies, 15–18
  market trends, 19–23
advertising (motorcycle industry), 31, 32, 35
aerospace industry, 166
agriculture, 21, 51
aircraft industry, 46, 59, 61
AJS, 27, 36
algorithms
  computer, 172, 233
  dispatching, 233, 235–40
Allen Bradley network, 129–30, 132–4
American Printed Circuit Company, 63–4
American Standard Code for Information Interchange (ASCII), 276
Andon system, 154, 157
animation, simulators with, 248, 251–2
anticipated delay reports, 154, 157
Applicon, 273, 276
Artificial Intelligence, 252
Asia, 29, 32
assembly, fixed position, 181
assembly, flexible, 109–10, 116
  design of, 100, 120–6,
assets, 35, 55
assignment techniques (job/cell), 145–6
Associated Motor Cycles, 34, 35–6, 41
Australia, 29
Austria, 30
AUTOFACT conferences, 273–5
automated materials handling system, 179, 232–41
automation levels (in FMS), 115–18
Autotrol, 276
'awareness' programmes, 17

Babcock and Wilcox (USA), 56–7
backlog (material handling), 234–8, 240
Baker, K. R., 146
Bank of England, 9, 13
Barbosa, L. C., 266
Barnett marques, 35, 36
batch production, 121, 224, 232
batch size, 8, 224, 226, 227, 229–31
Bausch and Lomb, 276
Becker, G., 295
Belmann, 255
Bendix Corporation, 273
Berlin University, 219
Birmingham University, 7
Black, J., 178, 196
BMW, 30
Boston Consulting Group, 33, 39–40
branch-and-bound techniques, 147
Britain
  engineering industry, 2–3, 7, 9–26
  exports, 18, 25, 58–61
  manufacturing, 9–20, 23, 51–4, 58–61
  motorcycle industry, 7–8, 27–42
  productivity, *see* productivity (UK)
  TMD (Factory A), 207, 209–14 *passim*
British Motor Cycle Industries Association, 28
Browne, J., 99–100, 102, 111
Brunn, P. J., 301, 302
BSA, 27, 28, 34–41 *passim*
Buchanan, J. T., 266
buildings (layout), 184, 186–7, 194
Burbridge, J. L., 191
Business Monitor, 40
Buzacott, J. A., 112, 268
Buzen, J. P., 244

CADCAM system, 165–8, 169–70, 172
  integration, 169, 179, 272–7

CADCAM *(cont.)*
  production engineering in, 179, 278–92
CALMA, 273, 276, 277
CAN-Q, 244, 246
Canada, 16, 29, 30
capacity planning
  decision-making, 178, 206–11
  information constraints, 178, 196–203
  Kanban/MRP II, 154, 156, 160
capital
  constraints (inventory), 265, 267–8
  investments, *see* investment
CAPS (simulation system), 232, 240
car industry, 13, 27–8, 36, 39, 92, 166, 168
Carrick, P., 40
Carrie, A. S., 192
Castellani, G., 268
CATV technology, 130
Causes of the Slow Rate of Economic Growth in the UK (Kaldor), 51
cellular manufacturing, 137–8, 224–5
  cell characteristics, 141–3, 144–5
  control, 100–1, 128–32, 135, 139–43, 146, 149
  job characteristics/density, 143–5
  loading, 101, 139, 140, 144–6, 149
  scheduling, 101, 139, 140, 144–9
Chakravarty, A. K., 267
Charles, R. (of Wadkin), 46
chemicals industries, 11, 13
Choe, U.C., 267
Christmas tree problem, 263
Clark, A. J., 254
CNC machines, 46–7, 49–50, 179
coal industry, 14
combinatorial scheduling, 147
communication
  adaptor modules, 129–30, 131
  controller modules, 130, 131–2, 136
  LANs and, *see* local area networks
  plant level, 127–8
  programmable controllers, 128–9, 130–1, 136
communications technology, 21–2
competition
  focused factory and, *see* focused manufacturing
  foreign, 21–3, 25–8, 30–2, 44
  priorities, 78, 79–80
component complexity, 301–2, 303, 304
component geometry, 280–3, 287–9, 290

computer
  -aided design, 101, 164–72, 177
  -aided manufacture, 99, 101–2, 164–72
  algorithm, 172, 233
  control, 100–1, 127–36, 172
  FMS concept, *see* flexible manufacturing systems
  see also CADCAM system; hardware; software
Computer-aided Programming for Simulation (CAPS), 232, 240
Computer Analysis of Networks of Queues (CAN–Q), 244, 246
Computervision, 273, 276, 279
consumerism, 11, 13, 14, 20, 22, 36
control
  cellular manufacturing, 100–1, 128–32, 135, 139–43, 146, 149
  centralized/decentralized, 83–7, 89, 94–5
  flexible assembly system, 122–4
  inventory, 179, 254–68
  machine, system, 100–1, 127–32
  market demand, 101, 151–63
  process, system, 100–1, 132–6
Control Data Corporation, 273, 276
Conway, R. W., 146
corporate strategy
  focused manufacturing and, 65, 70–1, 77–8, 81, 93
  manufacturing structure and, 52–8
  organization and, 81, 93, 95
  Wadkin's, 45–6
cost-effectiveness
  CAD system, 167–8
  machine-utilization, 300–1
costs, 19
  inventory system, 256, 258–9, 263
  materials handling, 192–4, 195
cranes, computer-controlled, 99, 101, 108, 110

Das, C., 265
data, 130, 134
  integration (CADCAM), 179, 272-7
Dave, U., 266
Davies, B. J., 279
Davies, I., 35
Day, J. E., 146
decision-making, 55, 81–2
  decentralized, 83–7, 89, 94–5
  operations management, 178, 204–14

Index

plant layout, 178, 181–95
dedicated FMS, 115
defence industries, 61, 166
deliveries, 53, 54, 143, 144
demand (factors)
  dynamic, models, 265–6
  seasonality, 36, 37, 263
  trends, 263–4
departments, layout problems and, 190–1, 195
design, 53, 56, 66, 103–4, 112
  automated materials handling, 179, 232–41
  computer-aided, 101, 164–72, 177
  flexible assembly, 100, 120–6
  machine tool, 8, 46, 49, 50
  motorcycle, 34, 35–6
  plant layout, 177, 178, 181–95
  system, 178–9, 242–52
  see also CADCAM system
desirability (capacity planning), 208, 209–11
detailed discrete simulations, 244, 246–8, 251–2
deterministic models, 258, 262
devaluation, 265, 268
developing countries, 29, 31, 60
devolution policy (at Wadkin), 45, 48
dispatching algorithm, 233, 235–40
Distribution Resource Planning, 162
diversification patterns, 78, 79
Dixon, F. (of Wadkin), 48
Dodgson, F., 294, 301
dominant orientation (management), 78–9
Donaldson, W. S., 266
Downstream Pull, 236, 237–8
'drop dead dates', 161
Dubois, D., 111
Dudley, N. A., 295
due date (CM system), 143, 144
Duermeyer, B. L., 266
Dunnett, P. J. S., 28
dynamic demand models, 265–6
dynamic dimensioning, 165
dynamic programming, 255, 264, 267–8

economic policy (effects), 36–7
economies of scale, 31, 36, 63, 74
economy, UK, 9–20, 23, 51–4, 58–61
ECSL, 240
education, 61
EEC, 11, 14, 60

electrical machinery, 13
electronic data processing equipment, 215, 219–20, 223
employees, 23, 51–2
employment, 14–15, 29, 38
Employment, Department of, 10, 38
energy, 20, 21
Energy, Department of, 273
engineering, 66
  dimension, 7, 8, 23–5
  exports (value), 58–61
  Finniston Report, 2–3, 7, 9–26
  mechanical, 18, 166–72
  motorcycle industry, 7–8, 27–42
  production, 179, 201–2, 278–92
  TMD Ltd, 207, 209, 210–11, 212–14
  Wadkin's, 8, 43–50
Engineering in Britain, West Germany and France (Saunders), 58
environmental factors, 52, 53
EOQ model, 258–9, 261, 266, 268
Erhardt, R., 265
Eskicioglu, H., 279
Europe, 29–30
expansion, plant layout and, 186, 187, 194
expansion flexibility, 113–14
exports, 11–14, 18, 49, 58–61
Extended Control and Simulation Language, 240

facilities decisions, 82
factory, focused, *see* focused manufacturing
Fanuc (Fuji complex), 109, 118
feasibility (capacity planning), 208, 290, 211
Ferrant Cetec system, 279
finance/financing, 23, 55
  see also investment
financial planning (in MRP II), 162
Finniston Report (1980), 2–3, 7, 9–26, 99
First-Come-First-Served (FCFS), 148
First-In-Shop-First-Out (FISFO), 148
flexibility, 99–100, 111–12, 115, 117
  plant layout, 188–90
  technical investment, 217, 229
  volume, 78, 80, 113, 114
flexible assembly cell, 116, 118
flexible assembly system, 100, 109–10, 116–17, 120–6
flexible machining cell, 116

flexible machining system, 116–17, 118
flexible manufacturing systems (FMS)
  classification, 100, 115–18
  in Japan, 99, 103–10
  modelling, 179, 242, 244, 246, 252
  simulation, 179, 236, 244, 249, 252
  software packages, 178, 215–31, 249, 252
flexible transfer line, 117, 118
flexible transfer multi-line, 117, 118
flow shops, modified, 146, 147
FOA (backlog), 237
'Focused Factory, The' (Skinner), 8, 54, 62–75
focused manufacturing, 62, 75, 77, 83
  basic concepts, 64–6
  growth (impact), 93–5
  management approach, 69–71, 72, 73
  process, 8, 86–92, 94, 95
  product, 8, 84–95 *passim*
  productivity and, 63, 64, 66–9
  PWP approach, 71–4
food resources, 21
Foster, G., 43
France, 15, 18, 29, 30, 31, 51–2, 58–60
free trade policy, 28
Freeland, J. R., 265
Friedman, M., 266
Fuji, 32
Fuji (Fanuc), 109, 118
functional layout, 101, 137, 138
furniture industry, 44, 49

gas industry, 14
GATT, 11
GDP, 14, 51
gearshop, Westland, 196–9, 201–2
Gelders, L. F., 255
General Electric (USA), 56
General Simulation Program, 247
Generalized Modelling System, 244–6
geometric modelling, 172, 178
geometry, component, 280–3, 287–90
Gerber, 273, 276
Germany, 15–16, 18–19, 28, 30, 51–2, 58–60, 118
Gerwin, D., 112
glass container industry, 132–6
Goddard, M. (at Wadkin), 44–50 *passim*
Goddard, W., 101, 151
Gordon, W. J., 244
government, 36–7, 60–1
  see also taxation

Goyal, S. K., 267
Graftek, 276
Grant, G., 41
graphics
  CADCAM system, 169, 179, 272–7
  Shapes program, 286–90
Graves, S. C., 146
Greene, T. J., 101, 137
Groover, M. P., 115
group cell techniques, 181
group technology, 137, 181, 185
growth, corporate attitude, 78, 79
growth, impact on organization, 93–4
guarantees, 20, 46
Gupta, N. K., 265

Hadley, G., 255, 261–2, 263, 267
Hagan, P. C., 269
Hall, M. (at Wadkin), 47–8
Hanlon, P. D., 127
Hannam, R. G., 179, 278, 279–80, 294
Hanssmann, F., 254, 255, 261, 267
hardware, 99, 101, 103
Harley Davidson, 30, 31
Harris (of Westinghouse), 255
Hatvany, J., 101, 164
Hayes, R. H., 8, 76
Henery, R. J., 266
Heriot–Watt University, 279
heuristic sequencing, 145, 146, 147
Hewlett-Packard, 80
hire purchase, 28, 37
Hollier, R. H., 178, 181
Honda, 32, 33, 35, 40, 41
Hopwood, B., 35, 36
Hottenstein, M. P., 146
housebuilding sector, 44
Hout, T. M., 31
Hutchinson, G. K., 179, 232

IGES, 169, 179, 272–7
imports, 11, 13, 18
  motorcycles, 27–42 *passim*
in-process workers, 305
incomes, personal, 11, 14
industrial relations, 16, 38, 44, 300
industrialization (implications), 19, 23
Industry, Department of, 10, 192–4
industry, UK (structure), 15
inflation, 44, 264
information, 21–2, 154, 157
  capacity planning, 178, 196–203
infrastructure decisions, 82

Index

Initial Graphics Exchange Specification, 169, 179, 272-7
international trade, 10-14, 23, 29-30
  comparisons, 16, 21, 22
inventory
  control, 179, 254-68
  management, *see* Kanban system; manufacturing resource planning
investment, 15-17
  focused factory, 63, 66, 68, 69, 72, 74
  motorcycles, 36-7, 41, 42
  planning, technical, 215-31
Italy, 30, 31

Jackson, J. R., 244
Jaiswal, M. C., 266
Japan, 13, 15, 16, 46, 50, 61
  FMS in, 99, 103-10, 118
  Kanban in, *see* Kanban system
  motorcycle industry, 27-9, 32-5, 41-2
Job-Priority Loading, 145-6
job characteristics, 143-4, 148
job density, 144-5
job flexibility, 112
job mix/routing, 143, 144
job shop, 185, 194
  materials handling, 179, 232-41
  scheduling, 140-1, 143, 146-8
job types, 141, 143, 144
joint-ordering systems, 265, 266-7

Kaldor, N., 51, 61
Kanban Cards, 154-6, 157, 158, 159-60
Kanban system, 101, 162-3
  deliveries, 153, 160-1
  limitations, 158-60
  MRP II versus, 151, 154-7
Kawasaki, 32, 33, 41
Kay, J. M., 179, 242, 250
Kelly, J. W. E., 31
Kicks, P., 266
Kilmartin, B. R., 179, 294
Koa, P. C., 267
Korgaonker, M. G., 267
Kottas, J. F., 265
Krauskopf, B., 276
Kruse, W. K., 265

labour, 15-17, 37, 41-2, 51-2
  personnel policies, 55-6, 60
Lagrange's multiplier, 260, 267

Last-In-System-Last-Out (LISLO), 148
lathe operations, 295, 298-300, 301-2, 305, 306-7
Lau, H., 265
layout, *see* plant layout
learning (market element), 54
leisure (motorcycles), 28, 32, 36
Leonard, R., 296
Lev, B., 268
Levary, R. R., 266
Lewis, W. C., 279
Liberatore, M. J., 265
line layout, 101, 137, 138
living standards (UK), 25
loading technique, 101, 139, 140, 145-6, 149
local area networks, 172
  glass-container industry, 101, 132-6
  manufacturing cell, 100-1, 127-31
Loughborough University, 132, 133
Lucas, 41

McAuto Unigraphics, 273, 276
Machine File (Westland), 198, 199, 202
Machine-Priority Loading, 145-6
machine tools, 8, 43-50, 59
  planning, 219, 220-1, 222
machinery for special industry, 58, 59
machines
  control systems, 100, 127-32
  flexibility, 112, 114, 116-18, 142
  manufacturing cells, 101, 137, 140, 142-6, 149
  numerically controlled, *see* NC machines
  Shapes program, 280-3, 286-91
  types, 142-3, 144-5
  utilization, 179-80, 294-307
  vertical CNC, 46, 47, 49-50
machining, flexible, 109-10, 116-18
machining system, planning, 217-22
Magaziner, I. C., 31
Magson, D. W., 265
Makita Electric Works Ltd, 162
Mallin, S. J., 100, 101, 120
management, 23, 24, 78-80
  approach (focused factory), 69-75
Management Today, 8, 58
Mandelbaum, M., 112
Manning File (Westland), 198, 199
Mantra Datavision, 276-7
manufacturing
  cellular, *see* cellular manufacturing

manufacturing (*cont.*)
  computer-aided, 99, 101–2, 164–72
  computer-integrated, *see* CADCAM
  control, *see* control
  economies (market trends), 19–23
  flexible, *see* flexible manufacturing systems
  focus, *see* focused manufacturing
  functions (in MRP II/Kanban), 154–7
  mission, 8, 77, 80–3, 89, 91, 93
  operating system, 204, 205
  organization, *see* organization
  strategy, 54, 78–80
  structure, 52–7, 67–8
  system design, 178, 242–52
  task, 52, 55–7
  UK, 9–20, 23, 51–4, 58–61
Manufacturing and Consulting Services, 273
manufacturing resource planning (MRP II), 101, 152, 153, 163, 197
  advantages, 161–2
  Kanban versus, 151, 154–7
market, 65, 78, 185–6, 212
  strategies, 24, 52, 55, 57–8
  success (elements), 53–4
  trends, 19–23
marketing, 88, 213
marques (motorcycles), 35, 36
master production schedules, 154–60
Matchless, 27
materials, 78
  raw, 10, 11, 21
  requirements, 154, 155–7, 264
materials handling, 115, 118. 222
  automated, 179, 232–41
  costs, 192–4, 195
mathematical modelling, *see* modelling, mathematical
mathematical programming, 147
Maxwell, W. L., 146
MBH, 41, 42
mechanical engineering, 18, 166–70, 171, 172
mergers (motorcycle industry), 36
Meriden, 33, 34, 36, 38
metalworking machinery, 58, 59
microcomputers, 167–8, 172
microelectronics, 21, 60
microprocessors, 52, 242
Miller, L. W., 146
Mills, R. I., 247, 252
mining industry, 51

Misra, R. B., 268
Mitsubishi, 32, 105
mix flexibility, 112
modelling, mathematical
  EOQ, 258–9, 261,266, 268
  goemetric, 172, 178
  inventory control, 179, 254–68
  systems design, 178, 243–6, 250–2
  3-D, 164–5, 171, 273, 274
modified flow shops, 146, 147
monitoring (production), 131–2
Monte Carlo sampling, 147
moped industry, 29, 30, 31, 36, 40
Mori Seiki (Japan), 105–6, 107
motorcycle industry (UK demise), 7–8
  Japan and, 27–35 *passim*, 41–2
  United States and, 27–31, 35–7, 39
MRP II, *see* manufacturing resource planning (MRP II)
MSC Incorporated, 276
Muhlemann, A. P., 268
multiline approach, 100, 117
multiprocessor-based control system, 133–4, 135
multirobot assembly cell, 249
Mumford, R. J., 265
Muther, R., 185

Nahimias, S., 266
National Bureau of Standards, 272, 276
National Commission on Productivity (USA), 62
NC machines, 219
  supervision, 297–300, 305–6
  utilization, 179–80, 294–307
NCGA Exposition, 273
NEDO, 17–18
New, C., 51
New Zealand, 29
Newell, G. F., 244
newsboy problem, 255, 263, 265
Nicol, L. M., 178, 181
non-price factors, 19, 20
North Sea Oil, 10, 14
Norton, 27, 36, 41
nuclear power industry, 53, 56–7
Nutt, J. (at Wadkin), 44, 48–9

OECD (output), 15
oil industry, 10, 14
Open Shop Order System (OSO), 197, 198–9, 202
Open University, 2, 3

Index

Operational Research, 254, 265
operations, 114, 144
   management, 178, 204–14
   time (SOT/T), 145, 146
organization, 56, 76
   focus approach, 83–92, 95
   growth (impact), 93–5
   manufacturing mission, 8, 80–3
   process focus, 8, 86–92, 95
   product focus, 8, 87–92, 95
   strategy (basic elements), 77–80
output (UK), 15, 53–4, 154–5
   performance indicators, 12–14
   see also productivity
overmanning, 16, 37

Packard, D., 80
Page, E., 267
pallet systems, 104–8 *passim*
part family (definition), 137
Patel, L. K., 266
Paul, R. J., 267
perishables, models for, 265, 266
personnel policies, 55–6, 60
PFO (backlog), 238
Phelps, R. I., 266
planning
   capacity, *see* capacity planning
   machining system, 217–21
   plant layout, 178, 181–95
   production engineering, 279–80
   technical investment, 215–31
plant and equipment technology, 55
plant layout, 177, 181–95
   simulation, 178, 225–9
plant within a plant (PWP), 71–4
Platt Saco Lowell, 295, 307
PLS model, 258–9
Plummer, J. C. S., 179, 278, 280, 291
policy-making, 206, 210–11
political trends, 21, 22, 23
pollution, 20, 52
Porteus, E. L., 265
preference (capacity planning), 208, 210–11
preference ranking, 237, 238–9
prices, 17–18, 25, 54
Prime Medusa, 276
priority procedure, 234–6, 238, 239
probabilistic models, 255
process, 181, 226
   control systems, 132–6
   flexibility, 112, 114

   focus, 8, 86–92, 94, 95
   technology, 22, 65
processing time (CM system), 143, 144
product
   design, *see* design
   flexibility, 78, 80, 112, 114
   focus, 8, 65, 84–6, 87–92, 93–5
   layout, 181
   market trends, 20, 22, 24
   master schedules, 154–6, 158–60
   proliferation, 68–9
   quality, 17–19, 53
   strategy, 54, 55
production, 19, 55, 114, 255
   control, 131–2, 201
   methods (motorcycles), 39–42
   planning, *see* Kanban system; manufacturing resources planning
   planning/control (TMD), 213–14
production engineering, 179, 201, 202, 278–92
Production Flow Analysis, 191
productivity (UK), 15–17, 137
   motorcycle, 33, 37–8, 39–40
productivity (USA), 62–4, 66–9, 74
professionalism, plant, 68
profitability, 15–17
programmable controllers, 128–31, 136
PTW (backlog), 238
public expenditure, 60
purchase tax, 28, 37
purchasing, 87, 88

quality levels (focused factory), 65–6
queuing network (system design), 244–6
queuing theory (scheduling), 8, 147

random FMS, 115
Rathmill, K., 111
rationalization (at Wadkin), 45, 47
raw materials, 10, 11, 21
Ray, W. D., 265
recession, 186, 187, 194
redundancies, 53, 60, 186
regional policy, 28, 60, 61
remainder cell, 137, 140, 143
Renault Machine Outils, 117
research and development, 61
Resh, M., 266
resources, basic, 21, 55
   raw materials, 10, 11, 21
Ritchie, E., 266

Robinson, L. (at Wadkin), 48
robots, 99, 109–10, 116, 249
  pick-and-place, 128–9, 130
Rogers, N. M., 27
Routing File (Westland), 198–200, 202
routing flexibility, 113, 114
Royal Enfield, 27, 34

Sackett, P. J., 100, 101, 120
Sadowski, R. P., 101, 137
safety standards, 20
Sahili, A., 127
Sandia National Laboratories, 273
Saunders, C., 58
SCAMP system, 115
scheduling, 172
  heuristic sequence theory, 145–7
  job-shop, 140–1, 143, 146–8
  modified flow shop, 146, 147
  technique, 101, 139, 140, 146–9
Schmenner, R. W., 8, 76
Schmitt, R., 171
Schrady, D. A., 267
Science and Engineering Research Council, 291
scooter industry, 31, 36, 40
seasonality (demand), 36, 37, 263
sensitivity analysis, 244–5
sequencing, heuristic, 145, 146, 147
service departments, 20, 32, 68, 205
services sector, 10–11
Sethi, S., 111
Shah, R., 99, 100, 101, 103
Shah, Y. K., 266
shape elements, 286, 291–2
Shapes program, 280–91 *passim*
sheet-metal shop, 232–41
shipbuilding industry, 59, 60, 166
shortest operation time (SOT), 148
  truncated (SOT/T), 145, 146
shortest processing time (SPT), 148
Shunk, D. L., 141
Silver, E. A., 266
Sims, B. (at Wadkin), 45, 46
simulation, 145, 147–8, 200–1
  automated materials handling, 179, 232–41
  CAPS system, 232, 240
  layout/workflow, 178, 225–9, 233
  techniques, 178, 243–4, 246–52
  3-D, 171, 249
simulators
  with animation, 244, 248, 251–2

  detailed discrete, 244, 246–8, 251–2
  specific, 244, 248–50, 252
Skinner, W., 8, 54, 62, 77, 83, 89
SLAM simulation model, 145
Smith, B., 179, 272
Smith, B. M. D., 27, 39
Smith, W. A., 279
social trends, 21, 22, 52, 53
software
  CAD systems, 168–9, 172, 177
  LAN, 100, 127–35
  packages (FMS), 178 215–31, 249, 252
  packages (system design), 245, 247–52
  Shapes program, 280–91 *passim*
Solberg, J. J., 244
Soyster, A. L., 268
standardization (CADCAM), 290
Stanley Electric, 162
Stecke, K., 111, 118
steel industry, 13
sterling, 14, 44
stochastic models, 258, 261–3, 265
storage areas, 115
  see also inventory
strict liability (manufacturers), 22
'Structure and Design of Manufacturing Systems' (OU course), 2
Stuttgart University, 219
Subramanyan, E. S., 268
Sunbeam, 27
Sundstrand/Caterpillar DNC line, 117
supervision (NC machines), 297, 298, 299, 300, 305–6
supply (in operating system), 204, 205
Sury, R., 295
Suzuki, 32, 33, 41
swing (bar stock), 284, 286, 287
Systematic Layout Planning, 185
systems approach, 1–2, 55
  materials handling, 193–4
  NC machine utilization, 179–80, 294–307
systems design, 172, 178, 242–52

Tadikamalla, P. R., 265, 266
task focusing, 8, 63–75
taxation, 28, 37, 61
team work, 152, 163
technical investment planning (of FMS), 215–31
technology, 24, 39–41, 52, 65, 78, 86
  constraints, 55, 60

Index

developments, layout and, 185–6
low level (exports), 58–61
new, 19, 21–2, 177–8
systems approach, 179–80, 294–307
telecommunications, 22, 52–3, 60
Texas Instruments, 79, 80
textile industry, 59
textile machinery, 294–307
Thornley, B. (at Wadkin), 49
3-D modelling, 164–5, 171, 273, 274
3-D simulation, 171, 249
Time and Attendance System (T & A), 197, 198–9
TMD Limited, 207, 209, 210–11, 212–14
Tocher, K. D., 247
tools and tooling, 66, 249–50
   CADCAM system, 279–90
Toyota, 152–6, 158–63 *passim*
trade unions, 38, 300
transducer assembly, 120
transportation, 22, 204, 205, 239
Triumph, 27, 34, 35, 36, 38, 41
truncation (dual sequencing rule), 148
TUC, 9
Turner, E., 35
turnkey systems, 169
TWA (backlog), 237

UMIST, 279, 291, 295
unemployment, 22, 25, 52, 53
unit values, 18, 25, 58–61
United States, 16, 49, 61, 118
   focused manufacturing, 8, 62–4, 66–9, 74–5
   IGES, 169, 179, 272–7
   motorcycle industry, 27–31, 35–7, 39
   MRP II, *see* manufacturing resource planning (MRP II)
Upendra, D., 266
Urgeletti Tinarelli, G., 179, 254, 267, 268
USSR, 29

Valtis Spanopoulos, N. P., 268
value added, 17, 25
Van Nunen, J. A. E. E., 267
Van Wassenhove, L. N., 255

vehicle licensing, 28
Veinott, A. F., 254
Venn diagram, 303
vertical CNC machines, 46, 47, 49–50
vertical integration, 93, 94
Vettin, G., 178, 215
Villiers, 34, 35, 41
Volpato, M., 268
volume constraint, 265, 267–8
volume flexibility, 78, 80, 113, 114

Wadkin (of Leicester), 43–50
wages, 38
Wagner, H., 255
Walmsley, A. J., 250
Wang, S. S., 266
Warnecke, H. J., 178, 215
warranties, 20, 46
Weiss, H. J., 266
Wellington, J., 179, 272
Wessels, J., 267
Western Electric (USA), 52–3
Westinghouse (USA), 56, 255
Westland Helicopters, 178, 196–203
Weston, R. H., 100, 101, 127
Whitin, T. M., 254, 255, 261–3, 267
Wild, R., 178, 204
Williams, J. M., 192
Wilson, R. H., 255
Wilson's model, 254–5, 257–64, 268
woodworking machinery, 8, 43–50
work-piece
   flow system, 215–20, 222–5, 230
   medium-sized (FMS), 104–7
   simulation, 226–8, 229, 244
work flow, 178, 225–9, 233
work station, 237
   assembly, 100, 121, 122, 124–6
   CAD, 101, 167–8
   system design, 244–6, 249, 251
   technical investment (of FMS), 216–18, 223–4, 227–8
workers, *see* labour
workshop scheduling, 172

Yamaha, 32, 33, 41
Yamazaki, 107–8